£5·00

KU-692-856

HARVARD ECONOMIC STUDIES

VOLUME CXXVI

The studies in this series are published by the Department
of Economics of Harvard University. The Department
does not assume responsibility for the views expressed.

Consumer Demand in the United States: Analyses and Projections

H. S. HOUTHAKKER

LESTER D. TAYLOR

SECOND AND ENLARGED EDITION

HARVARD UNIVERSITY PRESS

Cambridge, Massachusetts

1970

Distributed in Great Britain by Oxford University Press, London

Library of Congress Catalog Card Number: 79–95915

SBN 674–16601–9

Printed in the United States of America

Preface to the Second and Enlarged Edition

Shortly after the first edition of this study appeared in 1966 the Department of Commerce published extensive revisions in the National Income Accounts, including all of the constant dollar consumption data that underlay the empirical analyses of the book. We had known for some time that these revisions were in the offing and had in fact delayed publication during 1965 on the expectation that the revisions would become available earlier than they did, but we finally decided not to wait and to publish the results as they stood. However, since we had an agreement with the Interagency Growth Study to re-estimate the equations and redo the projections for 1970 when the revised data became available, it was natural to think in terms of a second edition almost from the start.

A second motive for a second edition was our progress in extending the dynamic theory to an additive system of demand equations which we have been able to apply to data of Canada, Sweden, and the Netherlands as well as to data of the United States. This material forms the basis of the present Chapter 5 and is entirely new in this edition. An analysis of the data from the 1960–1961 survey of consumer expenditures conducted by the Bureau of Labor Statistics and the Department of Agriculture is also new in this edition and is presented in Chapter 6. Still other new material is scattered throughout Chapters 4 and 7.

Despite the expanded scope of this edition, the basic dynamic model of the first edition is still the workhorse. The revised data upset none of the conclusions of the first edition, and indeed show the basic model to even better advantage. Whereas 72 of 83 equations for individual PCE categories were dynamic in the first edition, 79 out of 81 are dynamic with the revised data. More use is made of the Bergstrom model in this edition and, since 1970 is nearly upon us, the projections are extended to 1975.

The format of this edition is little changed from that of the first. The material in Chapter 2 of the first edition has been moved to Chapters 1 and 4, and what were Chapters 3, 4, and 5 are now Chapters 2, 3, and 4. As has already been mentioned, the present Chapters 5 and 6 are new, and the material on aggregate consumption and saving now forms Chapter 7. The concluding chapter is now Chapter 8. Except for the saving equations in

Chapter 7, the period of observation in nearly all cases is 1929–1964 for United States equations. The saving equations were the last to be estimated and use data through 1966.

In addition to those mentioned in the preface of the first edition, we have become indebted to Elizabeth Carroll and Ann Walka for what turned out to be a massive programming task in estimating the additive model of Chapter 5, to William Barger for programming the cross-section data used in Chapter 6, to Isabelle Whiston for supervising the vast majority of computations, to Suresh Tendulkar for his work in revising the aggregate consumption and saving equations, to Albert Eckstein and David Warner for general research assistance, and to Thomas T. Schweitzer of the staff of the Economic Council of Canada for providing us with a list of the embarrassingly large number of misprints and errors in the first edition. Kotaro Tsujimura, who directed the Japanese translation of the first edition, also pointed out a number of errors, and we have benefited from constructive criticisms by reviewers of our book, especially those of George Perry. To Christina Anderson, Helen Bigelow, Suellen Birnie, Mary Louise Fisher, Donna Frazier, Jacqueline Parsons, and Susan I. Tomkin fell the onerous task of typing the manuscript at various stages. Financial support has been provided by the National Science Foundation and the Bureau of Labor Statistics of the United States Department of Labor, who financed the calculations of Chapter 3 and part of those of Chapter 6. Portions of those two chapters have been supplied to the Department as reports under the contract. Once again we are grateful to the Bureau of Labor Statistics for allowing publication of these results, and also to the Office of Business Economics of the Department of Commerce for giving us access to unpublished data. Neither these agencies nor the organizations with which we are now affiliated should be held responsible for the contents of this book.

Washington, D.C.   H.S.H.
Ann Arbor, Michigan   L.D.T.
March 1969

Preface to the First Edition

In the modern economy the decisive voice in the level and composition of output belongs to consumers. Of the goods and services produced in the United States, some 65 percent are ultimately sold to consumers, as compared with 21 percent to the government and 14 percent to business for investment. To understand the past and future development of the economy as a whole, it is therefore essential to study the pattern of consumption. This is the primary purpose of the present book.

We approach the analysis of consumer demand through the historical record, which is available from 1929 on. For each of 83 items of consumption we estimate demand equations are used in turn to project consumption in 1970 under certain assumptions. Underlying our procedure is a belief in the basic relationships that determine actual patterns of demand. This belief is supported by the satisfactory agreement of our equations with the observations, but it may come as a surprise to those who think of the consumer either as inherently capricious or as the passive victim of advertising and the arbitrary dictates of fashion. The length of women's skirts or of automobile fenders, or the distribution of the toothpaste market between Brand X and Brand Y, would indeed be hard to analyze by our methods, but our concern is not with such details. We work with a breakdown of consumption in which fashion and product differentiation do not show up to any great extent.

This book is addressed to readers of three types. The general economist, we hope, will be interested in the dynamic theory of demand set out in Chapter 1, in at least a few of the results for particular commodities set out in Chapter 4 and discussed in Chapter 5, and perhaps most of all in the analysis of total consumption and savings in Chapter 6. Those interested in particular industries or groups or products, or in forecasting generally, may find Chapters 4 and 5 rewarding. The specialist in econometric methods, finally, is encouraged to turn to Chapters 1, 3, and 7.

It goes without saying that an undertaking as large as ours has benefited from the assistance and advice of numerous others. Most of the work was carried out at the Harvard Economic Research Project, of which Wassily Leontief is Director. Elizabeth W. Gilboy, Associate Director, shared in the supervision and was in charge of administrative aspects. Charlotte Taskier, a staff member of the Project, devoted much time to problems of data interpretation and classification. Karen R. Polenske, Yoel Haitovsky, Madabushanam V. Chari, Armando Lago, Barclay M. Hudson, and Judith L. Rice provided conscientious and imaginative research assistance. Apart from the above, useful advice and other help was also received from Jack Alterman, W. Duane Evans, and Hyman B. Kaitz of the Bureau of Labor Statistics and from Thomas A. Wilson, Clopper Almon, Jr., Richard Oveson, and Ronald Bodkin. Patricia M. Anderson provided invaluable programming assistance. Alvene P. Williams, Elizabeth Barnes, Marie-Claire Sempé, Beverlee Bell, Susan I. Tomkin, Lyndia Harvey, Mary Louise Fisher, Laura P. Hoffman, and Carolyn Mullins gave able and cheerful secretarial assistance.

Most of the research on this book was done under contract with the United States Department of Labor, which gave us access to unpublished data mostly originating in the Department of Commerce and provided certain assumptions for use in the 1970 projections. Earlier versions of Chapters 1, 2, 3, and 4 were supplied to the Department as reports under the contract. We are grateful to the Bureau of Labor Statistics for permitting their publication. It is to be understood that the Bureau does not endorse any of the opinions, methods, and conclusions contained in this book; we bear sole responsibility.

Cambridge, Mass.   H.S.H.

June 1965   L.D.T.

Contents

Expenditure Categories in Chapter 3 and its Appendix

Introduction

This monograph is first of all an econometric demand study designed for projecting all items of United States private consumption expenditure (PCE) in future years. It presents the results of research originally undertaken under a contract between the U.S. Bureau of Labor Statistics and the Harvard Economic Research Project; this work was started in the spring of 1962 and completed in the summer of 1964. Subsequent work under a later contract was completed in the summer of 1967. General financial support for this, the second, edition of the study has been provided by the National Science Foundation. The projection of the PCE items is one of several components of the Interagency Growth Study, a comprehensive investigation of the quantitative structure of the American economy in conditions of full employment and steady growth. Since these components are interrelated, the projections had to be flexible enough to fit in with a variety of assumptions concerning the determinants of demand. This means, in fact, that a system of demand functions had to be estimated. The classification of consumption in this system is virtually the same as in the annual PCE table published by the U.S. Department of Commerce, which is the principal source of data. Pending completion of the other components of the Interagency Growth Study, the Bureau of Labor Statistics provided us with four sets of tentative assumptions for which preliminary projections of the pattern of consumer demand were reported in the first edition of this monograph. The present edition extends these projections to 1975. We have also investigated the relation between total PCE or saving and personal disposable income.

Practical considerations have necessarily had a large influence on the design and development of this study. Since one of its main results had to be a set of plausible projections for 1970, the sobering test of common sense was applied at nearly every step of the empirical research, so that the demand equations finally reported in Chapter 3 are the result of a long process of experimentation and elimination. For several items, ten or more equations were estimated and projected before a final equation was selected. In this selection process the plausibility of the projection (often a matter of opinion) was only one of the criteria; the economic and statistical characteristics of each equation were usually given greater weight.

Apart from this primary objective, the present study also pursues more strictly scientific goals. The analysis of consumer demand is one of the most developed branches of econometrics, actively practiced in North America, and no less so in Europe and Asia. To see what progress its students have made, we venture to suggest a comparison of our results with the pioneering work of Schultz (1938)[1] and perhaps with the more recent but already classic investigations of Wold and Juréen (1953) and Stone (1954). If we have been able to advance beyond these illustrious predecessors, it may be mostly because of a greater attention to the dynamic aspects of demand, though improvements in basic data and computing techniques have certainly contributed as well. There is of course nothing new in emphasizing the role of time in demand analysis, but the means of translating this emphasis into an adequate and workable method have only become available in the last few years, thanks to the work of Koyck (1954), Nerlove (1958), Stone and Rowe (1960), and others. It is also only recently that the quantitative importance of dynamic effects has been fully recognized; some evidence on this may be found in Houthakker (1965).

The dynamic model on which most of our work is based generalizes an idea long adopted in demand studies for durables: that current purchases depend not only on current income and prices, but also on the pre-existing inventory of the item in question. Current purchases then are regarded as an attempt to bring inventories in line with some desired or equilibrium level. It follows also that the effect of, say, a change in income can be analyzed into a short-term effect (the change in current purchases for given stocks) and a long-term effect (the change in purchases after stocks have reached the desired level). In the case of durables, the short-term effect will be greater than the long-term effect.

This idea can easily be extended to nondurable commodities, where habit formation is the exact counterpart of stock adjustment. Although the "inventories" can no longer be given a concrete interpretation, the formal difference between habit formation and stock adjustment is only in the sign of the parameter relating stocks to current purchases. For habit-forming commodities, the long-term effect of a change in income is larger than the short-term effect, and their consumption is less dependent on income change than are purchases of durables. In our model the concept of habit formation, studied earlier by Duesenberry (1949), Farrell (1952), Brown (1952), Tsujimura and Sato (1964), and others, becomes amenable to more conclusive analysis than had hitherto been possible, and our empirical results show it to be of very wide applicability.

The implementation of our dynamic model raises various problems of

---

[1] All citations in this form are to the list of references at the back of the volume.

statistical technique, some of which are discussed in this book. In particular, we have made much use of an estimation method, developed by Taylor and Wilson (1964), for equations containing lagged valued of the dependent variable and autocorrelated errors. Projection from dynamic equations also raises difficult problems which, in the absence of sufficiently pertinent theory, we have often had to resolve by Monte Carlo experiments. Students of econometric methods may also be interested in the estimating techniques that we developed in order to take into account an identifying restriction on the estimating equation of our dynamic model and to estimate our additive model of Chapter 5 and in our principal component analysis of 36 items of consumption from the 1960–1961 Survey of Consumer Expenditures in Chapter 6, which confirms the use of total PCE as the budget constraint with cross-section data.

We shall now summarize the eight chapters of the book. Chapter 1 deals mostly with the economic background. It explains why time-series analysis has been preferred over cross-section analysis, sets out the basic dynamic model of demand mentioned above (both formally and by numerical examples) with its various special cases, and presents an alternative and simpler dynamic model that has been used for a few commodities. It also goes into the consequence of using per capita rather than aggregate data.

Chapter 2 is devoted to statistical problems, particularly those arising in projection. It contains a brief description of the Taylor-Wilson method of "three-pass least squares," compares the merits of different estimation and projection techniques by Monte Carlo experiments, discusses the method used in estimating the parameters of the dynamic model when there is an identifying restriction on the estimating equation, and discusses the "adding-up problem," which arises from the failure of our system of demand functions to equate the sum of the individual demand projections to the given total PCE.

Chapter 3 contains the main results of our work: the demand equations for 82 commodities as finally selected. All but two of the final equations are dynamic (with habit formation predominant) and rely on total PCE for most or all of their explanatory power. In nearly all instances the goodness of fit, plausibility of the estimated parameters, and the autocorrelation in the disturbances range from satisfactory to excellent, but a number of problem items remain. Each commodity is discussed in some detail. In Chapter 4 some broader conclusions are drawn from the results of Chapter 3, and two sets of projections for 1970 and 1975 for the 82 commodities are presented and discussed. As a test of the equations, forecasts are made for 1965 (which was not included in the period of fit). Although there are some large discrepancies between the forecasted and actual values, the test provides encouragement concerning the usefulness of our approach. The question of whether total

PCE or income should be the budget constraint is also investigated in this chapter using a disaggregation of PCE into 11 (rather than 82) commodities, and these equations are tested with data for 1965, 1966, and 1967.

The dynamic model is extended in Chapter 5 to an additive system of demand functions derived from a quadratic utility function. The utility function is in fact a dynamic version of the function first proposed by Gossen in 1854. The model is applied to data of Canada, the Netherlands, and Sweden, as well as of the United States. The results for the United States corroborate those obtained with the nonadditive model, while the results for the other countries confirm that dynamic elements in consumer behavior know no country borders. Estimates of quantities that are proportional to the marginal utility of total expenditure arise from the estimation of the additive model, and these too are discussed in Chapter 5.

Chapter 6 turns away from time-series analysis and focuses on the data obtained in the 1960–1961 Survey of Consumer Expenditures. A reconciliation of these data with the OBE time-series data for 1960 and 1961 is undertaken, and large discrepancies are revealed, not only for individual items of expenditure but for total PCE and income as well. A principal component analysis of 36 items of expenditure shows quite conclusively that total PCE rather than income is the predominant factor in accounting for variation in cross-section consumption data. Double logarithmic equations relating expenditure to PCE and family size for 50 categories of consumption, estimated from the survey data, are also presented in this chapter, and an attempt is made to incorporate a dynamic element into the analysis by making use of information on income change from the preceding year. The chapter concludes with a comparison for a limited number of commodities of the PCE elasticities obtained from the cross-section data with those obtained from the OBE time-series data.

Chapter 7 deals with total PCE as a function of personal disposable income (the "consumption function"). The basic data are annual for 1929–1964 and quarterly for 1947–1964. The basic dynamic model is again found to give good results, but even better results are obtained with a variant of the model which views saving as the accumulation of nondepreciating assets. A number of different definitions of saving are investigated with this model, and data from the flow-of-funds and the Securities and Exchange Commission are analyzed in addition to those collected by OBE. Chapter 8 is an evaluation of the results as a whole.

In several respects this book is a counterpart to an earlier one in which one of the present authors participated (Prais and Houthakker, 1955). There consumption patterns were analyzed from cross-section data, mostly British, here from time series, mostly American. The first point of similarity between the two works is that, although the general approach in each is suggested by economic theory, it is kept flexible enough so as not to become a straitjacket. Second, while novel statistical techniques are developed and applied in both, neither is exclusively nor primarily methodological: the substantive results are an end in themselves and not merely an illustration of the methods. In fact, both originated in requests from government departments interested in concrete economic problems.[2] Third, in both studies the whole range of consumers' expenditure is covered, not just the foodstuffs and durables that have received most attention in the literature. Fourth, in each a large body of public but partly unpublished data is investigated by appropriate econometric methods, requiring teamwork and the use of highspeed computers. It is indicative of the advance in research technology that 15 years ago the use of computers in economics was an innovation, which had to be explained in some detail, whereas now it has become commonplace. Last, but not least, the influence of Richard Stone can be traced in both monographs.

We hope that the present work will be of use to economists in business and government as well as to our academic colleagues. Although painfully aware of the weaknesses of our results and the shortcomings of our methods, we believe that many of our demand equations and projections deserve to be taken seriously; whenever we were left dissatisfied with our results, we have said so. At the same time, nothing would please us more than that our work inspire others to do better, whether or not they choose to follow our tracks.

[2] This is not apparent in the earlier study, but see Houthakker and Tobin (1952).

1

The Economic Background

The projection of consumer demand is more than the mechanical extrapolation of past trends; it has to be based on analysis. If projections under alternative assumptions are required, it is necessary to establish how consumer expenditures respond to changes in their main economic determinants (incomes and prices). Hence the appropriate tool of analysis is regression analysis, which permits estimation of the effect of these determinants on the basis of past experience.

The emphasis is on time-series analysis, though some use was also made of cross-section data in the early stages of the inquiry and, mainly for comparison, in Chapter 6. The reasons for relying primarily on time-series analysis were both theoretical and practical. In the first place, cross-section analysis, except under rather heroic assumptions, will not provide information on the influence of prices, which may be of importance in long-term projections. In the second place, some of the notorious difficulties associated with time series can be overcome by the use of recently developed devices, which are more fully explained in Chapter 2. In the third place, the household surveys of the Bureau of Labor Statistics, on which the cross-section analysis would have had to depend, are hard to reconcile with the time series of the Office of Business Economics, as is shown for the 1960–1961 survey in Chapter 6. Finally, it has been realized increasingly in recent years that the income elasticities provided by cross-section and time-series analyses are conceptually different, and that the latter are probably more suitable for projection over time.[1]

I. The Time-Series Analysis: General Considerations

The research strategy followed in this study was initially determined by practical considerations. Since plausible projections had to be produced within a limited period of time, there was not much opportunity for experimentation with novel ideas and methods. The emphasis had to be on estimation rather than on the testing of hypotheses and the development of new

[1] See Meyer and Kuh (1957), Friedman (1957), Modigliani and Brumberg (1954). For a recent attempt to use cross-section analysis for projection see C. Almon (1966).

techniques, which are the usual objectives of academic research. It would not have been efficient, however, to concentrate entirely on the routine application of standard methods to the problem at hand, for it is well known that the results thus obtained may be unsatisfactory in important respects. Consequently, we tried to improve upon these methods without venturing so far into uncharted territory as to endanger the attainment of the ultimate goal. As we gained confidence in the new approach we turned increasingly to further refinements intended to relate it more closely to economic theory (see Chapters 5 and 7).

The standard approach to demand analysis,[2] which was also the starting point of the present study, involves the estimation of the following demand equation:

$$(1) \qquad q_{it} = f_i(x_t, p_{it}, z_{1t}, z_{2t}, \ldots, z_{nt}, u_{it})$$

where q_{it} is per capita consumption of the ith commodity in year t, f_i is a function whose mathematical form is to be specified later, x_t is a measure of per capita real disposable income, p_{it} is the deflated price of the ith commodity, $z_{1t}, z_{2t}, \ldots, z_{nt}$, are any other explanatory variables, and u_{it} is a disturbance term representing both the effect of variables that are not explicitly introduced into the equation and errors of measurement in q_{it}. Among the additional predictors, $z_{1t}, z_{2t}, \ldots, z_{nt}$, may be such variables as the price of one or more substitutes or complements of the ith commodity, lagged values of x_t or p_{it}, a time trend, and many other types. The shortness of economic time series and the lack of independent variation limits the number of predictors that can be usefully introduced. Sometimes even p_{it}, or more rarely x_t, does not contribute enough to the explanation of q_{it} to be retained as an explicit predictor.

Some of the difficulties associated with this approach are:

(a) The explanatory variables x_t and p_{it} (and possibly some of the z's) are not truly exogenous; at least in theory, they are jointly determined with the q_{it}. The demand equation (1) is really only one in a system of equations, which for estimation purposes should be treated as a whole. In particular, it is necessary in principle to specify for each commodity not only a demand equation but a supply equation as well, and to estimate them simultaneously. Unfortunately simultaneous-equation techniques have so far only rarely led to convincing results in demand analysis. This appears to be due in large part to the failure of economic theory to formulate an adequate supply equation (except for crops, which are not immediately relevant to the markets for consumer goods). In the absence of such an equation, simultaneous estimation is virtually impossible, and the use of single-equation estimation is unavoidable in demand analysis at the present time. In the discussion of the

[2] Among others, see Wold and Jureen (1953), Stone (1954), Ferber and Verdoorn (1962).

regression equations for the individual items of expenditure (see Chapter 3), the occurrence of simultaneous-equation bias will be pointed out whenever it appears to have affected the results.

(b) The mathematical form of the demand equation cannot be specified *a priori* in the present state of the art. It is therefore advisable to try out different forms, especially those obtainable by logarithmic transformations of one or more of the variables. The following four forms were originally used in connection with nearly all commodities:

linear: $q = \alpha + \beta x + \gamma p$
semi-logarithmic: $q = \alpha + \beta \log x + \gamma \log p$
double-logarithmic: $\log q = \alpha + \beta \log x + \gamma \log p$
inverse semi-logarithmic: $\log q = \alpha + \beta x + \gamma p.$

For convenience other variables and subscripts have been suppressed. Other things being equal, the mathematical form giving the best fit to the observations was retained. For most commodities, however, the dynamic model discussed in the next section was applied and, since this is compatible only with a linear demand equation, there was no possibility of experimenting with transformations of the variables. Experience with the static model suggested that nonlinear equations frequently fit better than the linear one, but that the difference in fit (as measured by the correlation between actual and calculated values of the observations in arithmetic units) was relatively minor. This probably is explained by the fact that in time series (as opposed to cross-section data) the explanatory variables do not vary over a wide range, so that a linear approximation is usually quite satisfactory. Hence the dynamic model does not appear to be seriously weakened by its limitation to the linear form.

(c) The decision as to which predictors are to appear explicitly in a regression equation is also somewhat arbitrary in the absence of a generally agreed criterion. Although the frequently followed rule of regarding a regression coefficient as "insignificant" if it is less than twice its standard error may have some conventional usefulness in the testing of hypotheses, it is irrelevant in a projecting context. The rule followed in the present study is to retain a regression coefficient if it exceeds its standard error, provided its sign is theoretically correct. This is tantamount to minimizing the estimated variance of the projection. If the sign is wrong (in particular a positive own-price elasticity), further efforts to improve the equation are indicated.

As it happens, few instances of unacceptable signs were encountered, though this is not necessarily a reason for self-congratulation; it may be due in part to the way in which the price variables were derived. The undeflated price series for each commodity was the result of dividing expenditure at current prices by expenditure at constant prices. Hence if the constant-price expenditure figure was too high for some reason, the derived price figure would be too low. The correlation between quantity (represented by expenditure at constant prices) and price is therefore biased in the negative direction, and this bias may also have influenced the regression coefficients of prices.

(d) Probably the most serious defect of the standard approach to demand analysis is its static character, which is not essentially changed by the arbitrary inclusion of lagged income or prices as predictors. The effect of a change in, say, income is in general neither immediate nor delayed by a year or some other fixed interval; it is more likely to be spread out over some considerable period of time.[3] Fortunately, methods for dealing with these so-called distributed lags have been developed during the last few years; their economic rationale and application to the present study will be discussed in the next section.

A related difficulty, which also appears to be resolved (or at least mitigated) by these new methods, has to do with the disturbance term u_{it} in equation (1). The residuals in estimated regression equations of this type often show considerable autocorrelation, usually of the positive variety (if the actual observation in year t is higher than predicted, the same tends to be true in year $t + 1$). This does not bias the estimates of the parameters, but it does play havoc with the standard errors that are important for deciding which predictors to include. Autocorrelated residuals also cause problems in projecting; this is discussed more fully in Chapter 2.

II. *The Basic Dynamic Model (State Adjustment)*

The dynamic models used in this study express the generally accepted idea that current decisions are influenced by past behavior. To make this idea operational, the basic dynamic model postulates a particular type of relationship between the past and the present. The effect of past behavior is assumed to be represented entirely by the current values of certain "state variables," of which inventories are a concrete (but not the only) example. The basic dynamic model may therefore be said to represent *state adjustment*, in contrast to an alternative model of flow adjustment described in section V below. These state variables themselves are in turn changed by current decisions, and the net result is that of a "distributed lag": current behavior depends on

[3] The necessity of a dynamic approach has long been recognized in analyses of the demand for automobiles. Applications to a wider range of commodities were first made by Richard Stone and his associates—for instance, Stone and Croft-Murray (1959). The dynamic model used here differs from Stone's in several respects but is similar to one proposed by Nerlove (1960). In this chapter we shall not formulate the dynamics of demand in terms of the theory of consumer's choice, but this is done for a special case in Chapter 5; see also Houthakker (1962).

all past values of the predetermined variables, though more on recent values than on very remote ones.

A simple example will illustrate the principles involved. Let $q(t)$ be an individual's demand for clothing during a very short time interval around t, let $x(t)$ be his income during that interval, and let $s(t)$ be his inventory of clothes at time t. More exactly, let $q(t)$ be the rate of demand at time t and $x(t)$ be the rate of income at that time. All other variables are ignored for the time being. Then the basic assumption is that

$$(2) \qquad\qquad q(t) = \alpha + \beta s(t) + \gamma x(t)$$

so that the individual's current demand for clothing depends not only on his current income, but also on his stock of clothing. We may expect that, for a person with given tastes and given income, the more clothes he has to begin with, the fewer he will buy currently. In the case of a durable commodity such as clothing [4] the stock coefficient β will therefore be negative, but it will now be shown that equation (2) may also hold for other types of commodities if we allow a more general interpretation of $s(t)$. In fact the equation can represent not only the stock-adjustment behavior just described, but also habit formation or inertia, which is apparently a more widespread phenomenon.

Consider a commodity of which consumers do not normally hold physical inventories of any significance, say tobacco. By all accounts tobacco consumption is habit-forming, which means that it does not adjust immediately to changes in income (or in prices, for that matter) and that current consumption is positively influenced by consumption in the more or less recent past. In this case we can say metaphorically that the consumer has built up a psychological stock of smoking habits. His current consumption will be affected by that stock (or, if one prefers, "state variable") just as it is for clothing, but the sign of β will now be positive: the more he has smoked in the past, the more he will smoke currently (tastes and income again being given).

The question arises at once: How can we measure such a psychological stock? It will be shown in a moment that under certain reasonable assumptions there is no need to measure it, because $s(t)$ can be eliminated from the regression equation. Yet it should be stressed first that this difficulty is not peculiar to habit-forming commodities, but arises almost as strongly for durable commodities such as clothing.[5] In the latter case we cannot measure $s(t)$ simply by the number of suits, shirts, and such, for some of these may be worn out and due for replacement; moreover, their heterogeneity also makes

---

[4] The Department of Commerce in its PCE table does not classify clothing as durable, because its normal lifetime is not long enough. But for present purposes it may be so regarded, especially in view of our empirical results (item 2.3).

[5] In fact, there is often no *a priori* basis for deciding whether, in the demand for a commodity, habit formation or stock adjustment will predominate.

direct measurement hard. Clearly some depreciated measure of inventories is needed, but the appropriate depreciation rates are usually not known *a priori* and would have to be either estimated from the data or guessed. Hence even for durables, where the state variable has a concrete interpretation, it is desirable to eliminate it.

This can be done in the following manner. First consider the accounting identity

$$(3) \qquad \dot{s}(t) = q(t) - w(t)$$

where $\dot{s}(t)$ stands for the rate of change in the (physical or psychological) stock around time t and $w(t)$ stands for the average "using up" or "depreciation" of that stock at the same time. From now on, moreover, we shall assume that

$$(4) \qquad w(t) = \delta s(t)$$

where δ is a constant depreciation rate. Hence the rate of depreciation at any time t is proportional to the stock at that time. The assumption of proportionality corresponds to the "declining balance" method of depreciation, which has been found realistic in many practical situations.[6] Combining (3) and (4) we find that

$$(5) \qquad \dot{s}(t) = q(t) - \delta s(t).$$

Integration of equation (5) shows, incidentally, that

$$(6) \qquad s(t) = \int_{-\infty}^{t} q(u)e^{\delta(u-t)}du$$

or, in words, the state variable at any time is equal to the sum of the discounted flows bought up to that time. This formula applies equally well to durable as well as to habit-forming commodities. Next eliminate $s(t)$ from (5) by using (2):

$$(7) \qquad \dot{s}(t) = q(t) - \frac{\delta}{\beta}[q(t) - \alpha - \gamma x(t)].$$

Now differentiate (2) with respect to time and substitute (7) for $\dot{s}(t)$:

$$(8) \qquad \dot{q}(t) = \beta\left[q(t) - \frac{\delta}{\beta}(q(t) - \alpha - \gamma x(t))\right] + \gamma\dot{x}(t).$$

After simplification this expression becomes

$$(9) \qquad \dot{q}(t) = \alpha\delta + (\beta - \delta)q(t) + \gamma\dot{x}(t) + \gamma\delta x(t),$$

which is a first-order differential equation involving only the observable quantities q and x.

---

[6] In equation (56) of this chapter, an entirely different interpretation of δ will be given.

The short-term derivative of consumption with respect to income is given by γ, the coefficient of $x(t)$ in (2) and $\dot{x}(t)$ in (9). "Short-term" in this context is taken to mean the instantaneous adjustment in consumption before the state variables have a chance to adjust. It is also possible to calculate a long-term derivative, which is equal to the entire change in demand associated with a once-and-for-all change in income, including any indirect effects through changes in the state variables.

More precisely, we can define a long-term equilibrium in which q, s, and x all remain constant over time. These long-term levels will be denoted by $\hat{q}$, $\hat{s}$, and $\hat{x}$. Then it follows from (5) that, since $\dot{s}(t) = 0$,

$$(10) \qquad\qquad \hat{q} = \delta\hat{s}.$$

Substitution into (2) gives

$$(11) \qquad\qquad \hat{q} = \alpha + \frac{\beta}{\delta}\hat{q} + \gamma\hat{x}$$

and hence, assuming $\beta \neq \delta$,

$$(12) \qquad\qquad \hat{q} = \frac{\alpha\delta}{\delta - \beta} + \frac{\gamma\delta}{\delta - \beta}\hat{x}.$$

The long-run derivative of q with respect to x is given by the coefficient of $\hat{x}$. (If $\beta = \delta$ the long-run equation does not exist.)

Using (10) and (11) we find similarly that

$$(13) \qquad\qquad \hat{s} = \frac{\alpha}{\delta - \beta} + \frac{\gamma}{\delta - \beta}\hat{x},$$

which implies, after some manipulation, that

$$(14) \qquad\qquad q(t) - \hat{q} = \beta\{s(t) - \hat{s}\}$$

or, in words: *the deviation of current purchases from their long-term level is proportional to the deviation of the state variable from its long-term level.* Both long-term levels are calculated for the current income, but otherwise (14) is independent of income. This formula provides additional justification for the name "state-adjustment model." It also brings out the importance of the coefficient β: if β is negative, purchases are above their long-term level if the inventory is below its long-term level, but if β is positive, the two deviations have the same sign.

Perhaps of greater interest than the above interpretation of the long-term derivative, which in essence takes the dynamic approach of this section to its static limits, is another interpretation in the context of steady (linear) growth defined as a development in which the derivatives of q, s, and x remain constant over time.[7] In formula:

---

[7] In the theory of economic growth, more emphasis is put on exponential growth, in which the proportional increase per period is constant. Such growth is somewhat harder

(15) $$\dot{q}(t) = g_q; \quad \dot{x}(t) = g_x; \quad \dot{s}(t) = g_s \quad \text{for all } t.$$

It then also follows that

(16) $$g_s = q(t) - \delta s(t),$$

which upon differentiating with respect to time yields

(17) $$g_q = \delta g_s,$$

while from (2)

(18) $$g_q = \beta g_s + \gamma g_x.$$

Hence, again assuming $\beta \neq \delta$,

(19) $$g_q = \frac{\gamma}{1 - \beta/\delta} g_x = \frac{\gamma\delta}{\delta - \beta} g_x$$

in agreement with (12). The case $\delta = 0$ will be discussed in Chapter 7.

III. A Finite Approximation of the Dynamic Model

As indicated above, equation (9) contains only the observable quantities q and x. However, in order to estimate the parameters α, β, γ, and δ from annual or quarterly observations, the continuous model must be approximated by one involving discrete intervals of time. This has to be done with some care; the common practice in economics of simply replacing derivatives by finite differences is a source of unnecessary inaccuracy.

To begin with, we define

(20) $$\bar{q}_{t_0} = \int_{t_0}^{t_0 + \tau} q(t)\, dt.$$

That is, if $q(t)$ is the rate of consumption per unit time, dt, then $\bar{q}_{t_0}$ is the corresponding total consumption in a longer time interval, τ. Similarly, define

(21) $$\bar{x}_{t_0} = \int_{t_0}^{t_0 + \tau} x(t)\, dt; \qquad \bar{s}_{t_0} = \int_{t_0}^{t_0 + \tau} s(t)\, dt.$$

However, since $s(t)$ is a stock level at time t, the integral $\bar{s}_{t_0}$ is interpreted differently from $\bar{q}_{t_0}$ and $\bar{x}_{t_0}$. In particular, we can interpret $\bar{s}_{t_0}/\tau$ as the average stock level within the time interval $(t_0, t_0 + \tau)$. Finally, the changes in the variables within each period are defined by

(22) $$\Delta^* q_{t_0} = q(t_0 + \tau) - q(t_0); \qquad \Delta^* s_{t_0} = s(t_0 + \tau) - s(t_0); \text{ etc.}$$

---

to fit in with the linear demand function (2), since a linear function of an exponential function is not itself an exponential function. As it happens, linear growth had been postulated by the Bureau of Labor Statistics for the present projection study. Exponential growth is discussed in Chapter 7, under special assumptions.

If (2) is integrated over time from t_0 to $t_0 + \tau$, the structural equation becomes[8]

(23) $$\bar{q}_{t_0} = \alpha\tau + \beta\bar{s}_{t_0} + \gamma\bar{x}_{t_0}.$$

Similarly, in period $(t_0 + \tau, t_0 + 2\tau)$,

(24) $$\bar{q}_{t_0+\tau} = \alpha\tau + \beta\bar{s}_{t_0+\tau} + \gamma\bar{x}_{t_0+\tau}.$$

The within-period change in the level of stock is

(25) $$\Delta^*s_{t_0} \equiv \bar{q}_{t_0} - \delta\bar{s}_{t_0},$$

and similarly,

(26) $$\Delta^*s_{t_0+\tau} \equiv \bar{q}_{t_0+\tau} - \delta\bar{s}_{t_0+\tau}.$$

Subtracting (23) from (24) gives

(27) $$\bar{q}_{t_0+\tau} - \bar{q}_{t_0} = \beta(\bar{s}_{t_0+\tau} - \bar{s}_{t_0}) + \gamma(\bar{x}_{t_0+\tau} - \bar{x}_{t_0}).$$

Moreover, we can infer from (23) and (24):

(28) $$\bar{s}_{t_0+\tau} = \frac{1}{\beta}(\bar{q}_{t_0+\tau} - \alpha\tau - \gamma\bar{x}_{t_0+\tau});$$

(29) $$\bar{s}_{t_0} = \frac{1}{\beta}(\bar{q}_{t_0} - \alpha\tau - \gamma\bar{x}_{t_0}).$$

If (28) and (29) are used to replace $\bar{s}_{t_0+\tau}$ and $\bar{s}_{t_0}$ in (25) and (26), we get

(30) $$\Delta^*s_{t_0+\tau} = \bar{q}_{t_0+\tau} - \frac{\delta}{\beta}(\bar{q}_{t_0+\tau} - \alpha\tau - \gamma\bar{x}_{t_0+\tau});$$

(31) $$\Delta^*s_{t_0} = \bar{q}_{t_0} - \frac{\delta}{\beta}(\bar{q}_{t_0} - \alpha\tau - \gamma\bar{x}_{t_0}).$$

The difference $\bar{s}_{t_0+\tau} - \bar{s}_{t_0}$ between the two periods may be approximated by

(32) $$\bar{s}_{t_0+\tau} - \bar{s}_{t_0} \sim \frac{\tau}{2}(\Delta^*s_{t_0+\tau} + \Delta^*s_{t_0}),$$

an approximation that will be more accurate the closer the behavior of the stock variable is to linearity within the period. This is illustrated in Figure 1.1.

The solid curve represents the actual function, $s(t)$, while the dotted line represents the linear approximation to it. The area under the actual curve is given by

(33) $$\bar{s}_{t_0} = \int_{t_0}^{t_0+\tau} s(t)\,dt,$$

---

[8] An alternative and shorter derivation, for which we are indebted to Robert Dorfman, starts from the differential equation (9) and then applies the approximation of (32) to q and x rather than to s, thus leading directly to (37).

Figure 1.1

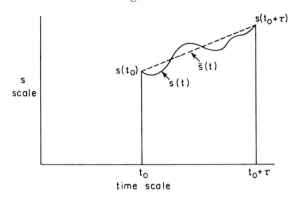

while the area under the linear approximation is equal to

$$(34) \qquad \tau s(t_0) + \frac{\tau}{2}[s(t_0 + \tau) - s(t_0)] = \frac{\tau}{2}[s(t_0 + \tau) + s(t_0)].$$

Hence the difference $\bar{s}_{t_0+\tau} - \bar{s}_{t_0}$ is approximately equal to

$$(35) \qquad \frac{\tau}{2}[s(t_0 + 2\tau) + s(t_0 + \tau) - s(t_0 + \tau) - s(t_0)] = \frac{\tau}{2}[\Delta^* s_{t_0+\tau} + \Delta^* s_{t_0}].$$

Assuming that the approximation is good enough for practical purposes, we can write (27) as

$$(36) \quad \bar{q}_{t_0+\tau} - \bar{q}_{t_0} = \frac{\tau}{2}\beta(\Delta^* s_{t_0+\tau} + \Delta^* s_{t_0}) + \gamma(\bar{x}_{t_0+\tau} - \bar{x}_{t_0})$$

$$= \frac{\tau}{2}\beta\left[\bar{q}_{t_0+\tau} - \frac{\delta}{\beta}(\bar{q}_{t_0+\tau} - \alpha\tau - \gamma\bar{x}_{t_0+\tau}) + \bar{q}_{t_0} \right.$$

$$\left. - \frac{\delta}{\beta}(\bar{q}_{t_0} - \alpha\tau - \gamma\bar{x}_{t_0})\right] + \gamma(\bar{x}_{t_0+\tau} - \bar{x}_{t_0}),$$

which upon simplification and rearrangement becomes

$$(37) \quad \bar{q}_{t_0+\tau} = \frac{\alpha\delta\tau^2}{1 - \frac{\tau}{2}(\beta - \delta)} + \frac{1 + \frac{\tau}{2}(\beta - \delta)}{1 - \frac{\tau}{2}(\beta - \delta)}\bar{q}_{t_0}$$

$$+ \frac{\gamma\left(1 + \frac{\tau\delta}{2}\right)}{1 - \frac{\tau}{2}(\beta - \delta)}\bar{x}_{t_0+\tau} - \frac{\gamma\left(1 - \frac{\tau\delta}{2}\right)}{1 - \frac{\tau}{2}(\beta - \delta)}\bar{x}_{t_0}.$$

Equation (37) is the discrete analogue to equation (9), and once τ is specified only the observable quantities q and x are involved. If we establish our time scale so that $\tau = 1$ and remove the bars for notational ease, then we have

$$(38) \quad q_t = \frac{\alpha\delta}{1 - \frac{1}{2}(\beta - \delta)} + \frac{1 + \frac{1}{2}(\beta - \delta)}{1 - \frac{1}{2}(\beta - \delta)} q_{t-1}$$

$$+ \frac{\gamma\left(1 + \frac{\delta}{2}\right)}{1 - \frac{1}{2}(\beta - \delta)} x_t + \frac{\gamma\left(1 - \frac{\delta}{2}\right)}{1 - \frac{1}{2}(\beta - \delta)} x_{t-1}.$$

Finally, for computational reasons it is convenient to write x_t as $(x_t - x_{t-1}) + x_{t-1} \equiv \Delta x_t + x_{t-1}$, which transforms (38) into [9]

$$(39) \quad q_t = \frac{\alpha\delta}{1 - \frac{1}{2}(\beta - \delta)} + \frac{1 + \frac{1}{2}(\beta - \delta)}{1 - \frac{1}{2}(\beta - \delta)} q_{t-1}$$

$$+ \frac{\gamma\left(1 + \frac{\delta}{2}\right)}{1 - \frac{1}{2}(\beta - \delta)} \Delta x_t + \frac{\gamma\delta}{1 - \frac{1}{2}(\beta - \delta)} x_{t-1}.$$

This is the equation actually used for estimation.

Equation (39) shows how the parameters α, β, γ, and δ of the structural equations enter the estimating equation. These four parameters can in fact be recomputed from the four coefficients of (39), which for convenience we shall rewrite as [10]

[9] Note that the economist's convention of writing Δx_t as $x_t - x_{t-1}$ is now being used. The difference Δ between the means in two periods is not to be confused with the change Δ^* within a period. From now on Δ^* will no longer be needed.

[10] Griliches (1967, p. 34) has observed that equation (40) could also arise from a static equation with first-order autocorrelation in the errors:

$$(1') \qquad\qquad q_t = a + bx_t + u_t$$

$$(2') \qquad\qquad u_t = cu_{t-1} + v_t,$$

where v_t is a "well-behaved" error term. If $(1')$ and $(2')$ are combined so as to eliminate u, the resulting expression is

$$(3') \qquad\qquad q_t = a(1 - c) + cq_{t-1} + bx_t - bcx_{t-1} + v_t,$$

which has the same form as (40) with

$$(4') \qquad A_0 = a(1 - c); \quad A_1 = c; \quad A_2 = b; \quad A_3 - A_2 = -bc.$$

If $(1')$ and $(2')$ together provide the correct specification, then it follows from $(4')$ that $A_3 - A_2$ must be equal to $-A_1 A_2$. This in turn implies that

$$(5') \qquad\qquad 1 - A_1 = A_3/A_2$$

or

$$(6') \qquad\qquad 1 - \frac{1 + \frac{1}{2}(\beta - \delta)}{1 - \frac{1}{2}(\beta - \delta)} = \frac{\delta}{1 + \frac{\delta}{2}},$$

which (after some manipulation) reduces to

$$(7') \qquad\qquad -\beta + \delta = \delta.$$

Expression $(7')$ implies that β must equal zero for all δ, a result which is hardly surprising and which can also be derived directly by comparing $(1')$ with (2). Thus, it follows that the static model with autoregressive errors is simply a special case of our basic model. In the empirical work that follows, however, there are only a few cases where dynamic adjustment appears to be absent.

$$(40) \qquad q_t = A_0 + A_1 q_{t-1} + A_2 \Delta x_t + A_3 x_{t-1}.$$

It can then be easily verified that (apart from estimating errors)

$$(41) \qquad \alpha = \frac{2A_0(A_2 - \frac{1}{2}A_3)}{A_3(A_1 + 1)};$$

$$(42) \qquad \beta = \frac{2(A_1 - 1)}{A_1 + 1} + \frac{A_3}{A_2 - \frac{1}{2}A_3};$$

$$(43) \qquad \gamma = \frac{2(A_2 - \frac{1}{2}A_3)}{A_1 + 1};$$

$$(44) \qquad \delta = \frac{A_3}{A_2 - \frac{1}{2}A_3}.$$

Equation (23) shows that the short-term derivative of q with respect to x, is equal to γ, the same as with the continuous model. From (23) and (25) we see that, when q, s, and x remain constant over time, the long-term derivative is given by $\gamma\delta/(\delta - \beta)$, again the same as with the continuous model. Similarly, with the case of steady (linear) growth where it is now assumed that q, s, and x each increase by a constant absolute amount per period, it can easily be shown that

$$(45) \qquad g_q = \frac{\gamma\delta}{\delta - \beta} g_x$$

where $g_q = q_t - q_{t-1}$, $g_x = x_t - x_{t-1}$, and $g_s = s_t - s_{t-1} = \Delta s_t$ for all t.

The foregoing will be illustrated by two examples, referring to food purchased for home use (excluding alcoholic beverages) and to clothing (including luggage). These are, respectively, items 1.1 and 2.3 in the National Income Accounts. The estimated equation for food was [11]

$$(46) \qquad \hat{q}_t = 29.074 + .6044q_{t-1} + .1128\Delta x_t + .0528x_{t-1},$$

where q and x are per capita figures measured in constant (1954) dollars; prices do not appear in this equation since their influence was found to be statistically insignificant. From (41) through (44) it follows that

$$(47) \qquad \hat{\alpha} = 59.28; \qquad \hat{\beta} = .118; \qquad \hat{\gamma} = .108; \qquad \hat{\delta} = .614.$$

(The "hats" denote estimates.) It appears therefore, since $\hat{\beta} > 0$, that aggregate food buying is habit-forming (though this conclusion can really be established only by considering the standard error of $\hat{\beta}$). So there is justification for introducing a "psychological stock of food-buying habits." In the

[11] The equations (46), (49), and (81) used here as examples have been taken unchanged from the first edition. The revised equations for these items will be found in Chapter 3.

present case this stock depreciates rather rapidly, as can be seen by the large size of δ.

The short-term effect of total consumer expenditure on food expenditure is measured by $\hat{\gamma}$, while the long-term effect is given by

$$(48) \qquad \frac{\hat{\gamma}\hat{\delta}}{\hat{\delta} - \hat{\beta}} = \frac{A_3}{1 - A_1} = .133.$$

The instantaneous effect of a one-dollar increase in total expenditure on food purchases is therefore equal to 10.8 cents. After one year the accumulated effect, measured by A_2, is 11.3 cents, and in subsequent years there is a further increase of 2.0 cents $(.113 + .020 = .133)$. We shall have more to say about (46) in a moment.

The estimated equation for clothing was

$$(49) \qquad \hat{q}_t = 17.595 + .6243q_{t-1} + .0763\Delta x_t + .0173x_{t-1},$$

with

$$(50) \qquad \hat{\alpha} = 84.5902; \qquad \hat{\beta} = -.2065; \qquad \hat{\gamma} = .0833; \qquad \hat{\delta} = .2561$$

as the corresponding estimates of the structural coefficients. We see that on balance clothing is subject to an inventory effect $(\hat{\beta} < 0)$; hence the earlier discussion treating clothing as a durable good had justification. The estimate of the long-run total-expenditure coefficient is

$$(51) \qquad \frac{\hat{\gamma}\hat{\delta}}{\hat{\delta} - \hat{\beta}} = .04605,$$

which is about half the short-run effect. This means that the immediate effect of an increase in total expenditure is to increase the stock of clothing; however, in subsequent periods the higher stock tends to decrease the flow of purchase.

We shall now use the equations for food and clothing to illustrate the behavior over time of our dynamic model. For this purpose we take the actual values of q_t in 1961 (as they were used in Chapter 4 of the first edition) and extrapolate q_t as a function of x_t under four different assumptions (see Table 1.1 and Figure 1.2; the figure also includes housing, which is discussed in section VI).

In this table, Case 1 corresponds to a stationary level of total PCE, and thus brings out the approach to a long-run equilibrium of the kind defined by equation (10). We observe that food consumption rises substantially at first, but at a diminishing rate. At the end of the decade it is close to its equilibrium value according to (11), which in this case becomes

$$(52) \qquad \hat{q} = 73.49 + .13347\hat{x}.$$

For $\hat{x} = 1657$, this gives $\hat{q} = 294.63$. Similarly for clothing,

Figure 1.2a

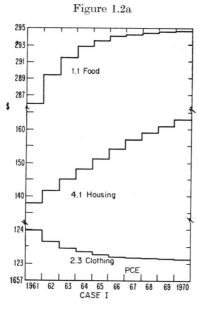

CASE I

(53) $$\hat{q} = 46.83 + .04605\hat{x}.$$

For $\hat{x} = 1657$, this gives $\hat{q} = 123.13$; clothing consumption, however, is falling throughout the decade. This means, of course, that in 1961 food consumption was below, and clothing consumption above, its equilibrium level. It will be shown in a moment that these relative positions of the 1961 level are not altogether accidental. Before leaving Case 1 it should be noted that

(54) $$\Delta q_t = A_1 \Delta q_{t-1},$$

as can easily be proved from equation (40).

Case 2 represents steady linear growth, equivalent to the average growth rate in aggregate PCE that was used as one assumption in Chapter 4. Each year PCE is increased by about \$54.22 to reach \$2145 in 1970. Both food and clothing consumption increase every year, but at a decreasing rate. At the end of the period, Δq_t is close to the equilibrium growth given by (45), which equals \$7.24 for food and \$2.50 for clothing. The interested reader may like to verify that in Case 2

(55) $$\Delta q_t - \Delta q_{t-1} = A_1(\Delta q_{t-1} - \Delta q_{t-2}),$$

in contrast with (54).

Perhaps the most remarkable feature of Case 2 is that the 1970 values of q_t are not close to the static equilibrium levels $\hat{q}$, given by (52) and (53); the latter, for $x_t = 2145$, are respectively 359.78 and 145.61. The 1970 figure for

Figure 1.2b

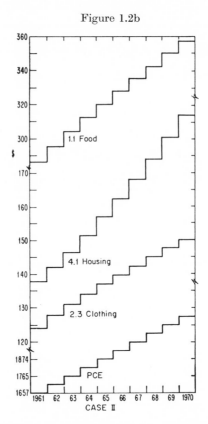

CASE II

food falls short of this level; that for clothing exceeds it. Here we can observe the implications of habit formation and stock adjustment: food is below its $\hat{q}$ because PCE is rising and current consumption is held back by the lower levels of the past; but in clothing these lower levels imply that inventories have not reached the currently desired level, so that relatively more has to be bought to bring inventories up to that level. And now it is also clear why in 1961 food consumption was below, and clothing consumption above, the $\hat{q}$ for that year, as we saw in Case 1. One reason (perhaps not the only one) is that per capita PCE had been rising for a few years up to 1961.

Case 2 further suggests that clothing is relatively more responsive to changes in PCE than food. This is also clear from equations (46) and (49): the ratio A_2/A_3 is twice as large for clothing as for food.[12] This ratio in turn determines δ, as can be seen if (44) is rearranged to give

$$(56) \qquad\qquad 1/\delta = A_2/A_3 - 1/2.$$

---

[12] Actually food and clothing are rather moderate examples of habit formation and stock adjustment, respectively. We chose those two, rather than more extreme instances, because they are large items with very simple dynamic equations.

Table 1.1. Equation (40): Behavior of Consumption over Time

Year	x_t	Item 1.1 (food)		Item 2.3 (clothing)	
		q_t	Δq_t	q_t	Δq_t
		Case 1			
1961	1657	286.05	—	123.98	—
1962	1657	289.45	+3.40	123.66	−.32
1963	1657	291.51	+2.06	123.46	−.20
1964	1657	292.75	+1.24	123.34	−.12
1965	1657	293.50	+.75	123.26	−.08
1966	1657	293.96	+.46	123.21	−.05
1967	1657	294.23	+.27	123.18	−.03
1968	1657	294.40	+.17	123.16	−.02
1969	1657	294.50	+.10	123.15	−.01
1970	1657	294.56	+.06	123.15	−.01
		Case 2			
1961	1657	286.05	—	123.98	—
1962	1711.22	295.57	+9.52	127.80	+3.82
1963	1765.44	304.18	+8.61	131.12	+3.32
1964	1819.66	312.25	+8.07	134.13	+3.01
1965	1873.88	319.99	+7.74	136.94	+2.81
1966	1928.10	327.53	+7.54	139.64	+2.70
1967	1982.32	334.95	+7.42	142.27	+2.63
1968	2036.55	342.30	+7.35	144.85	+2.58
1969	2090.78	349.61	+7.31	147.39	+2.54
1970	2145	356.89	+7.28	149.92	+2.53
		Case 3			
1961	1657	286.05	—	123.98	—
1962	1657	289.45	+3.40	123.66	−.32
1963	1711.22	297.62	+8.17	127.60	+3.94
1964	1711.22	299.31	+1.69	126.86	−.74
1965	1711.22	300.33	+1.02	126.40	−.46
1966	1657	294.83	−5.50	121.97	−4.43
1967	1657	294.76	−.07	122.41	+.44
		Case 4			
1961	1657	286.50	—	123.98	—
1962	1711.22	295.57	+9.52	127.80	+3.82
1963	1765.44	304.18	+8.61	131.12	+3.32
1964	1765.44	306.14	+1.96	130.00	−1.12
1965	1711.22	301.20	−4.94	125.16	−4.84
1966	1711.22	301.47	+.27	125.34	+.18
1967	1765.44	307.75	+6.28	129.59	+4.25
1968	1819.66	314.41	+6.66	133.18	+3.61

Figure 1.2c

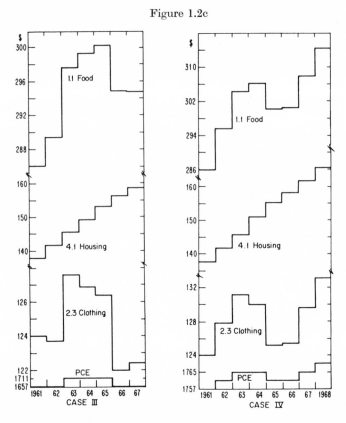

Consequently δ is smaller the greater the effect of a one-dollar change in PCE compared to that of a dollar's difference in past PCE. This interpretation of δ is independent of the original one in (4) as the depreciation rate of a physical or psychological stock.

Further evidence on the short-term effects of habit formation and stock adjustment is provided by Cases 3 and 4 of Table 1.1. In Case 3 PCE first remains stationary, then increases by the same amount as in Case 2, remains stationary again, and finally returns to its initial level. Food consumption rises during the first two periods of stationary PCE, when clothing consumption is falling. In the third stationary period, food consumption is higher than in the first, even though PCE is the same, because of the habit-forming effect of higher consumption in the second stationary period. Clothing consumption, on the contrary, is lower finally than initially, because stocks have been built up in the second period. Case 4 represents growth interrupted by a recession. Its analysis is in line with the preceding remarks; we leave it to the interested reader.

It is now time to reintroduce the demand predictors other than x that have been ignored up to this point. We shall consider only price p and the error term u, since the treatment of any additional variables will be clear by analogy.[13]

The basic equation becomes

(57) $$q_t = \alpha + \beta s_t + \gamma x_t + \eta p_t + u_t,$$

while the stock identity remains valid as it stands. The derivation of an estimating equation similar to (39) need not be given in full, for no new questions of principle come up. The result is

(58) $$q_t = A_0 + A_1 q_{t-1} + A_2 \Delta x_t + A_3 x_{t-1} + A_4 \Delta p_t + A_5 p_{t-1} + v_t,$$

where A_0, A_1, A_2, and A_3 have the same meaning as before and

(59) $$A_4 = \frac{\eta\left(1 + \dfrac{\delta}{2}\right)}{1 - \frac{1}{2}(\beta - \delta)};$$

(60) $$A_5 = \frac{\eta\delta}{1 - \frac{1}{2}(\beta - \delta)}.$$

The v_t is an error term defined by

(61) $$v_t = \frac{\left(1 + \dfrac{\delta}{2}\right)u_t - \left(1 - \dfrac{\delta}{2}\right)u_{t-1}}{1 - \frac{1}{2}(\beta - \delta)}.$$

It will be noted that A_4 and A_5 differ from A_2 and A_3 only in that γ is replaced by η; this means among other things that, parallel to (12) and (45), the long-term derivative of q with respect to p is given by $\eta\delta/(\delta - \beta)$, so that the lagged effect of a change in any predictor is distributed in the same manner as it is for x. Furthermore it also means that two different estimates of δ can be derived from (56), since in addition to (44) we have (apart from sampling errors):

(62) $$\delta = \frac{A_5}{A_4 - \frac{1}{2}A_5}.$$

These two estimates are not necessarily the same, so that δ is "overidentified." An iterative technique for arriving at the best single estimate of δ has therefore been devised and is discussed in the next chapter.

Also it appears that the error term v_t in (58) is now no longer nonautocorrelated, as is usually assumed for u_t in (57). This has been a long-standing problem with models of the distributed-lag and stock-adjustment types.

---

[13] The single exception to this is the dummy variable d_t introduced to separate the prewar years from the postwar years. (This is discussed in Chapter 2.) Since $d_t = d_{t-1}$, the dummy variable enters (58) as $A_6 d_t$, where $A_6 = \xi\delta[1 - \frac{1}{2}(\beta - \delta)]$ and ξ is the coefficient of d_t in the structural equations.

However, a recently developed technique for dealing with errors distributed as in (61) has been applied in the present investigation; this technique is discussed in Chapter 2.

IV. Special Cases of the Dynamic Model

In the course of estimating equation (58) for the several commodities, four special cases emerged that we shall now discuss separately. With a few commodities A_1 was found to be close to one, thereby implying that β is close to δ. In this case the equation can be simplified by putting $A_1 = 1$ and transferring the second term to the left-hand side so that the equation becomes

$$(63) \qquad q_t - q_{t-1} = A_0 + A_2 \Delta x_t + A_3 x_{t-1} + A_4 \Delta p_t + A_5 p_{t-1} + v_t.$$

Note that in this situation the long-term interpretation of the model breaks down because of the required division by $\delta - \beta$ (compare equations [12] and [45]). This is elaborated further below.

The second special case occurs when A_2 and A_4 do not differ significantly from A_3 and A_5, respectively. This implies that $\delta = 2$ and means that equation (58) becomes

$$(64) \qquad\qquad q_t = A_0 + A_1 q_{t-1} + A_2 x_t + A_4 p_t + v_t,$$

which includes only the current levels of total expenditure and prices. The case $\delta = 2$ appears to be of some importance as a special limiting case. As can be seen from (10) in long-term equilibrium δ can be interpreted as a consumption-inventory ratio. Then $\delta = 2$ would arise with a commodity with a lifetime of one year that is bought once a year. Admittedly, this is a polar example and would be unlikely to occur with broadly defined consumption categories. Indeed, when habit formation is permitted this interpretation loses much of its force; a more plausible interpretation is given below.

The third special case of the dynamic model arises when A_3 and A_5 do not differ significantly from zero, but when A_2 and A_4 do. This implies that δ is close to zero. Assuming that δ is in fact zero involves eliminating the intercept, x_{t-1}, and p_{t-1} from (58)—that is, A_0, A_3, and A_5 are assumed to equal zero. The long-run interpretation of the model becomes implausible with this case, for in long-run equilibrium $\delta = 0$ implies $\hat{q} = 0$ (compare [10]), a result that would be reasonable only with a markedly inferior good; moreover, as can be seen from (41), α becomes indeterminate. Consequently an alternative interpretation of this case is in order (see section II of Chapter 7).[14]

---

[14] Gollnick (1968) has pointed out that this special case (with an intercept in the estimating equation) can also arise from a linear static model with a linear trend.

The last special case of the dynamic model is a rather peculiar one and may possess only limited economic interest. It is conceivable that a commodity will have a zero or even a negative short-run income coefficient, but nevertheless a positive one in the long run. This case arises when A_3 is large relative to A_2, and where A_2 may even be negative. If A_2 does not differ from zero, the elimination of x_t from the model involves assuming $\delta = -2$. However, as was the case of $\delta = 2$, the interpretation of β and δ is not clear in this situation.

Note that the four special cases have in common the fact that a particular value of δ is involved; moreover, for each of these values of δ, the interpretation of the model is strained. In particular, the long-run interpretation of the model breaks down completely with case one and becomes implausible with case two, while the interpretation of δ becomes hazy with cases three and four. These observations suggest that an alternative formulation of the set of underlying structural equations might be in order.

This is possible in cases two and four, $\delta = 2$ and $\delta = -2$. The differential equations corresponding to these two cases have been elusive, but to recast the equations in the framework of a meaningful discrete process is a straightforward exercise.

The case $\delta = 2$ corresponds to the classical geometric distributed-lag model as formulated by Koyck (1954) and others. We formulate the model as a single equation:

$$(65) \qquad q_t = \alpha + \beta \sum_{i=0}^{\infty} \lambda^i x_{t-i}.$$

We now subtract

$$(66) \qquad \lambda q_{t-1} = \lambda \alpha + \beta(\lambda x_{t-1} + \lambda^2 x_{t-2} + \cdots)$$

from (65):

$$(67) \qquad q_t - \lambda q_{t-1} = (1 - \lambda)\alpha + \beta x_t,$$

or

$$(68) \qquad q_t = (1 - \lambda)\alpha + \lambda q_{t-1} + \beta x_t,$$

which conforms to equation (64), with prices and the error term omitted.

Similarly, the case $\delta = -2$ corresponds to a geometric distributed-lag model with a complete lapse of one time period; that is, the structural equation is

$$(69) \qquad q_t = \alpha + \beta \sum_{i=1}^{\infty} \lambda^{i-1} x_{t-i}.$$

If we apply the "Koyck transformation" in the same manner as above, we obtain

$$(70) \qquad q_t = (1 - \lambda)\alpha + \lambda q_{t-1} + \beta x_{t-1},$$

which corresponds to the basic equation with $A_2 = 0$ (again with prices and the error term omitted).

It is apparent from previous considerations that prices are treated in a manner parallel to income, so that their inclusion does not create any problem. Similarly the addition of the error term does not raise any new questions of principle.

To recapitulate, we have found in the empirical part of the study that there are four values of δ which have particular significance.[15] These are $\beta = \delta$ and $\delta = 2$, 0, and -2, respectively, which in turn corresponds to $A_1 = 1$, $A_2 = A_3$ (and $A_4 = A_5$), $A_3 = 0$ (and $A_5 = 0$), and $A_2 = 0$ (and $A_4 = 0$). At this point we abandoned the original interpretation of the set of structural equations and reformulated them in order to provide a more plausible interpretation of two of the special cases. In the empirical work in Chapter 3 these cases will be noted as they occur.

V. An Alternative Dynamic Model (Flow Adjustment)

In several of the habit-forming commodities analyzed in Chapter 3, our basic dynamic equation (40) implies values of the depreciation rate δ that at first sight seemed implausibly high.[16] This gave rise to the suspicion that we might be estimating something that is indeterminate because the basic equation does not hold even approximately for certain commodities. An alternative dynamic model has therefore been considered, which was suggested to us by A. R. Bergstrom of the London School of Economics.

In the "Bergstrom model" the state variables do not appear. Rather than as a process of adjustment in physical or psychological stocks, the dynamics of consumption are viewed as an attempt on the part of consumers to bring their actual consumption closer to some desired level, which is determined by PCE (and possibly by other variables as well). To distinguish it from our basic dynamic model we shall refer to the Bergstrom model also as the *flow-adjustment* model. In its continuous form the model consists of

(71) $$\dot{q} = \theta(\hat{q} - q);$$

(72) $$\hat{q} = \xi + \mu x.$$

Again $\dot{q}$ is the rate of change of consumption over time, and q is the desired level of consumption.

[15] Still another case turned up in an equation that was not retained because of other defects. This was the case $\delta - \beta + 2$, corresponding to $A_1 = 0$, which does not appear to be of interest. Finally, it should be noted that the static model discussed in footnote 10 above, that is, $A_3 - A_2 = -A_1 A_2$, is also a special case.

[16] They seemed high in comparison with the depreciation rates for durables, but our experience suggests that high values of δ are normal in the case of habit formation. We are unable to agree, however, with a suggestion made by Carl Christ (1967) to the effect

With our usual approximation,

(73) $$q_t - q_{t-1} = \tfrac{1}{2}(\Delta^* q_t + \Delta^* q_{t-1}),$$

the estimating equation becomes

(74) $$q_t = A_0^* + A_1^* q_{t-1} + A_2^*(x_t + x_{t-1}).$$

In this case

(75) $$A_0^* = \frac{\theta \xi}{1 + \tfrac{1}{2}\theta};$$

(76) $$A_1^* = \frac{1 - \tfrac{1}{2}\theta}{1 + \tfrac{1}{2}\theta};$$

(77) $$A_2^* = \frac{\theta \mu}{1 + \tfrac{1}{2}\theta};$$

(78) $$\theta = \frac{2(1 - A_1^*)}{1 + A_1^*};$$

(79) $$\xi = \frac{A_0^*}{1 - A_1^*};$$

(80) $$\mu = \frac{2A_2^*}{1 - A_1^*}.$$

In terms of the basic equation (40) the flow-adjustment model corresponds to $A_2 = 2A_3$, so that δ is indeterminate according to (56). The model was used for fourteen commodities, and it was tried without success for several other items.

As a numerical example similar to those in Table 1.1, we shall take 4.1 (owner-occupied housing), even though it is a somewhat extreme case of habit formation. However, 4.1 is not only a large item and a suitable counterpart to 1.1 and 2.3, but it also possesses some very interesting features (see Table 1.2 and Figure 1.2). The four cases considered are the same as in Table 1.1. The equation for 4.1 used in the first edition was

(81) $$q_t = -6.9625 + .9205 q_{t-1} + .00658(x_t + x_{t-1}),$$

where the terms with d_t and z_t given have been absorbed into the intercept (with $d_t = 1$ and z_t equal to its historical mean). The corresponding equation for desired consumption is

(82) $$\hat{q} = -87.58 + .1655x,$$

which for 1961 ($x = 1657$) gives $\hat{q} = 186.65$.

---

that what we call habit formation is merely a matter of high depreciation rates. Christ apparently regards inventory adjustment as applying to all commodities, but in the case of services it is hard to see what inventory adjustment means. Moreover, equation (14) above leaves no doubt that the adjustment coefficient β rather than the depreciation rate δ is the crucial parameter.

Table 1.2. Equation (74): Behavior of Consumption over Time

| | Item 4.1: owner-occupied housing | | | | | |
| | Case 1 | | | Case 2 | | |
Year	x_t	q_t	Δq_t	x_t	q_t	Δq_t
1961	1657	137.84	—	1657	137.84	—
1962	1657	141.73	+3.89	1711.22	142.08	+4.24
1963	1657	145.31	+3.58	1765.44	146.70	+4.62
1964	1657	148.60	+3.29	1819.66	151.66	+4.96
1965	1657	151.63	+3.03	1873.88	156.94	+5.28
1966	1657	154.42	+2.79	1928.10	162.51	+5.57
1967	1657	156.99	+2.57	1982.32	168.35	+5.84
1968	1657	159.35	+2.36	2036.55	174.44	+6.09
1969	1657	161.53	+2.18	2090.78	180.76	+6.32
1970	1657	163.53	+2.00	2145	187.29	+6.53
	Case 3			Case 4		
1961	1657	137.84	—	1657	137.84	—
1962	1657	141.73	+3.89	1711.22	142.08	+4.24
1963	1711.22	145.66	+3.87	1765.44	146.70	+4.62
1964	1711.22	149.64	+3.98	1765.44	151.31	+4.61
1965	1711.22	153.30	+3.66	1711.22	155.19	+3.88
1966	1657	156.31	+3.01	1711.22	158.41	+3.22
1967	1657	158.73	+2.42	1765.44	161.73	+3.32
1968	—	—	—	1819.66	165.50	+3.77

The most striking pattern of all four cases in Table 1.2 is the rise in consumption in every year without exception. This is, of course, due mostly to the large shortfall of actual compared to desired consumption in 1961, which cannot be made up quickly because of the slow adjustment ($\theta = .0828$). In the ten years covered by Case 1 only a little more than half of this shortfall is made good. Indeed, in the earlier years of Case 2 the rise in consumption is not much greater than in Case 1, though later on Case 2 shows a more rapid rise. In 1970, however, actual consumption at \$187.29 is still very much below the desired level of \$267.42 at a PCE of \$2145; the shortfall is even greater than in 1961, both in dollars and in percentage terms. The fluctuations in PCE of Cases 3 and 4 have almost no effect on housing consumption, which rises inexorably. Even the annual increase is only slightly affected by the changes in PCE.

A noteworthy advantage of the flow-adjustment model is that, unlike the state-adjustment model, it can be put in double-logarithmic form. For this purpose, the variables, q, $\hat{q}$, and x are simply replaced by $\log q$, $\log \hat{q}$, and $\log x$, while $\dot{q}$ is replaced by $\partial \log q / \partial t$. The parameters θ, ξ, and μ then become elasticities. This dynamic double-log model has not been used in the present work,[17] but it has been found useful in the study of imports.

VI. The Use of Per Capita Figures

In the calculations reported in this book—except for certain derived projections in Chapter 4 and for the analysis at the end of Chapter 7—consumption, total PCE, and similar variables are expressed in per capita terms. This is necessary partly because the underlying theory of consumer choice refers primarily to individuals, and partly because per capita relationships are likely to be more meaningful and stable than relationships between aggregates. Thus the fact that aggregate PCE has risen by 5 percent does not lead to any conclusions about, say, food consumption unless we know how much of the rise is due to population growth and how much to an increase in per capita PCE. To take two polar cases, if all the aggregate increase reflects population growth, food consumption may be expected to rise by the same 5 percent, but if population remains constant the rise in food consumption is determined by its elasticity with respect to per capita PCE, so that it may be no more than about 3 percent. The use of aggregate PCE in static models is legitimate only if the elasticity of the item considered is close to one.

The use of per capita figures raises two difficulties, however. In the first place, it is not strictly correct to give all persons equal weight irrespective of age and sex; as is well known, in principle one should use a different scale of weights (or "equivalent adult scale") for each commodity, with a "general scale" for PCE. But the limited evidence there is on these scales (see Prais and Houthakker, 1955) suggests that equal-weight scales do not produce too much distortion; moreover, the age and sex distribution of the population is fairly stable. For the few commodities where the problem appeared to be more serious, we have special demographic variables to achieve the desired correction (for instance, the percentage of the population over eighteen or on farms).

The second difficulty is connected with the state-adjustment model developed in this chapter. The basic behavior equation (2) is unaffected, but the accounting identity (3) holds only if population is constant. If it is not, the per capita stocks will be affected also by population changes. To see more clearly how this works out, let us put S for the aggregate stock and π for population, so that

$$(83) \qquad\qquad S = \pi s.$$

[17] See, however, section IV of Chapter 4.

Also writing Q for aggregate consumption and W for aggregate "using up," it is still true that

$$(84) \qquad\qquad \dot{S} = Q - W.$$

But differentiation of (83) gives

$$(85) \qquad\qquad \dot{S} = \dot{\pi}s + \pi\dot{s},$$

and by virtue of (2) and the definitions of S, Q, and W we get

$$(86) \qquad\qquad \pi\dot{s} = Q - W - \dot{\pi}s;$$

hence

$$(87) \qquad\qquad \dot{s} = q - w - \frac{\dot{\pi}}{\pi}s.$$

Now we introduce two special assumptions. The first is identical with (4), which defines the depreciation rate. The second lets population grow at a constant percentage rate ψ:

$$(88) \qquad\qquad \pi(t) = \pi_0 e^{\psi t},$$

where $\pi_0 = \pi(0)$. Consequently

$$(89) \qquad\qquad \frac{\dot{\pi}}{\pi} = \psi$$

and (87) become

$$(90) \qquad\qquad \dot{s} = q - \delta s - \psi s.$$

The effect of exponential population growth, then, is to replace (5) by

$$(91) \qquad\qquad \dot{s} = q - (\delta + \psi)s.$$

Fortunately the difference between δ and $(\delta + \psi)$ is quite small. The average rate of population growth was 1.3 percent from 1929 to 1964, so that all estimated δ's in Chapters 3 and 7 should really be increased by about .013. For most items δ is much larger than this, and the correction is negligible compared to the errors in the estimation of δ; we have therefore not made it. However, in two important cases where the estimated δ is small (namely automobiles and savings), we have noted this "population effect," and in section II of Chapter 7 we have analyzed it explicitly. The results of that section do not suggest that the population effect is of much quantitative importance.

2

Problems of Estimation and Projection

The discussion until now has centered largely on models and data. Since the objective of the investigation was to provide a set of projections for 1970 and 1975 of the components of PCE, the methods employed and some problems encountered in preparing the projections will be discussed in this chapter. The projections themselves will be discussed in Chapter 4.

Projection with the static model is essentially a trivial exercise, for the value of the predictors (or their logarithms, as the case may be) have only to be substituted into the equation. Since the estimating form of the dynamic model is a first-order difference equation, either the projection must be built up year by year from some initial conditions, or else a solution must be obtained for the difference equation and the projection made from the solution. Though these procedures are equivalent in principle, projecting from the solved equation is likely to involve more rounding error, and thus we have chosen to build up the projections year by year. Since we shall have occasion later to use the solution of the dynamic model, however, we will give it here:

$$(1) \quad q_{1975} = [A_0 + A_6 + A_2 q + A_3(x_{1964} + 10q) + A_4 h + A_5(p_{1964} + 10h)]$$

$$\times \left[\frac{1 - A_1^{11}}{1 - A_1}\right] + \frac{11 A_1^{11}}{1 - A} - \frac{A_1(1 - A_1^{11})}{(1 - A_1)^2} (A_3 q + A_5 h)$$

$$+ A_1^{11} q_{1964} + \sum_{i=1}^{11} A_1^{11-i} v_{1964+i},$$

where $q = \Delta x_i$ and $h = \Delta p_i$ for all i, and A_6 is the coefficient of the war-dummy variable.

Since 1964 is the most recent experience in the model, the 1964 values have been used for initial conditions; among other things, to use an earlier year would imply a higher variance, about which more will be said below. The only point at issue is how to treat the error in the dependent variable for 1964. Clearly it should be taken into account, for to ignore it by using the regression value for 1964 would entail throwing away valuable information. We could force the 1964 value to lie on the regression line by incorporating the 1964 error into the intercept. If past experience is any guide, however, the data for 1964 will probably still undergo some revision, and hence should not be given undue weight. Therefore we have used the actual 1964 value of the dependent variable as an initial condition and have not altered the intercept of the estimated equation. Other than for those equations without intercepts, this means that the projections are tied to the means of the historical period.

The sequence of topics in this chapter is as follows. The impossibility of providing a classical measure of the efficiency of the projections from the dynamic model and the problem of autocorrelated residuals are discussed in sections I and II. A difficulty encountered in projecting from the three-pass equation is treated in section III, while the results of a Monte Carlo experiment designed to resolve this difficulty are presented in section IV. Sections V and VI present a solution to the overidentification problem when prices are included in the dynamic model and formulas for approximate standard errors of the structural coefficients. Section VII then discusses the adding-up problem, and a final observation is noted at the end.

I. *The Projecting Variance*

Except for the special case where $\beta = \delta$ is assumed, it is not possible to provide an estimate of the standard error of the projection with the dynamic model. This problem is not peculiar to our dynamic model, but rather is a general problem with all such models, and this can be illustrated with the following simple dynamic equation:

$$(2) \qquad y_{t+1} = \xi + \lambda y_t + \kappa x_{t+1} + u_{t+1}.$$

If we assume $x_{t+1} = x_t + h$ for all t, the general solution for (2) can be written

$$
\begin{aligned}
(3) \quad y_{t+n} = {} & \xi(1 + \lambda + \lambda^2 + \cdots + \lambda^n) + \lambda^n y_t \\
& + \kappa(\lambda^n + 2\lambda^{n-1} + 3\lambda^{n-2} + \cdots + (n-1)\lambda + n)hx_t \\
& + \sum_{i=1}^{n} \lambda^{n-i} u_{t+i}.
\end{aligned}
$$

The projection for y_{t+n} will be

$$
\begin{aligned}
(4) \quad \hat{y}_{t+n} = {} & a(1 + b + b^2 + \cdots + b^n) + b^n y_t \\
& + c(b^n + 2b^{n-1} + \cdots + (n-1)b + n)hx_t,
\end{aligned}
$$

and the variance of the projection is

$$
\begin{aligned}
(5) \quad E(y_{t+n} - \hat{y}_{t+n})^2 = {} & E[(a - \xi)^2 + (ab - \xi\lambda)^2 + \cdots \\
& + (ab^n - \xi\lambda^n)^2 + (b^n - \lambda^n)^2]y_t^2 \\
& + [n^2(c - \kappa)^2 + c^2(b^n - \lambda^n)^2 \\
& \quad + 4c^2(b^{n-1} - \lambda^{n-1})^2 + \cdots \\
& \quad + (n-1)^2 c^2(b - \lambda)^2]h^2 x_t^2 \\
& + \left[\sum_{i=1}^{n} \lambda^{n-1} u_{t+i}\right]^2 + \text{cross-product terms.}
\end{aligned}
$$

It is seen immediately that the terms involving powers of the coefficients are not estimable from the data in the usual manner; indeed it is not clear that they can be estimated even in principle.

The problem disappears if it is assumed that $\lambda = 1$; that is, if y_t is moved to the left-hand side in (2). The solution becomes

$$(6) \qquad y_{t+n} = n\xi + y_t + n\kappa x_t + \frac{n(n-1)}{2}\kappa h + \sum_{i=1}^{n} u_{t+i},$$

with

$$(7) \qquad \hat{y}_{t+n} = na + y_t + ncx_t + \frac{n(n-1)}{2} ch$$

as the corresponding projection. Hence

$$(8) \qquad E(y_{t+n} - \hat{y}_{t+n})^2 = n^2 \operatorname{var} a + n^2 x_t^2 \operatorname{var} c$$
$$+ h^2 \frac{(n(n-1))^2}{4} \operatorname{var} c + n\sigma^2 + \text{covariance terms},$$

where σ^2 is the variance of u. Each of these variances and covariances can be estimated directly from the data. This case has practical interest also for the dynamic model when $\beta = \delta$ fits the hypothesis of (6). Accordingly, standard errors can be obtained for the projections from the equations in this category. Unfortunately, these are the only dynamic equations for which this can be done.

Nonetheless, it is possible to offer several remarks of a qualitative nature regarding the projecting variance of the other dynamic models. First, Stone and Prais (1953) have pointed out that, as long as the coefficient of the lagged dependent variable is positive but less than one, the resulting contribution of the stochastic element in the projecting variance is considerably lessened. To see this, we note that the contribution of the error term in (5), if $\lambda = 1$, is $n\sigma^2$, while it is

$$[(1 - \lambda^{2n})/(1 - \lambda^2)]\sigma^2 < n\sigma^2 \quad \text{if } 0 \leq \lambda < 1.$$

Also, $\lambda = 1$ is ordinarily only an assumption. As a result, (8) is correspondingly understated because λ has a variance that is not taken into account. Theil (1961), among others, has suggested a method whereby an *a priori* distribution on λ can be used in estimation. However, this has not been tried here.[1] These two observations suggest that the projecting variance for the dynamic models in which $\lambda = 1$ is not assumed is smaller, other things being equal, than for those in which $\lambda = 1$ is assumed.

---

[1] In a recent demand study, Barten (1964) has made considerable use of *a priori* information in the form of restrictions on own- and cross-price and income elasticities.

Third, the projecting variance for the dynamic model is much more sensitive to the length of the projection period than for a corresponding static model. This is because of the accumulating effect of the errors in the dynamic model, which is not present in the static model. The result is that, for a given R^2, the projecting variance of the static model is likely to be smaller than for the dynamic model. However, it must be remembered that one of the other major sources of error in a projection is not being measured. The error that results from a misspecified model does not enter the classical measure of the projecting variance. The classical formula only measures the errors of estimation on the hypothesis that the specified relationship is correct. There is considerable reason to believe on both the theoretical and the empirical level that the dynamic model is a more adequate representation of reality than is a static model. Indeed, much of this monograph provides evidence to this effect. Hence, for a given R^2, the "true" projecting variance of the static model is understated relative to the dynamic model.

Since we are unable to provide estimates of the projecting variances for the dynamic model, we have had to rely on the standard error of the estimate for assessing the efficiency of the projections. This statistic, which is an estimate of the standard deviation of the error term in the regression equation, is useful in evaluating year-to-year changes and in choosing among alternative equations having the same dependent variable.

Finally, there is the problem of autocorrelation, which merits a section of its own.

II. Problems of Autocorrelation

It is an established fact that autocorrelation in the error term leads in most instances to an underestimate of σ^2 when the method of least squares is used to estimate the parameters. Correspondingly, the classical formula will understate the true projecting variance, and this will be so regardless of whether the static or the dynamic model is being used. Malinvaud (1961), in an important early Monte Carlo study of forecasts made from distributed-lag models, found that the forecasting variance increased sharply upon the introduction of autocorrelation in the error term, with the increase being more marked the longer the forecast interval. It is easy to see why this is the case: with the effect of errors being spread out over succeeding periods, an error in period t affects the level of the dependent variable in $t + 1$ directly, as well as through the level of the dependent variable in t. If a large error (or errors) should occur in the early part of the projection period, a projection based on the assumption that the errors are identically zero could be either seriously overstated or understated. Hence the presence of autocorrelation not only leads to an underestimate of the true forecasting variance but to an increase in this variance as well.

Autocorrelation has been detected much less with the dynamic model than with the static model. This is primarily because the dynamic model is a more adequate specification. Moreover, where there is autocorrelation the three-pass method used to estimate the dynamic model usually succeeds in greatly reducing it. As a result, the dynamic model, owing to the lack of auto-correlation, will give more efficient projections than the static model.

Autocorrelation in the error term may imply bias in the projection as well as inefficiency. This arises because of the presence of the lagged value of the dependent variables as a predictor. The autocorrelation leads to a biased estimate of A_1 in equation (1.57),[2] which if there are no offsetting biases in the other coefficients is sufficient to give a biased projection.[3]

It was indicated in Chapter 1 that, even if u_t in (1.57) is nonautocorrelated, v_t in (1.61) will be autocorrelated. To see this, we note that the asymptotic covariance of v_t and v_{t-1} is given by

$$(9) \quad E(v_t v_{t-1}) = E \frac{\left(1 + \frac{\delta}{2}\right)u_t - \left(1 - \frac{\delta}{2}\right)u_{t-1}}{1 - \frac{1}{2}(\beta - \delta)} \cdot \frac{\left(1 + \frac{\delta}{2}\right)u_{t-1} - \left(1 - \frac{\delta}{2}\right)u_{t-2}}{1 - \frac{1}{2}(\beta - \delta)}$$

$$= \frac{\left(\left[\frac{\delta}{2}\right]^2 - 1\right)\sigma^2}{(1 - \frac{1}{2}[\beta - \delta])^2} \neq 0 \quad \text{unless } \delta = 2.$$

With the case of first-order autocorrelation in u, we have

$$(10) \quad E(v_t v_{t-1}) = \frac{2(1 + \delta^2/4)\sigma_{tt-1}}{(1 - \frac{1}{2}[\beta - \delta])^2} + \frac{\left(\left[\frac{\delta}{2}\right]^2 - 1\right)\sigma^2}{(1 - \frac{1}{2}[\beta - \delta])^2} \neq 0$$

unless

$$\frac{2(1 + \delta^2/4)\sigma_{tt-1}}{(1 - \frac{1}{2}[\beta - \delta])^2} = \frac{-\left(\left[\frac{\delta}{2}\right]^2 - 1\right)\sigma^2}{(1 - \frac{1}{2}[\beta - \delta])^2},$$

where σ_{tt-1} is the covariance between u_t and u_{t-1}. We assume, of course, that $1 - \frac{1}{2}(\beta - \delta) \neq 0$ in both (9) and (10).

---

[2] This is discussed in the next section. References such as (1.57) are to equations in another chapter, in this case Chapter 1, equation (57).

[3] In a recent paper Orcutt and Winokur (1969) present some Monte Carlo results showing that least-squares bias does not lead to forecasting bias in the model with only y_{t-1} as a predictor. Our Monte Carlo results in section V show, however, that there is a least-squares forecasting bias with the dynamic model of this book.

In terms of the Durbin–Watson statistic,

$$D.W. = \frac{\sum (\hat{v}_{t+1} - \hat{v}_t)^2}{\sum \hat{v}_t^2}$$

(assuming $(T-1)/T \cong 1$ where T is the number of observations)

(11)
$$E(D.W.) \cong 2 - \frac{\left(\frac{\delta}{2}\right)^2 - 1}{(1 + \delta^2/4)}$$

in the nonautocorrelated case, and

(12)
$$E(D.W.) \cong 2 + 2 \frac{(1 + \delta^2/4)\sigma_{tt-1} - (1 - \delta^2/4)\sigma^2}{(1 - \delta^2/4)\sigma_{tt-1} - (1 + \delta^2/4)\sigma^2}$$

in the autocorrelated case.

Unfortunately, a direct test for autocorrelation in u_t is not possible, for a direct estimate of u_t is not obtained; but an indirect test can be devised. When u_t is nonautocorrelated, the autoregression coefficient of v_t is not a free parameter, but depends on β and δ. Given the estimates of β and δ, the Durbin–Watson coefficient can be adjusted and used as a crude test for autocorrelation in u_t. Suppose that $\beta = .14$ and $\delta = .30$, then the expected value of the $D.W.$, assuming no autocorrelation in u_t, should be

(13)
$$E(D.W.) \cong 2 - \frac{.3^2/4 - 1}{.3^2/4 + 1} \cong 2.96.$$

Hence, if u_t is not autocorrelated, the $D.W.$, for these values of β and δ, should be in the neighborhood of 2.96.

Further experiment with combinations of β and δ on the assumption of zero autocorrelation in u_t indicates that the expected value of the $D.W.$ ranges between 2.6 and 3.0. Moreover, it can be shown without difficulty that $\sigma_{tt-1} > 0$ (positive first-order autocorrelation in u_t) implies a lower value for the $D.W.$, while $\sigma_{tt-1} < 0$ implies a higher value.[4] Thus, values of the $D.W.$ either near or below two indicates presence of positive autocorrelation in u_t. The fact that so many of our dynamic equations had $D.W.$'s in either the "acceptable" range or below suggests that the assumption of zero auto-correlation in u_t is generally untenable.[5] Yet, for a number of reasons, this test should be taken with a grain of salt. The two most important are: (1) the autoregressive parameters of v_t add a further restriction on the estimates of β and δ, which is not taken into account, and (2) the distribution of the "adjusted" $D.W.$ is unknown. In fact, the significance limits of the $D.W.$

[4] Assuming $\delta > 0$.
[5] We have used the range 1.6 to 2.4 for the "acceptable" region as a rough rule of thumb.

corresponding to v_t tabulated by Durbin and Watson (1951) are inappropriate because of the presence of q_{t-1} as a predictor.

We have indicated that the three-pass method used to estimate the dynamic model is designed to eliminate the autocorrelation in v_t, so that in principle the adverse effects of autocorrelation on the projections are overcome. As is often the case, however, with the solving of one problem another appears: how does one treat the three-pass variable in the projection period? Since this question is not dealt with in the Taylor–Wilson paper (1964), it will be discussed here. First we shall outline the three-pass estimation method.

III. Projection by the Three-Pass Method

With least squares, it is a well-known result that the presence of autocorrelation in the error term of a model containing a lagged value of the dependent variable as a predictor leads to an inconsistent estimate of the coefficient of the lagged value.[6] This arises because the composite error term of the model is necessarily correlated with the lagged dependent variable, thereby violating one of the basic assumptions of least squares.

Let the model under consideration be

$$(14) \qquad y_t = ay_{t-1} + bx_t + cx_{t-1} + u_t,$$

where

$$(15) \qquad u_t = du_{t-1} + \epsilon_t.$$

For convenience, y and x are assumed to be measured from their means so that the intercept disappears; ϵ_t is assumed to be a random error term with a constant variance for all t. If u_t were a known variable, (14) and (15) could be combined and

$$(16) \qquad y_t = ay_{t-1} + bx_t + cx_{t-1} + du_{t-1} + \epsilon_t$$

estimated directly with no problem of inconsistent estimates; but u_t is unknown so that this is not possible. Still it is possible to get an estimate of u_{t-1} which under certain conditions[7] converges stochastically to u_{t-1}, and

[6] See, for instance, Klein (1958).

[7] These conditions are that x_t must be nonautocorrelated and that x_{t-1} must be excluded from (14). It is an interesting result that, if x_{t-1} is included in the model, even when x is nonautocorrelated, the estimates of a and c will be inconsistent. For additional discussion, see Taylor and Wilson (1964).

With economic time series, the usual situation is that x_t is autocorrelated, and so we assume this to be the case in what follows. Also, because the estimating equation of the dynamic model includes x_{t-1}, we keep x_{t-1} in (14). This means that the three-pass estimates of a and c are still inconsistent. However, Monte Carlo studies indicate that the small sample bias is moderate. (The results that follow are stated without proof; proofs are in Taylor and Wilson.)

a consistent estimate of a can be obtained. We shall now show how such an estimate of u_{t-1} can be derived.

Pass 1. Equation (14) is estimated by least squares ignoring the auto-correlated error term:

$$(17) \qquad\qquad y_t = a_1 y_{t-1} + b_1 x_t + c_1 x_{t-1} + r_t,$$

where r_t is the calculated residual. If we treat u_{t-1} as an omitted variable and take the probability limit[8] of r_t, we get

$$(18) \qquad \operatorname{plim} r_t = y_t - \operatorname{plim} a_1 y_{t-1} - \operatorname{plim} b_1 x_t - \operatorname{plim} c_1 x_{t-1}$$
$$= y_t - (a + dg) y_{t-1} - b x_t - (c + dh) x_{t-1},$$

where g and h are the partial regression coefficients of y_{t-1} and x_{t-1} in the "auxiliary" regression of u_{t-1}, the omitted variable, on y_{t-1}, x_t, and x_{t-1}.[9]

If (18) is subtracted from (14), we obtain after rearrangement

$$(19) \qquad\qquad u_t = \operatorname{plim} r_t + dg y_{t-1} + dh x_{t-1}.$$

Upon substitution of (19) for u_t in (16), the "true" model becomes

$$(20) \quad y_t = a y_{t-1} + b x_t + c x_{t-1} + d \operatorname{plim} r_{t-1} + d^2 g y_{t-2} + d^2 h x_{t-2} + \epsilon_t.$$

Pass 2. Largely for reasons of reducing multicollinearity, we now subtract $b_1 x_t$ and $c_1 x_{t-1}$ from y_t, where b_1 and c_1 are the estimates of b and c from pass 1, and estimate the following equation by least squares:

$$(21) \qquad y_t - b_1 x_t - c_1 x_{t-1} = a^* y_{t-1} + d^* r_{t-1} + (d^2 g)^* y_{t-2} + \epsilon_t^*.$$

Note from (18) that b_1 is a consistent estimate of b; the same is not true for c_1. Asymptotically, (21) can be written as

$$(22) \quad y_t - b x_t - c x_{t-1} = a^* y_{t-1} + d^* \operatorname{plim} r_{t-1} + (d^2 g)^* y_{t-2} + dh x_{t-1} + \epsilon_t^*.$$

Equation (21) will be the same equation asymptotically as (20) only if

$$\epsilon_t^* = d^2 h x_{t-2} - dh x_{t-1} + \epsilon_t.$$

Hence two relevant variables, x_{t-1} and x_{t-2}, have been omitted from (21). As a result, the probability limit of the estimate of a^* is

$$(23) \qquad\qquad \operatorname{plim} a_2 = a - dhm + d^2 hn.$$

where m and n are the partial regression coefficients of y_{t-1} in the "auxiliary" regressions of x_{t-1} and x_{t-2}, the omitted variables, on y_{t-1}, r_{t-1}, and y_{t-2}.

---

[8] The probability limit of a random variable z is defined as the value to which z converges with probability one as the number of observations becomes indefinitely large. We assume that these probability limits exist.

[9] The theorem being used here relates to the impact of an omitted variable (or variables, as the case may be) on the estimated coefficients of explanatory variables included in the regression. A full discussion of the theorem is found in Theil (1961, pp. 326–327). A statement and proof of the theorem can also be found in Griliches (1961).

We now take b_1 and c_1 together with a_2 and compute

(24) $$\hat{u}_t = y_t - a_2 y_{t-1} - b_1 x_t - c_1 x_{t-1},$$

which is an estimate of u_t in (14).

Pass 3. If $\hat{u}_t$ is lagged one period and substituted for u_{t-1} in (16), we have

(25) $$y_t = ay_{t-1} + bx_t + cx_{t-1} + d^{**}u_{t-1} + \epsilon_t^{**},$$

which is the equation estimated in pass 3. If $\hat{u}_{t-1}$ were to converge stochastically to u_{t-1}, thereby implying $\epsilon_t^{**} \rightarrow \epsilon_t$, the least-squares estimates of all the coefficients in (25) would be consistent. But owing to the asymptotic expression for ϵ_t^{**} involving y_{t-2} and x_{t-2}, only the estimate of b is consistent.

It can be shown that the asymptotic expression for $\hat{u}_{t-1}$ is

(26) $$\text{plim } \hat{u}_{t-1} = u_{t-1} - (d^2hn - dhm)y_{t-2} - dhx_{t-2}$$

which means that the probability limit of the pass-3 estimate of a is

(27) $$\text{plim } a_3 = a + (d^3hn - d^2hm)e + dhf,$$

where e and f are the partial regression coefficients of y_{t-1} in the "auxiliary" regressions of y_{t-2} and x_{t-2} (the variables omitted from [25]) on y_{t-1}, x_t, x_{t-1}, and $\hat{u}_{t-1}$. The Taylor–Wilson Monte Carlo experiments indicate that the bias in a_3 is slight, thereby indicating that the three-pass method is appropriate for estimating the dynamic model.

At the same time, it is evident that the use of the method poses a problem when it comes to projecting from the estimated equation: except for the historical period, $\hat{u}_{t-1}$ is an unknown quantity.[10] The question emerges of how to project this unknown quantity. One impulse is to say assume z_t to be identically zero in the projection period. However, asymptotic theory tells us that this is clearly an inappropriate assumption because the expected value of z_t, assuming $E(u) = 0$, is

(28) $$E(z_t) = (dhm - d^2hn)E(y) - dhE(x),$$

which in general differs from zero.

While this possibility is quickly dismissed, at least four other alternatives require more detailed examination. These include: (1) assume that z takes on its historical mean in the projection period; (2) compute z year by year in the projection period according to its asymptotic formula; (3) use the least-squares equation; (4) abandon the idea of making the projection from the estimating equation by instead building up the implicit "stocks" and returning to the original structural equation to make the projection.

Unfortunately, existing theory is a poor guide in assessing these alternatives; moreover, there is no body of accumulated experience to draw upon.

[10] Hereafter, $\hat{u}_{t-1}$ will be referred to as z_t.

So it seemed prudent to take an empirical approach to the problem by running several Monte Carlo experiments using the alternatives, and then choosing the projection form of the equation on the basis of the Monte Carlo results. The experiments and results are described in the next section.

IV. Monte Carlo Forecasting Experiments

The following model has been used in the Monte Carlo experiments:

$$(29) \qquad q_t = 25 + .14s_t + .10x_t + \epsilon_t;$$

$$(30) \qquad \dot{s}_t = q_t - .30s_t.$$

Of 50 observations per sample, 52 samples were generated using a Gaussian random-number generator. In order to give the model some economic flavor, a long historical series for national income of the United Kingdom [11] that begins at 1870 was used for the x series. This series was, of course, fixed in repeated samples.

The stock series was constructed observation by observation, using the approximation for $s_t - s_{t-1}$ assumed in (1.32) above; that is, we used

$$(31) \qquad s_t - s_{t-1} = \tfrac{1}{2}(q_t - .30s_t + q_{t-1} - .30s_{t-1}).$$

The first two samples were discarded, as were the first nine observations of each sample, in order to remove the possible effects of atypical initial conditions for q and s. Observations 11–40, with observation 10 as the initial value, were used to estimate the coefficients in

$$(32) \qquad q_t = A_0 + A_1 q_{t-1} + A_2 x_t + A_3 x_{t-1} + u_t,$$

by both ordinary least squares (OLS) and the three-pass method (3PLS). The estimated equations were then used to forecast observations 41–49; these correspond to the nine years between 1961 and 1970 over which the actual projections were initially made.

The results of the four Monte Carlo experiments performed are summarized in Tables 2.1, 2.2, and 2.3. Tables 2.1 and 2.2 indicate the bias in the mean values of the coefficients, while Table 2.3 gives the mean value of the forecasts for each of the nine periods in the forecast interval for the alternative experiments.

Experiment 1 uses the estimating equation of the model to make the forecasts—that is, (32). The "actual" value of z, computed from the last observation of the historical period, has been used for z in the first forecast, while the historical mean of z computed from the sample is used thereafter.

[11] The source is Prest (1948).

Experiment 2 also uses the estimating equation to make the forecasts. However, after using the computed value of z for the first forecast, values of z computed according to the asymptotic (28) are used thereafter.

Experiment 3 uses the structural equation with estimates of the structural coefficients computed from estimates of $A_0, \ldots, A_3$ to make the forecasts. The implicit stocks are built up one observation at a time, using the estimated depreciation rate and the actual values of q. For the initial value of s, it is assumed that there is no error in the first observation.[12]

Experiment 4 also uses the structural equation for making the forecasts; the structural coefficients are re-estimated directly by using the computed stocks in the structural equation.

Table 2.1. Estimates of the Coefficients of the Estimating Equation

Coefficient	Actual	OLS	σ_A	3PLS	σ_A
A_0	6.9444	11.7225	4.8179	10.1389	4.575
A_1	.8519	.8366	.0181	.8468	.0518
A_2	.1065	.1033	.0176	.1050	.0161
A_3	$-.0787$	$-.0751$	.0177	$-.0770$	.0175
A_4	—	—	—	$-.4638$	.1384
R^2	—	.9685	—	.9740	—
$D.W.$	—	2.8095	—	2.3105	—

Note. The OLS and 3PLS estimates are the means of the 50 samples. The "actual" values are computed from α, β, γ, and δ, using formulas (1.41)–(1.44). A_4 is the coefficient of z_t. The σ_A's are empirical standard errors computed from the 50 samples.

As is to be expected, the bias in the estimates of the coefficients are smaller with 3PLS (three-pass least squares) than with OLS (ordinary least squares). However, with exception of the intercept which may appear to be an anomaly, the biases, even for OLS, are small. The large bias in the estimates of the intercept can be traced to the fact that, although the bias in the other coefficients is slight, the mean values of q and x are not. This results in a considerable bias in the estimates of the intercept.

Since ϵ_t is nonautocorrelated, the error term of the estimating equation will have negative autocorrelation. The mean value of 2.8095 for the OLS $D.W.$ agrees reasonably well with its expected value of 2.96 (see equation [13] above), though there is a downward bias. This bias is no doubt owing to the presence of q_{t-1} as a predictor.

---

[12] It would be more in keeping with the theory of least squares if the initial value were chosen so that the mean came out without error. But it is impossible to pinpoint a particular year with this assumption.

Table 2.2 gives the estimates in terms of the structural coefficients. The numbers in columns two and three are derived from the information in columns three and four of Table 2.1, using formulas of Chapter 1. The

Table 2.2. Estimates of the Coefficients of the Structural Model

Coefficient	Actual	Indirect		Direct	
		OLS	3PLS	OLS	3PLS
α	25.00	39.8934	2.9873	32.5617	23.2514
β	.14	.1510	.1527	.1411	.1447
γ	.10	.0972	.0984	.0975	.0956
δ	.30	.3292	.3203	.3292	.3203
		Standard Errors			
α		18.0970	.6908	44.4183	53.3986
β		.0722	.0605	.0160	.1931
γ		.0192	.0168	.0043	.0108
δ		.0742	.0780	.0742	.0780

Note. The entries in this table are means of the 50 samples. The estimates in column 5 are obtained by using the 3PLS estimates of the estimating equation in building up the stocks. The standard errors are empirical standard errors computed from the 50 samples. δ is not re-estimated when the structural equation is estimated directly.

numbers in columns four and five are direct estimates of the structural coefficients obtained from building up the implicit stocks and then re-estimating equation (29) directly. The formula used to build up the stocks is

$$(33) \qquad s_t = \frac{1}{2\left(1 + \frac{\delta}{2}\right)} (q_t + q_{t-1}) + \frac{\left(1 - \frac{\delta}{2}\right)}{\left(1 + \frac{\delta}{2}\right)} s_{t-1},$$

where $\hat{\delta}$ is the derived estimate of δ. This formula is obtained from (31).

We see from Table 2.2 that, of the estimates derived from the coefficients of the estimating equation (columns two and three), the largest bias is in the estimate of α and that the estimates of β and δ are obviously biased upward. 3PLS slightly reduces the bias in the estimates of γ and δ, but increases it slightly in the estimate of β. The estimate of δ is of central importance, since it is used directly in building up the stocks.

When the structural coefficients are estimated directly by using the built-up stocks in the structural equation (columns four and five), the bias in both the 3PLS and OLS estimates of γ is reduced.[13] Indeed it practically disappears in the OLS estimate. On the whole, when standard errors are considered, the results indicate that the OLS estimates are better than those of 3PLS when the structural equation is re-estimated directly.

Table 2.3 presents the forecasts from the various experiments. A careful look at this table shows three major results: (1) the forecasts from the

Table 2.3. Forecasts

		Experiment						
		1		2	3		4	
Forecast number	Actual	OLS	3PLS	3PLS	OLS	3PLS	OLS	3PLS
1	419.93	419.40	420.02	420.02	447.01	428.38	445.71	447.19
2	431.95	430.05	431.24	465.46	464.93	444.57	462.29	464.40
3	451.01	446.94	448.92	514.07	487.21	466.67	483.63	486.27
4	466.53	462.04	464.92	570.24	507.54	487.59	503.27	506.57
5	459.30	455.14	458.69	611.48	505.43	486.34	500.59	505.06
6	497.37	492.00	496.90	705.14	545.36	528.13	540.28	545.17
7	555.44	547.69	554.51	824.64	606.33	592.05	601.45	606.58
8	628.08	617.79	627.16	971.57	683.13	672.81	678.71	684.06
9	723.94	711.34	724.13	1157.63	784.67	779.52	780.99	786.45

Note. The forcasts are the means of the 50 samples. The different experiments are described above. The least-squares forecasts for 2 are the same as for 1.

structural equation (experiments 3 and 4) have a considerable upward bias; (2) an even larger upward bias is evident in the 3PLS forecasts of experiment 2, thereby implying that computing z according to its asymptotic formula is unadvisable; (3) the 3PLS forecasts of experiment 1 are practically unbiased. At the same time, the OLS forecasts of this experiment possess a bias of less than 2 percent in the final period, a fact that precludes summary rejection of the OLS equation for projection. It is clear, however, that we can confine our attention to experiment 1.

The forecasting variances and mean-square errors for experiment 1 are tabulated in Table 2.4. The OLS forecasts are more efficient on the whole than the 3PLS forecasts, both in terms of variance and of mean-square error. The 3PLS forecasts are more efficient for the first two periods, a result that is of particular interest for short-term forecasting, but the 3PLS variances are about double the OLS variances in the final four periods. It should be noted that for both methods the variances roughly double from one period

[13] The 3PLS estimates in this case refer to using the stocks computed with 3PLS estimates from Table 2.1.

Table 2.4. Forecast Variances and Mean-Square Errors for Experiment 1

Forecast number	Variance		Mean-square error	
	OLS	3PLS	OLS	3PLS
1	43.6060	30.8228	21.2419	12.7102
2	37.2938	37.4843	28.6574	26.5668
3	69.8600	91.3961	53.2950	65.0194
4	77.7388	133.0116	68.0292	117.8909
5	55.4643	163.4204	54.9008	154.6348
6	118.0343	280.5748	109.3807	295.1619
7	267.3773	582.9199	283.7307	614.8230
8	605.0296	1230.9009	598.4442	1206.5326
9	1126.3272	2273.4368	1155.3163	3209.4873

Note. The variance is defined as $\sum (p_i - a_t)^2/50$ where p_i is the predicted and a_i is the actual value. The mean-square error is defined as $\sum (p_i - a)^2/50$ where a is the mean of the actual values for the 50 samples. That the mean-square error on occasion is smaller than the variance is because of our somewhat different definition of the variance.

to the next from the sixth period on. The increase in the variance for the 3PLS forecasts over the first five periods is in rough agreement with the results of Malinvaud (1961) for models without autocorrelation in the error term.[14]

Further insight can be gained into our model by breaking the forecasting variance down into the part due to the error term of the true model and the part due to the errors of estimation. This can be done as follows. If the true coefficients were used in the forecasting equation, the forecasting variance would be due entirely to the random term of the model, which from equation (1) would be equal to

$$(34) \qquad E\left[\sum_{i=1}^{T} A_i^{T-i} v_i\right]^2 = \sigma^2(1 + A_1^2 + A_1^4 + \cdots + A_1^{2T-2})$$

for $T = 1, 2, \ldots, 9$. Now:

$$(35) \qquad \sigma^2 = E(v_t^2) = E\left[\frac{\left(1 + \frac{\delta}{2}\right)u_t - \left(1 - \frac{\delta}{2}\right)u_{t-1}}{1 - \frac{1}{2}(\beta - \delta)}\right]^2$$

$$= \frac{\left(1 + \frac{\delta}{2}\right)^2 + \left(1 - \frac{\delta}{2}\right)^2}{(1 - \frac{1}{2}(\beta - \delta))^2} \sigma^2.$$

[14] It is somewhat surprising in view of Malinvaud's results to find that the variances of the OLS forecasts for the first five periods are so small. Malinvaud found that the variances increase significantly when the error term is autocorrelated. However, his results are for a model with positive autocorrelation, while in our model, since we have assumed ϵ_t to be nonautocorrelated, v_t has negative autocorrelation. Negative autocorrelation, depending on the autocorrelation in the independent variables, may lead to a reduced forecasting variance. See Malinvaud (1966, chap. 12).

In generating the samples, $\sigma_\epsilon^2 = 16$; hence with $A_1 = .8519$, $\beta = .14$, and $\delta = .30$, we have $\sigma^2 = 28.05$. If we subtract (34) from the forecasting variance for each T, we are left with the part of the variance due to the errors in estimating the coefficients. This breakdown is given in Table 2.5.

We see that for 3PLS forecasts the errors of estimation dominate the forecasting variance from the sixth period on, and from the seventh period on for OLS. The "negative" contribution of the errors of estimation in two of the first four periods may be attributed to any one or all of three reasons: (1) negative covariances between the estimates of the regression coefficients; (2) negative autocorrelation in the error term (especially for the OLS forecasts); or (3) an unusual drawing of actual error terms.

Table 2.5. Breakdown of Forecasting Variances for Experiment 1

	Forecast number								
Variances	1	2	3	4	5	6	7	8	9
OLS	42.61	37.29	69.86	77.74	55.46	118.03	267.38	605.03	1126.33
3PLS	30.82	37.48	91.40	133.01	163.42	280.57	582.92	1230.90	2273.44
Variance due to true model	28.05	48.41	62.42	73.14	80.92	86.57	90.66	93.64	95.79
Variance due to errors of estimation									
OLS	15.56	−13.12	7.44	4.60	−25.46	31.46	176.72	511.39	1030.54
3PLS	2.77	−12.93	28.98	59.87	82.50	194.00	492.16	1237.16	2177.65

Note. The variances are the same as in Table 2.4. The variance due to the true model is calculated according to formula (35) with $A_1 = .8519$ and $\sigma^2 = 28.05$. The variance due to the errors of estimation is then obtained as a residual.

Table 2.6 presents the Theil U for each of the individual samples in experiment 1. The Theil U is a statistic that measures the goodness of fit of a set of forecasts with the actual values and is defined as

$$(36) \qquad U = \frac{[\sum (P_i - A_i)^2]^{1/2}}{\sqrt{\sum P_i^2} + \sqrt{\sum A_i^2}},$$

where P is the predicted value and A is the actual value. U must lie between zero and one. A value of zero denotes a perfect forecast, while one denotes the other extreme.[15]

In general the individual forecasts are very good, for with the exception of the 3PLS forecasts for number 46, the values of U are all less than .04. The mean values are .0133 and .0172 for OLS and 3PLS, respectively. The larger

[15] For an extensive discussion of U, see Theil (1961, pp. 31–42).

value of U of the 3PLS forecasts corresponds to their larger forecasting variance, which we had noted earlier.

At this point it will be useful to summarize the results thus far:

1. We have found that the estimating equation is the best form of the model for making the projections.

2. The best way to project the z variable is to use its value computed from the last observation of the historical period for the first forecast, and its historical mean thereafter.

3. The forecasts from the 3PLS equation are essentially unbiased, while the OLS forecasts are biased downward.

4. The 3PLS forecasts are less efficient than those of OLS, although for both the forecasting variance increases sharply from the sixth period on.

Our remaining task is to choose between the 3PLS and OLS equations for making the projections. On a criterion of unbiasedness 3PLS is the choice,

Table 2.6. Theil U for Experiment 1

Forecast number	OLS	3PLS	Forecast number	OLS	3PLS
1	.0087	.0042	26	.0280	.0287
2	.0050	.0198	27	.0057	.0218
3	.0261	.0149	28	.0173	.0272
4	.0202	.0039	29	.0046	.0107
5	.0193	.0225	30	.0254	.0206
6	.0131	.0303	31	.0104	.0061
7	.0128	.0267	32	.0050	.0048
8	.0315	.0123	33	.0182	.0115
9	.0077	.0050	34	.0112	.0090
10	.0143	.0277	35	.0086	.0097
11	.0076	.0333	36	.0051	.0233
12	.0029	.0044	37	.0160	.0373
13	.0115	.0066	38	.0268	.0298
14	.0015	.0061	39	.0308	.0181
15	.0095	.0079	40	.0135	.0150
16	.0126	.0214	41	.0254	.0223
17	.0222	.0173	42	.0060	.0078
18	.0049	.0107	43	.0055	.0050
19	.0044	.0141	44	.0118	.0109
20	.0149	.0166	45	.0207	.0284
21	.0123	.0233	46	.0260	.0829
22	.0014	.0246	47	.0153	.0134
23	.0094	.0067	48	.0138	.0188
24	.0019	.0034	49	.0132	.0036
25	.0017	.0074	50	.0100	.0203

while on criteria of efficiency or smallest mean-square error we would use OLS. Which criterion do we use in choosing? To make the choice properly, we actually need more information; we need, among other things, to know how and under what circumstances the projections are to be used. Ideally we should know the utility function (or, alternatively, the loss function) of the user (or users) of the projections, from which we could derive the trade-off between smaller variance and increased bias. Given this knowledge we could then choose the method of projection that maximized the user's utility.

Since the projections were prepared for a government agency for inclusion in a comprehensive economy-wide model intended for a variety of uses, it is not possible to be very specific about the disutilities associated with increased variance and increased bias. However, in a context where considerable experimentation and simulation is to take place and where a large number of projections are involved, it would appear that being correct on the average (unbiasedness) is more important than a smaller variance (but with bias) or even a smaller mean-square error.[16]

Although this does not provide a rigorous justification for using 3PLS, it does provide some. Moreover, since up to now 3PLS has been tested only by Monte Carlo techniques, this creates a good chance to try the method in the real world, particularly since little will be lost by doing so. Hence we have used 3PLS to project 36 of the 82 consumption categories. The OLS equations have been used wherever the *D.W.* coefficient was initially in the "acceptable" range.[17]

V. A Problem of Overidentification

It was indicated in Chapter 1 that δ becomes overidentified when prices are included as a predictor in the dynamic model. One estimate of δ can be derived from $\delta/(1 + \delta/2) = A_3/A_2$, and a separate independent estimate from $\delta/(1 + \delta/2) = A_5/A_4$. For these two estimates of δ to be consistent, simple algebra shows that the following must hold:

$$(37) \qquad A_2A_5 = A_3A_4.$$

There are several approaches that could be pursued in deriving estimates of the coefficients in equation (1.58) under restriction (37). A simple yet

---

[16] These last two paragraphs have only touched upon a very difficult and complex topic. The reader is urged to consult Theil (1961, chaps. 7–9), Meyer and Glauber (1964, chap. 10), and Christ (1956) for further discussions.

[17] It should be noted that in principle the projections from the OLS equations could be adjusted upward so as to overcome the downward bias. However, this would require the dubious assumption that the bias in the real world is in the same direction as in our Monte Carlo model.

effective procedure we have used is to view the estimation problem as one of constrained least squares. Alternatively, this can be seen as an exercise in quadratic programming.

Proceeding formally, consider the following expression:

$$(38) \quad \phi = \sum (q_t - A_0 - A_1 q_{t-1} - A_2 \Delta x_t - A_3 x_{t-1} \\ - A_4 \Delta p_t - A_5 p_{t-1})^2 - 2\kappa (A_2 A_5 - A_3 A_4),$$

where κ is a Lagrangian multiplier associated with the restriction on the coefficients. By differentiating (38) partially with respect to each of the parameters, including κ, a system of seven estimating equations is obtained:

$$(39)$$

$$
\begin{bmatrix}
T & q_{-1} & x & x_{-1} & p & p_{-1} \\
q_{-1} & q_{-1}^2 & q_{-1}x & q_{-1}x_{-1} & q_{-1}p & q_{-1}p_{-1} \\
x & q_{-1}x & x^2 & xx_{-1} & xp & xp_{-1}+\kappa \\
x_{-1} & q_{-1}x_{-1} & xx_{-1} & x_{-1}^2 & x_{-1}p-\kappa & x_{-1}p_{-1} \\
p & q_{-1}p & xp & x_{-1}p-\kappa & p^2 & pp_{-1} \\
p_{-1} & q_{-1}p_{-1} & xp_{-1}+\kappa & x_{-1}p_{-1} & pp_{-1} & p_{-1}^2
\end{bmatrix}
\begin{bmatrix}
\hat{A}_0 \\
\hat{A}_1 \\
\hat{A}_2 \\
\hat{A}_3 \\
\hat{A}_4 \\
\hat{A}_5
\end{bmatrix}
$$

$$
=
\begin{bmatrix}
q \\
qq_{-1} \\
qx \\
qx_{-1} \\
qp \\
qp_{-1}
\end{bmatrix}
$$

$$\hat{A}_2 \hat{A}_5 - \hat{A}_3 \hat{A}_4 = 0.$$

(The summation signs and the subscript t have been dropped for convenience; T is the number of observations.)

We see that κ enters four of the first six equations as either an addition or a subtraction to the cross-products between the total expenditure and price terms. A nonzero value of κ amounts to adjusting the covariance, and hence the correlation, between total expenditure and price. Note that once a value for κ is specified, the first six equations are linear in the regression coefficients.

If the first six equations are solved for $A_0, \ldots, A_5$ in terms of κ, it is possible to define a function

$$(40) \qquad\qquad \theta(\kappa) = A_2 A_5 - A_3 A_4.$$

The object is to find a solution for $\theta(\kappa) = 0$. Unfortunately, the functional form of θ is both unknown and nonlinear, so that an immediate solution of

$\theta(\kappa) = 0$ is not evident. As a result, the procedure we follow is to approximate $\theta(\kappa)$ by a linear function, $\theta^*(\kappa)$, by solving the first six equations for two arbitrary values of κ, κ_1, and κ_2, and then evaluating $\theta(\kappa_1)$ and $\theta(\kappa_2)$. Given these values of θ, κ_3 for $\theta^*(\kappa_3) = 0$ is obtained. Again κ_3 is used to solve the first six equations for new values of $A_0, \ldots, A_5$. Then A_2, A_3, A_4, and A_5 are substituted in (40) to see if in fact $\theta(\kappa_3)$ does equal $\theta^*(\kappa_3)$. In other words we have

(41) $$\theta(\kappa_1) = \theta^*(\kappa_1) \quad \text{and} \quad \theta(\kappa_2) = \theta^*(\kappa_2),$$

so that the objective is to have

(42) $$\theta(\kappa_3) = \theta^*(\kappa_3) = 0.$$

If equality is not attained, the entire procedure is repeated using the value of κ suggested by the first iteration, and so on.

The mechanics of the technique are illustrated graphically in Figure 2.1, where it is assumed that the correct value of κ is reached in two iterations. The solid line is the true θ, while the hatched line is θ_1^* and the dotted line is θ_2^*. (Note: the shape of the "true" θ in this diagram is completely arbitrary and is used only for illustrative purposes.)

The validity of the method depends, of course, upon the eventual converging of the process. Although there is no guarantee of convergence—indeed, $\theta(\kappa)$ may not even possess a real root—our experience has been that a fairly rapid one can be expected. Moreover, multiple roots are possible (although they have never knowingly been encountered), in which case the smallest root would seem the one to use.[18]

The procedure just outlined was the one used in the first edition of this book. In the present edition, in place of approximating $\theta(\kappa)$ by a linear function we have used a quadratic approximation, and this gives a faster

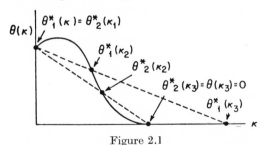

Figure 2.1

[18] In an extensive study of the roots of $\theta(\kappa)$ using Belgian data, Professor Paul Mathieu of the Facultés Universitaires in Namur has found that a large number of real roots do in fact exist, there nearly always being one for a small value of κ. Unfortunately, however, this root, which is the one that we would like to have, is generally difficult to find for it usually follows a very high value of $\theta(\kappa)$. We are grateful to Professor Mathieu for making his results available to us through correspondence.

convergence. Occasionally, the linear approximation still has to be used when neither of the quadratic roots is real, but this is no trouble since the scheme is mechanized: if there are no real roots, the program switches automatically to a linear approximation.

To derive the variance–covariance matrix of the regression coefficients when the identifying restriction is taken into account, it will be useful to rewrite the normal equations in (39) as

$$(43) \qquad (X'X + \kappa D)\hat{A} = X'q,$$

where D is an appropriate matrix of 0's, 1's, and -1's. Therefore $\hat{A}$ is equal to

$$
\begin{aligned}
(44) \quad \hat{A} &= (X'X + \kappa D)^{-1}X'q \\
&= (X'X + \kappa D)^{-1}X'(XA + v) \\
&= (X'X + \kappa D)^{-1}X'XA + (X'X + \kappa D)^{-1}X'v.
\end{aligned}
$$

Taking the expected value of $\hat{A}$, we obtain [since $E(v) = 0$]

$$(45) \qquad E(\hat{A}) = (X'X + \kappa D)^{-1}X'XA.$$

The variance–covariance matrix of A then is given by

$$
\begin{aligned}
(46) \quad E[\hat{A} - E(A)][\hat{A} - E(A)]' &= E(X'X + \kappa D)^{-1}X'vv'X(X'X + \kappa D)^{-1} \\
&= (X'X + \kappa D)^{-1}X'E(vv')X(X'X + \kappa D)^{-1} \\
&= \sigma^2(X'X + \kappa D)^{-1}X'X(X'X + \kappa D)^{-1},
\end{aligned}
$$

assuming $E(vv') = \sigma^2 I$.

Of the 79 dynamic models estimated in the study, 23 have been estimated using constrained least squares. In order further to illustrate the method, the equations for item 1.5 (tobacco) are presented and briefly discussed here. (Note that $\kappa = 0$ corresponds to ignoring the identifying restriction.)

$\kappa = 0$ (constraint ignored)

$$(47) \quad q_t = 16.475 + .7513q_{t-1} + .00516\Delta x_t + .00491x_{t-1} - .1874\Delta p_t$$
$$\quad\quad (4.722) \quad (.0955) \quad\quad (.00326) \quad\quad (.00151) \quad\quad (.0359)$$
$$\quad\quad - .1356p_{t-1} + 2.3191d_t + .2791z_t$$
$$\quad\quad (.0359) \quad\quad (1.1574) \quad (.1317)$$
$$\quad \delta_1 = 1.8149 \quad\quad \delta_2 = 1.1334 \quad\quad R^2 = .993 \quad\quad D.W. = 1.65$$

$\kappa = -249.80$ (constrained least squares)

$$(48) \quad q_t = 16.642 + .7512q_{t-1} + .00629\Delta x_t + .00467x_{t-1} - .1796\Delta p_t$$
$$\quad\quad (4.765) \quad (.0964) \quad\quad (.00326) \quad\quad (.00149) \quad\quad (.0347)$$
$$\quad\quad - .1333p_{t-1} + 2.1297d_t + .2832z_t$$
$$\quad\quad (.0353) \quad\quad (1.1312) \quad (.1326)$$
$$\quad\quad \delta = 1.1800 \quad\quad R^2 = .993 \quad\quad D.W. = 1.61$$
$$\quad\quad (1.1587)$$

(The symbols and notation are explained at the beginning of Chapter 3.)

These equations were selected because the discrepancy in the unrestricted estimates is among the smallest of the 23 categories. Often it is much larger. The final δ lies between δ_1 and δ_2, which is as would be expected, but is closer to δ_2 than to δ_1, reflecting the fact that the price terms are more significant on balance than the income terms. The size of κ is of some interest, since it can, loosely speaking, be interpreted as a measure of the compatibility of the model and the data.[19] A small value of κ is to be preferred, for this means that the data are nearly consistent (in terms of identifiability) with the model as they stand. A large value of κ indicates the opposite and means, among other things, that the empirical covariance between total expenditure and prices must be altered considerably. Indeed, κ has on some occasions been so large that the resulting estimates were implausible, and we had to abandon the model. Of course, it could be in these cases that smaller roots which would have given more reasonable estimates were missed, but this we have no way of knowing.

A formal procedure for testing the compatibility of the data and the identifiability constraint is available. It will be shown in the next section how approximate variances and covariances of the structural coefficients can be derived, and these can be used to test the hypothesis that δ_1 is equal to δ_2. We have not done this, however, preferring instead to view δ_1 equal to δ_2 as an *a priori* restriction rather than a hypothesis to be tested.

VI. *Approximate Variances and Covariances of the Structural Coefficients*

Since the structural coefficients are not estimated directly, their standard errors can only be approximated indirectly. We will now show how, by using a device that is more or less part of the folklore of statistics, this can be done. For convenience, let

$$(49) \qquad B = \begin{bmatrix} b_1 \\ b_2 \\ b_3 \\ b_4 \\ b_5 \end{bmatrix} = \begin{bmatrix} \alpha \\ \beta \\ \gamma \\ \eta \\ \delta \end{bmatrix}.$$

[19] This creates the problem of deciding when κ is to be considered "small." One possibility is to look at the size of κ relative to some measure of the "size" of $(X'X - \kappa D)$, say the trace. However, we have not pursued this beyond looking at the absolute value of κ.

Then we can rewrite equations (1.41)–(1.44) as

(50) $b_i = f_i(A) \qquad i = 1, 5,$

and also

(51) $\hat{b}_i = f_i(\hat{A}) \qquad i = 1, 5,$

where as before, the "hats" denote estimates. Expanding $\hat{b}_i$ in a Taylor series around its true value, b_i, we obtain

(52) $\hat{b}_i = b_i + \sum_j (A_j - \hat{A}_j) \dfrac{\partial \hat{b}_i}{\partial \hat{A}_j} + \text{higher order terms.}$

Dropping the higher-order terms and taking b_i over the left-hand side, we have

(53) $\hat{b}_i - b_i = \sum_j (A_j - \hat{A}_j) \dfrac{\partial \hat{b}_i}{\partial \hat{A}_j}.$

From here it follows that asymptotically the variance of $\hat{b}_i$ will be approximately equal to

(54) $E(\hat{b}_i - b_i)^2 = \sum_j (\hat{A}_j - A_j)^2 \dfrac{\partial \hat{b}_i}{\partial \hat{A}_j}$

$$+ 2 \sum_j \sum_{\substack{k \\ j \neq k}} E(\hat{A}_j - A_j)(\hat{A}_k - A_k) \dfrac{\partial \hat{b}_i}{\partial \hat{A}_j} \dfrac{\partial \hat{b}_i}{\partial \hat{A}_k};$$

and the covariances:

(55) $E(\hat{b}_i - b_i)(\hat{b}_j - b_j) = \sum_k \sum_m E(\hat{A}_k - A_k)(\hat{A}_m - A_m) \dfrac{\partial b_i}{\partial A_k} \dfrac{\partial b_i}{\partial A_m}.$

Given the variance–covariance matrix of $\hat{A}$ and the partial derivatives, which can be calculated from equations (1.41)–(1.44), equations (54) and (55) give approximate variances and covariances of the structural coefficients. It should be emphasized, however, that these formulas are only strictly valid as asymptotic approximations, for although $\hat{A}$ is unbiased B is merely consistent. For finite samples, therefore, formula (54) must be viewed as an approximation to the mean-square error, and for this reason we have not relied very heavily on the standard errors of the structural coefficients for guidance.

VII. The Adding-up Problem

At this point we should recall that the independent variable in the analysis is total consumption expenditure rather than disposable income. The exceptions to this are in categories 1.4 (food produced and consumed on the farm) and 4.3 (space rental value of farm housing), for which disposable farm income is used in place of total PCE. Since total expenditure in 1970 and 1975 is taken as given, the exercise is to allocate the aggregate among the components rather than to project the aggregate itself. This means that care must be taken to ensure that we do not allocate either more or less than we have at the start: the individual items should add up to the total. If each equation were static, linear, and had the same set of predictors, then additivity would be assured and there would be no problem.[20] But one equation is nonlinear, 79 are dynamic, and with 82 categories[21] and only 32 observations, it is impossible for all equations to include the same set of predictors. Hence our set of demand functions is not additive.

But fortunately this has not been much of a problem. It was decided at the outset that, if the discrepancy were on the order of 4 percent or less, the projections would be adjusted in order to make them add up, and that this would be done by adjusting the independent variable (PCE), downward if the projections are too high and upward if too low. An alternative would be to alter each projection directly by the percentage that the sum of the projections is off. Unlike adjusting the independent variable, however, this method does not take into account different total expenditure elasticities in allocating the discrepancy.

Adjusting the independent variable, moreover, is more in line with the theory of consumer choice. When a set of demand functions is derived from an ordinal utility function, it is the marginal utility of income that ensures consistency. When the consumer is in equilibrium, we have $MU_i/P_i = \lambda$ for all i, where λ is the marginal utility of income. If expenditure for the individual items should add up to more than the total, this means, assuming the second order conditions hold, that λ can effectively be increased by reducing income (or total expenditure). In other words, our procedure reduces the marginal utility of income in the eyes of the consumer by reducing (in effect) the amount of income he sees. The correct way, of course, would be to increase λ directly, but this cannot be done with the present model because it is not derived from a utility function. This defect is overcome in Chapter 5 where the dynamic notions of Chapter 1 are incorporated into a quadratic utility function. Demand theory also requires that the expenditures add up in current, rather than in constant, dollars.

---

[20] This is, of course, only one of the possible functional forms that possesses the adding-up property. See Nicholson (1949), Prais (1952), Stone (1954), Prais and Houthakker (1955), Leser (1963), and Chapter 7 below for discussions of other functional forms that satisfy the criterion, as well as the criterion itself.

[21] No equation has been estimated for item 2.4 (standard clothing issued to military personnel).

Formally, the procedure that we use here is: (1) project the PCE items ignoring the adding-up constraint; (2) multiply each projection by its relative price; (3) adjust the 1975 total PCE by the amount of the discrepancy; (4) project again, and so forth, continuing until the projections sum to the original 1975 level of total PCE. Our experience has been that the projections converge within three or four iterations. In addition to making the projections add up in 1975 we also force them to add up in each intervening year as well.

3

Demand Equations for Individual Items of Expenditure

This chapter contains the empirical results obtained from applying our theory and methods to 82 categories of personal consumption expenditure in the United States. The results for the categories are presented individually here, while a more aggregative discussion is found in Chapter 4. The projections are also presented and discussed in Chapter 4.

The principal results in this chapter are the regression equations used in making the projections and occasionally an alternative equation. In addition, the elasticities with respect to total expenditure and price both for the short and the long run are given. Except for the double-logarithmic static equation, these elasticities have been calculated at the means of the respective variables. For the dynamic equations, the coefficients of the structural equation and their approximate standard errors have also been computed. For each equation we also give the "standard error of the estimate," which is the estimated standard deviation of the residuals. It is of some usefulness in evaluating the accuracy of year-to-year changes projected from the equation, and in comparing different equations for the same item.

I. Data

The principal source of data was the United States Department of Commerce, which has published annual data on 84 different categories of PCE from 1929 to date. These published data, which usually appear in each July issue of the *Survey of Current Business*, are in current dollars; constant-dollar figures (in prices of 1958) are not published in the same detail, because they are not considered as reliable, but they were made available by the Office of Business Economics in the form of worksheets. In a few instances the unpublished data gave more commodity detail than is published.

All calculations reported in this study are in terms of constant dollars, both for the dependent variables and for total expenditure. The current-dollar figures have been used only to obtain price indices (base 1958) for each category of expenditures by dividing the constant-dollar amount into the current-dollar amount. These price indices are therefore so-called implicit deflators which means that (unlike the Consumer Price Index) the weights of the various components of each category shift over time. The individual price series were deflated by the price index for total PCE derived in the same manner, thus giving a set of relative price indices.

The Department of Commerce data have been taken as they came, without any attempt at adjustment.[1] The projections presented in Chapter 4 are therefore directly comparable with the actual data that will be published in 1970 and 1975, except for changes in Commerce Department estimating procedures between now and 1975 and for revisions in already published data. In particular it appears that Commerce Department data on consumption are less accurate after 1958 than before, since the 1958 Census of Manufactures is the most recent one used for deriving these data. Consequently considerable revisions in the figures for 1959–1964 are expected when the data using the 1963 Census become available. The bulk of the empirical work in this study was completed by June, 1967.

It may be appropriate at this point to insert some comments on the quality of the Commerce Department data for PCE. Since for most commodities they are the only figures available, there is no basis for discussing their accuracy without a great deal of additional research. It is clear that some series are more reliable than others, but no attempt has been made to classify the series by accuracy, for such an attempt would not have improved the projection exercise. There is always a temptation to attribute unsatisfactory regression results to defects in the data, though it is equally conceivable that crude data give higher correlations: everything depends on how the data were derived. Indeed, it should be emphasized that many of the data series are themselves the result of more or less indirect estimating procedures, and that regression analysis of such series may on occasion amount to nothing more than an ex-post reconstruction of these procedures.[2]

Some of the PCE series are greatly influenced by the bookkeeping conventions on which the United States National Accounts are based, so that their interpretation in terms of actual transactions is often difficult. One important example is the space rental value of owner-occupied dwellings, not to be confused with the housing expenditure of homeowners;[3] another is the

---

[1] There is one difference from the published classification. Alcohol had been separated out from items 1.1 and 1.2 and is treated here as a distinct category, which we have numbered 1.0.

[2] A general ex-ante description of these procedures may be found on pp. 103–122 of *National Income*, 1954 ed. (a supplement to the *Survey of Current Business*), but it usually does not give enough detail to permit an independent derivation of the individual series, which no doubt also reflect a certain amount of expert judgment.

[3] *National Income*, p. 46.

"expense of handling life insurance," which represents expenditures by life insurance companies rather than by households.[4] Perhaps the most debatable item of this type is "services furnished without payment by financial intermediaries other than life insurance companies," amounting to well over $5 billion in 1961, which is merely a bookkeeping entry designed to offset an anomaly in the treatment of interest elsewhere in the accounts.[5] It is wholly out of line with any realistic estimate of the net cost of handling checks for nonbusiness accounts; indeed, it exceeds the total operating cost (excluding interest) of all commercial banks by a considerable margin. For projection purposes, however, any doubts about the meaning of the consumption categories have been rigorously suppressed.

Another factor limiting the usefulness of the Commerce Department data is the uneven fineness with which expenditures are broken down. Huge undivided aggregates such as "food purchased for off-premise consumption," amounting to $61 billion in 1961, contrast with such minute items as "purchased intercity transportation other than by rail, bus or air," amounting to $22 million. These are admittedly extreme examples; most of the individual items are between $1 and $5 billion, which is a reasonable range. However, a further breakdown of the food item and a few others would greatly increase the value of the published PCE table. To conclude these critical remarks, however, we wish to put on record our conviction that the Commerce Department data, for all their weaknesses, are derived with unusual conceptual clarity, painstaking care, and keen critical judgment. We certainly do not wish to leave the impression that our work is built on sand.

Some remarks about the period of observation underlying the regressions are in order here. Except for the two cases noted in our footnote, this was 1929–1964 excluding the war years 1942–1945, leaving 32 years in all (in the dynamic models discussed in Chapter 1 the observations for 1929 and 1946 are lost by differencing).[6] The reasons for omitting the war years are obvious, but it is possible to question the inclusion of the prewar period on the grounds that it is too remote. The main advantage of including this period is that it nearly doubles the number of observations, which are always at a premium in time-series analysis.[7] It also increases the range of variation of the predictors and thus increases the confidence with which the regression coefficients can be used for projection. Furthermore, as indicated, the PCE data from 1959 on are subject to revision and therefore should not be given undue weight.

[4] *Ibid.*, p. 48.   [5] *Ibid.*, pp. 46–47.

[6] The exceptions are alcoholic beverages, for which there were no data prior to 1933 since the Commerce Department figures do not cover illicit transactions, and the space rental of farmhouses which are analyzed only from 1935 on, since there was no farm-income series for earlier years.

[7] A fresh reading of Yule's classic paper (1926) on spurious correlation and the dangers inherent in using short-time series will help to bring home the points of this paragraph.

Moreover, there is another reason for keeping the prewar years, which has to do with our extensive use of the dynamic model in the study. The dynamic model, it will be recalled, is basically a process whereby physical and psychological stocks are adjusted to income. In the postwar period, the dependent variables, as well as income, in many instances have been dominated by strong trends so that an equilibrium between stocks and income may never have been reached. In particular this would be true if, over a considerable portion of the period, there was for some reason or another a constraint upon supply. Since we are ignoring supply in our analyses, it becomes important, if the dynamic model is to be valid for projection, that somewhere in the experience used to estimate the model there should exist "near equilibriums" between stocks and income. This is where the experience of the 1930's comes to the fore: at the low (relative) levels of income prevailing in the early thirties, the existing levels of stocks probably came close in many instances to being equilibrium amounts.

On the other hand, it is conceivable that consumers' tastes changed markedly as a result of World War II, which would render the prewar experience irrelevant. There is no convincing indication that any major change has occurred, but in the regressions this possibility was allowed for to some extent by the introduction of a "dummy variable," which permits demand to have a different level (but not a different response to income or price changes) in the postwar years compared to the prewar years. For many commodities this dummy variable turned out to be insignificant, even under the rather generous criteria adopted in this study (see section I of Chapter 1).

As part of the investigation, however, an equation for each category has also been estimated from postwar data only, and several have been used in the projections. A complete listing and a short discussion of these equations is given in the appendix to this chapter.

The data underlying all of the equations used in making the projections are described in the next section. They include revisions published through 1966. Static models for each category have also been estimated with the revised (August, 1965) PCE data, but there was little point in tabulating the equations since in virtually all cases they were inferior to the dynamic equations. The reader interested in comparing static and dynamic equations is referred to the first edition of this monograph.

II. *Variables*

The usual approach in demand analysis is to set out a relationship between quantity consumed and prices, with disposable income as the relevant budget variable. However, rather than using disposable income we have used total consumption expenditure as the independent variable. This is in keeping with the end objective of the investigation, which is to take a given level of total PCE in 1970 and allocate it optimally among its components. In the early days of demand analysis, particularly in budget inquiries, investigators often had to use total expenditure rather than income because typically income information was not given, nor could it be derived.[8] Hence the use of total expenditure is not novel.

There is, moreover, a more sophisticated reason for using total expenditure, even in the face of availability of income data. This is the argument that, at least over short periods of time, consumers have more control over their expenditures than over their receipts of income, so that total expenditure is a better measure of the "true" income of the consumer. It is an easy extension to interpret this argument as a variant of the permanent-income hypothesis made popular in recent years by Modigliani and Brumberg (1954), Friedman (1957), and their followers. We postpone further discussion of this topic until Chapter 6. We mention it here only to point out that the use of total expenditure is in keeping with such a hypothesis.

The intercepts of the regression equations have been estimated as the coefficients of a dummy variable that takes the value 1 for all observations. This allows the intercept to be treated like any other explanatory variable in an equation. Accordingly, the intercept has been suppressed whenever it did not exceed its standard error.

Finally, there remain only the predictors that have been used in isolated instances. These are treated when the equations in which they appear are discussed. The sources for these variables, as well as for the variables discussed above, are given in the data appendix.

III. Notation

For convenience the following symbols and notations are used throughout this chapter:

q_t per capita personal consumption expenditure in question in year t (1958 dollars)

Δq_t $q_t - q_{t-1}$

x_t total per capita personal consumption expenditure in year t (1958 dollars)

Δx_t $x_i - x_{t-1}$

p_t relative price in year t of the good in question (1958 = 100), calculated as the implicit deflator for that good divided by the implicit deflator for total PCE

[8] See, among others, Allen and Bowley (1935) and Prais and Houthakker (1955).

Δp_t $p_t - p_{t-1}$

d_t dummy variable used to separate the pre-World War II years from those following; takes the value 1 for 1929–1941 and 0 for 1946–1964

z_t 3-pass variable (only in connection with 3PLS, see below)

R^2 coefficient of multiple determination, defined as the square of the correlation between the actual and predicted values in their original units (i.e., in 1958 dollars) (except for first-difference equations, where it refers to first differences)

S_e standard error of the estimate

$\bar{q}$ mean per capita expenditure during the period of observation

$D.W.$ Durbin–Watson coefficient.

Other variables are defined as they appear. The parameters of the dynamic model are defined next (these are, of course, estimates, but the "hats" have been suppressed).

α intercept (an asterisk indicates that α is indeterminate)

β stock coefficient

γ short-run coefficient of total expenditure

γ' long-run coefficient of total expenditure

η short-run elasticity with respect to total expenditure

η' long-run elasticity with respect to total expenditure

λ short-run relative price coefficient

λ' long-run relative price coefficient

σ short-run relative price elasticity

σ' long-run relative price elasticity

δ depreciation rate

ξ intercept in the flow-adjustment model

θ adjustment coefficient in the flow-adjustment model

μ total expenditure coefficient in the flow-adjustment model

ζ relative price coefficient in the flow-adjustment model

For the dynamic models, the estimation method is indicated by OLS (ordinary least squares) or 3PLS (three-pass least squares).

Graphs of actual and computed values for each of the 82 items of expenditure accompany the discussion. The key to these graphs is as follows:

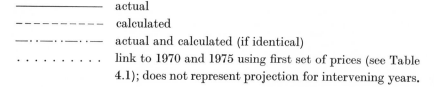

——————————   actual

– – – – – – – – –   calculated

—··—··—··—   actual and calculated (if identical)

· · · · · · · · · ·   link to 1970 and 1975 using first set of prices (see Table 4.1); does not represent projection for intervening years.

IV. Equations

1.0 ALCOHOLIC BEVERAGES

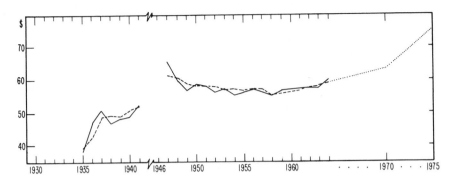

State-adjustment model; $\delta = 2$ OLS

$$q_t = 56.49 + -.3635q_{t-1} + .0146x_t + 1.0462(\% \text{ pop.} \geq 18)_t$$
$$\quad\quad (33.05) \quad\quad (.1073) \quad\quad (.0049) \quad\quad (.4633)$$

$R^2 = .924$ $S_e = 1.66$ $\bar{q} = 55.08$ $D.W. = 1.90$

$\alpha = -41.43$ $\beta = 1.0664$ $\gamma = .0107$ $\gamma' = .0229$
$\quad (26.97)$ $\quad (.2308)$ $\quad (.0044)$ $\quad (.0044)$

$\lambda = -$ $\lambda' = -$ $\delta = 2$

$\eta = .2898$ $\eta' = .6207$ $\sigma = -$ $\sigma' = -$

In the basic data made available to us, alcoholic beverages had been separated out of items 1.1 and 1.2 in the published PCE table. We first estimated this equation using the population over age 18 as the deflator rather than total population. The R^2 was higher and we did not need to restrict δ. However, this procedure posed a serious problem in the interpretation of total PCE (we should have PCE just for those over 18), so it was dropped. The Bergstrom model was also tried, but without success.

1.1 FOOD PURCHASED FOR OFF-PREMISE CONSUMPTION (EXCLUDING ALCOHOLIC BEVERAGES)

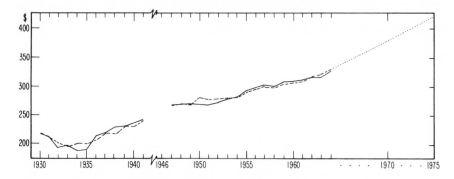

State-adjustment model   OLS

$$q_t = 31.76 + .5695q_{t-1} + .1029\Delta x_t + .0580x_{t-1}$$
$$(11.81) \quad (.1545) \quad\quad (.0186) \quad\quad (.0212)$$

$R^2 = .990$	$S_e = 4.49$	$\bar{q} = 262.27$	$D.W. = 1.79$
$\alpha = 51.56$	$\beta = .2365$	$\gamma = .0942$	$\gamma' = .1348$
(18.09)	(.2774)	(.0251)	(.0065)
$\lambda = -$	$\lambda' = -$	$\delta = .7851$	
		(.4780)	
$\eta = .4972$	$\eta' = .7115$	$\sigma = -$	$\sigma' = -$

As indicated above, alcoholic beverages have been excluded from this category. The relative price was dropped from the dynamic model when the own-price elasticity turned out to be positive. Food consumed in the home is seen to be subject to some habit formation ($\beta > 0$), although the habit wears off quite rapidly, as evidenced by the rather large value of δ. The total expenditure elasticities are consistent with those obtained in other studies, both for the United States and for other countries.[9]

[9] See, for instance, Crockett (1960).

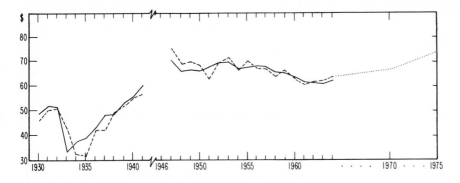

State-adjustment model; $\delta = 0$ OLS

$$q_t = -.9741 q_{t-1} + .0668 \Delta x_t - 1.3862 \Delta p_t$$
$$\quad\quad (.0120) \quad\quad (.0163) \quad\quad (.3413)$$

$R^2 = .916$	$S_e = 3.64$	$\bar{q} = 58.92$	$D.W. = 2.06$
$\alpha = *$	$\beta = -.0262$	$\gamma = .0677$	$\gamma' = -$
	$(.0123)$	$(.0167)$	
$\lambda = -1.4044$	$\lambda' = -$	$\delta = 0$	
$(.3464)$			
$\eta = 1.6126$	$\eta' = -$	$\sigma = -2.2703$	$\sigma' = -$

Restaurant meals have one of the highest short-run own-price elasticities in the study, and the short-run total expenditure is also quite high. Unlike food prepared in the home, consumers (figuratively) treat eating-out as a durable good, for β is slightly negative.

1.3 FOOD FURNISHED GOVERNMENT (INCLUDING MILITARY) AND COMMERCIAL EMPLOYEES

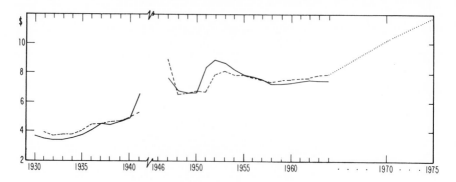

State-adjustment model   3PLS

$$q_t = .4862q_{t-1} + .00347\Delta x_t + .00239x_{t-1} + .2144z_t$$
$$\qquad (.1111) \qquad\quad (.00280) \qquad\;\; (.00060) \qquad (.2137)$$

$R^2 = .894$	$S_e = .62$	$\bar{q} = 6.17$	$D.W. = 1.69$
$\alpha = 0$	$\beta = .3602$	$\gamma = .0031$	$\gamma' = .0046$
	(1.3593)	$(.0038)$	$(.0003)$
$\lambda = -$	$\lambda' = -$	$\delta = 1.0516$	
		(1.4144)	
$\eta = .6799$	$\eta' = 1.0342$	$\sigma = -$	$\sigma' = -$

When the own relative price was included in the dynamic model, the coefficients were both positive, so prices were deleted. This equation should be interpreted with due regard for the peculiar nature of the commodity; the item does not reflect the decisions of private households, but of employers.

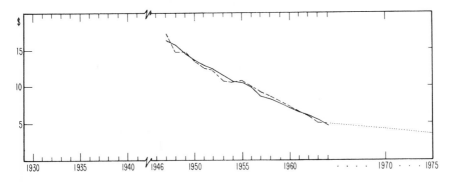

Flow-adjustment model   OLS   Postwar

$$q_t = 42.38 + .6817 q_{t-1} - .00788(x_t + x_{t-1})$$
$$(23.94) \quad (.1520) \qquad (.00641)$$

$R^2 = .754$ $S_e = 3.45$ $\bar{q} = 85.21$ $D.W. = 1.91$

$\xi = -1.0242$ $\theta = .3786$ $\mu = -.0495$
    $(.0140)$ $(.2150)$ $(.0317)$

$\zeta = —$ $\eta = -.6052$ $\sigma = —$

The farm population is used as the deflator for this item and disposable farm income is the independent variable. (The projections in Table 4.4, however, are in terms of the total population.) The relative price had the wrong sign when it was included in the Bergstrom model. Equations were also estimated with data going back to 1935 (disposable farm income is unavailable before then), but farm income as well as the relative price was insignificant.

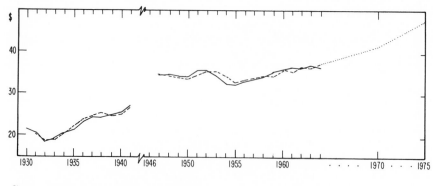

State-adjustment model   3PLS

$$q_t = 16.64 + .7512q_{t-1} + .00629\Delta x_t + .00467x_{t-1} - .1796\Delta p_t - .1333p_{t-1}$$
$$(4.77) \quad (.0964) \qquad (.00326) \qquad (.00149) \qquad (.0347) \qquad (.0353)$$

$$+ 2.1297d_t + .2832z_t$$
$$(1.1372) \quad (.1326)$$

$R^2 = .993$	$S_e = .60$	$\bar{q} = 30.00$	$D.W. = 1.61$
$\alpha = 16.11$	$\beta = .8958$	$\gamma = .0045$	$\gamma' = .0188$
(15.20)	(1.1345)	(.0039)	(.0055)
$\lambda = -.1290$	$\lambda' = -.5357$	$\delta = 1.1800$	
(.0306)	(.1913)	(1.1587)	
$\eta = .2075$	$\eta' = .8615$	$\sigma = -.4556$	$\sigma' = -1.8919$

Tobacco consumption, as would be expected, is subject to considerable habit formation, although the large δ indicates that the habit tends to wear off rapidly. The approximate standard errors for both coefficients, however, are quite large. Total expenditure and price are both important predictors, and there is substantial price elasticity in the long run, in contrast to the PCE elasticity which is less than one in the long as well as the short run.

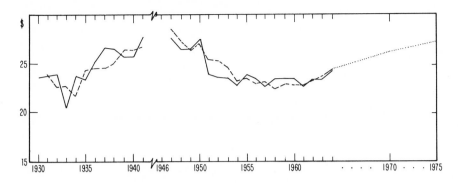

State-adjustment model; $\delta = 0$ 3PLS

$$q_t = .9592q_{t-1} + .0162\Delta x_t - .2355\Delta p_t - .3100z_t$$
$$\quad\quad (.0144) \quad\quad\quad (.0046) \quad\quad\quad (.0860) \quad\quad\quad (.1698)$$

$R^2 = .707$	$S_e = 1.03$	$\bar{q} = 24.36$	$D.W. = 2.03$
$\alpha = *$	$\beta = -.0417$	$\gamma = .0165$	$\gamma' = -$
	$(.0150)$	$(.0047)$	
$\lambda = -.2404$	$\lambda' = -$	$\delta = 0$	
$(.0876)$			
$\eta = .9433$	$\eta' = -$	$\sigma = -.9135$	$\sigma' = -$

Because of the low R^2 and the assumption $\delta = 0$, this equation leaves much to be desired. Inclusion of the per capita stock of automobiles suggested by an earlier static model increases the R^2 to .78, but the projections from this equation, given below, are implausibly high.

State-adjustment model; $\delta = 2$ OLS

$$q_t = 29.6229 + .2462q_{t-1} + .0190x_t - .2389p_t - 61.5020(\text{car stocks per capita})_t$$
$$\quad (3.9033) \quad (.1361) \quad\quad (.0041) \quad\quad (.0477) \quad\quad (18.7426)$$

$R^2 = .776$	$S_e = .86$	$\bar{q} = 24.36$	$D.W. = 2.19$
$\alpha = 23.77$	$\beta = .7904$	$\gamma = .0153$	$\gamma' = .0252$
(5.35)	$(.3505)$	$(.0047)$	$(.0039)$
$\lambda = -.1917$	$\lambda' = -.3169$	$\delta = 2$	
$(.0429)$	$(.0868)$		
$\eta = .8798$	$\eta' = 1.4547$	$\sigma = -.7299$	$\sigma' = -1.2069$

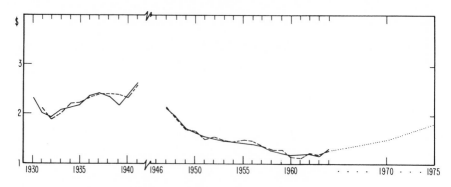

State-adjustment model   3PLS

$$q_t = 1.0305 + .6721q_{t-1} + .000698\Delta x_t + .000299x_{t-1} - .0258\Delta p_t$$
$$ (.4213) \quad (.0611) \qquad (.000309) \qquad\quad (.000129) \qquad\quad (.0067)$$

$$- .0111p_{t-1} + .3690d_t + .1858z_t$$
$$ (.0033) \qquad\;\; (.0647) \quad\;\; (.2558)$$

$R^2 = .986$	$S_e = .06$	$\bar{q} = 1.77$	$D.W. = 2.00$
$\alpha = 2.2628$	$\beta = .1525$	$\gamma = .00066$	$\gamma' = .00091$
(2.2360)	$(.5104)$	$(.00040)$	$(.00048)$
$\lambda = -.0243$	$\lambda' = -.0337$	$\delta = .5447$	
$(.0080)$	$(.0084)$	$(.5120)$	
$\eta = .5206$	$\eta' = .7230$	$\sigma = -1.3067$	$\sigma' = -1.8147$

As with 2.1, there was some evidence from the static model that the stock of automobiles has had an important influence on this item, but the above equation appears to be quite satisfactory.

2.3 CLOTHING, INCLUDING LUGGAGE[10]

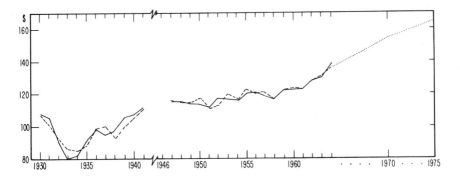

State-adjustment model   OLS

$$q_t = 11.594 + .7599q_{t-1} + .0862\Delta x_t + .0100x_{t-1}$$
$$(7.181)\quad (.1152)\qquad (.0152)\qquad (.0050)$$

$R^2 = .953$	$S_e = 3.14$	$\bar{q} = 111.86$	$D.W. = 1.90$
$\alpha = 107.48$	$\beta = -.1503$	$\gamma = .0923$	$\gamma' = .0415$
(53.58)	$(.0844)$	$(.0160)$	$(.0082)$
$\lambda = -$	$\lambda' = -$	$\delta = .1226$	
		$(.0807)$	
$\eta = 1.1423$	$\eta' = .5131$	$\sigma = -$	$\sigma' = -$

These results indicate that clothing, on balance, acts like a durable good, for β is negative. The total expenditure elasticities appear reasonable, but the depreciation rate seems too low. The relative price, when it was included in the model, was unimportant.

In addition to the equation for total clothing, equations for women's clothing (2.3a) and men's clothing (2.3b) have also been estimated separately:

2.3a Women's Clothing (including luggage)
State-adjustment model   OLS

$$q_t = .6010q_{t-1} + .0403\Delta x_t + .0187x_{t-1} + 3.6586d_t$$
$$(.1175)\qquad (.0108)\qquad (.0057)\qquad (1.4619)$$

$R^2 = .958$	$S_e = 2.26$	$\bar{q} = 70.23$	$D.W. = 1.72$
$\alpha = 0$	$\beta = .1075$	$\gamma = .0386$	$\gamma' = .0470$
	$(.2509)$	$(.0140)$	$(.0010)$
$\lambda = -$	$\lambda' = -$	$\delta = .6059$	
		$(.3966)$	
$\eta = .7614$	$\eta' = .9256$	$\sigma = -$	$\sigma' = -$

2.3b Men's Clothing (including luggage)
State-adjustment model   OLS

$$q_t = .8832q_{t-1} = .0414\Delta x_t + .00251x_{t-1} + 1.4517d_t$$
$$(.0610)\qquad (.0042)\qquad (.00167)\qquad (.7150)$$

[10] For a discussion of this equation, see also section III of Chapter 1.

$$R^2 = .936 \qquad S_e = .96 \qquad \bar{q} = 41.63 \qquad D.W. = 2.80$$

$$\alpha = 0 \qquad \beta = -.0615 \qquad \gamma = .0426 \qquad \gamma' = .0215$$
$$(.0251) \qquad (.0044) \qquad (.0033)$$

$$\lambda = — \qquad \lambda' = — \qquad \delta = .0625$$
$$(.0461)$$

$$\eta = 1.4166 \qquad \eta' = .7142 \qquad \sigma = — \qquad \sigma' = —$$

Here we see the interesting result that, unlike men's clothing, purchases of women's clothing are subject to habit formation. Although this may confirm some long-held suspicions, the habit is dissipated quite rapidly, and, even in the long run, the total expenditure elasticity of women's clothing is less than one. For men's clothing, the PCE elasticity may be a bit high in the short run, but seems reasonable in the long run. The depreciation rate, however, is clearly implausibly low, and this accounts for the low δ in the equation for total clothing.

2.4 STANDARD CLOTHING ISSUED TO MILITARY PERSONNEL

Owing to the peculiar nature of this commodity, no equation was estimated. Instead, the 1965 level has been used for both 1970 and 1975.

2.5 AND 2.6 CLOTHING UPKEEP AND LAUNDERING IN ESTABLISHMENTS

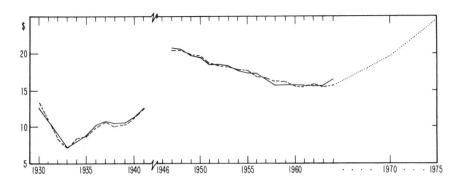

State-adjustment model; $\beta = \delta$ OLS

$$\Delta q_t = .00770\Delta x_t + .00151x_{t-1} - .1448\Delta p_t - .0285p_{t-1} + 1.6165d_t$$
$$\qquad\quad (.00145) \qquad (.00041) \qquad (.0175) \qquad (.0065) \qquad (.3519)$$

$R^2 = .909$	$S_e = .28$	$\bar{q} = 14.53$	$D.W. = 1.56$
$\alpha = 0$	$\beta = \delta = .2180$	$\gamma = .00695$	$\gamma' = -$
	$(.1232)$	$(.00153)$	
$\lambda = -.1306$	$\lambda' = -$	$\delta = -$	
$(.0163)$			
$\eta = .6534$	$\eta' = -$	$\sigma = -.9293$	$\sigma' = -$

Despite the lack of long-run elasticities (because of the assumption $\beta = \delta$), the dynamic model works very well for the total of these two items. Both PCE and the relative price are highly significant, habit formation is plausible, and the R^2 is rather remarkable in light of the dependent variable being a first difference.

Since the Office of Business Economics combined these two categories starting in 1962, it is no longer possible to estimate equations for them separately.

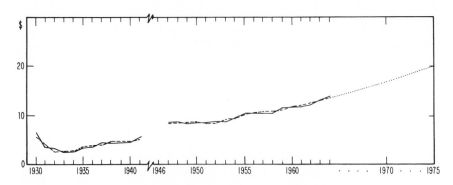

State-adjustment model   OLS

$$q_t = .5635q_{t-1} + .00646\Delta x_t + .00406x_{t-1} - .0297\Delta p_t - .0186p_{t-1}$$
$$\quad\quad\;\; (.0867) \qquad\quad (.00143) \qquad\quad (.00077) \qquad (.0099) \qquad (.0034)$$

$R^2 = .992$ $S_e = .34$ $\bar{q} = 7.82$ $D.W. = 2.26$

$\alpha = 0$ $\beta = .3577$ $\gamma = .00567$ $\gamma' = .00929$

           $(.7301)$ $(.00190)$ $(.00032)$

$\lambda = -.0260$ $\lambda' = -.0427$ $\delta = .9160$

   $(.0129)$ $(.0036)$ $(.8333)$

$\eta = 1.0025$ $\eta' = 1.6447$ $\sigma = -.4100$ $\sigma' = -.6726$

Despite their durable nature, the positive β for watches and (especially) jewelry, although tempered by a large approximate standard error, seems plausible. The large depreciation rate, however, indicates that the habit quickly wears off. Ideally, this category and 2.8, which contains (among other things) jewelry and watch repair, should be estimated simultaneously. We made an early effort in this direction, but multicollinearity precluded success.

2.8 OTHER CLOTHING ACCESSORIES, ETC.[11]

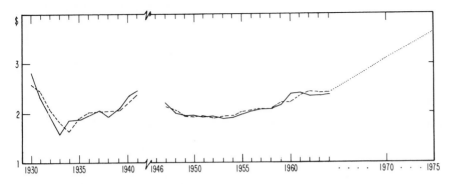

State-adjustment model　　OLS

$$q_t = -.2940 + .6674q_{t-1} + .0015\Delta x_t + .0006x_{t-1} + .3348d_t$$
$$\quad\ (.2765)\ \ (.1012)\qquad (.0006)\qquad (.0002)\qquad (.1254)$$

$R^2 = .819$	$S_e = .11$	$\bar{q} = 2.09$	$D.W. = 1.74$
$\alpha = -.7182$	$\beta = .0920$	$\gamma = .00143$	$\gamma' = .00176$
(.6360)	(.2999)	(.00069)	(.00054)
$\lambda = -$	$\lambda' = -$	$\delta = .4910$	
		(.3856)	
$\eta = .9472$	$\eta' = 1.1657$	$\sigma = -$	$\sigma' = -$

When prices were included in the dynamic model, both coefficients were positive and insignificant. The results indicate there is slight, though apparently insignificant, habit formation which wears off quickly. This is one of the few instances where the fit was poorer with the revised data than with those used in the first edition.

---

[11] Comprises watch, clock, and jewelry repairs, dressmakers and seamstresses not in shops, costumes and dress-suit rental, and miscellaneous services related to clothing.

3.1 TOILET ARTICLES AND PREPARATIONS

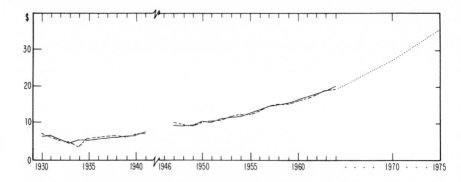

State-adjustment model; $\delta = 2$ OLS

$$q_t = .8769q_{t-1} + .0035x_t - .0353p_t + 1.7186d_t$$
$$\quad (.0553) \quad\quad (.0007) \quad\quad (.0061) \quad\quad (.3990)$$

$R^2 = .993$	$S_e = .42$	$\bar{q} = 10.58$	$D.W. = 2.07$
$\alpha = 0$	$\beta = 1.8689$	$\gamma = .00185$	$\gamma' = .0282$
	$(.0628)$	$(.00041)$	$(.0083)$
$\lambda = -.0188$	$\lambda' = -.2870$	$\delta = 2$	
$(.0035)$	$(.1181)$		
$\eta = .2453$	$\eta' = 3.7406$	$\sigma = -.1993$	$\sigma' = -3.0391$

This equation is substantially improved over the one that was obtained in the first edition of this book. PCE is now an important predictor, and the coefficient of q_{t-1} is no longer greater than one. However, habit formation is still considerable, and the long-run elasticities still reflect a strong trend in the dependent variable.

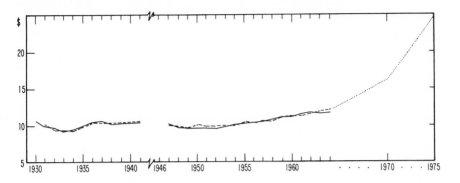

State-adjustment model   3PLS

$$q_t = -1.3683 + .6704q_{t-1} + .00731\Delta x_t + .00345x_{t-1} + 1.4580d_t + .2155z_t$$
$$(1.1605)\quad(.1386)\quad\quad(.00191)\quad\quad(.00151)\quad\quad\quad(.7356)\quad\quad(.1908)$$

$R^2 = .941$	$S_e = .40$	$\bar{q} = 10.73$	$D.W. = 2.03$
$\alpha = -2.6479$	$\beta = .2240$	$\gamma = .00668$	$\gamma' = .0105$
(1.7358)	$(.3294)$	$(.00247)$	$(.0020)$
$\lambda = -$	$\lambda' = -$	$\delta = .6187$	
		$(.4589)$	
$\eta = .8675$	$\eta' = 1.3598$	$\sigma = -$	$\sigma' = -$

When the relative price was included in the dynamic model, both price coefficients were negative, but less than their standard errors. This item is also subject to habit formation, although its influence is not as strong as with 3.1.

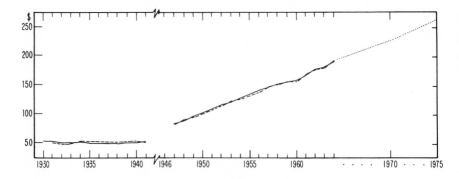

State-adjustment model; $\delta = 2$ 3PLS

$$q_t = .9439q_{t-1} + .01014x_t - .0625p_t + .3755z_t$$
$$(.0162)\qquad (.00102)\quad (.0052)\quad (.1941)$$

$R^2 = .999$	$S_e = .85$	$\bar{q} = 102.87$	$D.W. = 1.69$
$\alpha = 0$	$\beta = 1.9423$	$\gamma = .00522$	$\gamma' = .1808$
	$(.0171)$	$(.00055)$	$(.0422)$
$\lambda = -.0322$	$\lambda' = -1.1139$	$\delta = 2$	
$(.0028)$	$(.2848)$		
$\eta = .0707$	$\eta' = 2.4495$	$\sigma = -.0351$	$\sigma' = -1.2150$

In interpretating the results for this category it should be kept in mind that this is entirely an imputed item and therefore does not reflect any actual expenditures. The strong habit formation could conceivably reflect a supply constraint at some time during the period, say following the war and lasting till 1957 or 1958. The Bergstrom model also works quite well for this item. Indeed, in terms of fit and projections, there is little to choose between the two models, and so we will give the Bergstrom model here for reference.

Flow-adjustment model   3PLS

$$q_t = .9457q_{t-1} + .00506(x_t + x_{t-1}) - .0301(p_t + p_{t-1}) + .3650z_t$$
$$(.0134)\qquad (.00050)\qquad\qquad (.0028)\qquad\qquad (.1695)$$

$R^2 = .999$	$S_e = .98$	$\bar{q} = 102.87$	$D.W. = 1.91$
$\xi = 0$	$\theta = .0558$	$\mu = .1864$	
	$(.0142)$	$(.0368)$	
$\zeta = -1.1104$	$\eta = 2.6045$	$\sigma = -1.2711$	
$(.2422)$			

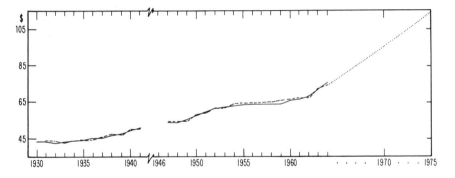

Flow-adjustment model   3PLS

$$q_t = -2.8328 + .8118q_{t-1} + .00580(x_t + x_{t-1}) - .00856(p_t + p_{t-1})$$
$$(2.1398) \quad (.0870) \qquad\quad (.00159) \qquad\qquad\quad (.00767)$$

$$+ 3.4403d_t + .8573z_t$$
$$(.9283) \quad (.1946)$$

$R^2 = .996$	$S_e = .64$	$\bar{q} = 56.09$	$D.W. = 2.53$
$\xi = -.7391$	$\theta = .2078$	$\mu = .0617$	
(.1457)	(.1060)	(.0138)	
$\zeta = -.0910$	$\eta = 1.5315$	$\sigma = -.1839$	
(.1017)			

This equation, though plausible on its face, has some problems. The dependent variable has a very strong postwar trend, and the result of this is to make the parameter estimates extremely sensitive to revisions in the data. For example, it was impossible to obtain a plausible equation with the 1965 revisions, but the 1966 revisions gave the above equation. The large coefficient on z_t and the high $D.W.$ may reflect this to an extent. At one point we tried combining this item with 4.1 and then deriving 4.2 as a residual, but the resulting projections were implausible.[12]

[12] We might note in passing that it is impossible to test for a price substitution between 4.1 and 4.2, since the same deflator is used for both. This is a weakness of the Commerce Department figures on housing. Since owner-occupied dwellings (mostly one-family houses) are different in kind from rental dwellings (mostly apartments), and are also located in different areas (relatively more in suburbs, for instance), it is unlikely that their rental value has evolved in the same manner as that of rented dwellings.

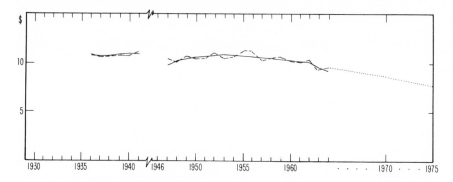

Flow-adjustment model   3PLS   1935–1964

$$q_t = .9241q_{t-1} + .00397(x_t + x_{t-1}) - .0178(p_t + p_{t-1}) - .3005z_t$$
$$\quad (.0511) \quad\quad (.00147) \quad\quad\quad (.0073) \quad\quad\quad (.1695)$$

$R^2 = .997$ $S_e = 1.95$ $\bar{q} = 83.40$ $D.W. = 2.25$

$\xi = 0$ $\theta = .0789$ $\mu = .1046$
$\quad\quad\quad (.0552) \quad\quad (.0654)$

$\zeta = -.4674$ $\eta = 1.1283$ $\sigma = -.6044$
$\quad (.3239)$

As with item 1.4 (food produced and consumed on farms), the farm population is the deflator for this category and disposable farm income the independent variable.[13] Since the latter is unavailable prior to 1935, the function has been fitted to the period 1935–1964.

[13] Although the equation for this category was estimated using the farm population as the deflator, the projections in Table 4.6 have been converted to per capita terms using the total population.

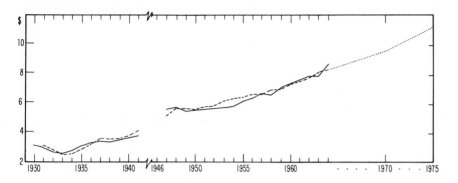

Flow-adjustment model   3PLS

$$q_t = -1.9753 + .1999q_{t-1} + .00195(x_t + x_{t-1}) + .5003z_t$$
$$\quad\;\; (.6031)\;\; (.3053) \qquad\quad (.00060) \qquad\qquad\quad (.3770)$$

$R^2 = .986$	$S_e = .23$	$\bar{q} = 5.29$	$D.W. = 1.50$
$\xi = -.6639$	$\theta = 1.3337$	$\mu = .00487$	
$(.0681)$	$(.8481)$	$(.00061)$	
$\zeta = -$	$\eta = 1.2735$	$\sigma = -$	

The own-price elasticity was positive when prices were included in this model. They were negative but insignificant in the dynamic model with $\delta = 2$. Note, in contrast to the other rent categories, the large adjustment coefficient (θ) for this item. Indeed, it may be implausibly large.

[14] Comprises transient hotels, tourist cabins, clubs, schools, and institutions.

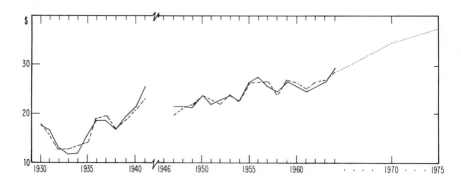

State-adjustment model   OLS

$$q_t = 1.2326 + .8348q_{t-1} + .0376\Delta x_t + .0013x_{t-1}$$
$$\qquad(.8099)\quad(.1088)\qquad(.0039)\qquad(.0016)$$

$R^2 = .967$	$S_e = .89$	$\bar{q} = 21.44$	$D.W. = 1.90$
$\alpha = 36.73$	$\beta = -.1435$	$\gamma = .0402$	$\gamma' = .00817$
(52.54)	$(.0876)$	$(.0041)$	$(.00510)$
$\lambda = -$	$\lambda' = -$	$\delta = .0366$	
		$(.0464)$	
$\eta = 2.5975$	$\eta' = .5275$	$\sigma = -$	$\sigma' = -$

Other than an implausibly small depreciation rate, this equation is quite good. The stock coefficient is negative, as it should be, and the PCE elasticities seem reasonable. With prices in the model, δ converged to a negative value and the coefficient of q_{t-1} was greater than one.

In view of the insignificant coefficient for x_{t-1}, a model with $\delta = 0$ has also been estimated:

State-adjustment model; $\delta = 0$ 3PLS

$$q_t = .9533q_{t-1} + .0421\Delta x_t - .2257\Delta p_t + .5641d_t - .2153z_t$$
$$\qquad(.0128)\qquad(.0035)\qquad(.0566)\qquad(.2608)\qquad(.1938)$$

$R^2 = .979$	$S_e = .74$	$\bar{q} = 21.44$	$D.W. = 1.75$
$\alpha = {}^*$	$\beta = -.0478$	$\gamma = .0431$	$\gamma' = -$
	$(.0134)$	$(.0037)$	
$\lambda = -.2311$	$\lambda' = -$	$\delta = 0$	
$(.0584)$			
$\eta = 2.7803$	$\eta' = -$	$\sigma = -1.0126$	$\sigma' = -$

This is actually a better equation than the one given first, for the R^2 is higher and it includes the relative price. The assumption $\delta = 0$, however, is clearly a defect.

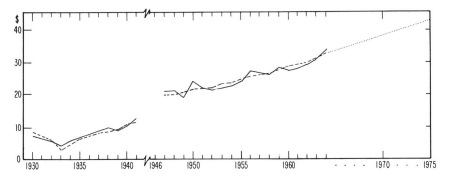

Static model   linear
$$q_t = 10.200 + .0151x_t - .0882p_t - 5.1357d_t$$
$$(6.845) \quad (.0027) \quad (.0234) \quad (.9374)$$

$R^2 = .991$	$S_e = .93$	$\bar{q} = 17.84$	$D.W. = 1.66$
$\alpha = -$	$\beta = -$	$\gamma = -$	$\gamma' = -$
$\lambda = -$	$\lambda' = -$	$\delta = -$	
$\eta = 1.1827$	$\eta' = -$	$\sigma = -.6337$	$\sigma' = -$

The dynamic model for this category gives an unusual result in that the coefficient of q_{t-1} is negative, though not significantly so. This implies an implausibly large negative stock coefficient and an equally implausible depreciation rate. The equation is given below.

State-adjustment model   OLS
$$q_t = -.0349q_{t-1} + .0268\Delta x_t + .0191x_{t-1} - .0709\Delta p_t - .0505p_{t-1} - 4.5307d_t$$
$$(.1094) \quad (.0037) \quad (.0022) \quad (.0577) \quad (.0101) \quad (.7219)$$

$R^2 = .993$	$S_e = .86$	$\bar{q} = 17.84$	$D.W. = 1.67$
$\alpha = 0$	$\beta = -1.0391$	$\gamma = .0358$	$\gamma' = .0185$
	(1.4091)	$(.0083)$	$(.0005)$
$\lambda = -.0947$	$\lambda' = -.0488$	$\delta = 1.1057$	
$(.1194)$	$(.0072)$	(1.4677)	
$\eta = 2.7232$	$\eta' = 1.4037$	$\sigma = -.6743$	$\sigma' = -.3476$

It is unfortunate that for this important item, which is undoubtedly durable, a satisfactory dynamic equation could not be found.[15]

---

[15] One reason may be that there was unusually rapid technological change in this category, which our model does not take into account.

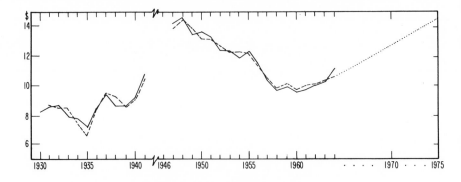

State-adjustment model; $\delta = 2$ 3PLS

$$q_t = 22.425 + .2457q_{t-1} + .00434x_t - .2166p_t + .4744z_t$$
$$(2.404) \quad (.0770) \qquad (.00051) \quad (.0241) \quad (.1045)$$

$R^2 = .977$	$S_e = .34$	$\bar{q} = 10.43$	$D.W. = 2.14$
$\alpha = 18.00$	$\beta = .7889$	$\gamma = .00348$	$\gamma' = .00575$
(2.98)	(.1984)	(.00061)	(.00030)
$\lambda = -.1739$	$\lambda' = -.2871$	$\delta = 2$	
(.0293)	(.0149)		
$\eta = .4692$	$\eta' = .7749$	$\sigma = -1.5448$	$\sigma' = -2.5512$

The results show this item to be subject to considerable habit formation, which in turn wears off very rapidly. Note also the high price elasticities. Other than having implausibly large long-run elasticities, the postwar data also give a good equation, and it is offered as an alternative.

State-adjustment model   3PLS   Postwar

$$q_t = .9384q_{t-1} + .01099\Delta x_t + .00381x_{t-1} - .1931\Delta p_t - .0669p_{t-1} - .4151z_t$$
$$(.0409) \qquad (.00253) \qquad (.00179) \qquad (.0368) \quad (.0317) \quad (.2956)$$

$R^2 = .978$	$S_e = .28$	$\bar{q} = 11.67$	$D.W. = 2.37$
$\alpha = 0$	$\beta = .3553$	$\gamma = .00937$	$\gamma' = .0618$
	(.4666)	(.00234)	(.0511)
$\lambda = -.1647$	$\lambda' = 1.0854$	$\delta = .4189$	
(.0427)	(.9350)		
$\eta = 1.3182$	$\eta' = 8.6858$	$\sigma = -1.3355$	$\sigma' = -8.7999$

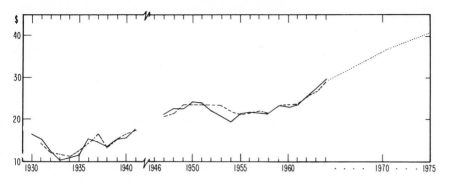

State-adjustment model 3PLS

$$q_t = .8373q_{t-1} + .02835\Delta x_t + .00269x_{t-1} + .3924z_t$$
$$\quad\quad (.1142) \quad\quad (.00421) \quad\quad (.00173) \quad\quad (.1875)$$

$R^2 = .972$	$S_e = .89$	$\bar{q} = 19.50$	$D.W. = 2.22$
$\alpha = 0$	$\beta = -.0774$	$\gamma = .0294$	$\gamma' = .0166$
	$(.0676)$	$(.0044)$	$(.0227)$
$\lambda = -$	$\lambda' = -$	$\delta = .0997$	
		$(.0737)$	
$\eta = 2.0879$	$\eta' = 1.1759$	$\sigma = -$	$\sigma' = -$

When prices were included in the model, their coefficients, although negative, were insignificant. The above equation, however, seems to be quite good. There is inventory adjustment, as is to be expected, and, in view of the fact that this category includes items such as floor covering, mirrors, and picture frames, the depreciation rate does not appear out of line, and the PCE elasticities are reasonable.

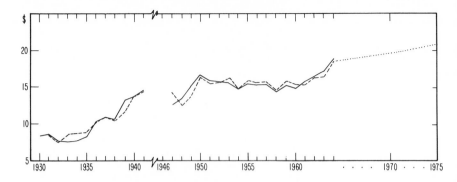

State-adjustment model   3PLS

$$q_t = .4551q_{t-1} + .01747x_t + .00342x_{t-1} + .4825d_t + .5887z_t$$
$$\qquad (.1736) \qquad (.00332) \qquad (.00117) \qquad (.2464) \qquad (.2700)$$

$R^2 = .954$	$S_e = .73$	$\bar{q} = 13.35$	$D.W. = 1.75$
$\alpha = 0$	$\beta = -.5318$	$\gamma = .0216$	$\gamma' = .00628$
	$(.2674)$	$(.0053)$	$(.00085)$
$\lambda = -$	$\lambda' = -$	$\delta = .2172$	
		$(.0894)$	
$\eta = 2.2298$	$\eta' = .6466$	$\sigma = -$	$\sigma' = -$

Among the items included in this category are piece goods allocated to house-furnishing use (other than bedding and floor coverings), brushes, brooms, and lampshades; these are durables that are by and large necessities —hence the substantial negative stock coefficient, along with a high short-run but low long-run total-expenditure elasticity, is what we should expect. Moreover, the estimated depreciation rate is reasonable.

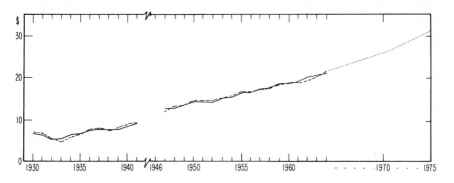

State-adjustment model   OLS

$$q_t = -3.0053 + .5860q_{t-1} + .0103\Delta x_t + .0062x_{t-1} - .5143d_t$$
$$(1.5648) \quad (.0980) \qquad (.0018) \qquad (.0018) \qquad (.3755)$$

$R^2 = .995$	$S_e = .38$	$\bar{q} = 12.68$	$D.W. = 1.80$
$\alpha = 4.4414$	$\beta = .3312$	$\gamma = .00909$	$\gamma' = .0149$
(1.5195)	(.2452)	(.00214)	(.0016)
$\lambda = -$	$\lambda' = -$	$\delta = .8523$	
		(.3322)	
$\eta = .9929$	$\eta' = 1.6227$	$\sigma = -$	$\sigma' = -$

The own-price elasticity was positive when the relative price was included
in the dynamic model. Other than perhaps having stronger habit formation
than one would expect, this equation does not have any obvious defects.

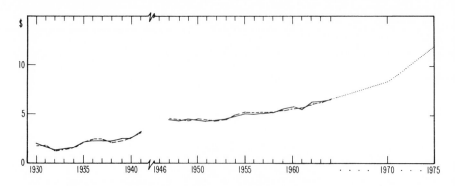

State-adjustment model   OLS

$q_t = -.7149 + .3756 q_{t-1} + .00468 \Delta x_t + .00331 x_{t-1} - .0212 \Delta p_t - .0149 p_{t-1}$
         (.4691)   (.1898)   (.00078)   (.00100)   (.0075)   (.0079)

$R^2 = .994$ $S_e = .14$ $\bar{q} = 4.01$ $D.W. = 1.75$

$\alpha = -.9529$ $\beta = .1830$ $\gamma = .00441$ $\gamma' = .00530$
    (1.3237)   (1.0586)   (.00106)   (.00141)

$\lambda = -.0199$ $\lambda' = .0239$ $\delta = 1.0908$
    (.0110)   (.0084)   (1.4073)

$\eta = 1.5211$ $\eta' = 1.8277$ $\sigma = -.4693$ $\sigma' = -.5638$
    (1.4073)

The results indicate this commodity to be subject to moderate habit formation, which wears off very rapidly. Note also the relatively high total-expenditure elasticities and significant but much smaller own-price elasticities.

86

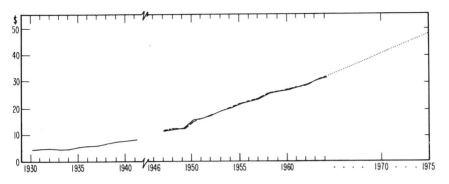

State-adjustment model; $\delta = 2$ **OLS**   Postwar

$$q_t = 3.7139 + .8725q_{t-1} + .00328x_t - .0504p_t$$
$$ (2.8139) \quad (.0470) \qquad\quad (.00140) \quad\; (.0250)$$

$R^2 = .999$	$S_e = .16$	$\bar{q} = 21.80$	$D.W. = 2.32$
$\alpha = .7565$	$\beta = 1.9216$	$\gamma = .00175$	$\gamma' = .0258$
(1.7093)	(.0855)	(.00079)	(.0051)
$\lambda = -.0269$	$\lambda' = -.3952$	$\delta = 2$	
(.0139)	(.1232)		
$\eta = .1319$	$\eta' = 1.9364$	$\sigma = -.1289$	$\sigma' = -1.8926$

The postwar equation was chosen over the equation for the entire period, which is given below, because of the significant price elasticities. Other than this, there is little difference between the two models.

State-adjustment model   **OLS**   1929–1964

$$q_t = .9646q_{t-1} + .0021\Delta x_t + .0012x_{t-1} - .7645d_t$$
$$ (.0076) \qquad (.0006) \qquad\;\; (.0001) \qquad (.0782)$$

$R^2 = .999$	$S_e = .15$	$\bar{q} = 12.42$	$D.W. = 2.17$
$\alpha = 0$	$\beta = .7500$	$\gamma = .00151$	$\gamma' = .0330$
	(.3267)	(.00063)	(.0044)
$\lambda = -\!\!-$	$\lambda' = -\!\!-$	$\delta = .7860$	
		(.3265)	
$\eta = .1371$	$\eta' = 2.9916$	$\sigma = -\!\!-$	$\sigma' = -\!\!-$

In the first edition of this book, a marginal price was used in place of the implicit deflator, and this was significant in the dynamic model. With the revised data, however, the marginal price had negative coefficients, but they were insignificant.

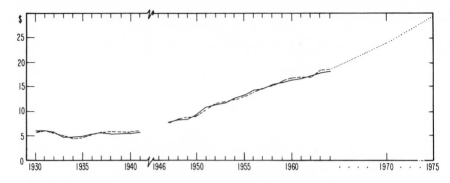

Flow-adjustment model   OLS

$$q_t = -1.8084 + .8984q_{t-1} + .00114(x_t + x_{t-1})$$
$$(.3824)\quad (.0319)\qquad (.00024)$$

$R^2 = .997$	$S_e = .25$	$\bar{q} = 10.06$	$D.W. = 1.77$
$\xi = -.6439$	$\theta = .1071$	$\mu = .0224$	
$(.0484)$	$(.0354)$	$(.0030)$	
$\zeta = -$	$\eta = 3.1087$	$\sigma = -$	

The relative price and total PCE are very highly correlated, with the result that both cannot be in the model at the same time. The equation with the relative price in place of total PCE is given below. The implausibly large long-run elasticity is due to β and δ being nearly identical.

State-adjustment model   OLS

$$q_t = 1.6803 + .9889q_{t-1} - .0158\Delta p_t - .0092p_{t-1}$$
$$(.6178)\quad (.1780)\qquad (.0077)\qquad (.0065)$$

$R^2 = .998$	$S_e = .24$	$\bar{q} = 10.06$	$D.W. = 2.09$
$\alpha = 2.0528$	$\beta = .8119$	$\gamma = -$	$\gamma' = -$
(1.7891)	$(.7196)$		
$\lambda = -.0112$	$\lambda' = -.8264$	$\delta = .8231$	
$(.0067)$	(1.5962)	$(.7173)$	
$\eta = -$	$\eta' = -$	$\sigma = -.1458$	$\sigma' = -10.7386$

As with electricity, a marginal price is probably more appropriate than the implicit deflator. Our efforts to construct one, however, were unsuccessful. The adjustment coefficient of about .10 with the Bergstrom model appears to be smaller than one might expect (though the PCE elasticity seems high), but this could reflect a supply constraint at some time during the historical period. The high PCE elasticity is the result of a strong trend in the dependent variable; if computed near the end of the period, the elasticity would be lower.

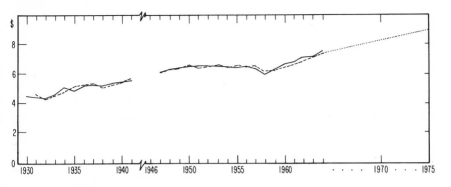

State-adjustment model   3PLS

$$q_t = 1.8084 + .5112q_{t-1} + .00345\Delta x_t + .00123x_{t-1} - .0116\Delta p_t - .0041p_{t-1}$$
$$\quad (1.3996) \quad (.3242) \qquad (.00182) \qquad (.00076) \qquad (.0076) \qquad (.0049)$$
$$\quad + .4644z_t$$
$$\quad (.3359)$$

$R^2 = .977$	$S_e = .14$	$\bar{q} = 5.93$	$D.W. = 1.78$
$\alpha = 5.5208$	$\beta = -.2133$	$\gamma = .00376$	$\gamma' = .00252$
(6.6271)	$(.4182)$	$(.00271)$	$(.00028)$
$\lambda = -.0126$	$\lambda' = -.0084$	$\delta = .4335$	
$(.0101)$	$(.0055)$	$(.9080)$	
$\eta = .8746$	$\eta' = .5861$	$\sigma = -.2028$	$\sigma' = -.1359$

It is surprising to find a negative stock coefficient for this item; casual observation suggests that lawn watering and car washing (and perhaps even taking a bath) are habit forming; however, the estimates of the structural parameters have large approximate standard errors, as tends to be true where prices appear in the dynamic model.

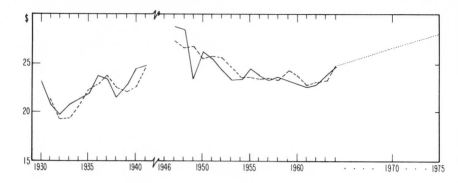

State-adjustment model; $\delta = 0$ 3PLS

$$q_t = .9869q_{t-1} + .01259\Delta x_t - .1676\Delta p_t - .2210z_t$$
$$\quad\quad (.0111) \quad\quad (.00550) \quad\quad (.0820) \quad\quad (.2060)$$

$R^2 = .720$	$S_e = 1.18$	$\bar{q} = 23.60$	$D.W. = 2.03$
$\alpha = *$	$\beta = -.0131$	$\gamma = .0126$	$\gamma' = -$
	$(.0112)$	$(.0056)$	
$\lambda = -.1687$	$\lambda' = -$	$\delta = 0$	
$(.0823)$			
$\eta = .7514$	$\eta' = -$	$\sigma = -.7317$	$\sigma' = -$

This is one of the poorer equations in terms of R^2 in the study and also one of the few for which the R^2 fell significantly with the revised data. Before being constrained at zero, δ had converged to a small negative value. This implied, among other things, a negative long-run PCE elasticity and positive long-run price elasticity. Although the former is plausible, x_{t-1}, p_{t-1}, and δ were all insignificant, and so $\delta = 0$ was assumed.

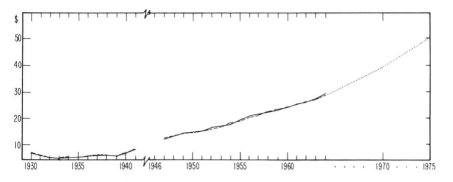

State-adjustment model; $\beta = \delta$ OLS

$$\Delta q_t = .00385\Delta x_t + .00128x_{t-1} - .0366\Delta p_t - .0122p_{t-1} + .4970d_t$$
$$\quad\quad (.00113) \quad\quad (.00024) \quad\quad (.0092) \quad\quad (.0038) \quad\quad (.3104)$$

$R^2 = .877$ $S_e = .23$ $\bar{q} = 14.40$ $D.W. = 2.01$

$\alpha = 0$ $\beta = \delta = .4007$ $\gamma = .00320$ $\gamma' = -$
            $(.2546)$ $(.00118)$

$\lambda = -.0305$ $\lambda' = -$ $\delta = \beta$
   $(.0084)$

$\eta = .3158$ $\eta' = -$ $\sigma = -.2556$ $\sigma' = -$

Apart from the indeterminacy in the long-run arising from the assumption $\beta = \delta$, this is a satisfactory result, particularly in view of the dependent variable being a first difference. Habit formation is present, which is to be expected, and both PCE and prices are significant. However, the elasticity with respect to total PCE looks rather low, even for the short-run. The opposite is the case in the Bergstrom model, which works quite well in the postwar period, and this equation follows.

Flow-adjustment model   3PLS   Postwar

$$q_t = -14.068 + .5497q_{t-1} + .00798(x_t + x_{t-1}) - .0137(p_t + p_{t-1}) - .2853z_t$$
$$\quad (3.553) \quad (.0926) \quad\quad (.00151) \quad\quad\quad (.0116) \quad\quad\quad (.2327)$$

$R^2 = .999$ $S_e = .21$ $\bar{q} = 20.14$ $D.W. = 2.12$

$\xi = -.9336$ $\theta = .5811$ $\mu = .0354$
   $(.0156)$ $(.1542)$ $(.0017)$

$\zeta = -.0607$ $\eta = 2.8173$ $\sigma = -.2970$
   $(.0501)$

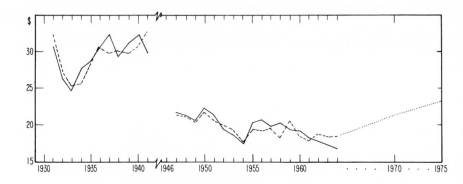

State-adjustment model; $\delta = 0$ OLS

$$q_t = .9468q_{t-1} + .0314\Delta x_t - .1823\Delta p_t$$
$$(.0168) \qquad (.0062) \qquad (.1205)$$

$R^2 = .949$	$S_e = 1.33$	$\bar{q} = 23.67$	$D.W. = 2.40$
$\alpha = *$	$\beta = -.0546$	$\gamma = .0323$	$\gamma' = -$
	$(.0177)$		
$\lambda = -.1873$	$\lambda' = -$	$\delta = 0$	
$(.1239)$			
$\eta = 1.8875$	$\eta' = -$	$\sigma = -.6635$	$\sigma' = -$

In the first edition the distribution of income appeared in place of the relative price, but still under the assumption that $\delta = 0$. It is fortunate that the relative price has become significant with the revised data since the Commerce Department series on the distribution of income is no longer available. The equation is little changed in its other aspects, however, and so the earlier equation is reproduced here for reference.

State-adjustment model; $\delta = 0$ OLS 1929–1961 (unrevised data)

$$q_t = .9699q_{t-1} + .0303\Delta x_t + .0186\Delta(\text{income dist.})_t$$
$$(.0108) \qquad (.0052) \qquad (.0126)$$

$R^2 = .952$	$S_e = -$	$\bar{q} = 23.67$	$D.W. = 2.17$
$\alpha = *$	$\beta = -.0306$	$\gamma \text{ (upper)} = .0102$	$\gamma \text{ (lower)} = .0085$
$\lambda = -$	$\lambda' = -$	$\delta = 0$	
$\eta = -$	$\eta' = -$	$\sigma = -$	$\sigma' = -$

One would expect the difference between the marginal propensities to consume of the two income groups to be larger than the above equation indicates.[16] This is probably because of the absence of prices. The distribution of income is no doubt picking up much of the price effect, but this could be merely a statistical illusion.

[16] The distribution of income variable in the above equation is defined as the difference between $\frac{1}{5}$ times the mean income of the top fifth of income receivers and $\frac{4}{5}$ times the mean income of the bottom four-fifths. The means were constructed from unpublished data provided by the Bureau of Labor Statistics by graphical interpolation on double logarithmic paper. With this definition, the different marginal propensities to consume are derived as follows:

Let x be the mean income (or PCE) for the top group and x_2 the mean income (or PCE) for the bottom group. Then the overall mean is $(x_1 + 4x_2)/5$, while by definition the income distribution measure is $(x_1 - 4x_2)/5$. Hence in the regression

$$y = a + b\left(\frac{x_1 + 4x_2}{5}\right) + c\left(\frac{x_1 - 4x_2}{5}\right)$$

the MPC of the upper group is $(b + c)/5$, while it is $4(b - c)/5$ for the lower group.

In terms of the equation for domestic services, therefore:

$$\gamma \text{ (upper)} = \frac{2}{1.9699} \frac{[.0303 + 1.063(.0186)]}{5} = .0102$$

$$\gamma \text{ (lower)} = \frac{2}{1.9699} \cdot \frac{4}{5}[.0303 - 1.063(.0186)] = .0085,$$

where 1.063 is the factor for adjusting disposable income to total expenditure while leaving the overall equation unchanged.

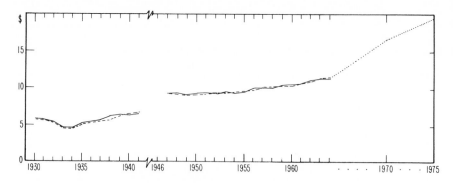

State-adjustment model   3PLS

$$q_t = .6932q_{t-1} + .00401\Delta x_t + .00234x_{t-1} - .0134\Delta p_t - .0078p_{t-1} - .3104z_t$$
$$\quad (.2238) \qquad (.00119) \qquad (.00172) \qquad\qquad (.0288) \qquad (.0062) \qquad\quad (.3052)$$

$R^2 = .997$	$S_e = .15$	$\bar{q} = 8.30$	$D.W. = 1.63$
$\alpha = 0$	$\beta = .4600$	$\gamma = .00336$	$\gamma' = .00762$
	(3.6143)	$(.00104)$	$(.00035)$
$\lambda = -.0112$	$\lambda' = -.0254$	$\delta = .8224$	
$(.0360)$	$(.0054)$	(3.9165)	
$\eta = .5577$	$\eta' = 1.2657$	$\sigma = -.1272$	$\sigma' = -.2885$

The large positive stock indicates that there is a good deal of inertia and habit formation present in the consumption of the items in this category. But the habit wears off rapidly, for the depreciation rate is quite large. Note that the own-price elasticity only borders on significance; prices could have been left out with little overall effect on the results.

[17] Comprises maintenance services for appliances and house furnishings, moving and warehouse expenses, postage and express charges, premiums for fire and theft insurance less claims paid, and miscellaneous household-operation services.

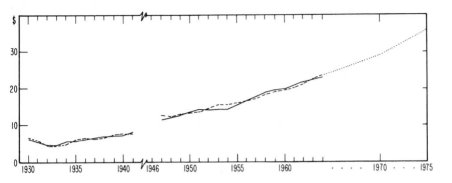

State-adjustment model   OLS

$$q_t = -1.4777 + .9322q_{t-1} + .0064\Delta x_t + .0019x_{t-1}$$
$$(1.1293) \quad (.0805) \qquad (.0018) \qquad (.0015)$$

$R^2 = .996$	$S_e = .42$	$\bar{q} = 12.52$	$D.W. = 1.74$
$\alpha = -4.4543$	$\beta = .2732$	$\gamma = .00563$	$\gamma' = .0275$
(1.4894)	$(.2343)$	$(.00181)$	$(.0117)$
$\lambda = —$	$\lambda' = —$	$\delta = .3434$	
		$(.3092)$	
$\eta = .6221$	$\eta' = 3.0422$	$\sigma = —$	$\sigma' = —$

The price coefficients were insignificant when the relative price was included in the dynamic model, and the own-price elasticity was positive in the static model.

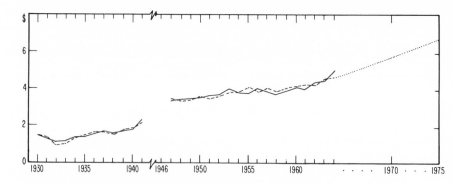

State-adjustment model   OLS

$$q_t = .5939q_{t-1} + .00283\Delta x_t + .00122x_{t-1} - .0090\Delta p_t - .0039p_{t-1}$$
$$\quad\ (.1978)\qquad (.00082)\qquad (.00044)\qquad (.0016)\qquad (.0016)$$

$R^2 = .990$	$S_e = .14$	$\bar{q} = 3.00$	$D.W. = 1.92$
$\alpha = 0$	$\beta = .0405$	$\gamma = .00279$	$\gamma' = .00301$
	$(.5234)$	$(.00102)$	$(.00011)$
$\lambda = -.0088$	$\lambda' = —$	$\delta = .5501$	
$(.0072)$		$(.7018)$	
$\eta = 1.2883$	$\eta' = 1.3906$	$\sigma = -.3681$	$\sigma' = -.3973$

The small positive (though insignificant) stock coefficient may appear to be an anomaly, for the products included in this category are certainly of a durable nature and would be expected to have a negative stock coefficient. However, these products are not ordinary durable goods; the purchase of eyeglasses, etc., are near necessities, although in the long run an increase in income means that new and better frames, or even contact lenses, can be purchased. This is consistent with a positive stock coefficient.

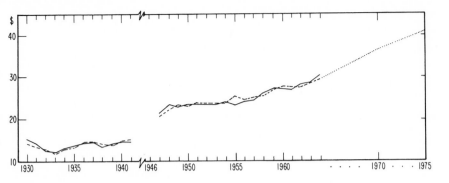

State-adjustment model; $\delta = 2$ 3PLS

$$q_t = .6108q_{t-1} + .00657x_t - 1.2507d_t + .2242z_t$$
$$\quad\ (.1064) \qquad (.00168) \qquad (.3080) \quad\ (.1947)$$

$R^2 = .990$	$S_e = .64$	$\bar{q} = 20.66$	$D.W. = 2.00$
$\alpha = 0$	$\beta = 1.5168$	$\gamma = .00408$	$\gamma' = .0169$
	$(.1640)$	$(.00131)$	$(.0009)$
$\lambda = $ —	$\lambda' = $ —	$\delta = 2$	
$\eta = .2770$	$\eta' = 1.1465$	$\sigma = $ —	$\sigma' = $ —

Habit formation is strong, but wears off quickly for this item. The price coefficients had mixed signs and were insignificant when the relative price was included in the model.

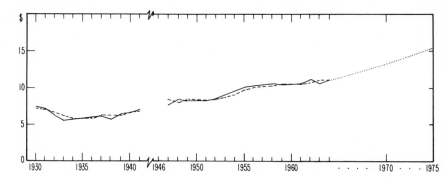

State-adjustment model   OLS

$$q_t = .6737q_{t-1} + .0029\Delta x_t + .0020x_{t-1}$$
$$\quad\quad (.0992) \quad\quad (.0013) \quad\quad (.0006)$$

$R^2 = .978$	$S_e = .30$	$\bar{q} = 8.38$	$D.W. = 2.18$
$\alpha = 0$	$\beta = .6342$	$\gamma = .00230$	$\gamma' = .00604$
	$(.9155)$	$(.00171)$	$(.00013)$
$\lambda = -$	$\lambda' = -$	$\delta = 1.0241$	
		(1.0193)	
$\eta = .3799$	$\eta' = .9976$	$\sigma = -$	$\sigma' = -$

Habit formation characterizes the behavior for the use of dentist's services: the short-run effect of an increase in income is most likely to have interim repairs made (which would probably be made anyway), while gold fillings, new plates, or false teeth are obtained in the long run.

The own-price elasticity was negative but insignificant in the dynamic model, though significant in the static model.

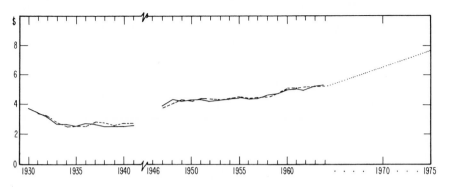

Flow-adjustment model 3PLS

$$q_t = .7113q_{t-1} + .000536(x_t + x_{t-1}) - .0016(p_t + p_{t-1}) + .1699z_t$$
$$\quad\ (.0731) \qquad\quad (.000105) \qquad\qquad\quad (.0006) \qquad\qquad\quad (.1922)$$

$R^2 = .982$ $S_e = .13$ $\bar{q} = 3.92$ $D.W. = 1.97$

$\xi = 0$ $\theta = .3374$ $\mu = .00371$
$\qquad\qquad\quad (.0998) \qquad\quad (.00041)$

$\zeta = -.0109$ $\eta = 1.3289$ $\sigma = -.2708$
$\ (.0053)$

The dynamic model with prices excluded indicated strong habit formation in the consumption of this item, but the Bergstrom model is better.

[18] Comprises services of osteopathic physicians, chiropractors, chiropodists and podiatrists, private-duty trained nurses, and miscellaneous curative and healing professions.

6.6 PRIVATE HOSPITALS AND SANITARIUMS

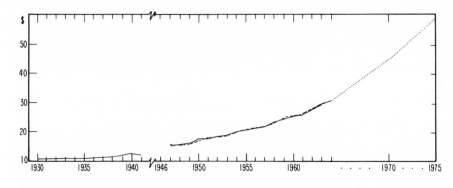

State-adjustment model   OLS   Postwar

$$q_t = -6.2246 + .8875q_{t-1} + .0077\Delta x_t + .0058x_{t-1}$$
$$ (4.8878) \quad (.1681) \qquad (.0036) \qquad (.0052)$$

$R^2 = .996$	$S_e = .36$	$\bar{q} = 22.29$	$D.W. = 2.11$
$\alpha = -5.4431$	$\beta = 1.0925$	$\gamma = .00505$	$\gamma' = .0514$
(3.2780)	(1.2465)	(.00305)	(.0315)
$\lambda = -$	$\lambda' = -$	$\delta = 1.2117$	
		(1.3968)	
$\eta = .3651$	$\eta' = 3.7114$	$\sigma = -$	$\sigma' = -$

The postwar equation was chosen when all attempts to find a plausible equation for the entire period failed. Expenditures for this item bore little relation to total PCE prewar, and show a strong trend in the postwar period. The high long-run PCE elasticity reflects this trend; it would be lower if computed nearer the end of the period. The own-price elasticity was positive when the relative price was included in the model.

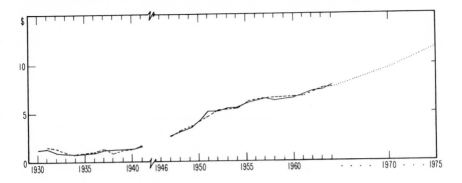

State-adjustment model   3PLS

$$q_t = .8245q_{t-1} + .00231\Delta x_t + .00101x_{t-1} - .0103\Delta p_t - .0045p_{t-1} - .2674z_t$$
$$\quad (.0532) \qquad (.00071) \qquad (.00029) \qquad (.0024) \qquad (.0014) \qquad (.2149)$$

$R^2 = .997$	$S_e = .16$	$\bar{q} = 3.88$	$D.W. = 1.74$
$\alpha = 0$	$\beta = .3697$	$\gamma = .00197$	$\gamma' = .00577$
	$(.5104)$	$(.00081)$	$(.00043)$
$\lambda = -.0088$	$\lambda' = -.0257$	$\delta = .5620$	
$(.0026)$	$(.0029)$	$(.5584)$	
$\eta = .6900$	$\eta' = 2.0162$	$\sigma = -.3136$	$\sigma' = -.9162$

No comment is needed about the equation for this item, for it is plausible
in nearly every aspect.

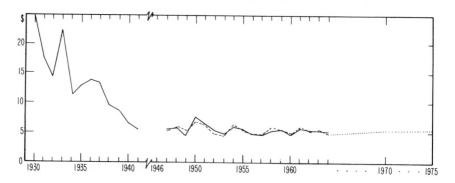

Static model   double logarithmic   Postwar

$\ln q_t = 22.761 - 2.956 \ln x_t + .6340 \ln \text{(shares traded on NYSE per capita)}_t$
            (3.056)   (.428)   (.0955)

$R^2 = .775$ $S_e = .06$ $\bar{q} = 5.37$ $D.W. = 1.81$

$\alpha = -$ $\beta = -$ $\gamma = -$ $\gamma' = -$

$\lambda = -$ $\lambda' = -$ $\delta = -$

$\eta = -2.956$ $\eta' = -$ $\sigma = -$ $\sigma' = -$

It seems strange that the results indicate the services in this category to be an inferior good. Nevertheless, the fact stands that the per capita consumption of this item has decreased nearly sevenfold since 1929; exactly why this is so is not clear. One early idea was that, once the amount of wealth per capita was taken into account, the total-expenditure coefficient would become positive. Accordingly, a wealth variable was constructed and tried in both the static and dynamic models, but without success.

Another idea was that the strong emergence of mutual and other investment funds in recent years was an important contributory factor in the decline of brokerage charges, and a variable representing the importance of these funds was tried in both the dynamic and the static model. The results were very disappointing, however, as can be seen from the following.

State-adjustment model   OLS   Postwar

$q_t = 17.912 + .136q_{t-1} + .0019\Delta x_t - .0098x_{t-1} - 3.442\Delta M_t + 1.096M_{t-1}$
        (7.353)   (.174)   (.0056)   (.0060)   (1.096)   (.878)

$R^2 = .547$ $S_e = -$ $\bar{q} = 5.37$ $D.W. = 2.05$

[M is the percentage of shares listed on NYSE held by mutual funds (in value terms).]

The fact remains, therefore, that despite considerable effort we are unable to explain the puzzling behavior of this item. Neither of the above equations gave plausible projections.

7.2 BANK SERVICE CHARGES, TRUST SERVICES, AND SAFE-DEPOSIT-BOX RENTAL

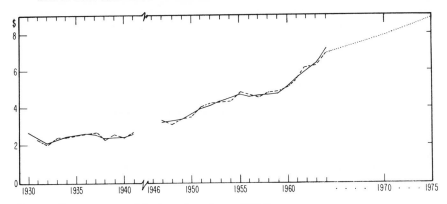

State-adjustment model; $\beta = \delta = 0$ 3PLS

$$\Delta q_t = .0011\Delta x_t - .0243\Delta p_t - .0620d_t + .6870z_t$$
$$\quad\quad\quad (.0006) \quad\quad (.0041) \quad\quad\; (.0389) \quad\; (.0964)$$

$R^2 = .847$	$S_e = .10$	$\bar{q} = 3.78$	$D.W. = 1.84$
$\alpha = *$	$\beta = \delta = 0$	$\gamma = -$	$\gamma' = .00107$
			$\quad\;\;\; (.00057)$
$\lambda = -.0243$	$\lambda' = -$	$\delta = 0$	
$\quad\;\;\; (.0041)$			
$\eta = .4025$	$\eta' = -$	$\sigma = -.5334$	$\sigma' = -$

This is the first of several models with $\beta = \delta$ that have been estimated with 3PLS. The 3-pass variable, z_t, is first estimated with A_1 as a free parameter, and then used as an independent variable with Δq_t as the dependent variable. It should also be noted that although we describe $\beta = \delta = 0$ as a special form of the dynamic model, it is really the linear static model in first differences.

103

7.3 SERVICES FURNISHED WITHOUT PAYMENT BY FINANCIAL INTERMEDIARIES

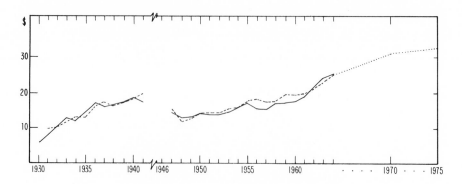

State-adjustment model; $\delta = 2$ 3PLS

$$q_t = -3.2187 + .2647q_{t-1} + .0122x_t + 6.0353d_t + .4376z_t$$
$$\quad\quad (2.1524) \quad (.0740) \quad\quad (.0015) \quad\quad (.8412) \quad\quad (.1588)$$

$R^2 = .925$	$S_e = .81$	$\bar{q} = 21.67$	$D.W. = 2.13$
$\alpha = 2.5450$	$\beta = .8372$	$\gamma = .00964$	$\gamma' = .0166$
(1.6783)	(.1851)	(.00154)	(.0018)
$\lambda = -$	$\lambda' = -$	$\delta = 2$	
$\eta = .6229$	$\eta' = 1.0714$	$\sigma = -$	$\sigma' = -$

The relative price added little to the explanation when it was included in the dynamic model. Because of the fictitious nature of this category, already emphasized in Chapter 2, this equation should be viewed with caution.

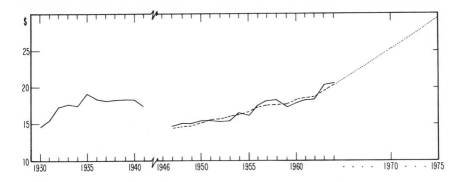

Flow-adjustment model   **OLS**   Postwar

$$q_t = -2.5447 + .0803q_{t-1} + .0056(x_t + x_{t-1})$$
$$(1.4634) \quad (.2243) \qquad (.0013)$$

$R^2 = .928$	$S_e = .52$	$\bar{q} = 17.02$	$D.W. = 1.90$
$\xi = .7179$	$\theta = 1.7027$	$\mu = .0122$	
$(.1165)$	$(.7686)$	$(.0010)$	
$\zeta = -$	$\eta = 1.1642$	$\sigma = -$	

Given the implausibly large adjustment coefficient, this equation is not very impressive; indeed, this carries over to the item itself, for it is not a true consumption good in the sense that it enters independently into the consumer's bundle of expenditures (see Chapter 2). The price elasticities had mixed signs when relative price was in the model.

The dynamic model for the entire period is given below; it was not used because of the poor fit.

State-adjustment model   **OLS**   1929–1964

$$q_t = .9868q_{t-1} - .0070\Delta x_t + .0005x_{t-1}$$
$$(.0331) \qquad (.0028) \qquad (.0004)$$

$R^2 = .829$	$S_e = .69$	$\bar{q} = 17.26$	$D.W. = 2.19$
$\alpha = 0$	$\beta = -.0832$	$\gamma = -.00730$	$\gamma' = .0382$
	$(.0904)$	$(.00285)$	$(.0671)$
$\lambda = -$	$\lambda' = -$	$\delta = -.0698$	
		$(.0588)$	
$\eta = -.5857$	$\eta' = 3.0672$	$\sigma = -$	$\sigma' = -$

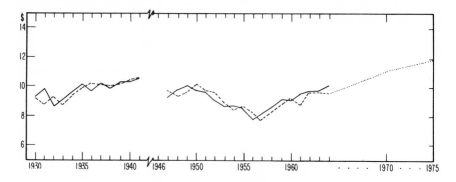

State-adjustment model; $\beta = \delta = 0$ OLS

$$\Delta q_t = \underset{(.00141)}{.00292}\Delta x_t - \underset{(.022)}{.044}\Delta p_t$$

$R^2 = .229$	$S_e = .38$	$\bar{q} = 9.49$	$D.W. = 2.14$
$\alpha = *$	$\beta = \delta = 0$	$\gamma = .00292$	$\gamma' = -$
		$(.00141)$	
$\lambda = -.0444$	$\lambda' = -$	$\delta = 0$	
$(.0216)$			
$\eta = .4264$	$\eta' = -$	$\sigma = -.3707$	$\sigma' = -$

Our efforts to find an adequate equation for this category cannot be termed a success. Inspection of a scatter diagram quickly dismissed the distribution of income as being of importance, and attempts to find additional explanatory variables were equally unpromising. It may be worth noting that per capita expenditure on this item varied very little from 1929, the high being \$10.62 in 1941 and the low \$7.98 in 1956 (1958 dollars). Given this small range of variation, the low R^2, which is about .75 in terms of levels, is perhaps not surprising.

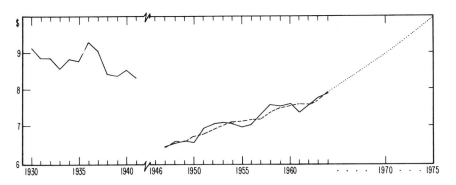

Flow-adjustment model   OLS   Postwar

$$q_t = 1.4155 + .4597q_{t-1} + .0008(x_t + x_{t-1})$$
$$ (.4955) \quad (.1669) \qquad (.0003)$$

$R^2 = .936$ $S_e = .12$ $\bar{q} = 7.17$ $D.W. = 1.82$

$\xi = -3.4069$ $\theta = .7402$ $\mu = .00285$

    (2.8708)   (.3132)   (.00037)

$\zeta = -$ $\eta = .6462$ $\sigma = -$

The relative price was insignificant when included in the above model. With the dynamic model using data over the entire period, the price elasticities were negative, but the coefficient of q_{t-1} was greater than one. The model was then estimated with $\beta = \delta = 0$ and is given below:

State-adjustment model; $\beta = \delta = 0$ OLS

$$\Delta q_t = .00271\Delta x_t - .0369\Delta p_t$$
$$ (.00078) \qquad (.0135)$$

$R^2 = .385$ $S_e = .20$ $\bar{q} = 7.17$ $D.W. = 2.29$

$\alpha = *$ $\beta = \delta = 0$ $\gamma = .0027$ $\gamma' = -$

                                   (.0008)

$\lambda = -.0369$ $\lambda' = -$ $\delta = 0$

    (.0135

$\eta = .4811$ $\eta' = -$ $\sigma = -.4742$ $\sigma' = -$

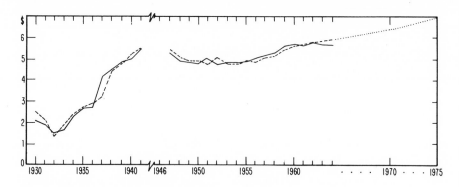

State-adjustment model; $\beta = \delta = 0$. OLS

$$\Delta q_t = .00216\Delta x_t - .0845\Delta p_t + .1941d_t$$
$$(.00096) \qquad (.0232) \qquad (.0750)$$

$R^2 = .527$	$S_e = .26$	$\bar{q} = 4.45$	$D.W. = 1.89$
$\alpha = *$	$\beta = \delta = 0$	$\gamma = .00216$	$\gamma' = —$
		$(.00096)$	
$\lambda = .0845$	$\lambda' = —$	$\delta = 0$	
$(.0232)$			
$\eta = .6900$	$\eta' = —$	$\sigma = -1.9382$	$\sigma' = —$

Considering the heterogeneous nature of this item, this equation, with its R^2 of .53 in first differences, and significant short-run PCE and price elasticities, looks reasonable.

---

[19] Comprises total payments to labor unions minus cash benefits, employment-agency fees, employees' payments to professional associations, miners' expenditures (for explosives, lamps, and smithing), money-order fees, classified advertisements, net purchases from pawnbrokers and miscellaneous secondhand stores, and other personal business services.

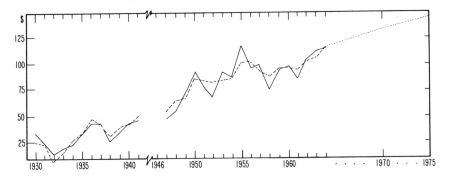

State-adjustment model   OLS

$$q_t = .4298q_{t-1} + .2102\Delta x_t + .0293x_{t-1} - 14.0534d_t$$
$$\quad\quad (.0933) \quad\quad (.0293) \quad\quad (.0051) \quad\quad (3.2246)$$

$R^2 = .957$	$S_e = 7.19$	$\bar{q} = 66.12$	$D.W. = 2.20$
$\alpha = 0$	$\beta = -.6408$	$\gamma = .2610$	$\gamma' = .0513$
	$(.1566)$	$(.0436)$	$(.0021)$
$\lambda = —$	$\lambda' = —$	$\delta = .1569$	
		$(.0402)$	
$\eta = 5.4645$	$\eta' = 1.0749$	$\sigma = —$	$\sigma' = —$

The price elasticities were negative but insignificant when the relative price of automobiles was included in the model. In the first edition of this book, some success was attained with using an average price per new car sale in place of the implicit deflator which is ordinarily used. However, the strong shift to compacts in recent years creates obvious difficulties for an index of this type and so we have not used it here.

Though the R^2 could be higher, the above equation is acceptable in its other aspects. The stock coefficient is strongly negative, and the influence of total PCE is much stronger than that of prices. Both of these are expected results. The short-run total PCE elasticity, though large, is consistent with those obtained by Suits (1958). The depreciation rate of .16, implying an average lifetime of about six years, agrees well with other information on deterioration and depreciation.[20]

[20] This compares with values of .16 and .25 for 1952 and 1955 that Houthakker and Haldi (1960) found from used-car prices.

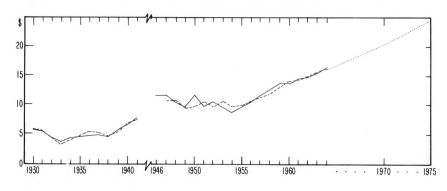

State-adjustment model   OLS

$$q_t = .6643q_{t-1} + .00980\Delta x_t + .00427x_{t-1} - .0703\Delta p_t - .0306p_{t-1} + 1.5747d_t$$
$$\qquad (.1272) \qquad (.00296) \qquad (.00144) \qquad (.0323) \qquad (.0110) \qquad (.7197)$$

$R^2 = .977$	$S_e = .64$	$\bar{q} = 9.12$	$D.W. = 2.04$
$\alpha = 0$	$\beta = .1534$	$\gamma = .00921$	$\gamma' = .0127$
	$(.4604)$	$(.00372)$	$(.0019)$
$\lambda = -.0661$	$\lambda' = -.0913$	$\delta = .5568$	
$(.0387)$	$(.0306)$	$(.5372)$	
$\eta = 1.3976$	$\eta' = 1.9290$	$\sigma = -.8624$	$\sigma' = -1.1904$

In interpreting this equation it should be borne in mind that β is the coefficient of a state variable, which should not necessarily be identified with the existing inventory of tires, etc. This state variable may well have a closer connection with the existing inventory of cars. If so, the sign of β makes sense: the more cars there are, the more people will spend on tires and the like.

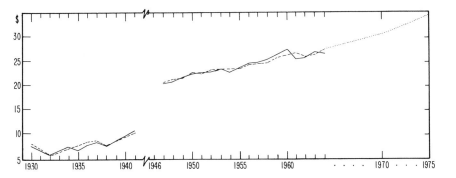

State-adjustment model   OLS

$$q_t = 4.2747 + .6391q_{t-1} + .0119\Delta x_t + .00140x_{t-1} - .0666\Delta p_t$$
$$\quad (2.1570) \quad (.2401) \quad\quad (.0026) \quad\quad (.00364) \quad\quad (.0660)$$
$$\quad - .0230p_{t-1} + 3.1173d_t$$
$$\quad\quad (.0247) \quad\quad (2.2481)$$

$R^2 = .995$	$S_e = .64$	$\bar{q} = 17.58$	$D.W. = 2.08$
$\alpha = 12.47$	$\beta = -.0222$	$\gamma = .0120$	$\gamma' = .0114$
(26.23)	$(.7087)$	$(.0033)$	$(.0038)$
$\lambda = -.0672$	$\lambda' = -.0638$	$\delta = .4182$	
$(.0704)$	$(.0918)$	$(.8920)$	
$\eta = .9429$	$\eta' = .8955$	$\sigma = -.4002$	$\sigma' = -.3801$

The relative price coefficients, it will be noted, are hardly significant, and prices could therefore be left out of the model with very little effect on the projections. The model with prices excluded is given below:

State-adjustment model   OLS

$$q_t = 2.9201 + .5029q_{t-1} + .0127\Delta x_t + .00553x_{t-1} - 4.8663d_t$$
$$\quad (1.5906) \quad (.1688) \quad\quad (.0026) \quad\quad (.00269) \quad\quad (1.4187)$$

$R^2 = .995$	$S_e = .63$	$\bar{q} = 17.58$	$D.W. = 1.87$
$\alpha = 6.9626$	$\beta = -.1035$	$\gamma = .0132$	$\gamma' = .0111$
(6.5738)	$(.2039)$	$(.0036)$	$(.0023)$
$\lambda = -$	$\lambda' = -$	$\delta = .5581$	
		$(.3661)$	
$\eta = 1.0389$	$\eta' = .8764$	$\sigma = -$	$\sigma' = -$

111

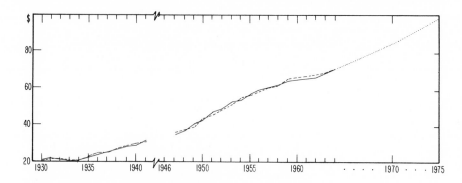

State-adjustment model   OLS

$$q_t = .8913q_{t-1} + .0185\Delta x_t + .0046x_{t-1} - 1.4435d_t$$
$$(.0244)\phantom{q_{t-1}} (.0032) (.0008)\phantom{x_{t-1}} (.3614)$$

$R^2 = .998$	$S_e = .76$	$\bar{q} = 43.25$	$D.W. = 2.00$
$\alpha = 0$	$\beta = .1691$	$\gamma = .0172$	$\gamma' = .0424$
	$(.0599)$	$(.0034)$	$(.0024)$
$\lambda = -$	$\lambda' = -$	$\delta = .2840$	
		$(.0710)$	
$\eta = .5493$	$\eta' = 1.3572$	$\sigma = -$	$\sigma' = -$

The stocks implicit in this item are presumably automobiles, which is consistent with a positive β. The habit formation may also indicate that more costly autos are purchased in the long run. The price elasticities were negative, but insignificant, when the relative price was in the model.

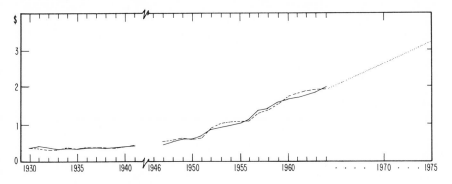

State-adjustment model; $\delta = 2$ 3PLS

$$q_t = -.1889 + .9278q_{t-1} + .000198x_t + .3341z_t$$
$$\quad\;\; (.0572) \quad (.0420) \qquad (.00006) \qquad (.2188)$$

$R^2 = .995$	$S_e = .04$	$\bar{q} = 0.85$	$D.W. = 1.80$
$\alpha = -.0980$	$\beta = 1.9251$	$\gamma = .000103$	$\gamma' = .00274$
$(.0312)$	$(.0452)$	$(.000031)$	$(.00104)$
$\lambda = -$	$\lambda' = -$	$\delta = 2$	
$\eta = .1677$	$\eta' = 4.4758$	$\sigma = -$	$\sigma' = -$

The own-price elasticities were positive when the relative price was included in the model. The implausibly high long-run PCE elasticity is mainly due to a strong trend in the dependent variable and would be smaller if computed near the end of the period.

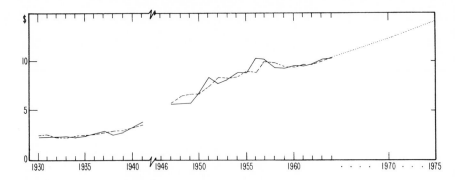

State-adjustment model   OLS

$$q_t = .6953q_{t-1} + .0022\Delta x_t + .0017x_{t-1} - .9002d_t$$
$$ (.0837) \quad\quad (.0017) \quad\quad (.0004) \quad\quad (.2751)$$

$R^2 = .985$	$S_e = .41$	$\bar{q} = 6.14$	$D.W. = 2.12$
$\alpha = 0$	$\beta = .8616$	$\gamma = .00165$	$\gamma' = .000559$
	(1.5160)	$(.00202)$	$(.000265)$
$\lambda = -$	$\lambda' = -$	$\delta = 1.2211$	
		(1.5261)	
$\eta = .3708$	$\eta' = 1.2596$	$\sigma = -$	$\sigma' = -$

The strong habit formation for this item may stem from either or both of the following reasons: (1) more expensive automobiles are purchased in the long run, with correspondingly higher insurance rates; (2) there are more accidents as the number of cars increases. Both reasons would be consistent with an interpretation of the "stock" as the stock of autos. This in turn would be consistent with the results of the static model of the first edition, where per capita stocks of autos were found to be important, together with PCE and prices.

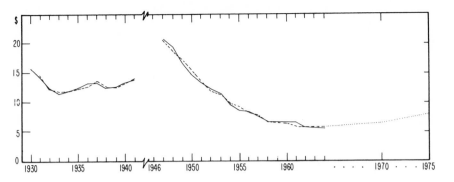

State-adjustment model   3PLS

$$q_t = .9039q_{t-1} + .00605\Delta x_t + .00107x_{t-1} - .0828\Delta p_t - .0147p_{t-1}$$
$$(.0301)\qquad (.00253)\qquad (.00098)\qquad (.0197)\qquad (.0158)$$
$$+ 1.5180d_t + .2097z_t$$
$$(.7031)\quad (.1728)$$

$R^2 = .997$	$S_e = .27$	$\bar{q} = 11.40$	$D.W. = 1.91$
$\alpha = 0$	$\beta = .0933$	$\gamma = .00579$	$\gamma' = .0111$
	$(.3592)$	$(.00230)$	$(.0075)$
$\lambda = -.0793$	$\lambda' = -.1525$	$\delta = .1943$	
$(.0264)$	$(.1286)$	$(.3856)$	
$\eta = .7167$	$\eta' = 1.3785$	$\sigma = -.6221$	$\sigma' = -1.1967$

Although apparently insignificant, there is some habit formation in the use of local public transportation, probably through the influence of residential location patterns. It is of interest that the long-run elasticity is greater than one for both PCE and the relative price.

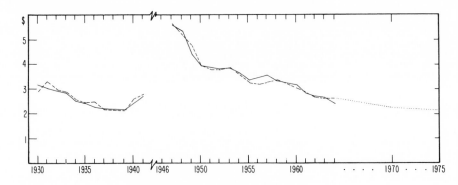

State-adjustment model; $\delta = 0$ OLS

$$q_t = .9318q_{t-1} + .0026\Delta x_t - .0203\Delta p_t + .1157d_t$$
$$\quad\quad (.0110) \quad\quad (.0008) \quad\quad (.0051) \quad\quad (.0574)$$

$R^2 = .963$ $S_e = .17$ $\bar{q} = 3.20$ $D.W. = 1.84$

$\alpha = *$ $\beta = -.0706$ $\gamma = .00265$ $\gamma' = —$
              $(.0118)$ $(.00081)$

$\lambda = -.0211$ $\lambda' = —$ $\delta = 0$
   $(.0053)$

$\eta = 1.1460$ $\eta' = —$ $\sigma = -.6299$ $\sigma' = —$

There is slight, though distinct, inventory adjustment in the use of taxi-
cabs, and both short-run elasticities are highly significant.

8.2c RAILWAY (COMMUTATION)

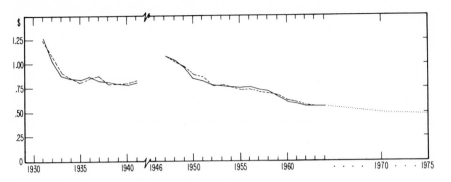

State-adjustment model   3PLS

$$q_t = .3090 + .8221q_{t-1} - .0067\Delta p_t - .0015p_{t-1} + .2955z_t$$
$$\quad\ (.0463)\ \ (.0360)\qquad (.0010)\qquad (.0003)\qquad (.1192)$$

$R^2 = .986$	$S_e = .02$	$\bar{q} = .82$	$D.W. = 2.25$
$\alpha = 1.3670$	$\beta = .0528$	$\gamma = -$	$\gamma' = -$
$(.4017)$	$(.0594)$		
$\lambda = -.00659$	$\lambda' = -.00837$	$\delta = .2481$	
$(.00104)$	$(.00167)$	$(.0729)$	
$\eta = -$	$\eta' = -$	$\sigma = -.7185$	$\sigma' = -.9127$

Next to 8.3d (other intercity transportation), this is the smallest category in the study. Total PCE was insignificant when it was included in the model, a not altogether surprising result. Commuting by railway is seen to be subject to habit formation, for β is positive, but the effect is small.

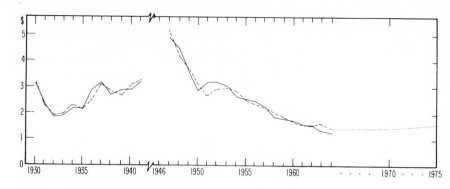

State-adjustment model   OLS

$$q_t = 1.3203 + .8399q_{t-1} - .0341\Delta p_t - .0112p_{t-1} + .5418d_t$$
$$\quad\;\;(.2996)\;\;(.0375)\quad\quad(.0061)\quad\quad(.0027)\quad\quad(.1395)$$

$R^2 = .956$	$S_e = .19$	$\bar{q} = 2.59$	$D.W. = 1.84$
$\alpha = 3.6535$	$\beta = .2188$	$\gamma = -$	$\gamma' = -$
(1.2509)	$(.1292)$		
$\lambda = -.0130$	$\lambda' = -.6099$	$\delta = .3928$	
$(.0064)$	$(.0226)$	$(.1345)$	
$\eta = -$	$\eta' = -$	$\sigma = -1.4151$	$\sigma' = -3.1948$

The two railway items are the only categories for which PCE was insignificant, although intercity rail travel appears as an inferior good in the postwar model, but the projections from this equation, given below, were negative. Even with an inferior good there can be habit formation; it simply means that with higher incomes consumers reduce their expenditures even more in the long run.

State-adjustment model   OLS   Postwar

$$q_t = 6.9310 + .6136q_{t-1} - .00274\Delta x_t - .00202x_{t-1} - .0374\Delta p_t - .0275p_{t-1}$$
$$\quad\;\;(3.8839)\;\;(.1343)\quad\quad(.00186)\quad\quad(.00113)\quad\quad(.0187)\quad\quad(.0199)$$

$R^2 = .976$	$S_e = .19$	$\bar{q} = 2.12$	$D.W. = 2.02$
$\alpha = 7.3767$	$\beta = .6856$	$\gamma = -.00215$	$\gamma' = -.00523$
(9.9360)	(1.8742)	$(.00211)$	$(.00134)$
$\lambda = -.0293$	$\lambda' = -.0713$	$\delta = 1.1646$	
$(.0230)$	$(.0394)$	(2.0165)	
$\eta = -1.3453$	$\eta' = -3.2708$	$\sigma = -1.1428$	$\sigma' = -2.7785$

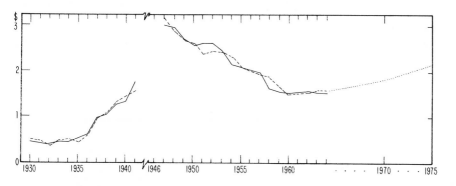

State-adjustment model   **OLS**

$$q_t = .9158q_{t-1} + .000282\Delta x_t + .000184x_{t-1} - .00339\Delta p_t - .00221p_{t-1}$$
$$(.0340) \qquad (.000623) \qquad (.000093) \qquad (.00169) \qquad (.00101)$$
$$+ .3585d_t$$
$$(.1133)$$

$R^2 = .986$	$S_e = .10$	$\bar{q} = 1.59$	$D.W. = 2.25$
$\alpha = 0$	$\beta = .8797$	$\gamma = .000198$	$\gamma' = .00218$
	(3.8075)	$(.000684)$	$(.00082)$
$\lambda = -.00239$	$\lambda' = -.0263$	$\delta = .9675$	
$(.00156)$	$(.0139)$	(3.8185)	
$\eta = .1720$	$\eta' = 1.8944$	$\sigma = -.1967$	$\sigma' = -2.1657$

Habit formation seems to be strong (although the approximate standard error is very large) in intercity bus travel.

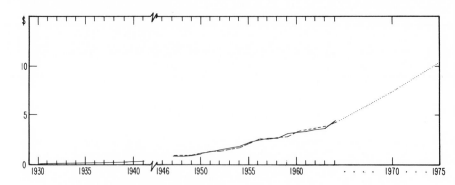

Flow-adjustment model   OLS   Postwar

$$q_t = -6.7047 + .3951q_{t-1} + .0025(x_t + x_{t-1})$$
$$(1.2841)\quad(.1286)\qquad(.0005)$$

$R^2 = .995$ $S_e = .09$ $\bar{q} = 2.30$ $D.W. = 1.93$

$\xi = -.8702$ $\theta = .8672$ $\mu = .00832$

   $(.0216)$ $(.2643)$ $(.0032)$

$\zeta = -$ $\eta = 5.8723$ $\sigma = -$

Air travel has had a strong trend in the postwar period, and this is reflected in the large PCE elasticity. With the relative price in the dynamic model, both elasticities were negative, but neither was significant over the entire period and only the short-run elasticity was significant in the postwar models.

The dynamic model over the entire period is also plausible, showing habit formation which wears off relatively slowly and having substantial PCE elasticities. The projections from it seemed implausibly low, however, and the postwar Bergstrom equation has been used instead. This equation is given below.

State-adjustment model   3PLS   1929–1964

$$q_t = -.3202 + .9489q_{t-1} + .00124\Delta x_t + .000304x_{t-1} + .3639z_t$$
$$(.1967)\quad(.0631)\qquad(.00047)\qquad(.000177)\qquad(.2457)$$

$R^2 = .996$ $S_e = .10$ $\bar{q} = 1.46$ $D.W. = 2.06$

$\alpha = -1.1826$ $\beta = .2254$ $\gamma = .00112$ $\gamma' = .00594$

   $(.5357)$ $(.1775)$ $(.00048)$ $(.00510)$

$\lambda = -$ $\lambda' = -$ $\delta = .2778$

                                  $(.2062)$

$\eta = 1.0679$ $\eta' = 5.6555$ $\sigma = -$ $\sigma' = -$

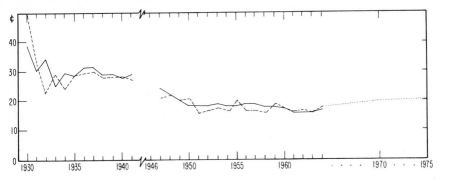

State-adjustment model; $\delta = 0$ OLS

$$q_t = .8928q_{t-1} + .0004\Delta x_t$$
$$\quad\;(.0244)\qquad (.0001)$$

$R^2 = .787$	$S_e = .03$	$\bar{q} = .23$	$D.W. = 2.10$
$\alpha = *$	$\beta = -.1132$	$\gamma = .00047$	$\gamma' = —$
	$(.0272)$	$(.00013)$	
$\lambda = —$	$\lambda' = —$	$\delta = 0$	
$\eta = 2.7059$	$\eta' =$	$\sigma = —$	$\sigma' = —$

Since this is a very small and inconsequential item, no effort was made to improve upon the above model.

[21] Comprises baggage charges, and coastal, inland-waterway, and ferry foot-passenger fares.

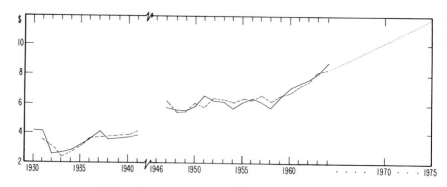

State-adjustment model   3PLS

$$q_t = -1.3275 + .4901q_{t-1} + .00621\Delta x_t + .00280x_{t-1} + .2128z_t$$
$$(.4243) \quad (.1538) \quad\quad (.00164) \quad\quad (.00081) \quad\quad (.2424)$$

$R^2 = .966$ $S_e = .35$ $\bar{q} = 5.33$ $D.W. = 1.98$

$\alpha = -3.0613$ $\beta = -.1024$ $\gamma = .00646$ $\gamma' = .00549$
    (1.1798) $(.2142)$ $(.00221)$ $(.00045)$

$\lambda = -$ $\lambda' = -$ $\delta = .5820$
                                      $(.3348)$

$\eta = 1.6726$ $\eta' = 1.4223$ $\sigma = -$ $\sigma' = -$

The results indicate the purchase of books and maps to be subject to some inventory adjustment; the stocks deteriorate quite rapidly, however, for δ is fairly large. Where the relative price was in the model, the price elasticities were negative, but insignificant.

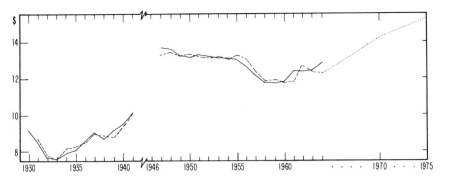

State-adjustment model; $\beta = \delta = 0$

$$\Delta q_t = .00309 \Delta x_t - .0493 \Delta p_t + .0519 z_t$$
$$\qquad\quad (.00121) \qquad (.0136) \qquad (.0549)$$

$R^2 = .633$	$S_e = .24$	$\bar{q} = 11.10$	$D.W. = 1.76$
$\alpha = *$	$\beta = \delta = 0$	$\gamma = .00309$	$\gamma' = -$
		$(.00121)$	
$\lambda = -.0493$	$\lambda' = -$	$\delta = 0$	
$(.0136)$			
$\eta = .3841$	$\eta' = -$	$\sigma = -.4185$	$\sigma' = -$

Ordinarily we would expect to find habit formation present for newspapers and magazines. However, when β and δ were unrestricted, the depreciation rate was negative and the coefficient of q_{t-1} was greater than one.

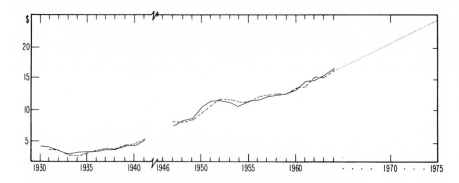

State-adjustment model   3PLS

$$q_t = .6547q_{t-1} + .00534\Delta x_t + .00446x_{t-1} - .0357\Delta p_t - .0298p_{t-1} + .3163z_t$$
$$\quad(.1479)\qquad(.00195)\qquad(.00172)\qquad\quad(.0313)\qquad\quad(.0114)\qquad\quad(.2574)$$

$R^2 = .993$ $\qquad S_e = .42$ $\qquad\qquad \bar{q} = 8.78$ $\qquad\quad D.W. = 2.00$

$\alpha = 0$ $\qquad\qquad \beta = 1.0138$ $\qquad\quad \gamma = .00376$ $\qquad\quad \gamma' = .0129$
$\qquad\qquad\qquad\quad (2.1611)$ $\qquad\qquad (.00257)$ $\qquad\qquad (.0009)$

$\lambda = -.0252$ $\qquad \lambda' = -.0864$ $\qquad \delta = 1.4312$
$\quad(.0364)$ $\qquad\qquad (.0098)$ $\qquad\quad (2.2528)$

$\eta = .5864$ $\qquad \eta' = 2.0107$ $\qquad\quad \sigma = -.2970$ $\qquad \sigma' = -1.0186$

This equation leaves some doubts, for though the fit is good and the
elasticities reasonable, the stock coefficient is implausibly large; little
explanation can be offered for this.

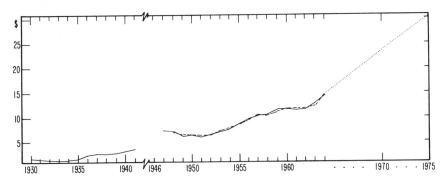

State-adjustment model   3PLS   Postwar

$$q_t = .7276q_{t-1} + .00978\Delta x_t + .00586x_{t-1} - .0984\Delta p_t - .0590p_{t-1} + .4067z_t$$
$$(.0713)(.00231)(.00092)(.0451)(.0085)(.1317)$$

$R^2 = .994$	$S_e = .24$	$\bar{q} = 9.27$	$D.W. = 2.30$
$\alpha = 0$	$\beta = .5403$	$\gamma = .00793$	$\gamma' = .0215$
	$(.5339)$	$(.00268)$	$(.0032)$
$\lambda = -.0798$	$\lambda' = -.2165$	$\delta = .8557$	
$(.0514)$	$(.0382)$	$(.5857)$	
$\eta = 1.3696$	$\eta' = 3.7162$	$\sigma = -.8804$	$\sigma' = -2.3889$

The postwar equation was chosen over the one for the entire period because the relative price was insignificant in the latter and because the standard error of the estimate was considerably smaller (see below). In other aspects, however, there is little difference between the two models. (The more plausible long-run PCE elasticity with the postwar equation reflects its being computed nearer the end of the period.)

State-adjustment model   3PLS   1929–1964

$$q_t = -5.1028 + .8331q_{t-1} + .00751\Delta x_t + .00461x_{t-1} + .8867d_t + .4312z_t$$
$$(1.4952)(.0841)(.00157)(.00137)(.3519)(.1661)$$

$R^2 = .994$	$S_e = .34$	$\bar{q} = 6.44$	$D.W. = 2.16$
$\alpha = -6.2896$	$\beta = .7031$	$\gamma = .00568$	$\gamma' = .0276$
(2.0008)	$(.3963)$	$(.00180)$	$(.0078)$
$\lambda = -$	$\lambda' = -$	$\delta = .8852$	
		$(.4583)$	
$\eta = 1.1970$	$\eta' = 5.8178$	$\sigma = -$	$\sigma' = -$

It might seem at first that the stock coefficient should be negative, since the items in this category are durables. However, sports equipment, pleasure boats, aircraft, etc., in many respects are luxuries in the short run and are complementary to leisure in the long run, and they are no doubt subject to substantial demonstration effects in the long run. Hence the long-run total-expenditure elasticity should be larger than in the short run.

9.5 RADIO AND TELEVISION RECEIVERS, RECORDS, AND MUSICAL INSTRUMENTS

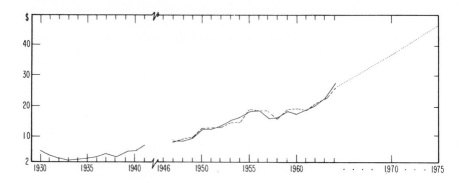

State-adjustment model   OLS   Postwar

$$q_t = -12.0273 + .6470q_{t-1} + .0406\Delta x_t + .0108x_{t-1}$$
$$(7.6382) \quad (.2160) \qquad (.0084) \qquad (.0067)$$

$R^2 = .961$	$S_e = 1.08$	$\bar{q} = 16.41$	$D.W. = 2.07$
$\alpha = -47.7599$	$\beta = -.1228$	$\gamma = .0428$	$\gamma' = .0305$
(12.1409)	$(.1648)$	$(.0110)$	$(.0056)$
$\lambda = -$	$\lambda' = -$	$\delta = .3058$	
		$(.2251)$	
$\eta = 4.1978$	$\eta' = 2.9950$	$\sigma = -$	$\sigma' = -$

The own-price elasticities were negative, but insignificant, when the relative price was in the model. The negative stock coefficient is what we would expect for this item, and the depreciation rate seems reasonable. The long-run PCE elasticity may be a bit high, but it would be lower if computed nearer the end of the period.

The relative price was also insignificant in the model for the entire period, and when it was left out of the model, the stock coefficient became positive. This equation, which is given below, has a higher R^2 than the one above, but the positive β is implausible.

State-adjustment model   OLS   1929–1964

$$q_t = -8.7552 + .7922q_{t-1} + .0183\Delta x_t + .00775x_{t-1} + 1.5466d_t$$
$$(4.6896) \quad (.1479) \qquad (.0046) \qquad (.00413) \qquad (1.1450)$$

$R^2 = .980$	$S_e = 1.11$	$\bar{q} = 11.54$	$D.W. = 1.53$
$\alpha = -18.25$	$\beta = .3035$	$\gamma = .0161$	$\gamma' = .0373$
(6.08)	$(.2669)$	$(.0052)$	$(.0118)$
$\lambda = -$	$\lambda' = -$	$\delta = .5355$	
		$(.3891)$	
$\eta = 1.9367$	$\eta' = 4.4713$	$\sigma = -$	$\sigma' = -$

A preliminary cross-section study indicated that several demographic variables may have an important influence on consumption in this category. These include age of head of household, tenure, class of residence, and size of family. However, none of these has been incorporated into the regression analyses because none shows enough year-to-year variation.

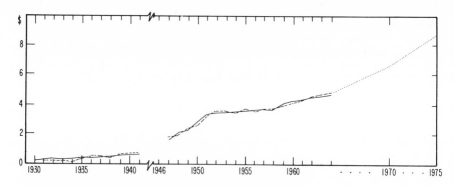

State-adjustment model   3PLS

$$q_t = .9324q_{t-1} + .00136\Delta x_t + .000605x_{t-1} - .0150\Delta p_t - .0067p_{t-1} + .1675z_t$$
$$(.0313) \qquad (.00076) \qquad (.000156) \qquad\quad (.0058) \qquad\quad (.0019) \qquad (.2209)$$

$R^2 = .995$ $S_e = .13$ $\bar{q} = 2.32$ $D.W. = 1.55$

$\alpha = 0$ $\beta = .5011$ $\gamma = .00110$ $\gamma' = .00894$
       $(.4964)$ $(.00076)$ $(.00269)$

$\lambda = -.0121$ $\lambda' = -.0986$ $\delta = .5711$
   $(.0053)$ $(.0372)$ $(.5055)$

$\eta = .6372$ $\eta' = 5.1978$ $\sigma = -.4711$ $\sigma' = -3.8427$

The stocks implicit in this category are undoubtedly radios and television sets, hence the positive β is to be expected. However, the long-run elasticities seem implausibly large.

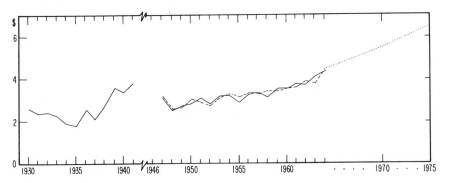

State-adjustment model   OLS   Postwar

$$q_t = .9559q_{t-1} + .00222\Delta x_t + .000301x_{t-1} - .0252\Delta p_t - .0034p_{t-1}$$
$$\quad\quad (.4286) \quad\quad (.00112) \quad\quad (.000952) \quad\quad (.0105) \quad\quad (.0018)$$

$R^2 = .925$ $\quad\quad S_e = .15$ $\quad\quad \bar{q} = 3.31$ $\quad\quad D.W. = 2.55$

$\alpha = 0$ $\quad\quad\quad \beta = .1000$ $\quad\quad\quad \gamma = .00212$ $\quad\quad\quad \gamma' = .00683$

$\quad\quad\quad\quad\quad\quad (.2016)$ $\quad\quad\quad\quad (.00115)$ $\quad\quad\quad (.04499)$

$\lambda = -.0240$ $\quad\quad \lambda' = -.0774$ $\quad\quad \delta = .1451$

$\quad (.0066)$ $\quad\quad\quad (.7303)$ $\quad\quad\quad (.6054)$

$\eta = 1.0312$ $\quad\quad \eta' = 3.3208$ $\quad\quad \sigma = -.8233$ $\quad\quad \sigma' = -2.6514$

These results indicate this item is influenced by habit formation which takes its time to wear off; hence the substantial long-run elasticities. The dynamic model for the entire period was considerably inferior to the equation above. It is given below.

State-adjustment model   OLS   1929–1964

$$q_t = -1.8994 + .4158q_{t-1} + .0026\Delta x_t + .0023x_{t-1} + .9892d_t$$
$$\quad\quad (.7740) \quad (.1862) \quad\quad (.0012) \quad\quad (.0007) \quad\quad (.3261)$$

$R^2 = .821$ $\quad\quad S_e = .29$ $\quad\quad \bar{q} = 3.04$ $\quad\quad D.W. = 2.09$

$\alpha = -1.5785$ $\quad\quad \beta = .8745$ $\quad\quad \gamma = .00195$ $\quad\quad \gamma' = .00402$

$\quad (1.4153)$ $\quad\quad\quad (1.6836)$ $\quad\quad\quad (.00176)$ $\quad\quad\quad (.00086)$

$\lambda = —$ $\quad\quad\quad \lambda' = —$ $\quad\quad\quad \delta = 1.6997$

$\quad\quad\quad\quad\quad\quad\quad\quad\quad\quad\quad\quad\quad (1.7952)$

$\eta = .8900$ $\quad\quad \eta' = 1.8333$ $\quad\quad \sigma = —$ $\quad\quad\quad \sigma' = —$

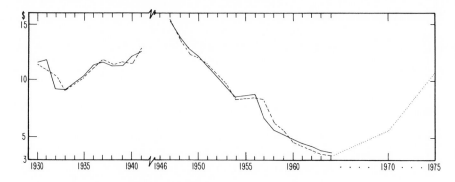

State-adjustment model   OLS

$$q_t = .8726q_{t-1} + .00665\Delta x_t + .00295x_{t-1} - .1012\Delta p_t - .0449p_{t-1} + 2.8193d_t$$
$$\quad\ (.0565) \qquad\ (.00374) \qquad (.00285) \qquad\ (.0862) \qquad\ (.0406) \qquad\ (1.5965)$$

$R^2 = .974$	$S_e = .58$	$\bar{q} = 9.41$	$D.W. = 2.01$
$\alpha = 0$	$\beta = .4344$	$\gamma = .00553$	$\gamma' = .0232$
	(1.1112)	$(.00516)$	$(.0150)$
$\lambda = -.0841$	$\lambda' = -.3526$	$\delta = .5705$	
$(.0747)$	$(.2197)$	(1.1585)	
$\eta = .8126$	$\eta' = 3.4075$	$\sigma = -.8748$	$\sigma' = -3.6685$

The large long-run PCE elasticity seems somewhat at odds with the sharp postwar trend downward in expenditures for this item. But this can partly be explained by an equally sharp increase in the relative price during that period.

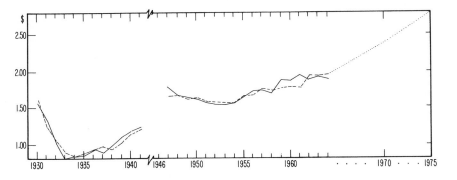

State-adjustment model   OLS

$$q_t = .6057q_{t-1} + .00089\Delta x_t + .00052x_{t-1} - .0031\Delta p_t - .0018p_{t-1}$$
$$(.0632) \qquad (.00031) \qquad (.00008) \qquad (.0031) \qquad (.0006)$$

$R^2 = .978$ $S_e = .06$ $\bar{q} = 1.46$ $D.W. = 1.61$

$\alpha = 0$ $\beta = .3446$ $\gamma = .00078$ $\gamma' = .0013$
             (1.2408) $(.00040)$ $(.0001)$

$\lambda = -.0027$ $\lambda' = -.0046$ $\delta = .8356$
     $(.0038)$ $(.0016)$ (1.2714)

$\eta = .7407$ $\eta' = 1.2604$ $\sigma = -.1827$ $\sigma' = -.3109$

The results show theater and opera to be subject to habit formation which wears off quite rapidly. The distribution of income, which was important in the static model, was tried in place of prices in an early dynamic model, but without success.

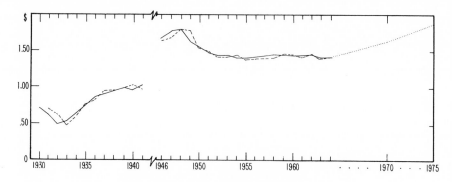

State-adjustment model; $\delta = 2$ 3PLS

$$q_t = .0709 + .9188q_{t-1} + .0000763x_t + .5072z_t$$
$$(.0510) \quad (.0493) \quad (.0000628) \quad (.1512)$$

$R^2 = .979$	$S_e = .06$	$\bar{q} = 1.23$	$D.W. = 2.08$
$\alpha = .0370$	$\beta = 1.9154$	$\gamma = .000040$	$\gamma' = .000940$
$(.0264)$	$(.0536)$	$(.000034)$	$(.000453)$
$\lambda = -$	$\lambda' = -$	$\delta = 2$	
$\eta = .0452$	$\eta' = 1.0697$	$\sigma = -$	$\sigma' = -$

This item, it is seen, has hardly any short-run response to a change in PCE; inertia is so prevalent that the response is almost entirely in the long run. Total PCE and the relative price are highly collinear for this item, and a model with price in place of PCE and $\delta = 0$ gives a slightly higher R^2 than the above equation. PCE seems more reasonable as a predictor, however.

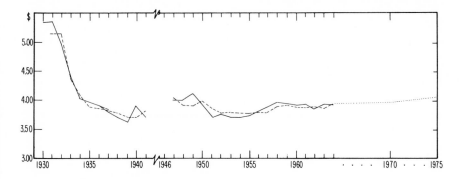

Flow-adjustment model   OLS

$q_t = 1.6419 + .5341q_{t-1} + .0000474(x_t + x_{t-1}) + .6333(\text{Prohibition dummy})_t$
   $(.3764)$ $(.0817)$ $(.0000352)$ $(.1239)$

$R^2 = .955$ $S_e = .10$ $\bar{q} = 4.02$ $D.W. = 2.14$

$\xi = -2.5578$ $\theta = .6074$ $\mu = .000203$
   $(.9134)$ $(.1388)$ $(.000200)$

$\zeta = -$ $\eta = .0706$ $\sigma = -$

The observations for the first four years (1929–1932) are markedly above
the pattern for the rest of the early part of the period. A probable explanation
is that this reflects one of the "legitimate" substitute forms of entertainment
during Prohibition. Accordingly, a dummy variable has been incorporated
into the model; it takes the value 1 for 1929–1932, and 0 thereafter.

133

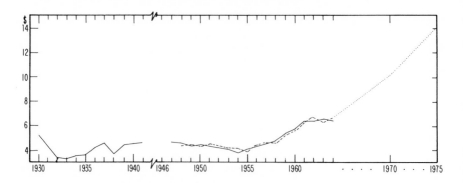

State-adjustment model   3PLS   Postwar

$$q_t - .7466 + .9095q_{t-1} + .00330\Delta x_t + .00151x_{t-1} + .9309z_t$$
$$(.6003)\ (.0712)\qquad (.00154)\qquad (.00046)\qquad (.2442)$$

$R^2 = .980$ $S_e = .16$ $\bar{q} = 4.96$ $D.W. = 2.38$

$\alpha = -1.3188$ $\beta = .4982$ $\gamma = .00267$ $\gamma' = .0167$
$\quad(.8002)$ $\quad(.4162)$ $\quad(.00164)$ $\quad(.0100)$

$\lambda = -$ $\lambda' = -$ $\delta = .5929$
$\qquad\qquad\qquad\qquad\qquad\qquad(.4381)$

$\eta = .8686$ $\eta' = 5.4354$ $\sigma = -$ $\sigma' = -$

The postwar equation was chosen over the equation for the entire period because it had a higher R^2. The latter equation, however, which is given below, has a more plausible long-run PCE elasticity. Habit formation is evident in both models, though stronger with the postwar. Price was insignificant in both.

State-adjustment model   3PLS   1929–1964

$$q_t = -1.1532 + .7350q_{t-1} + .00492\Delta x_t + .00168x_{t-1} + .6569d_t + .2636z_t$$
$$(.7469)\ (.1012)\qquad (.00124)\qquad (.00065)\qquad (.3275)\ (.1900)$$

$R^2 = .932$ $S_e = .27$ $\bar{q} = 4.62$ $D.W. = 1.96$

$\alpha = -3.2367$ $\beta = .1052$ $\gamma = .00471$ $\gamma' = .00633$
$\quad(1.4756)$ $\quad(.1946)$ $\quad(.00150)$ $\quad(.00169)$

$\lambda = -$ $\lambda' = -$ $\delta = .4107$
$\qquad\qquad\qquad\qquad\qquad\qquad(.2587)$

$\eta = 1.4237$ $\eta' = 1.9143$ $\sigma = -$ $\sigma' = -$

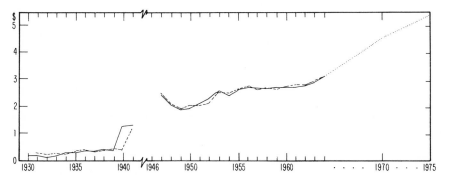

State-adjustment model   3PLS

$$q_t = -.8486 + .5389q_{t-1} + .00198\Delta x_t + .00138x_{t-1} - .1920d_t + .3701z_t$$
$$(.2832) \quad (.0927) \qquad (.00052) \qquad (.00027) \qquad (.1486) \quad (.1621)$$

$R^2 = .990$	$S_e = .11$	$\bar{q} = 1.77$	$D.W. = 2.19$
$\alpha = -1.0380$	$\beta = .4632$	$\gamma = .00168$	$\gamma' = .00298$
$(.4291)$	$(.5138)$	$(.00071)$	$(.00047)$
$\lambda = -$	$\lambda' = -$	$\delta = 1.0625$	
		$(.5180)$	
$\eta = 1.2843$	$\eta' = 2.2770$	$\sigma = -$	$\sigma' = -$

This item presents no apparent anomalies: the stock coefficient is positive, price is unimportant, and there is substantial PCE elasticity. However, it will be noted that the habit wears off quite rapidly.

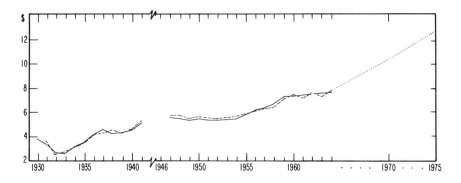

State-adjustment model   3PLS

$$q_t = .8034q_{t-1} + .00502\Delta x_t + .00163x_{t-1} - .0328\Delta p_t - .0106p_{t-1}$$
$$\quad\quad (.0897) \quad\quad (.00095) \quad\quad (.00073) \quad\quad (.0127) \quad\quad (.0084)$$
$$\quad + .4272d_t + .4603z_t$$
$$\quad\quad (.3398) \quad (.1887)$$

$R^2 = .989$	$S_e = .18$	$\bar{q} = 5.31$	$D.W. = 2.43$
$\alpha = 0$	$\beta = .1689$	$\gamma = .00467$	$\gamma' = .00828$
	$(.4602)$	$(.00101)$	$(.00252)$
$\lambda = -.0305$	$\lambda' = -.0541$	$\delta = .3869$	
$(.0136)$	$(.0394)$	$(.5143)$	
$\eta = 1.2112$	$\eta' = 2.1498$	$\sigma = -.5675$	$\sigma' = -1.0073$

Most of the items included in this category can be considered complementary with leisure; hence the positive stock coefficient and the substantial total-expenditure elasticities are appropriate.

[22] Comprises photo developing and printing, photographic studios, collectors' net acquisitions of stamps and coins, hunting-dog purchase and training, sports guide service, veterinary service, purchase of pets, camp fees, nonvending coin-machine receipts minus payoff, and other commercial amusements.

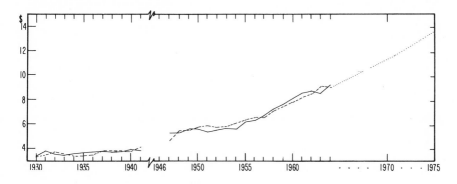

Flow-adjustment model   OLS

$$q_t = -.5703 + .8837q_{t-1} + .0005(x_t + x_{t-1})$$
$$ (.2551) \quad (.0719) \quad\quad (.0002)$$

$R^2 = .988$ $S_e = .22$ $\bar{q} = 5.54$ $D.W. = 1.99$

$\xi = -.3632$ $\theta = .1234$ $\mu = .00854$

$(.1034)$ $(.0811)$ $(.00220)$

$\zeta = -$ $\eta = 2.1512$ $\sigma = -$

The Bergstrom model is used for elementary and secondary education (10.2) as well as for higher education here, and the model seems plausible in both cases. In particular, the high PCE elasticity is to be expected, as is also the small adjustment coefficient. When included in the model, the relative price was insignificant and had the wrong signs.

137

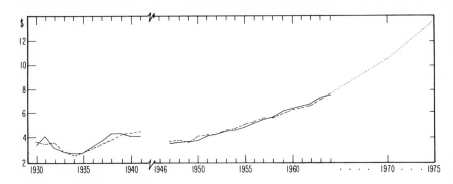

Flow-adjustment model   OLS

$$q_t = -3.5978 + .6084q_{t-1} + .0018(x_t + x_{t-1}) + 1.2887d_t$$
$$\quad\;\;(.8372)\quad(.0969)\quad\quad(.0004)\quad\quad\quad\quad(.3246)$$

$R^2 = .981$ $S_e = .20$ $\bar{q} = 4.60$ $D.W. = 1.96$

$\xi = -.7825$ $\theta = .4870$ $\mu = .0091$

   $(.0396)$ $(.1499)$ $(.0099)$

$\zeta = -$ $\eta = 2.7674$ $\sigma = -$

As for 10.1, the Bergstrom model results seem quite plausible for this item. The higher adjustment coefficient here than with higher education is reasonable, and the high PCE elasticity here is in keeping with its high value there. In the dynamic model the price elasticities were negative for this item, but they became insignificant when the identifying constraint on δ was taken into account, and this insignificance carried over to the Bergstrom model.

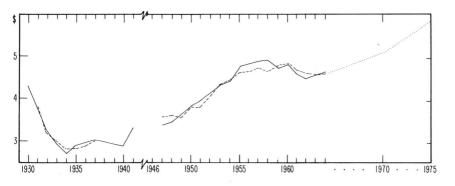

State-adjustment model   3PLS

$$q_t = 1.1571 + .7884q_{t-1} + .00121\Delta x_t + .000660x_{t-1} - .0254\Delta p_t$$
$$(.5013)\quad (.0768)\qquad (.00075)\qquad\quad (.000188)\qquad (.0092)$$
$$- .0139p_{t-1} - .2542z_t$$
$$\ (.0053)\qquad\ (.2165)$$

$R^2 = .975$	$S_e = .14$	$\bar{q} = 3.88$	$D.W. = 2.01$
$\alpha = 1.7219$	$\beta = .5149$	$\gamma = .000983$	$\gamma' = .00312$
	$(.7984)$	$(.000871)$	$(.00058)$
$\lambda = -.0206$	$\lambda' = -.0656$	$\delta = .7515$	
$(.0093)$	$(.0382)$	$(.8464)$	
$\eta = .3542$	$\eta' = 1.1251$	$\sigma = -.5182$	$\sigma' = -1.6459$

Given the heterogeneous collection of items included in this category (some of them purely conventional), the above dynamic equation appears plausible.

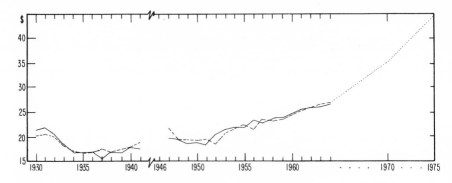

Flow-adjustment model   OLS

$$q_t = .7268q_{t-1} + .0037(x_t + x_{t-1}) - .0302(p_t + p_{t-1}) + 2.4909d_t$$
$$(.0820)\qquad (.0010)\qquad\qquad (.0147)\qquad\qquad (.9540)$$

$R^2 = .937$ $S_e = .87$ $\bar{q} = 20.69$ $D.W. = 1.67$

$\xi = 0$ $\theta = .3165$ $\mu = .0274$

                $(.1100)$ $(.0079)$

$\zeta = -.2212$ $\eta = 1.8456$ $\sigma = -1.0156$

$(.1305)$

This equation presents no apparent anomalies, although we might take the strong importance of the relative price to be somewhat surprising since the interpretation of a price for this item is far from clear.

140

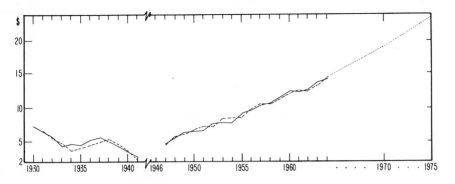

State-adjustment model; $\delta = 2$ 3PLS

$$q_t = .8583q_{t-1} + .00234x_t - .0170p_t + .1990z_t$$
$$\quad\;\; (.0576) \qquad (.00049) \qquad (.0034) \quad\;\; (.1735)$$

$R^2 = .976$	$S_e = .57$	$\bar{q} = 7.55$	$D.W. = 1.85$
$\alpha = 0$	$\beta = 1.8475$	$\gamma = .00126$	$\gamma' = .0165$
	$(.0667)$	$(.00030)$	$(.0043)$
$\lambda = -.0092$	$\lambda' = -.1201$	$\delta = 2$	
$(.0020)$	$(.0445)$		
$\eta = .2355$	$\eta' = 3.0873$	$\sigma = -.1351$	$\sigma' = -1.7707$

It is interesting to note the high long-run elasticities for foreign travel. There is substantial habit formation, as one would expect, but $\delta = 2$ means that the habit wears off very rapidly.

12.2 EXPENDITURES ABROAD BY U.S. GOVERNMENT PERSONNEL (MILITARY AND CIVILIAN)

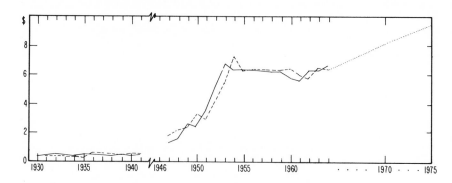

Flow-adjustment model   3PLS

$$q_t = .8171q_{t-1} + .000377(x_t + x_{t-1}) - .6977d_t + .2271z_t$$
$$\quad\quad (.0681) \quad\quad (.000111) \quad\quad\quad\quad (.2516) \quad (.1984)$$

$R^2 = .973$ $S_e = .48$ $\bar{q} = 3.23$ $D.W. = 2.04$

$\xi = 0$ $\theta = .2013$ $\mu = .00412$
                $(.0824)$ $(.00060)$

$\zeta = -$ $\eta = 1.7339$ $\sigma = -$

Ideally, expenditure for this item should be deflated by U.S. government personnel abroad, with total expenditure correspondingly being the total expenditure of these individuals. Unfortunately, these data are not available for each year of the period. Moreover, the category itself is ill-defined, for included within the category is a mixture of services, durable goods, and non-durable goods, which are classified by type of product in the domestic accounts. Accordingly, the above equation should be viewed with caution.

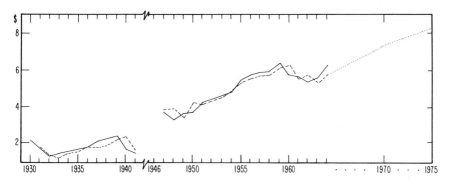

State-adjustment model   3PLS

$$q_t = .7596q_{t-1} - .00245\Delta x_t - .000785x_{t-1} + .4956d_t + .3130z_t$$
$$ (.1363) \qquad (.00138) \qquad (.000430) \qquad (.2291) \qquad (.2441)$$

$R^2 = .976$	$S_e = .30$	$\bar{q} = -3.74$	$D.W. = 2.05$
$\alpha = 0$	$\beta = .1079$	$\gamma = -.00234$	$\gamma' = -.00327$
	$(.2838)$	$(.00158)$	$(.00023)$
$\lambda = -$	$\lambda' = -$	$\delta = .3811$	
		$(.3778)$	
$\eta = .8590$	$\eta' = 1.1980$	$\sigma = -$	$\sigma' = -$

This category is now treated as a debit in the PCE table, hence the negative coefficients on total PCE are appropriate. Moderate habit formation seems plausible for this item, as does also the slightly elastic long-run PCE elasticity.

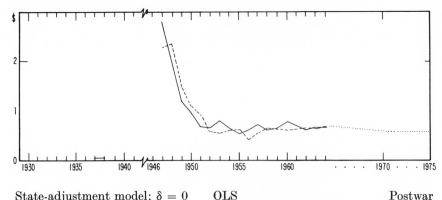

State-adjustment model; $\delta = 0$ OLS   Postwar

$$q_t = .8339 q_{t-1} - .0019 \Delta x_t - .0453 \Delta p_t$$
$$(.0502) \qquad (.0016) \qquad (.0338)$$

$R^2 = .862$ $S_e = .22$ $\bar{q} = -.91$ $D.W. = 1.64$

$\alpha = *$ $\beta = -.1812$ $\gamma = -.00210$ $\gamma' = -$
                $(.0597)$ $(.00175)$

$\lambda = -.0494$ $\lambda' = -$ $\delta = 0$
    $(.0371)$

$\eta = 3.7149$ $\eta' = -$ $\sigma = 5.5554$ $\sigma' = -$

There is little that can be said for this category, since it is a balancing item and, like 12.3, enters the PCE accounts as a debit. The price elasticity is perverse, as well as being implausibly large. The importance of PCE is also surprising; it perhaps measures world prosperity.

Appendix to Chapter 3

Equations Estimated with Postwar Data, 1946–1964

Nineteen sixty-four brings the number of postwar observations up to 19, which makes an analysis using only postwar data more feasible than was the case in the first edition when only 16 annual observations were available. We have already seen several postwar equations in Chapter 3, and in this appendix we present equations for all 82 commodities. But, apart from a general discussion, we have been content with just listing the results in tables. The coefficients for the estimating equations are tabulated in Table 3.1, while the structural coefficients and elasticities are given in Tables 3.2 and 3.3.

The first thing to observe is that the postwar equations as a group are not as good as the ones estimated with the prewar data included. The R^2's are typically lower, the coefficients less significant, and the structural coefficients less plausible. The major problem is that the postwar data are dominated to a considerable extent by trends, which results in extensive multicollinearity and values of A_1 for several equations that are greater than one. Because of the persistent upward movement in many of the consumption series (including the total), several equations are essentially trends and the PCE and price elasticities are highly suspect as a result.

Despite the generally poor quality of the postwar equations as a group (relative, that is, to the equations over the entire period), a number of them are better than their entire period counterparts either in terms of R^2, reasonableness of parameters, or plausibility of projections, and these equations have already been discussed. Altogether 12 postwar equations have been used in preparing the projections; these are marked with an asterisk in Table 3.1.

We might also note that the Bergstrom model finds more frequent use with the postwar data, being applied to 19 categories, in contrast to 10 for the data over the entire period. This no doubt reflects in part the prevalent trends already discussed in the postwar data, especially since the majority of the Bergstrom categories are services in which trends are strongest.

Perhaps the key lesson to be drawn from this exercise is the importance of the prewar data in estimating the parameters of the dynamic model. Sustained economic growth is fine from a social point of view, but it makes life difficult for the econometrician. The years during the Great Depression inject considerable independent movement into the data, leading to reduced multicollinearity and less pervasive trends. The end result is that the strong cyclical swings in the prewar data combine with the more trendlike variation in the postwar period to give the diverse behavior needed for estimation.

Table 3.1. Estimating Equations (1947-1964)

$$q_t = A_0 + A_1 q_{t-1} + A_2 \Delta X_t + A_3 X_{t-1} + A_4 \Delta p_t + A_5 p_{t-1} + A_6 z_t + u_t$$

Item	A_0	A_1	A_2	A_3	A_4	A_5	A_6	R^2	S_e	D.W.
1.0	−96.250 (45.197)	.5940 (.1334)	.0208 (.0073)	A_2	1.2885 (.5417)	A_4		.759	1.24	2.18
1.1	29.874 (17.813)	.5445 (.2139)	.07919 (.02438)	.05926 (.02773)			.5132 (.3582)	.982	3.07	2.27
1.2	125.85 (34.40)	.0937 (.2173)	.00332 (.00119)		−.9022 (.2626)	−.6342 (.2035)	.5379 (.3914)	.900	1.09	1.90
1.3	−5.9043 (3.0321)	.5130 (.1482)		A_2	.0384 (.0096)	A_4	.2673 (.2272)	.778	.36	2.44
1.4*	42.38 (23.94)	.6817 (.1520)	−.00788 (.00641)	$2A_2$				.755	3.45	1.91
1.5	43.715 (14.186)	.1452 (.2924)	.00440 (.00204)	$2A_2$	−.1464 (.0923)	$2A_4$	1.1095 (.4615)	.840	.64	2.34
2.1		.9671 (.0103)	.0219 (.0056)		−.2676 (.0846)			.845	.75	1.77
2.2	.6580 (.2074)	.6645 (.0260)			−.0227 (.0043)	−.0020 (.0018)		.990	.03	1.78
2.3		.7602 (.0888)	.0637 (.0183)	.0173 (.0067)				.894	2.39	2.23
2.4	No equation estimated									
2.5 ⎱ 2.6 ⎰	10.863 (5.409)	1.0407 (.0811)	.00853 (.00158)	A_2	−.2606 (.0644)	A_4 •	−.3625 (.2750)	.987	.20	2.09
2.7		.7017 (.0953)	.00868 (.00180)	.00306 (.00072)	−.0519 (.0218)	−.0183 (.0028)		.987	.24	2.21

146

2.8		1.0205 (.0113)	.00701 (.00228)	.00364 (.00141)	−.0224 (.0108)		.4328 (.2047)	.862	.08	2.09
3.1		.8802 (.0840)			−.0764 (.0206)	−.0396 (.0124)		.996	.23	2.07
3.2	−2.8105 (.8162)	.7211 (.1075)	.0037 (.0010)	A_2				.972	.28	2.11
4.1	−6.7109 (6.6962)	.9438 (.0294)	.0124 (.0064)	A_2				.999	.76	1.80
4.2	16.095 (6.015)	1.0748 (.1640)	.0037 (.0026)	$2A_2$	−.1614 (.0502)			.983	.82	1.62
4.3		.9404 (.0573)	.00222 (.00118)	$2A_2$		$2A_2$	−.2384 (.1927)	.994	2.25	2.26
4.4	−2.7245 (.7658)	.5979 (.1481)	.00518 (.00158)	A_2	−.0266 (.0148)	A_5	.2379 (.2237)	.980	.17	2.19
5.1	3.7007 (2.4225)	.5669 (.1951)	.03300 (.00676)	.00388 (.00321)				.895	.83	1.73
5.2	−17.596 (3.339)	−.0648 (.1194)	.0270 (.0034)	A_2				.943	1.01	1.62
5.3		.9384 (.0409)	.01099 (.00253)	.00381 (.00179)	−.1931 (.0368)	−.0669 (.0317)	−.4151 (.2956)	.978	.28	2.37
5.4		.8245 (.1129)	.03271 (.00659)	.00378 (.00176)			.5948 (.1964)	.906	.83	2.42
5.5		.6694 (.1637)	.01875 (.00620)	.00292 (.00157)				.698	.82	1.10
5.6	−8.5314 (2.0389)	.3038 (.1233)	.0123 (.0024)	A_2				.984	.38	1.53
5.7	−1.7077 (.5470)	.5198 (.1589)	.00336 (.00136)	.00260 (.00071)				.955	.17	1.79

(continued)

Table 3.1 (*continued*)

Item	A_0	A_1	A_2	A_3	A_4	A_5	A_6	R^2	S_e	D.W.
5.8a*	3.7139 (2.8139)	.8725 (.0470)	.00328 (.00140)	A_2	−.0504 (.0250)	A_4		.999	.16	2.32
5.8b		.9431 (.0293)	.0004 (.0001)	$2A_2$				.993	.29	1.92
5.8c		1.0849 (.0629)	.00392 (.00095)		−.0527 (.0135)		.2070 (.1794)	.928	.14	2.00
5.8d		.9465 (.0340)	.01370 (.00963)		−.1808 (.1123)		−.2550 (.2757)	.456	1.25	2.36
5.9	−14.068 (3.553)	.5497 (.0926)	.00798 (.00151)	$2A_2$	−.0137 (.0116)	$2A_4$	−.2853 (.2327)	.999	.21	2.12
5.10	21.104 (11.485)	.4620 (.2935)	.01111 (.00864)	.00486 (.00531)	−.4275 (.1669)	−.1869 (.1241)		.798	.86	2.31
5.11	1.9820 (1.5739)	.4734 (.2769)	.00581 (.00161)	.00482 (.00335)	−.0560 (.0291)	−.0464 (.0463)		.972	.15	1.65
6.1	−9.7794 (3.9249)	.6072 (.1624)	.00530 (.00209)	$2A_2$			.1766 (.2650)	.990	.39	1.80
6.2		.4990 (.2779)	.0030 (.0012)	.0012 (.0007)				.872	.16	1.79
6.3		.5256 (.2298)	.00488 (.00217)	$2A_2$			.3651 (.2494)	.933	.67	1.97
6.4		.7638 (.1671)	.0007 (.0005)	$2A_2$				.927	.34	1.91
6.5		.9830 (.0568)				−.0274 (.0184)	.2540 (.3252)	.898	.14	1.94

6.6*	-6.2246 (4.8878)	.8875 (.1681)	.0077 (.0036)	.0058 (.0052)				.996	.36	2.11
6.7		.7695 (.1027)	.00240 (.00150)	.00162 (.00071)	-.0142 (.0062)	-.0096 (.0055)	-.4751 (.3086)	.989	.18	1.81
7.1*†										
7.2		1.0466 (.0075)	.0016 (.0008)	$2A_2$	-.0416 (.0058)	$2A_4$		.993	.09	1.77
7.3	-16.556 (3.108)	.0419 (.0748)	.0144 (.0021)	$2A_2$	-.0472 (.0153)			.973	.49	1.75
7.4*	-2.5447 (1.4634)	.0803 (.2243)	.0056 (.0013)	$2A_2$				.928	.52	1.90
7.5		1.0226 (.0179)			-.0658 (.0472)			.728	.38	1.78
7.6*	1.4155 (.4955)	.4597 (.1669)	.0008 (.0003)	$2A_2$				.936	.12	1.82
7.7		.6214 (.0722)	.0006 (.0001)	$2A_2$				.919	.11	1.71
8.1a	23.368 (22.984)	.4858 (.1082)	.3676 (.0507)	.00890 (.01830)				.906	6.53	2.56
8.1b	-5.1618 (2.5175)	.7583 (.1378)	.0150 (.0062)	.0048 (.0022)				.908	.80	2.19
8.1c	2.5316 (2.2345)	.5076 (.2270)	.0091 (.0058)	.0058 (.0039)				.902	.75	2.05
8.1d		.9094 (.0532)	.01420 (.00629)	.00543 (.00100)			.1743 (.1885)	.995	.80	2.31
8.1e	-1.2790 (.5605)	.9893 (.1469)	.000507 (.000212)	$2A_2$			.2146 (.1161)	.991	.05	2.24

149

(continued)

Table 3.1 (continued)

Item	A_0	A_1	A_2	A_3	A_4	A_5	A_6	R^2	S_e	D.W.
8.1f		.7011 (.1063)	.0008 (.0003)					.898	.51	2.07
8.2a	8.2201 (2.4830)	.6427 (.0676)	.00472 (.00128)	A_2	−.1327 (.0292)	A_4	.6044 (.1774)	.999	.19	1.96
8.2b		.6228 (.1013)	.00489 (.00107)		−.0354 (.0097)		1.1478 (.3728)	.974	.13	1.91
8.2c	.5763 (.1844)	.7916 (.1404)			−.0054 (.0025)	−.0029 (.0010)	.3561 (.1343)	.989	.17	2.34
8.3a	6.9310 (3.8839)	.6136 (.1343)	−.00274 (.00186)	−.00202 (.00113)	−.0374 (.0187)	−.0275 (.0199)		.976	.19	2.02
8.3b		.9415 (.0131)	.0009 (.0007)					.963	.10	1.62
8.3c*	−6.7047 (1.2841)	.3951 (.1286)	.0025 (.0005)	$2A_2$				.995	.09	1.93
8.3d	No equation estimated									
9.1		.9793 (.0225)	.0082 (.0034)					.767	.46	1.67
9.2	6.2832 (3.8995)	.6764 (.1884)			−.0230 (.0177)	A_4		.819	.28	.92
9.3	−7.1806 (3.3415)	.5515 (.1907)	.00975 (.00417)	.00886 (.00363)			.3459 (.2264)	.963	.50	2.41
9.4*		.7276 (.0713)	.00978 (.00231)	.00586 (.00092)	−.0984 (.0451)	−.0590 (.0085)	.4067 (.1317)	.994	.24	2.30
9.5*	−12.027 (7.638)	.6470 (.2160)	.0406 (.0084)	.0108 (.0067)				.961	1.08	2.07

Eq.								R^2		
9.6	.9868 (.0262)		.00205 (.00144)		−.0184 (.0166)		.6714 (.2547)	.971	.18	2.06
9.7*	.9559 (.4286)		.00222 (.00112)	.00030 (.00095)	−.0252 (.0105)	−.0034 (.0018)		.925	.15	2.55
9.8a	.9507 (.0134)		.0044 (.0031)					.984	.49	1.92
9.8b	.7256 (.0977)		.000291 (.000102)					.859	.05	2.01
9.8c	.9852 (.0090)				−.0030 (.0036)		.3906 (.2471)	.864	.05	1.98
9.9	1.4197 (.7133)	.5912 (.1540)		.0001 (.0002)				.501	.08	1.78
9.10*	−.7466 (.6003)	.9095 (.0712)	.00330 (.00154)	.00151 (.00046) $2A_2$			.9309 (.2442)	.980	.16	2.38
9.11	.5225 (.3679)	.3481 (.0820)		.0011 (.0001) $2A_2$		−.0117 (.0025) $2A_4$		.959	.07	1.58
9.12	−1.5839 (.4498)	.7809 (.0837)	.00219 (.00052)				.4617 (.2363)	.984	.13	2.40
10.1	−1.8859 (1.5083)	.8822 (.1343)		.00090 (.00076) $2A_2$			.0275 (.2008)	.981	.21	1.99
10.2	.7194 (.0977)				−.0313 (.0111)		−.5802 (.1703)	.999	.05	2.24
10.3	1.0993 (.0521)		.00136 (.00098)		−.0141 (.0091)		.3326 (.1915)	.953	.13	2.03
11.0	−6.5671 (1.9378)	.3228 (.1373)		.00672 (.00123) $2A_2$				.946	.69	1.88
12.1	−6.7051 (3.0188)	.6617 (.1288)		.0063 (.0025) A_2				.989	.33	2.12

(continued)

Table 3.1 (continued)

Item	A_0	A_1	A_2	A_3	A_4	A_5	A_6	R^2	S_e	D.W.
12.2		.8267 (.1036)	.000921 (.000317)	A_2			.2078 (.1894)	.883	.60	2.18
12.3		.8636 (.1330)	−.00317 (.00253)	−.00062 (.00045)			.1417 (.2224)	.903	.32	1.94
12.4*		.8339 (.0502)	−.0019 (.0016)		−.0453 (.0338)			.862	.22	1.64

Note: Items with asterisk represent postwar equations that have been used in preparing the projections.

† $\ln q_t = 22.761 - 2.9557 \ln X_t + 0.6340 \ln$ (shares traded on NYSE/cap)$_t$.
$\quad\quad\quad$ (3.056) $\quad\quad$ (.4278) $\quad\quad\quad\quad$ (.0955)

Table 3.2. Structural Coefficients (1947–1964)

$$q_t = \alpha + \beta s_t + \gamma x_t + \lambda p_t$$
$$\Delta s_t = q_t - \delta s_t$$

Item	α	β	γ	γ'	λ	λ'	δ	η	η'	σ	σ'
1.0	-60.38 (29.76)	1.4907 (.2100)	.0131 (.0049)	.0513	.8083 (.3719)	3.1738 (.3719)	2	.3696	1.4513	.9249	3.6316
1.1	32.35 (24.52)	.6061 (.8319)	.0642 (.0337)	.1301			1.1959 (1.0809)	.3531	.7159		
1.2	212.33 (127.32)	-.5735 (.6754)			-1.0700 (.5066)	-.6997	1.0838 (.6499)			-1.6322	-1.0674
1.3	-3.9024 (1.9276)	1.3562 (.2589)	.0022 (.0008)	.0068	.0254 (.0072)	.0789	2	.4814	1.4955	.3698	1.1487
1.4	Flow-adjustment model										
1.5	Flow-adjustment model										
2.1	*	-.0334 (.0107)	.0223 (.0057)		-.2721 (.0854)		0	1.4872		-1.1211	
2.2	8.431 (8.026)	-.3093 (.0712)			-.0260 (.0053)	-.0061	.0938 (.0893)			-1.7486	-.4068
2.3	0	.0423 (.1196)	.0626 (.0212)	.0723			.3148 (.1968)	.8351	.9645		
2.4	No equation estimated										
2.5 ⎫ 2.6 ⎭	5.3231 (2.8041)	2.0399 (.0779)	.0042 (.0007)	-.2093	-.1277 (.0332)	6.3950	2	.3988		-.7291	
2.7	0	.0778 (.2486)	.0084 (.0022)	.0103 (.0011)	-.0502 (.0246)	-.0614 (.0174)	.4284 (.3102)	1.3017	1.5905	-.5447	-.6655

(continued)

Table 3.2 (*continued*)

Item	α	β	γ	γ'	λ	λ'	δ	η	η'	σ	σ'
2.8	*	.0203 (.0111)			−.0222 (.0107)	0				−1.0520	
3.1	0	.5725 (.5890)	.0055 (.0022)	.0304 (.0100)	−.0602 (.0240)	−.3305 (.1407)	.6999 (.6685)	.6493	3.5659	−.4407	−2.4202
3.2	−1.6329 (.5241)	1.6759 (.1451)	.0022 (.0007)	.0133			2	.3148	1.9430		
4.1	−3.4526 (3.4948)	1.9421 (.0311)	.0064 (.0034)				2	.0762	2.6331		
4.2	Flow-adjustment model										
4.3	Flow-adjustment model										
4.4	−1.7050 (.5910)	1.4968 (.2320)	.0032 (.0012)	.0129	−.0166 (.0098)	−.0661	2	.7999	3.1792	−.2370	−.9419
5.1	37.84 (50.02)	−.4280 (.2225)	.0397 (.0085)	.0090			.1248 (.1235)	2.6141	.5902		
5.2	−18.81 (5.38)	−.2772 (.5462)	.0289 (.0071)	.0253			2	1.8851	1.6556		
5.3	0	.3553 (.4666)	.0094 (.0023)	.0618 (.0511)	−.1647 (.0427)	−1.0854 (.9350)	.4189 (.4669)	1.3182	8.6858	−1.3355	−8.7999
5.4	0	−.0699 (.0829)	.0338 (.0073)	.0215			.1225 (.0678)	2.3677	1.5070		
5.5	0	−.2272 (.1444)	.0207 (.0074)	.0088 (.0074)			.1689 (.1265)	2.1550	.9188		
5.6	−6.5432 (2.1260)	.9322 (.2901)	.0095 (.0027)	.0177			2	.9386	1.7579		
5.7	1.7883 (1.1479)	.6248 (.9163)	.0027 (.0018)	.0054 (.0008)			1.2566 (.9690)	.8339	1.6585		

5.8a	.7565 (1.7093)	1.9216 (.0855)	.0017 (.0008)	.0425	−.0164 (.0153)	−.4179	2	.1228	3.1329	−.0757	−1.9309
5.8b	Flow-adjustment model										
5.8c	*	.0814 (.0578)	.00376 (.00093)		−.0505 (.0129)		0	.9256		−.6817	
5.8d	*	−.0163 (.0172)	.0115 (.0096)		−.2373 (.0987)		0	.7604		−.9638	
5.9	Flow-adjustment model										
5.10	51.59 (89.55)	−.1763 (.9803)	.0119 (.0109)	.0090	−.4570 (.2053)	−.3475	.5596 (1.1650)	.9797	.7449	−2.3249	−1.7678
6.1											
6.2	0	−.1736 (.3070)	.0032 (.0017)	.0024			.4948 (.4195)	1.3229	.9793		
6.3	Flow-adjustment model										
6.4	Flow-adjustment model										
6.5	*	−.0171 (.0578)			−.0276 (.0186)		0			−.5709	
6.6	−5.4431 (3.2780)	1.0925 (1.2465)	.0051 (.0031)	.0514			1.2117 (1.3968)	.3651	3.7114		
6.7	0	.7582 (1.7569)	.0018 (.0018)	.0070 (.0010)	−.0106 (.0054)	−.0415 (.0134)	1.0188 (1.8571)	.4895	1.9140	−.2040	−.7975
7.1	Static model										
7.2	*	.0456 (.0072)	.0015 (.0008)		−.0407 (.0056)		0	.5278		−.7410	
7.3	Flow-adjustment model										
7.4	Flow-adjustment model										
7.5	*	.0224 (.0175)			−.0650 (.0462)		0			−.6061	

(continued)

Table 3.2 (continued)

Item	α	β	γ	γ'	λ	λ'	δ	η	η'	σ	σ'
7.6	Flow-adjustment model										
7.7	Flow-adjustment model										
8.1a	1283.14 (3892.83)	−.6677 (.1608)	.4888 (.0727)	.0173			.0245 (.0521)	8.8408	.3131		
8.1b	−15.33 (8.25)	.1080 (.2661)	.0143 (.0074)	.0200			.3829 (.3167)	1.9647	2.7366		
8.1c	3.6020 (7.2336)	.2791 (1.1587)	.0082 (.0082)	.0117 (.0082)			.9324 (1.3923)	.5482	.7825		
8.1d	0	.3775 (.2688)	.0120 (.0066)	.0120 (.0066)	.0599		.4724 (.2734)	.3434	1.7090		
8.1e	Flow-adjustment model										
8.1f	Flow-adjustment model										
8.2a	5.0040 (1.6878)	1.5650 (.1003)	.0029 (.0008)	.0132	−.0808 (.0209)		2	.4890	2.2485	−.7696	−3.5386
8.2b		−.4648 (.1538)	.0060 (.0014)		−.0436 (.0108)		0	2.8050		−1.2435	
8.2c	.8725 (.7690)	.5047 (.5301)			−.0044 (.0028)	−.0140	.7373 (.6498)			−.5365	−1.7004
8.3a	7.3767 (9.9360)	.6856 (1.8742)	−.0021 (.0021)	−.0052 (.0013)	−.0293 (.0230)	−.0713 (.0394)	1.1646 (2.0165)	−1.3453	−3.2708	−1.1428	−2.7785
8.3b	*	−.0603 (.0139)	.0009 (.0007)				0	.6748			
8.3c	Flow-adjustment model										
8.3d	No equation estimated										
9.1	*	−.0209 (.0230)	.0083 (.0035)				0	2.0226			

156

Eq.											
9.2	3.7481	1.6139 (.2688)			-.0137 (.0119)		2			-.1007	-.5217
9.3	-5.5525 (4.1842)	1.0889 (1.4304)	.0069 (.0052)	.0198			1.6671 (1.5531)	.9074	2.6163	-.8804	-2.3889
9.4	0	.5403 (.5339)	.0079 (.0027)	.0215 (.0032)	-.0798 (.0514)	-.2165 (.0382)	.8557 (.5857)	1.3696	3.7162		
9.5	-47.76 (12.14)	-.1228 (.1648)	.0428 (.0110)	.0305			.3058 (.2251)	4.1978	2.9950		
9.6	*	-.0133 (.0265)	.0021 (.0015)		-.0185 (.0167)		0	.9037		-.4419	
9.7	0	.1000 (.2016)	.0021 (.0011)	.0068 (.0450)	-.0240 (.0066)	-.0774 (.7303)	.1451 (.6054)	1.0312	3.3208	-.8233	-2.6514
9.8a	*	-.0989 (.0147)	.0047 (.0033)				0	.9011			
9.8b	0	1.6820 (.1312)	.0002 (.0001)	.0011			2	.1604	1.0086		
9.8c	*	-.0149 (.0092)			-.0030 (.0036)		0			-.2147	
9.9	-.8922 (.5306)	2.5138 (.2433)	-.0001 (.0001)	.0002			-2	-.0248	.0970		
9.10	-1.3188 (.8002)	.4982 (.4162)	.0027 (.0016)	.0167 (.0100)			.5929 (.4381)	.8686	5.4354		
9.11	Flow-adjustment model										
9.12	-.8894 (.2771)	1.7540 (.1055)	.0012 (.0003)	.0100			2	.3214	2.6129		
10.1	Flow-adjustment model										
10.2	*	.3264 (.1321)			-.0365 (.0138)		0			-.6436	

(continued)

Table 3.2 (continued)

Item	α	β	γ	γ'	λ	λ'	δ	η	η'	σ	σ'
10.3	*	.0946 (.0473)	.0013 (.0009)		−.0134 (.0086)		0	.4757		−.2919	
11.0	Flow-adjustment model										
12.1	−4.0350 (2.1182)	1.5929 (.1866)	.0038 (.0018)	.0186			2	.6550	3.2175		
12.2	0	1.8102 (.1242)	.0005 (.0002)	.0053			2	.1558	1.6420		
12.3	0	.0694 (.2411)	−.0031 (.0028)	−.0045			.2157 (.2818)	.9670	1.4254		
12.4	*	−.1812 (.0597)	−.0021 (.0017)		−.0494 (.0371)		0	3.7149		5.5554	

Note: Items with asterisk indicate that α is indeterminate.

158

Table 3.3. Coefficients of Flow-Adjustment Model (1947–1964)

$$\Delta q_t = \theta(q_t - \hat{q}_t)$$
$$\hat{q}_t = \xi + \mu x_t + \zeta p_t$$

Item	ξ	θ	μ	ζ	η	σ
1.4	62.44	.4881 (.2359)	−.0826 (.0319)	−.0248 (.0157)	−1.0104	−.0579
1.5	51.14	1.4927 (.8918)	.0103 (.0058)	−.3424 (.2575)	.4819	−.9805
4.2	215.17	−.0721 (.1524)	−.0998 (.2810)	4.3160 (8.7443)	−2.5757	6.6847
4.3	0	.0614 (.0609)	.0744 (.0687)		.7707	
5.8b	0	.0586 (.0310)	.0146 (.0035)		1.7781	
5.9	−31.24	.5811 (.1542)	.0354 (.0017)	−.0607 (.0501)	2.8173	−.2970
6.1	−24.83	.4888 (.2514)	.0270 (.0024)		2.5799	
6.3	0	.6218 (.3950)	.0206 (.0032)		1.3257	
6.4	0	.2679 (.2149)	.0063 (.0004)		1.0547	
7.3	−17.28	1.8392 (.2578)	.0302 (.0030)	−.0986 (.0271)	2.1645	−.4012
7.4	−2.707	1.7027 (.7686)	.0122 (.0010)		1.1642	
7.6	2.620	.7402 (.3132)	.0029 (.0004)		.6462	
7.7	0	.4670 (.1098)	.0032 (.0001)		1.0014	
8.1e	−4.719	.1975 (.1485)	.0039 (.0006)		5.3178	
8.1f	0	.3514 (.1469)	.0057 (.0003)		1.0856	
8.3c	−.8702 (.0216)	.8672 (.2643)	.0083 (.0003)		5.8723	
9.11	.802	.9672 (.1805)	.0033 (.0003)	−.0360 (.0076)	2.0975	−1.4118
10.1	−16.01	.1251 (.1516)	.0154 (.0088)		3.6356	
11.0	9.669	1.0240 (.3139)	.0198 (.0019)		1.4365	

4

Discussion of the Demand Equations and Projections

This chapter discusses our empirical results and the projections to 1970 and 1975 from a broader perspective than was done in Chapter 3. Of particular interest are the success (or lack of it) of the dynamic model, the overall influence of habit formation on consumption, and the general influence of prices. These empirical questions, together with several related issues, are discussed in section I. Section II analyzes the projections to 1970 and 1975. Among other things, the growth rates implied by our projections are computed for each category. In analyzing the projections we also aggregate the 82 commodity categories into two larger classifications: the eleven-group aggregates (food, clothing, and so on) and the traditional aggregates of durables, nondurables, and services. Sections III and IV present tests of the performance of our equations in forecasting consumption in 1965, 1966, and 1967.

I. *An Overview of the Empirical Results*

One of the most striking results of the investigation is the large number of categories in which the dynamic model gave the best equation. Of the 81 equations, 79 are dynamic, including 14 Bergstrom models (although 4 equations have $\beta = \delta = 0$, which corresponds to the static model in first differences). Although this is the expected result, it nevertheless takes on added significance in view of the fact that the nature of the projection exercise precluded complete commitment to the dynamic model.

Another successful aspect of the dynamic model is that the harmful effects of autocorrelation in the error term have been largely sidestepped. This is attributable in large part to the superior specification of the dynamic equation, for only 36 of the 79 dynamic equations required 3PLS in estimation. To see that our early fear of facing a major problem of autocorrelation with the static model had substance, we need only note the very low $D.W.$'s for a large majority of the static equations presented in the first edition.

Item	Period*	Form*	Special case	3PLS†	Stock coefficient	PCE†	Prices†	R^2	D.W.
1.0	E	D	$\delta = 2$		1.0664	×		.924	1.90
1.1	E	D			.2365	×		.990	1.79
1.2	E	D	$\delta = 0$		−.0262	×	×	.916	2.06
1.3	E	D		×	.3602	×		.894	1.69
1.4	P	B				×		.754	1.91
1.5	E	D		×	.8958	×	×	.993	1.61
2.1	E	D	$\delta = 0$	×	−.0417	×	×	.707	2.03
2.2	E	D		×	.1525	×	×	.986	2.00
2.3	E	D			−.1503	×		.953	1.90
2.4	no equation estimated								
2.5 } 2.6	E	D	$\beta = \delta$		.2180	×	×	.909	1.56
2.7	E	D			.3577	×	×	.992	2.26
2.8	E	D	$\delta = 2$		.0920	×	×	.819	1.74
3.1	E	D			1.8689	×	×	.993	2.07
3.2	E	D		×	.2240	×		.941	2.03
4.1	E	D	$\delta = 2$	×	1.9423	×	×	.999	1.69
4.2	E	B		×		×	×	.996	2.53
4.3	E	B		×		×	×	.997	2.25
4.4	E	B		×		×		.986	1.50
5.1	E	D			−.1435	×		.967	1.90
5.2	E	L	$\delta = 2$			×	×	.991	1.66
5.3	E	D		×	.7889	×	×	.977	2.14
5.4	E	D		×	−.0774	×		.972	2.22
5.5	E	D		×	−.5318	×		.954	1.75
5.6	E	D			.3312	×		.995	1.80
5.7	E	D			.1830	×	×	.994	1.75
5.8a	P	D			1.9216	×	×	.999	2.32
5.8b	E	B				×	×	.997	1.77

(continued)

Table 4.1 (continued)

Item	Period*	Form*	Special case	3PLS†	Stock coefficient	PCE†	Prices†	R^2	D.W.
5.8c	E	D		×	−.2133	×	×	.977	1.78
5.8d	E	D	$\delta = 0$	×	−.0131	×	×	.720	2.03
5.9	E	D	$\beta = \delta$		.4007	×	×	.877	2.01
5.10	E	D	$\delta = 0$		−.0546	×	×	.949	2.40
5.11	E	D		×	.4600	×	×	.997	1.63
6.1	E	D			.2732	×		.996	1.74
6.2	E	D			.0405	×	×	.990	1.92
6.3	E	D	$\delta = 2$	×	1.5168	×		.990	2.00
6.4	E	D			.6342	×		.978	2.18
6.5	E	B		×		×	×	.982	1.97
6.6	P	D			1.0925	×		.996	2.11
6.7	E	D		×	.3697	×	×	.997	1.74
7.1	P	DL				×		.775	1.81
7.2	E	D	$\beta = \delta = 0$	×		×	×	.847	1.84
7.3	E	D	$\delta = 2$	×	.8372	×		.925	2.13
7.4	P	B				×		.928	1.90
7.5	E	D	$\beta = \delta = 0$			×	×	.229	2.14
7.6	P	B				×		.936	1.82
7.7	E	D	$\beta = \delta = 0$			×	×	.527	1.89
8.1a	E	D			.6408	×		.957	2.20
8.1b	E	D			.1534	×	×	.977	2.04
8.1c	E	D			−.0222	×	×	.995	2.08
8.1d	E	D			.1691	×		.998	2.00
8.1e	E	D	$\delta = 2$	×	1.9251	×		.995	1.80
8.1f	E	D			.8616	×		.985	2.12
8.2a	E	D		×	.0933	×	×	.997	1.91
8.2b	E	D	$\delta = 0$		−.0706		×	.963	1.84
8.2c	E	D		×	.0528		×	.986	2.25
	E	B							

Eq.	Period	Model	Constraint		Coefficient			R^2	D-W
8.3b	E	D			.8797	×	×	.986	2.25
8.3c	P	B				×		.995	1.93
8.3d	E	D	$\delta = 0$		−.1132	×		.787	2.10
9.1	E	D		×	−.1024	×		.966	1.98
9.2	E	D	$\beta = \delta = 0$	×	1.0138	×	×	.633	1.76
9.3	E	D		×	.5403	×	×	.993	2.00
9.4	P	D		×	−.1228	×	×	.994	2.30
9.5	P	D			.5011	×		.961	2.07
9.6	E	D		×	.1000	×	×	.995	1.55
9.7	P	D			.4344	×	×	.925	2.55
9.8a	E	D			.3446	×	×	.974	2.01
9.8b	E	D	$\delta = 2$		1.9154	×	×	.978	1.61
9.8c	E	D		×		×		.979	2.08
9.9	E	B			.4482	×		.955	2.14
9.10	P	D		×	.4632	×		.980	2.38
9.11	E	D		×	.1689	×	×	.990	2.19
9.12	E	D		×		×		.989	2.43
10.1	E	B				×		.988	1.99
10.2	E	B			.5149	×	×	.981	1.96
10.3	E	D		×		×	×	.975	2.01
11.0	E	B			1.8475	×	×	.937	1.67
12.1	E	D	$\delta = 2$	×		×		.976	1.85
12.2	E	B		×	.1079	×		.973	2.04
12.3	E	D		×		×		.976	2.05
12.4	P	D	$\delta = 0$	×	−.1812	×	×	.862	1.64

* Definitions of the symbols are:

    E   1929–1964
    P   1946–1964
    D   state-adjustment model
    B   flow-adjustment model
    L   linear
    DL   double logarithmic

† An "×" indicates that the equation has the characteristic.

In general, the R^2's of the equations are satisfactory, for they are typically very high. Fifty-eight of the 81 have $R^2 > .950$ and 68 have $R^2 > .900$ (see Table 4.1). For the equations with q_t as the dependent variable, the lowest R^2 with the dynamic equation is for item 2.1 ($R^2 = .707$), and there are only five equations with $R^2 < .800$. Moreover, five of the six equations estimated with Δq_t as the dependent variable have R^2's above .5.

However, high R^2's with time-series data are commonplace, so that this in itself is little reason for self-congratulation. More important in many respects is the statistical significance of the regression coefficients. On this score the results must also be termed a success, for in most equations the coefficients of q_{t-1} and Δx_1 are several times their standard errors, while the coefficient of p_t is typically $1\frac{1}{2}$ to $2\frac{1}{2}$ times its standard error.

As has been noted, one of the strong features of the dynamic model is that it enables the effect of habit formation to be clearly separated from the effect of inventory adjustment: $\beta > 0$ indicates presence of habit formation, while $\beta < 0$ indicates inventory adjustment. Hence it becomes an interesting exercise to analyze the stock coefficients of the dynamic equations in order to see whether habit formation or inventory adjustment predominates in United States consumption.

A count of signs of the stock coefficient in Table 4.1 shows that 46 are positive, 15 are negative, and 4 are zero.[1] The 46 categories subject to habit formation (by this criterion) accounted for 61.1 percent of total expenditure in 1964 (1958 dollars), while the commodities subject to inventory adjustment accounted for 27.7 percent.[2] Hence, even after allowing for the 16 categories for which stock coefficients are missing, habit formation quite clearly predominates in United States consumption.

It is difficult to say whether or not this is an expected result. Perhaps the surprising thing is the general strength of habit formation, and not its predominance as such. In a similar study of 64 categories of consumer expenditure in Sweden for the period 1931–1958, Taylor (1968) found habit formation to be much less pervasive, accounting for only about 40 percent of total Swedish consumption expenditure in 1958. Since incomes in Sweden over the period were roughly half those in the United States, these two results suggest that the strength of habit formation may be a positive function of the level of income. This could come about in two ways.

First, it is probably safe to say that each commodity has some forces making for inventory adjustment and some making for habit formation, and the single stock coefficient therefore reflects an amalgam of these opposing tendencies. For a durable good such as autos, inventory adjustment obviously

---

[1] This makes a total of 65; the other 14 dynamic equations are the Bergstrom model and thus do not have stock coefficients.

[2] Items 12.3 and 12.4 have been excluded in these calculations.

should prevail, although the opposite should be expected for, say, tobacco. As income grows, however, durable goods, as they account for increasingly smaller proportions of the consumer's budget, can come to be treated more and more like nondurables and services. We would therefore expect habit formation to become more important and the stock coefficient accordingly to be related positively to income.

The second way that habit formation and income can be related is through a changing consumption-mix as income grows. We have found that goods subject to habit formation, particularly services, tend to have larger long-run income elasticities than goods with negative stock coefficients (see Table 4.2), with the result that they assume an increasing share of total expenditure over time. In 1939, for example, the habit-forming categories accounted for only 52 percent of total expenditure.

We hasten to add, lest we give the impression that we are generalizing from the data of only two countries, that this positive relationship between habit formation and income is only a hypothesis. A great deal of further work with data of other countries will be required before we can be definitive.

Clearly the most important factor explaining the pattern of consumption in the United States is total expenditure. PCE is excluded from only two of the 81 categories: 8.2c (commuting by railway) and 8.3a (intercity railway travel), and neither of these is surprising. Moreover, 7.1 (brokerage charges and interest, and investment counseling) is the only category with a negative total-expenditure elasticity, although 8.3a, not surprisingly, is also indicated to be an inferior good with the postwar data. The results for 7.1, as was noted in Chapter 3, are among the most puzzling in the entire study.

Prices, on the other hand, are much less important than PCE in explaining United States consumption. Of the 81 equations, prices appear in only 44, and they barely border on significance in many of these. Moreover, as was noted in Chapter 1, the price coefficients may be biased in a negative direction because of the manner in which the price series are derived. In light of this possible bias, it is interesting to note that of the 44 categories with prices 26 are classified as services by the Department of Commerce.

The lack of a strong overall influence of prices is consistent with the predominance of habit formation. Prices should be expected to exert less of an influence on consumption at high levels of income because income becomes less of a constraining factor and more commodities become subject to habit formation. The results for Sweden noted above are consistent with this hypothesis, for, with inventory adjustment predominating prices appear in 46 of 64 Swedish equations.

Before moving on to the projections, we should point out that, though we are pleased in general with the set of equations, several equations leave a lot to be desired; equations for 1.4, 2.1, 5.2, 5.8d, 7.1, 7.2, 7.7, and 9.2 are clearly

Table 4.2. Elasticities for 82 PCE Categories

Item	Total expenditure		Price	
	Short-run	Long-run	Short-run	Long-run
1.0	.2898	.6207		
1.1	.4972	.7115		
1.2	1.6126		− 2.2703	
1.3	.6799	1.0342		
1.4	− .6052			
1.5	.2075	.8615	− .4556	− 1.8919
2.1	.9433		− .9135	
2.2	.5206	.7230	− 1.3067	− 1.8147
2.3	1.1423	.5131		
2.4	no equation estimated			
2.5⎫ 2.6⎭	.6534		− .9293	
2.7	1.0025	1.6447	− .4100	− .6726
2.8	.9472	1.1657		
3.1	.2453	3.7406	− .1993	− 3.0391
3.2	.8675	1.3598		
4.1	.0707	2.4495	− .0351	− 1.2150
4.2	1.5315		− .1839	
4.3	1.1283		− .6044	
4.4	1.2735			
5.1	2.5975	.5275		
5.2	1.1827		− .6337	
5.3	.4692	.7749	− 1.5448	− 2.5512
5.4	2.0879	1.1759		
5.5	2.2298	.6466		
5.6	.9929	1.6627		
5.7	1.5211	1.8277	− .4693	− .5638
5.8a	.1319	1.9364	− .1289	− 1.8926
5.8b	3.1087			
5.8c	.8746	.5861	− .2028	− .1359
5.8d	.7514		− .7317	
5.9	.3158		− .2556	
5.10	1.8875		− .6635	
5.11	.5577	1.2657	− .1272	− .2885
6.1	.6221	3.0422		
6.2	1.2883	1.3906	− .3681	− .3973
6.3	.2770	1.1465		
6.4	.3799	.9976		
6.5	1.3289		− .2708	
6.6	.3651	3.7114		
6.7	.6900	2.0162	− .3136	− .9162
7.1	− 2.9560			
7.2	.4025		− .5334	
7.3	.6229	1.0714		
7.4	1.1642			
7.5	.4264		− .3707	
7.6	.6462			
7.7	.6900		− 1.9382	
8.1a	5.4646	1.0749		

Table 4.2 (*continued*)

Item	Total expenditure Short-run	Long-run	Price Short-run	Long-run
8.1b	1.3976	1.9290	−.8624	−1.1904
8.1c	.9429	.8955	−.4002	−.3801
8.1d	.5493	1.3572		
8.1e	.1677	4.4758		
8.1f	.3708	1.2596		
8.2a	.7167	1.3785	−.6221	−1.1967
8.2b	1.1460		−.6299	
8.2c			−.7185	−.9127
8.3a			−1.4151	−3.1948
8.3b	.1720	1.8944	−.1967	−2.1657
8.3c	5.8723			
8.3d	2.7059			
9.1	1.6726	1.4223		
9.2	.3841		−.4185	
9.3	.5864	2.0107	−.2970	−1.0186
9.4	1.3696	3.7162	−.8804	−2.3889
9.5	4.1978	2.9950		
9.6	.6372	5.1978	−.4711	−3.8427
9.7	1.0312	3.3208	−.8233	−2.6514
9.8a	.8126	3.4075	−.8748	−3.6685
9.8b	.7407	1.2604	−.1827	−.3109
9.8c	.0452	1.0697		
9.9	.8686	5.4354		
9.10	1.4239	1.9143		
9.11	1.2843	2.2770		
9.12	1.2112	2.1498	−.5675	−1.0073
10.1	2.1512			
10.2	2.7674			
10.3	.3542	1.1251	−.5182	−1.6459
11.0	1.8456		−1.0156	
12.1	.2355	3.0873	−.1351	−1.7707
12.2	1.7339			
12.3	.8590	1.1980		
12.4	3.7149		5.5554	

cases in point. While reasons for the poor quality of these equations could undoubtedly be advanced, in the end we must acknowledge that our dynamic theory is still only a modest step forward.

II. *Projections for 1970 and 1975*

Since the initial purpose of the investigation was to provide projections for 1970 and 1975, it is appropriate to devote a section to an analysis of our projections. Two sets of projections have been made, corresponding to two alternative projections of relative prices. Essentially extrapolations of 1956–1964 trends through 1970, the first set of relative prices then assumes no further change between 1970 and 1975. The second set assumes no change at all in the relative prices, that is, 1964 values are used for both 1970 and 1975. As it turns out, only a few projections are sensitive to prices, so that the obviously unrealistic assumption of constancy over part or all of the projection period is not as serious as it might seem. The two sets of relative prices are given in Table 4.3.

Underlying the projections is the assumption that real GNP will grow at 4.3 percent per year (with 4 percent unemployment), and implicit in this is the same assumption for total PCE. These assumptions to 1970 are among those underlying the Interagency Growth Study[3] and we have extended

Table 4.3. Projected Relative Prices, 1970 and 1975

Item	Set I	Set II	Item	Set I	Set II	Item	Set I	Set II
1.0	95.3	99.6	5.8a	92.6	95.5	8.2b	121.8	115.4
1.1	93.0	95.6	5.8b	113.4	104.3	8.2c	136.1	115.6
1.2	113.4	107.3	5.8c	122.9	109.9	8.3a	97.7	95.3
1.3	86.1	91.3	5.8d	94.9	97.5	8.3b	99.8	99.8
1.4	80.5	86.8	5.9	97.1	97.1	8.3c	123.0	107.3
1.5	108.1	105.5	5.10	121.9	112.8	8.3d	85.9	93.1
2.1	107.7	103.3	5.11	114.7	110.5	9.1	107.5	104.6
2.2	110.2	107.8	6.1	92.0	91.3	9.2	107.8	104.6
2.3	94.5	98.0	6.2	105.8	103.1	9.3	88.3	93.3
			6.3	121.1	111.6	9.4	95.6	96.6
2.4	92.6	97.3	6.4	112.7	108.3	9.5	93.2	93.9
2.5 } 2.6 }	107.9	105.1	6.5	121.2	111.6	9.6	100.5	97.1
			6.6	129.0	117.5	9.7	97.3	100.6
2.7	78.3	89.1	6.7	121.0	107.9	9.8a	131.6	125.8
2.8	97.9	101.6	7.1	187.3	156.4	9.8b	129.1	124.1
3.1	94.3	95.3	7.2	89.7	87.4	9.8c	131.2	123.4
3.2	112.7	107.0	7.3	117.9	117.0	9.9	107.2	104.2
4.1	100.3	100.3	7.4	121.1	113.2	9.10	124.4	112.5
4.2	100.3	100.3	7.5	130.3	116.0	9.11	112.0	106.4
4.3	112.5	112.1	7.6	109.7	108.8	9.12	118.5	112.9
4.4	107.2	102.9	7.7	100.1	100.5	10.1	138.7	126.4
5.1	91.0	95.7	8.1a	93.7	94.4	10.2	119.2	111.3
5.2	66.9	83.2	8.1b	85.9	87.5	10.3	116.7	108.5
5.3	106.4	102.7	8.1c	106.0	103.2	11.0	102.3	100.7
5.4	89.9	94.2	8.1d	93.4	96.1	12.1	101.7	102.5
5.5	92.3	97.1	8.1e	85.2	93.1	12.2	87.1	93.8
5.6	91.7	94.0	8.1f	124.9	105.2	12.3	102.6	101.6
5.7	97.0	98.9	8.2a	125.8	113.3	12.4	93.8	96.5

Source: Set I, Bureau of Labor Statistics; Set II, 1964 relative prices.

[3] See *Projections 1970*, BLS Bulletin 1536 (1966) for a discussion of these assumptions.

them through 1975. The relative prices in 1970 have also been provided
the IAGS, and it was our decision to extend them to 1975. The Bureau of
Census Series A projections (as published in the *1966 Statistical Abstract)*
taken for the population (including armed forces overseas) in 1970 and 1975,
and the Census' projections of the percentage of the population 18 or older are
also used. For farm income, we have assumed that it will grow 6 percent
per year in real terms per farm capita through 1970, and 2.75 percent per
year between 1970 and 1975, and we have assumed that the farm population
as a percentage of the total will continue its long-term downward trend,
reaching 5.5 by 1970 and 4.7 by 1975. The values of all of these predictors
are given in Table 4.4.

Table 4.4 Values of the Predictors

Predictor	1964	1970	1975
Total PCE (billions of 1958 dollars)		$485.5	$608.6
Total population (millions)		209	228
Total PCE per capita (1958 dollars)	1945.67	2322.07	2669.30
Farm income per farm capita (1958 dollars)	1193.66	1693.80	1947.87
Farm population as percent of total population	6.7	5.5	4.7
Population 18 or older (percent of total population)	63.4	64.1	64.0

Source: PCE (1970): BLS; population: Bureau of the Census; all others: Houthakker
and Taylor.

Table 4.5 contains the intercepts for the equations estimated with 3PLS
to be used beginning with 1966. In addition to the constant term of the regression equation, the historical mean of the 3-pass variable times its
coefficient is included in these intercepts. (The actual value for z is used in
1965; these are also given in the table.)

The projections tabulated in Table 4.6 are in per capita terms, while those
in Table 4.7 have been multiplied by the projected population in 1970 and
1975 and thus are aggregates. Both tables are in 1958 dollars. The implied
rates of growth between 1964 and 1970 and 1970 and 1975 have also been
computed and are given in columns 6 and 7 of Table 4.6. Table 4.8 aggregates
the projections to more broadly defined commodity groups. As was noted in
Chapter 2, the projections add up to total expenditure in each intervening
year as well as in 1970 and 1975,[4] and, although exponential growth is

[4] The projections have been multiplied by their relative prices before being added up.
As a result they are additive in current dollars although the control total remains constant
dollar PCE.

Table 4.5. Intercepts for 3PLS Equations*

Item	1965	1966–1975	Item	1965	1966–1975
1.3	−.3828	−.2095	7.2	.4127	.1749
1.5	13.8349	14.6712	7.3	−2.8831	−3.3455
2.1	.5388	.5543	8.1e	−.1191	−.1649
2.2	1.0377	1.0296	8.2a	−.1610	−.2345
3.2	−2.1325	−1.9365	8.2c	.2743	.2556
4.1	4.1125	2.3581	9.1	−1.1252	−1.2714
4.2	−2.4872	−4.0286	9.2	−.0472	−.0575
4.3	13.1568	7.0169	9.3	.2380	.1135
4.4	−.3662	−1.1155	9.4	−1.3643	−.9759
5.3	22.1750	22.0080	9.6	−.0218	−.0093
5.4	−1.0405	−.9149	9.8c	−.0099	−.0028
5.5	3.2459	2.1999	9.10	−2.6957	−2.0405
5.8c	1.6204	1.5860	9.11	−1.1497	−1.0272
5.8d	.0545	−.0036	9.12	−.5161	−.3128
5.11	.1563	.0427	10.3	1.2463	1.2374
6.3	−.5389	−.5013	12.1	−.4317	−.1907
6.5	−.0478	−.0494	12.2	−.0208	−.0268
6.7	.0526	.0421	12.3	−.1050	.0020

* Equals $A_0 + a_7 z$; for 1965, $z = z_{1965}$; for 1966–1975, $z = \bar{z}$.

implicit in the figures for total PCE, linear growth has been assumed in deriving the projections—that is, once the levels of total PCE in 1970 and 1975 are given, the changes are allocated evenly over the interior years between 1964 and 1970 and 1970 and 1975.

The projections for brokerage charges (7.1) were finally obtained by assuming the constant dollar value to be $5.25 per capita in both 1970 and 1975. This was done after the projections from the equation for this item appeared to be implausibly high, a result which in view of the other problem encountered with this category (see the discussion in Chapter 3) is hardly surprising.

It was mentioned at the end of Chapter 1 that a good deal of emphasis was given to the projections in selecting the final set of equations. Hence, on the whole, we are comfortable with the projections. This does not mean that we are completely satisfied, for there are still several obvious problems. Perhaps the most blatant anomalies are the projections for domestic services (5.10) and motion pictures (9.8a), both of which appear to be unreasonably large. It is hard to visualize domestic services suddenly reversing its rather persistent downward postwar trend and attaining a level of expenditure in 1970 that is higher than any year since 1950, and it is equally difficult to take seriously a virtual tripling of expenditures on motion pictures between 1964 and 1975.

Table 4.6. Projections in 1970 and 1975 (per capita 1958 dollars)

Item	1964	1970		1975		Growth rate*		Equation†
		I	II	I	II	1964–1970	1970–1975	
1.0	59.73	65.50	66.78	72.71	74.22	1.5	2.1	1935–1964
1.1	311.24	353.68	362.02	393.16	403.11	2.2	2.1	E
1.2	67.48	76.80	78.82	84.37	83.81	2.2	1.9	E
1.3	6.68	8.76	9.24	10.05	10.63	4.6	2.8	E
1.4	4.24	4.08	4.40	3.31	3.56	−.6	−4.1	P
1.5	38.23	45.11	44.81	51.16	51.15	2.8	2.5	E
2.1	25.21	28.17	27.46	29.41	28.24	1.9	.9	E
2.2	1.40	1.65	1.68	1.95	1.98	2.8	3.4	E
2.3	137.14	145.93	149.50	155.73	159.91	1.0	1.3	E
2.4	.36	.34	.36	.34	.36	−.9	.0	
2.5 2.6	17.36	21.33	21.13	26.83	26.74	3.5	4.7	E
2.7	12.79	15.43	15.31	18.03	17.94	3.2	3.2	E
2.8	2.33	3.11	3.13	3.66	3.70	4.9	3.3	E
3.1	19.21	26.56	26.43	33.91	33.77	5.5	5.1	E
3.2	14.86	18.96	18.78	22.44	22.29	4.1	3.4	E
4.1	190.89	231.56	230.83	270.53	269.65	3.3	3.2	E
4.2	75.98	96.33	96.01	114.88	114.54	4.0	3.6	E
4.3	9.92	8.92	9.20	7.86	8.10	−1.8	−2.5	1935–1964
4.4	9.11	9.96	9.91	11.63	11.59	1.5	3.1	E
5.1	28.26	33.67	32.70	35.49	34.51	3.0	1.1	E
5.2	28.01	31.48	31.35	35.62	35.53	2.0	2.2	E
5.3	11.35	13.19	13.17	15.12	15.12	2.5	2.8	E
5.4	27.82	34.14	33.39	38.27	37.51	3.5	2.3	E
5.5	18.44	19.16	18.90	20.83	20.65	.6	1.7	E
5.6	19.78	24.84	24.65	29.23	29.09	3.9	3.3	E

(continued)

Table 4.6 (*continued*)

Item	1964	1970 I	1970 II	1975 I	1975 II	Growth rate* 1964–1970	Growth rate* 1970–1975	Equation†
5.7	6.67	8.58	8.51	10.26	10.21	4.3	3.6	E
5.8a	30.45	38.92	38.78	46.35	46.21	4.2	3.6	P
5.8b	19.08	25.14	25.06	31.30	31.20	4.7	4.5	E
5.8c	8.35	9.16	8.99	10.01	9.85	1.6	1.8	E
5.8d	24.04	26.43	26.00	27.57	26.91	1.6	.8	E
5.9	28.66	38.85	38.66	49.33	49.05	5.2	4.9	E
5.10	18.95	24.49	23.38	26.15	24.63	4.4	1.3	E
5.11	12.51	16.60	16.79	19.36	19.62	4.8	3.1	E
6.1	20.99	26.94	26.74	32.66	32.39	4.2	3.9	E
6.2	5.23	6.14	6.08	7.09	7.04	2.7	2.9	E
6.3	34.09	40.45	40.25	46.47	46.30	2.9	2.8	E
6.4	12.08	14.50	14.42	16.56	16.49	3.1	2.7	E
6.5	6.03	7.33	7.31	8.64	8.62	3.3	3.3	E
6.6	37.46	53.01	52.72	68.87	68.52	6.0	5.4	P
6.7	8.61	10.23	10.45	11.98	12.24	2.9	3.2	E
7.1	8.17	9.83	8.17	9.83	8.17	3.1	.0	E
7.2	6.25	7.84	7.67	8.85	8.64	3.8	2.5	
7.3	33.68	36.79	38.98	42.74	45.37	1.5	3.0	E
7.4	23.48	28.41	28.35	33.02	32.99	3.2	3.1	P
7.5	11.79	13.14	12.85	13.96	13.59	1.8	1.2	E
7.6	8.61	9.44	9.77	10.43	10.80	1.5	2.0	P
7.7	5.78	6.54	6.47	7.05	6.94	2.1	1.5	E
8.1a	110.50	124.95	123.05	137.42	136.50	2.1	1.9	E
8.1b	14.39	18.27	18.07	21.68	21.51	4.1	3.5	E
8.1c	27.55	32.55	32.28	36.13	35.92	2.8	2.1	E
8.1d	68.52	82.39	81.72	93.95	93.18	3.1	2.7	E
8.1e	1.84	2.45	2.44	3.03	3.02	4.9	4.3	E

8.1f	10.58	12.77	12.82	14.62	14.70	3.2	2.7	E
8.2a	6.11	7.26	7.07	9.22	9.00	2.9	4.9	E
8.2b	2.87	2.77	2.66	2.59	2.42	−.6	−1.3	E
8.2c	.65	.59	.58	.56	.56	−1.6	−1.0	E
8.3a	1.27	1.41	1.43	1.45	1.48	1.8	.6	E
8.3b	1.57	1.81	1.81	2.21	2.20	2.4	4.1	E
8.3c	4.77	8.02	7.99	10.96	10.94	9.0	6.4	P
8.3d	.16	.19	.18	.19	.17	2.9	.0	E
9.1	9.36	10.72	10.64	12.49	12.44	2.3	3.1	E
9.2	13.42	14.19	14.09	14.66	14.49	.9	.7	E
9.3	15.52	19.47	19.35	23.24	23.14	3.9	3.6	P
9.4	13.62	21.67	21.46	28.27	28.10	8.0	5.5	P
9.5	26.29	35.51	34.94	43.78	43.42	5.1	4.3	E
9.6	4.62	6.49	6.44	8.39	8.33	5.8	5.3	P
9.7	4.31	5.57	5.49	6.77	6.66	4.4	4.0	E
9.8a	4.48	7.52	7.34	13.42	13.24	9.0	12.3	E
9.8b	2.35	3.00	2.98	3.52	3.51	4.2	3.2	P
9.8c	1.78	2.00	2.05	2.28	2.33	2.0	2.7	E
9.9	4.04	4.17	4.14	4.24	4.21	.5	.3	E
9.10	7.23	12.08	10.81	17.12	15.35	8.9	7.2	E
9.11	3.36	5.06	4.78	6.14	5.81	7.1	3.9	E
9.12	8.77	12.08	11.63	14.92	14.40	5.5	4.3	E
10.1	11.77	15.95	14.52	19.13	17.41	5.2	3.7	E
10.2	8.54	12.87	11.99	16.41	15.30	7.1	5.0	E
10.3	5.10	6.02	5.94	6.90	6.91	2.8	2.8	E
11.0	26.80	36.59	36.14	45.38	44.94	5.3	4.4	E
12.1	14.49	19.35	19.40	24.29	24.34	4.9	4.7	E
12.2	6.16	7.08	7.61	8.22	8.85	2.3	3.0	E
12.3	−6.31	−7.55	−7.42	−8.52	−8.39	−3.0	−2.4	E
12.4	−.65	−.55	−.60	−.52	−.52	2.7	1.1	P

* Based on first set of prices.
† E: 1929–1964; P: 1946–1964.

Table 4.7. Projections in 1970 and 1975 (billions of 1958 dollars

Item	1964	1970*	1975*
1.0	11.47	13.69	16.58
1.1	59.79	73.92	80.64
1.2	12.96	16.05	19.24
1.3	1.28	1.83	2.29
1.4	.81	.85	.75
1.5	7.34	9.43	11.66
2.1	4.84	5.89	6.71
2.2	.27	.34	.44
2.3	26.34	30.50	35.51
2.4	.07	.07	.08
2.5 } 2.6 }	3.33	4.46	6.12
2.7	2.46	3.22	4.11
2.8	.45	.65	.83
3.1	3.69	5.55	7.73
3.2	2.85	3.96	5.12
4.1	36.67	48.40	61.68
4.2	14.60	20.13	26.19
4.3	1.91	1.86	1.79
4.4	1.75	2.08	2.65
5.1	5.43	7.04	8.09
5.2	5.38	6.58	8.12
5.3	2.18	2.76	3.45
5.4	5.34	7.14	8.73
5.5	3.54	4.00	4.75
5.6	3.80	5.19	6.66
5.7	1.28	1.79	2.34
5.8a	5.85	8.13	10.57
5.8b	3.67	5.25	7.14
5.8c	1.60	1.91	2.28
5.8d	4.62	5.52	6.29
5.9	5.51	8.12	11.25
5.10	3.64	5.12	5.96
5.11	2.40	3.47	4.41
6.1	4.03	5.63	7.45
6.2	1.00	1.28	1.62
6.3	6.55	8.45	10.60
6.4	2.32	3.03	3.78
6.5	1.16	1.53	1.97
6.6	7.20	11.08	15.70
6.7	1.65	2.14	2.73
7.1	1.57	2.06	2.24
7.2	1.20	1.64	2.02
7.3	6.47	7.69	9.74
7.4	4.51	5.94	7.53
7.5	2.26	2.75	3.18
7.6	1.65	1.97	2.38
7.7	1.11	1.37	1.61
8.1a	21.23	26.11	31.33
8.1b	2.76	3.82	4.94

(continued)

Table 4.7 (*continued*)

Item	1964	1970*	1975*
8.1c	5.29	6.80	8.24
8.1d	13.16	17.22	21.42
8.1e	.35	.51	.69
8.1f	2.03	2.67	3.33
8.2a	1.17	1.52	2.10
8.2b	.55	.58	.59
8.2c	.12	.12	.13
8.3a	.24	.29	.33
8.3b	.30	.38	.50
8.3c	.92	1.68	2.50
8.3d	.03	.04	.04
9.1	1.80	2.24	2.85
9.2	2.58	2.97	3.34
9.3	2.98	4.07	5.30
9.4	2.62	4.53	6.45
9.5	5.05	7.42	9.98
9.6	.89	1.36	1.91
9.7	.83	1.16	1.54
9.8a	.86	1.57	3.06
9.8b	.45	.63	.80
9.8c	.34	.42	.52
9.9	.78	.87	.97
9.10	1.39	2.52	3.90
9.11	.65	1.06	1.40
9.12	1.68	2.52	3.40
10.1	2.26	3.33	4.36
10.2	1.64	2.69	3.74
10.3	.98	1.26	1.57
11.0	5.15	7.65	10.35
12.1	2.78	4.04	5.53
12.2	1.18	1.48	1.87
12.3	− 1.12	− 1.58	− 1.94
12.4	− .12	− .11	− .12

* Based on first set of prices.

The explanation for motion pictures is rather simple, for this is one of the rare cases where the relative price is important enough quantitatively to have a significant effect on the projection. The relative price of motion pictures has increased sharply in recent years, and the slackening of this increase implicit in the projections of the relative prices leads to the projected upsurge in expenditures. To explain the "take-off" of domestic services, however, is more elusive. The relative price of domestic services has also increased substantially in the postwar period, and the price projections perhaps do not reflect this as strongly as they might. The quantitative impact of price, however, is not nearly as great as for motion pictures. The explanation appears

Table 4.8. Projections of Personal Consumption Expenditures in 1970 and 1975
(Eleven Groups and Durables, Nondurables, and Services)

Group	1958 dollars per capita			Growth rate (percent)	
	1964	1970*	1975*	1964–1970	1970–1975
Automobiles and parts	124.89	143.22	159.10	2.3	2.1
Furniture and household equipment	121.73	147.99	168.28	3.3	2.6
Other durable goods	41.00	53.96	65.88	4.7	4.1
Food and beverages	449.37	508.82	563.60	2.1	2.1
Clothing and shoes	162.71	174.44	185.48	1.2	1.2
Gasoline and oil	68.52	82.39	93.95	3.1	2.7
Other nondurable goods	186.12	223.38	257.99	3.1	2.9
Housing	285.90	346.77	404.90	3.3	3.1
Household operation	122.62	159.65	190.89	4.5	3.6
Transportation	57.37	69.82	80.96	3.3	3.0
Other services	324.38	411.70	498.51	4.1	3.9
Durables	287.62	345.17	393.26	3.1	2.6
Nondurables	866.72	989.03	1101.02	2.2	2.2
Services	790.27	987.94	1175.26	3.8	3.5
Total PCE†	1965.47	2322.07	2669.30	2.8	2.8

* Based on first set of prices.
† Components do not add to total PCE because of rounding.

instead to be in the fairly large short-run response to a change in total PCE. But, in view of the postwar behavior of expenditures for this item, this is also rather hard to rationalize.

In addition to 9.8a, it will be noted that growth rates (see Table 4.6) between 1964 and 1970 of 6 percent or more are projected for private hospitals and sanitariums (6.6), air travel (8.3c), durable toys and sports equipment (9.4), commercial participant amusements (9.10), pari-mutuel betting (9.11), and higher education (10.2). Of these, only 9.10 appears to be out of line with recent experience. The utilities, 5.8a, 5.8b, and 5.9, are projected to grow between 4.0 and 5.5 percent per year, as are also expenditures on radio and television sets (9.5). The large housing items, 4.1 and 4.2, are expected to grow at more modest rates, but still in excess of total PCE. Tobacco expenditures will just about keep pace with total PCE, but food and alcoholic beverages are expected to fall a little short. Expenditures on automobiles are also expected to lag behind the growth of the economy, but the autos sold will be more costly to operate. Furniture expenditures have an unusual pattern in that they are projected to decelerate appreciably between 1970 and 1975.

Generally the goods subject to habit formation have the highest projected growth rates, which is consistent, of course, with their typically higher long-run PCE elasticities. Comparing the growth rates between 1970 and 1975 with those between 1964 and 1970, there is no apparent pattern between habit formation and higher growth rates between 1970 and 1975, which might have been expected *a priori*. Holding relative prices constant after 1970, however, may upset any pattern that might be implicit.

To return to Table 4.6 for a moment, it will be observed that, on the whole, the projections are insensitive to the relative prices. About the only major exceptions to this are purchased food (1.2) and, as we have already noted, motion pictures (9.8a).

III. Predictions of Personal Consumption Expenditures for 1965

Since the only true test of an econometric model is to confront it with data that were not used in estimation, the data for 1965 were withheld in order to provide a forecasting test of the equations. The results are tabulated in Table 4.9. In analyzing these predictions, it would be misleading to compare directly the actual predicted levels; a more meaningful and stringent test is to compare the predicted change between 1964 and 1965 with the actual change. These values are given in columns three and four of the table.

Inspection of the table shows that with respect to *direction of change*, the equations correctly predict 61 of the 63 increases, and four of the 17 decreases.[5] This means that compared to naïve forecasting, that is, forecasting the 1964 level, our model does better in 65 of the 82 cases. With respect to levels, 48 are too high, 31 are too low, and three are correct.[6]

The largest overprediction is for food consumed at home (1.1), where the prediction is about $7.00 too high. If recent past experience is any guide, however, the 1964 figure will probably be revised upward. Other large over-forecasts are for 1.2 (purchased meals), 5.1 (furniture), 5.10 (domestic services), 8.1d (gasoline and oil), and 11.0 (religious and welfare expenditures), where the forecasts are all a dollar or more too high. Of these, 5.10 and 11.0 are the most disturbing, since substantial increases are predicted in the face of actual decline.

The largest underprediction is for new cars and net purchases of used cars, the forecast being only a little more than half the actual increase of nearly $20. In assessing this substantial discrepancy, however, it should be kept in mind

[5] A "no change" for the actual is excluded.
[6] The predictions have been made to add up.

Table 4.9. Predictions for 1965 (per capita 1958 dollars)

Item	Level		Change	
	Predicted	Actual	Predicted	Actual
1.0	62.09	61.99	1.70	1.60
1.1	340.73	332.72	15.17	7.16
1.2	66.93	65.13	4.04	2.24
1.3	8.18	7.31	.86	−.01
1.4	5.16	4.43	.28	−.45
1.5	36.26	36.77	.02	.53
2.1	25.52	24.50	1.12	.10
2.2	1.39	1.38	.09	.08
2.3	146.23	147.16	6.29	7.22
2.4	.37	.37	.07	.07
2.5⎫ 2.6⎭	17.11	17.06	.59	.54
2.7	15.11	15.69	.75	1.33
2.8	2.53	2.34	.24	.05
3.1	21.49	21.74	1.33	1.58
3.2	14.65	13.89	.76	.00
4.1	198.30	197.30	7.98	6.98
4.2	80.47	80.24	4.72	4.49
4.3	9.66	9.60	−.13	−.19
4.4	9.18	9.26	.33	.41
5.1	32.40	31.00	2.87	1.47
5.2	34.07	35.58	.40	1.91
5.3	11.51	11.64	.46	.59
5.4	31.86	31.49	2.33	1.96
5.5	20.35	20.46	1.36	1.47
5.6	22.36	21.53	1.32	.49
5.7	7.25	6.89	.51	.15
5.8a	33.53	33.11	1.65	1.23
5.8b	19.18	18.53	.89	.24
5.8c	7.79	7.84	.19	.24
5.8d	25.60	25.91	.94	1.25
5.9	31.33	31.95	1.81	2.43
5.10	18.50	16.06	1.70	−.74
5.11	12.12	11.72	.80	.40
6.1	24.24	24.35	1.25	1.36
6.2	5.28	5.60	.21	.53
6.3	31.59	32.22	1.04	1.67
6.4	11.65	11.54	.50	.39
6.5	5.58	5.69	.18	.29
6.6	34.10	34.03	2.22	2.15
6.7	8.33	8.41	.35	.43
7.1	5.25	5.81	.00	.69
7.2	7.73	7.75	.58	.60
7.3	29.73	31.71	.94	2.92
7.4	21.56	21.27	.82	.53
7.5	10.40	10.41	.24	.25
7.6	8.13	7.98	.22	.07
7.7	5.97	5.81	.22	.06

(continued)

Table 4.9 (*continued*)

Item	Level		Change	
	Predicted	Actual	Predicted	Actual
8.1a	128.10	136.96	11.04	19.90
8.1b	17.56	17.08	1.12	.64
8.1c	28.15	28.19	1.45	1.49
8.1d	74.44	73.29	3.14	1.99
8.1e	2.12	2.08	.14	.10
8.1f	10.54	10.15	.48	.09
8.2a	5.69	5.28	.30	−.11
8.2b	2.57	2.46	.80	−.03
8.2c	.54	.54	−.02	−.02
8.3a	1.41	1.21	.08	−.12
8.3b	1.60	1.54	.03	−.03
8.3c	5.04	5.08	.59	.63
8.3d	.20	.17	.03	.00
9.1	9.35	9.28	.40	.33
9.2	13.06	12.70	.23	−.13
9.3	17.58	17.31	.95	.68
9.4	15.86	15.03	1.76	.93
9.5	31.25	31.69	3.25	3.69
9.6	5.14	5.22	.38	.46
9.7	4.50	4.63	.22	.35
9.8a	3.05	3.34	−.51	−.22
9.8b	2.00	1.81	.11	−.08
9.8c	1.47	1.44	.03	.00
9.9	3.90	3.84	.02	−.04
9.10	6.43	6.31	.00	−.12
9.11	3.43	3.21	.27	.05
9.12	8.14	1.98	.37	.21
10.1	9.64	9.32	.33	.01
10.2	8.14	7.84	.58	.28
10.3	4.77	4.66	.07	−.04
11.0	28.16	25.99	1.55	−.62
12.1	14.73	15.13	.59	.99
12.2	6.85	7.18	.28	.61
12.3	−6.60	−6.35	−.39	−.14
12.4	−.79	−.65	−.12	.02

that 1965 was the best auto year in history and came on the heels of three successive boom years for Detroit which had increased car stocks to a record level in 1964 relative to income. Thus the $20 per capita increase in auto expenditures in 1965 was more than would normally be expected. Other substantial underpredictions are for 5.9 (telephone, telegraph, and wireless) and 7.3 (financial services furnished without payment).

On the brighter side, the forecasts for 2.2 (shoe repairs) are right on target, and those for 2.5, 2.6 (clothing upkeep and laundering in establishments, respectively), 5.8c (water), 7.2 (bank service charges, and so on), 8.1c (auto repair, and so on), 7.5 (legal services), and 8.1e (bridge, tunnel, ferry, and road tolls) are within $.05 of the actual change. After food and autos, the forecasts for the next two largest items, 2.3 (clothing) and 4.1 (space rental value of owner-occupied housing), although each is about $1.00 off, are quite good when viewed in relative terms. There are numerous others that also fall into this category. In particular, it should be noted that the equation for 9.8a (motion pictures) correctly anticipates the decrease in expenditures in 1965 (though it overdoes it). A sharp increase in the relative price is the principal reason for the decline.

As summary statistics for measuring the accuracy of the predictions, we have calculated the R^2 and Theil U between actual and predicted changes. The categories have been weighted by their respective (1965) budget shares in computing these statistics in order to compensate for the largest category being many times larger than the smallest. The R^2 is .88 and the Theil U is .28. The weighted R^2 thus is quite high for changes.

As a whole, the results from the accuracy analysis of the predictions for 1965 are favorable to the set of equations. Despite a few large errors and taken in conjunction with the results for broader groups of expenditure reported in the next section, they add to our confidence in the projections for 1970 and 1975, although it should be mentioned that they also tend to confirm our earlier reservations about the projections for domestic services (5.10) and 9.8a (motion pictures). To forestall any tendency to smugness, however, we must remember that no model can be adequately tested by data for only one year.

IV. Demand Equations for Broader Expenditures Groups

Although the breakdown of consumption into the 82 categories listed in Chapter 3 will probably be most useful in practical forecasting, it is of interest to consider broader classes of expenditures. To do so is also necessary in connection with the analyses of Chapter 5, where an additive dynamic model of consumer's choice is implemented, and where computational considerations limit the number of items rather severely. The nonadditive results of this section are therefore meant in part for comparison with the additive results reported in section VI of Chapter 5.

The Office of Business Economics regularly publishes data in current and constant dollars for 11 expenditure groups.[7] Each of these groups (which

[7] For very recent years these are available quarterly, but there are not yet enough quarterly observations for use with our models.

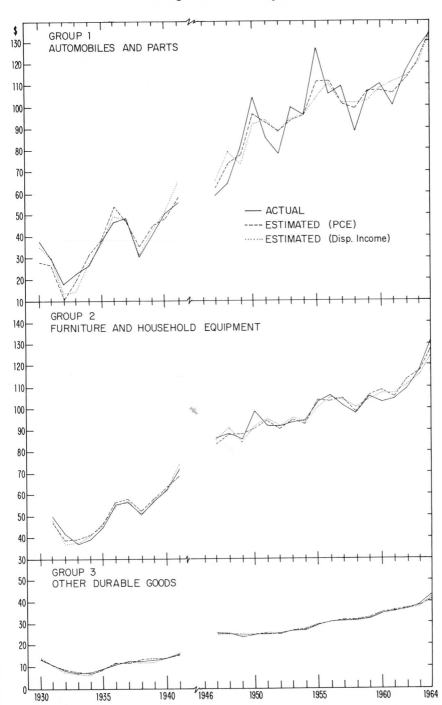

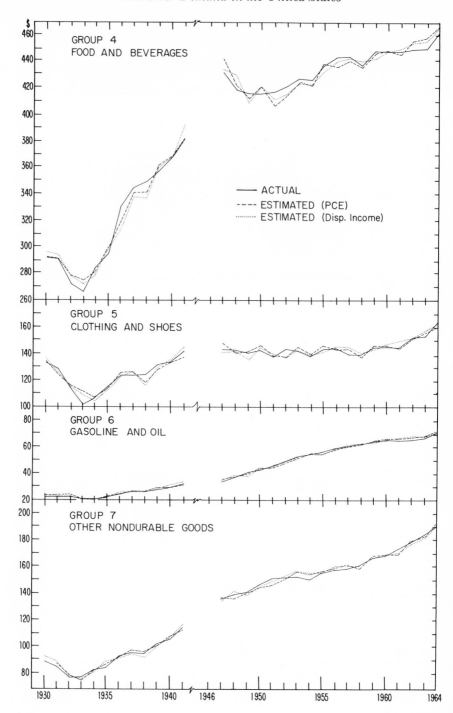

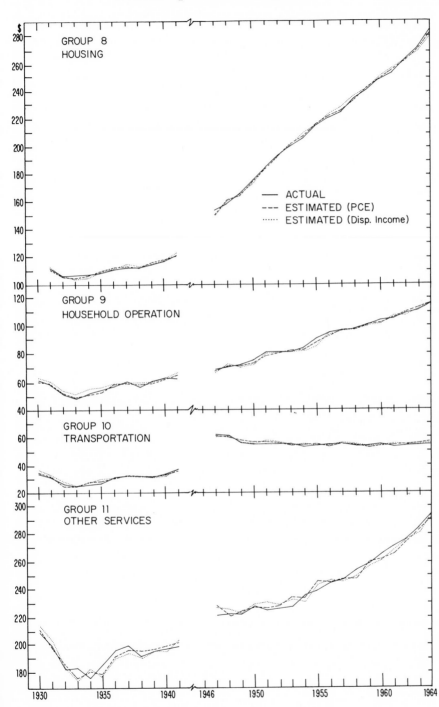

combine the 82 minor items) is composed entirely of durables, of nondurables, or of services, and in addition classifies expenditures by broad purposes. Thus transportation expenditures appear separately under durables (automobiles and parts), under nondurables (gasoline and oil), and under services.

Since it is easier to experiment with 11 items than with 82 we have run the equations with two different indicators of purchasing power: total PCE used throughout Chapter 2, and disposable personal income (DPI).[8] Apart from this variation we have used the basic state-adjustment model of Chapter 1 (some experiments with a flow-adjustment model will be briefly reported below); in particular, consumption and income are per capita in 1958 dollars, and prices are deflated as before. The period of observation is also the same. The final results using total PCE are given in Tables 4.10 and 4.11, and those using DPI in Tables 4.12 and 4.13. Charts similar to those presented in Chapter 3 for the 82 commodities are shown for PCE and also for DPI.

It will be seen from Table 4.10 and also from the group charts that there is not much difference between the PCE and the DPI equations as regards goodness of fit and serial correlation. Except for automobiles and clothing the fits are close in both cases, and the Durbin–Watson coefficients are in the acceptable range. PCE does better with automobiles, and DPI with clothing, but the differences in fit are small and cancel each other. From Chapter 3, we know that for these two items a satisfactory explanation is hard to obtain.

Some differences do appear, however, in the structural coefficients tabulated in Tables 4.11 and 4.13. Thus for DPI there are three cases in which δ had to be constrained (twice to zero and once to two) and one other (furniture) where it was unreasonably high. The δ's obtained with PCE are generally more plausible, though also rather high in the case of furniture and other durables. The β's estimated in the two sets of equations agree well with each other, except that for clothing the PCE equation shows inventory adjustment, while in the DPI model β is virtually zero. In neither set does "other durables" behave as a durable on our definition, but this agrees with the results of Chapter 3.[9]

We have also made projections for 1965, 1966, and 1967 from the two sets of 11 equations based on actual values for the lagged dependent variable and with additivity imposed according to the method of Chapter 2. The results, shown in Table 4.14, are interesting enough to be discussed in some detail. For automobiles the DPI equation is consistently closer to the mark; in fact, the PCE equation is too low in each of the three years. For furniture, on the other hand, the DPI equation performs very poorly indeed, while the PCE

---

[8] This was done partly in response to the doubts expressed by Perry (1967) concerning our emphasis on total PCE.

[9] Other durables consist of ophthalmic products, orthopedic appliances, wheel goods, durable toys, sports equipment, boats, and pleasure aircraft.

Table 4.10. Coefficients for Estimating Equation,* Nonadditive Model (United States: Eleven Groups)

Group	A_0	A_1	A_2	A_3	A_4	A_5	A_6	A_7	R^2	S_e	D.W.
Automobiles and parts		.4366 (.0936)	.2124 (.0290)	.0326 (.0057)			−14.8080 (3.3070)		.965	7.06	2.21
Furniture and household equipment	−27.17 (7.58)	.2510 (.1977)	.1151 (.0146)	.0657 (.0174)				.5269 (.2249)	.989	3.05	2.04
Other durable goods		.7042 (.1465)	.0177 (.0042)	.0109 (.0043)	−13.4869 (4.7057)	−8.3604 (2.6474)	3.0602 (.9338)		.996	.69	1.97
Food and beverages		.8874 (.0426)	.2039 (.0244)	.0270 (.0114)			12.2152 (2.3743)		.992	5.91	1.64
Clothing and shoes	17.01 (8.68)	.7845 (.0983)	.1100 (.0161)	.0075 (.0045)					.947	3.37	2.21
Gasoline and oil		.8795 (.0284)	.0173 (.0036)	.0064 (.0013)	−6.1115 (2.5768)	−2.2525 (.6068)			.998	.79	1.88
Other nondurable goods	−6.16 (3.89)	.7211 (.1383)	.0831 (.0087)	.0318 (.0158)				.3169 (.2309)	.998	1.83	2.10
Housing		.9265 (.0274)	.0221 (.0065)	.0157 (.0024)	−10.6610 (5.6020)	−7.5623 (.8084)		.3028 (.2472)	.999	1.40	1.97
Household operation		.9891 (.1132)	.0365 (.0091)	.0034 (.0069)	−31.0928 (21.3285)	−2.9015 (1.5143)			.997	1.28	1.83
Transportation	57.61 (16.66)	.2034 (.2145)	.0144 (.0058)	.0125 (.0041)	−40.9112 (7.4550)	−35.5118 (11.1098)	−8.9186 (2.7784)		.996	.94	1.68
Other services		.7081 (.0973)	.0955 (.0179)	.0447 (.0148)			7.2776 (3.7608)		.987	4.04	2.00

* $q_t = A_0 + A_1 q_{t-1} + A_2 \Delta x_t + A_3 x_{t-1} + A_4 \Delta p_t + A_5 p_{t-1} + A_6 d_t + A_7 z_t.$

Table 4.11. Structural Coefficients, Nonadditive Model (United States: Eleven Groups)

Group	α	β	δ		Income Derivative	Income Elasticity	Price Derivative	Price Elasticity
Automobiles and parts		-.6182 (.1533)	.1662 (.0415)	SR	.2731 (.0430)	5.06		
				LR	.0579 (.0021)	1.07		
Furniture and household equipment	-54.41 (10.02)	-.3992 (.2401)	.7983 (.3453)	SR	.1315 (.0233)	2.23		
				LR	.0877 (.0034)	1.49		
Other durable goods		.5512 (.6548)	.8983 (.8273)	SR	.0143 (.0060)	.88	-10.922 (4.963)	-.56
				LR	.0370 (.0048)	2.27	-28.262 (7.248)	-1.45
Food and beverages		.0225 (.0256)	.1419 (.0659)	SR	.2018 (.0260)	.72		
				LR	.2398 (.0136)	.85		
Clothing and shoes	270.15 (138.37)	-.1710 (.0833)	.0706 (.0503)	SR	.1190 (.0166)	1.20		
				LR	.0348 (.0101)	.35		
Gasoline and oil		.3236 (.2929)	.4518 (.3104)	SR	.0151 (.0038)	.48	-5.305 (2.741)	-.14
				LR	.0530 (.0035)	1.69	-18.691 (3.161)	-.48

Other nondurable goods	−15.15 (3.95)	.1483 (.1096)	.4724 (.2812)	SR	.0781 (.0099)	.81		
				LR	.1139 (.0042)	1.18		
Housing		1.0229 (1.0795)	1.0992 (1.0947)	SR	.0148 (.0067)	.12	−7.142 (5.813)	−.05
				LR	.2135 (.0587)	1.68	−102.95 (33.60)	−.66
Household operation		.0869 (.1906)	.0979 (.3009)	SR	.0350 (.0080)	.62	−29.805 (20.444)	−.39
				LR	.3111 (2.5852)	5.53	−264.98 (2637.0)	−3.44
Transportation	62.44 (67.07)	.2097 (1.7344)	1.5336 (2.2587)	SR	.0135 (.0101)	.41	−38.483 (11.272)	−.82
				LR	.0157 (.0026)	.47	−44.579 (4.245)	−.95
Other services		.2687 (.2358)	.6105 (.3511)	SR	.0857 (.0228)	.53		
				LR	.1531 (.0023)	.94		

Table 4.12. Coefficients for Estimating Equation* Using Disposable Income, Nonadditive Model (United States: Eleven Groups)

Group	A_0	A_1	A_2	A_3	A_4	A_5	A_6	A_7	R^2	S_e	D.W.
Automobiles and parts		.2530 (.1490)	.1197 (.0249)	.0558 (.0181)	-56.2812 (53.9492)	-26.2368 (22.2887)	-11.3804 (6.2678)		.949	8.93	2.21
Furniture and household equipment	-20.07 (8.55)	-.2534 (.2150)	.0762 (.0088)	.0862 (.0159)			-7.1678 (3.2415)	.7699 (.2821)	.989	3.04	1.60
Other durable goods		.8368 (.1027)	.0139 (.0019)	.0068 (.0026)	-13.3010 (3.6947)	-6.4465 (1.7509)	3.0026 (.8279)		.997	.66	1.81
Food and beverages		.8865 (.0460)	.1268 (.0170)	.0263 (.0114)			11.5033 (2.8405)		.991	6.46	1.75
Clothing and shoes		.7833 (.0645)	.0718 (.0087)	.0171 (.0054)			6.5771 (2.4057)		.956	3.11	2.21
Gasoline and oil	-4.39 (1.05)	.8529 (.0303)	.0134 (.0021)	.0080 (.0015)					.998	.76	1.96
Other nondurable goods		1.0087 (.0026)	.0523 (.0047)						.998	1.79	1.78
Housing		.9434 (.0323)	.0129 (.0021)	A_2	-6.5679 (.7647)	A_4		.1118 (.1997)	.999	1.54	1.75
Household operation		1.0196 (.0042)	.0170 (.0047)		-43.3828 (10.4839)				.995	1.64	1.61
Transportation	53.49 (13.96)	.2620 (.1766)	.0111 (.0032)	.0092 (.0029)	-36.5772 (7.0661)	-30.2902 (8.9040)	-9.1384 (2.4707)		.995	.94	1.78
Other services		.8955 (.0304)	.0717 (.0112)	.0154 (.0045)					.985	4.25	1.76

* $q_t = A_0 + A_1 q_{t-1} + A_2 \Delta x_t + A_3 x_{t-1} + A_4 \Delta p_t + A_5 p_{t-1} + A_6 d_t + A_7 z_t$.

188

Table 4.13. Structural Coefficients Using Disposable Income, Nonadditive Model (United States: Eleven Groups)

Group	α	δ		Income Derivative	Income Elasticity	Price Derivative	Price Elasticity
Automobiles and parts	−20.66 (7.79)	.6079 (1.1392)	SR	.1465 (.0423)	2.92	−68.896 (85.604)	−.87
			LR	.0747 (.0145)	1.49	−35.122 (26.514)	−.44
Furniture and household equipment		2.6020 (1.1762)	SR	.0887 (.0265)	1.62		
			LR	.0688 (.0039)	1.25		
Other durable goods		.6397 (.4663)	SR	.0115 (.0026)	.76	−10.973 (3.721)	−.56
			LR	.0414 (.0112)	2.73	−39.506 (17.685)	−2.03
Food and beverages		.2311 (.1128)	SR	.1205 (.0180)	.46		
			LR	.2314 (.0100)	.89		
Clothing and shoes		.2698 (.1156)	SR	.0709 (.0100)	.77		
			LR	.0787 (.0024)	.86		

(continued)

189

Table 4.13 (continued)

Group	α	β	δ		Income Derivative	Income Elasticity	Price Derivative	Price Elasticity
Gasoline and oil	-5.58 (1.29)	.6911 (.2231)	.8498 (.2421)	SR	.0101 (.0022)	.35		
				LR	.0542 (.0031)	1.86		
Other nondurable goods	*	.0086 (.0026)	0	SR	.0521 (.0047)	.59		
Housing		1.9417 (.0342)	2	SR	.0066 (.0011)	.06	-3.3797 (.4193)	-.02
				LR	.2271 (.1136)	1.96	-115.966 (61.967)	-.74
Household operation	*	.0914 (.0041)	0	SR	.0169 (.0047)	.32	-42.962 (10.358)	-.59
Transportation	59.99 (50.23)	.2437 (1.2565)	1.4133 (1.6262)	SR	.0103 (.0053)	.33	-33.966 (10.425)	-.73
				LR	.0124 (.0023)	.40	-41.042 (4.368)	-.88
Other services		.1302 (.0677)	.2405 (.0955)	SR	.0676 (.0121)	.45		
				LR	.1473 (.0051)	.97		

* Indicates that α is indeterminate.

Table 4.14. Comparative Forecasting Performance of the Eleven Equations Involving PCE or DPI

Group	1965			1966			1967		
	Actual	PCE	DPI	Actual	PCE	DPI	Actual	PCE	DPI
Automobile and parts	156.22	143.89	145.41	156.92	153.94	157.54	152.67	148.92	155.23
Furniture and household equipment	140.81	141.14	138.12	153.87	152.28	140.58	158.20	156.44	141.05
Other durable goods	45.22	45.40	46.04	51.29	48.27	48.99	52.23	52.71	53.80
Food and beverages	473.30	483.65	482.70	481.92	493.56	494.51	484.64	495.76	497.08
Clothing and shoes	171.64	172.17	175.06	182.82	176.88	181.77	182.81	182.16	187.87
Gasoline and oil	74.00	74.25	74.76	77.70	77.52	78.24	81.36	80.59	81.37
Other nondurable goods	198.88	199.92	198.92	207.19	208.88	207.30	210.93	214.28	212.54
Housing	298.57	296.57	296.16	308.25	307.24	308.24	314.89	316.56	317.88
Household operation	119.22	121.56	120.06	124.42	125.79	124.53	128.57	129.52	128.27
Transportation	56.53	56.81	56.57	57.89	57.90	57.76	61.27	58.26	58.04
Other services	309.37	307.04	308.35	319.93	318.99	320.63	333.97	326.43	327.27

equation is reasonably close. The defects of the DPI equation may be linked to the negative coefficient of q_{t-1} in the estimating equation, which in turn leads to the high estimate of δ mentioned already.[10] For other durables the PCE equations have a slight edge, as is also true for food where both equations give rise to consistent overprojections. In the case of clothing and of gasoline there is not much to choose between PCE and DPI, but in other nondurables DPI has a distinct advantage. For housing PCE is a little better, but for household operation and transportation DPI is. In the case of other services DPI is a little closer in every year.

Consequently, no clear-cut conclusion emerges from these projections. DPI is better in five cases and worse in four cases, with two standoffs. However, DPI is so poor in one case that the net effect can only be called a tie. It appears, therefore, that there are no major objections from an empirical point of view to our emphasis on PCE.[11]

Finally, we have to report briefly on another experiment with the 11 expenditure groups. This involved a double-logarithmic variant of the flow-adjustment model discussed in section V of Chapter 1. The linear version described in the equations can easily be turned into a double-logarithmic one by the substitution mentioned at the end of that section. Unfortunately the results were disappointing. For none of the 11 double-logarithmic equations was the fit as good as for the corresponding linear state-adjustment equations, and a number of anomalies appeared. We have therefore not pursued this approach.

---

[10] This is the case, referred to in footnote 15 of Chapter 1, where we were tempted to assume $A_1 = 0$.

[11] In Chapter 6 it will be shown that for the cross-section analysis PCE is definitely to be preferred, but this conclusion does not necessarily carry over to the time-series analysis.

5

An Additive Dynamic Model

It was noted in Chapter 2 that our dynamic model is not additive in the sense that projections from it necessarily add up to total expenditure. Although the material significance of this defect can be overemphasized, it is of considerable theoretical interest to have a model that is in line with the theory of consumer's choice. The present chapter, therefore, extends the notions of Chapter 1 to a set of additive dynamic demand functions. The additivity is achieved by deriving the functions from a quadratic utility function (in which state variables as well as flows appear explicitly as arguments) and then jointly estimating the functions subject to the usual budget constraint.[1]

A less obvious defect of the nonadditive model is also overcome by this model. The identifying restriction on δ in the nonadditive model forces the ratio between the long-run and short-run derivatives for prices to be the same as for income. This is an unreasonable restriction in many instances and therefore worth removing.

The first two sections of this chapter derive the model and discuss methods of estimation. Empirical results then follow in sections III and IV for the United States, Canada, Sweden, and Holland.[2] Estimates of the marginal utility of total expenditure for the four countries are presented in section V, and forecasts for the United States for 1965 are given in section VI. The chapter concludes with an evaluation of the model in section VII.

I. Derivation of the Model

Consider a consumer who can purchase n commodities and whose preferences may be described by a utility function of the form[3]

$$(1) \qquad \phi(q, s) = q'a + s'b + \tfrac{1}{2}q'Aq + q'Bs + \tfrac{1}{2}s'Cs$$

[1] The model presented here was first discussed by Houthakker in a paper delivered at the Econometric Society meetings in New York in 1961; an abstract was published in *Econometrica* (1962). We are indebted to Richard W. Parks for useful comments on an earlier version of this chapter, presented at the San Francisco meetings of the Econometric Society in 1966.

[2] We had intended also to present results for the United Kingdom for the period 1900–1964, but difficulties, which did not become apparent until just before the manuscript went to press, in splicing the Stone–Rowe series for 1900–1955 [Stone and Rowe (1966)] with past 1955 data from *National Income and Expenditure (Blue Book)* precluded their presentation here.

[3] The utility function is of course ordinal, not cardinal; a monotonic transformation does not affect the demand functions, but it will change the marginal utility of income.

where q and s are $(n \times 1)$ vectors of flows (purchases) and "state variables," respectively, a and b are constant vectors and A, B, and C are constant matrices; q and s are functions of time, which is treated as continuous. The interpretation of the state variables is the same as in Chapter 1, and as before there is one state variable for each flow. In this chapter we shall also assume that both A and B are diagonal and nonsingular, although this is not essential to the theory. This restriction amounts to assuming that the underlying preference ordering is directly additive;[4] it is, in fact, a dynamic version of the quadratic utility function proposed by Gossen in 1854.

As with the nonadditive model, we assume the state variables to be related to the flows through

(2) $$\dot{s} = q - Ds,$$

where D is also assumed to be diagonal and nonsingular. The final equation in the model is the budget constraint

(3) $$p'q = x.$$

Maximizing (1) subject to (3), we obtain

(4) $$a + Aq + Bs = \lambda p$$

where the L.H.S. represents the marginal utilities of the flows and λ the marginal utility of income. Solving for q, we find that

(5) $$q = A^{-1}(\lambda p - a - Bs).$$

Since the state variables are generally unobservable, we proceed, as before, to eliminate them by making use of equation (2). (That λ is not directly observable either can be ignored for the moment.) Replacing λp by p^* and differentiating (5) with respect to time, we have

(6) $$\dot{q} = A^{-1}(\dot{p}^* - B\dot{s}),$$

which upon using (2) becomes

(7) $$\dot{q} = A^{-1}[\dot{p}^* - B(q - Ds)].$$

From (4) we have

(8) $$s = B^{-1}(p^* - a - Aq),$$

hence

(9) $$\dot{q} = A^{-1}\{\dot{p}^* - B[q - DB^{-1}(p^* - a - Aq)]\},$$

which can be simplified to

(10) $$\dot{q} = -A^{-1}Da - (A^{-1}B + D)q + A^{-1}\dot{p}^* + A^{-1}Dp^*$$

(using the fact that $DB^{-1} = B^{-1}D$ since D and B are both diagonal).

[4] See Houthakker (1960).

Expression (10) is a system of first order differential equations in q and p^* Looking at the equation for the ith commodity $(i = 1, \ldots, n)$

(11) $\dot{q}_i = A_{ii}^{-1} D_{ii} a_i - (A_{ii}^{-1} B_{ii} + D_{ii}) q_i + A_{ii}^{-1} \dot{p}_{ii}^* + A_{ii}^{-1} D_{ii} p_{ii}^*,$

we see that $\dot{q}_i$ depends only on q_i itself and its own relative price in addition to λ. This of course follows from the independence (diagonality) assumptions on A, B, and D. Income, it will be observed, does not enter the equations directly, but only indirectly through λ, the marginal utility of income. In fact by multiplying both sides of (5) by p' we find that

(12) $$p'q = x = \lambda p' A^{-1} p - p' A^{-1} a - p' A^{-1} Bs$$

and consequently

(13) $$\lambda = \frac{x + p' A^{-1} a + p' A^{-1} Bs}{p' A^{-1} p}$$

so that λ, and hence every q_i, is a linear function of income.[5] This is a well known property of the quadratic preference ordering, valid also in the dynamic case.

It is evidently desirable that the differential equation (11) converge to a long-run solution $\hat{q}_i$ if prices and income are held constant. The conditions for this convergence are somewhat complicated, however, for even if prices and income are constant the state variables will change, by virtue of (2), as long as $q \neq \hat{q}$. Hence λ, which is a function of s according to (13), will only settle down at the same time as q so that p^* is not constant. It is therefore more convenient to consider the differential equation for s, the advantage being that λ, according to (13), is a linear function of s which is itself independent of λ. In the appendix to this chapter a sufficient condition for the stability of (11) is shown to be

(14) $A_{ii} < 0 \quad \text{and} \quad A_{ii} D_{ii} + B_{ii} < 0.$

The interpretation of this condition is immediate. The coefficients A_{ii} determine the marginal utilities of the flows, which are normally decreasing, so that the first part of the condition agrees with static theory. The depreciation rates D_{ii} are normally positive; consequently the second part puts a bound on the B_{ii}, which relate the marginal utilities of the flows to the state variables. If B_{ii} is negative, which is true for durables, the second part is vacuous; it is important only for habit-forming commodities, and says that habit

---

[5] In this respect and also in the linear dependence of q on s the additive model agrees with the basic model of Chapter 1. Note, however, that in the additive model q is not a linear function of p. The model of Chapter 1 may therefore be regarded as a linearized approximation of the additive model; as a result of the linearization, additivity is lost.

formation should not be so strong as to offset the combined effect of diminishing marginal utility and the depreciation rate. If the second part of the stability condition does not hold, we may say that addiction is present.

The procedure for deriving a finite approximation of this model is the same as was followed for the nonadditive model, so we will give only the essential steps there, using the same notation as in Chapter 1. Integrating (4) and (2) over the interval from t to $t + 1$, we have

(15) $$\bar{q}_t = A^{-1}(\bar{p}_t^* - a - B\bar{s}_t)$$

(16) $$\Delta^* s_t = \bar{q}_t - D\bar{s}_t,$$

so that

(17) $$\bar{q}_{t+1} - \bar{q}_t = A^{-1}[\bar{p}_{t+1}^* - \bar{p}_t^* - B(\bar{s}_{t+1} - \bar{s}_t)].$$

Then, using the approximation discussed in Chapter 1

(18) $$\bar{s}_{t+1} - \bar{s}_t \cong \tfrac{1}{2}(\Delta^* s_{t+1} + \Delta^* s_t),$$

we can write (14) as

(19) $$\begin{aligned}
\bar{q}_{t+1} - \bar{q}_t &= A^{-1}[\bar{p}_{t+1}^* - \bar{p}_t^* - \tfrac{1}{2}B(\Delta^* s_{t+1} + \Delta^* s_t)] \\
&= A^{-1}\{\bar{p}_{t+1}^* - \bar{p}_t^* - \tfrac{1}{2}B[\bar{q}_{t+1} + \bar{q}_t - D(\bar{s}_{t+1} + \bar{s}_t)]\} \\
&= A^{-1}\{\bar{p}_{t+1}^* - \bar{p}_t^* - \tfrac{1}{2}B \\
&\qquad [\bar{q}_{t+1} + \bar{q}_t - DB^{-1}(\bar{p}_{t+1}^* + \bar{p}_t^* - 2a - A(\bar{q}_{t+1} + \bar{q}_t))]\}
\end{aligned}$$

[since $\bar{s}_t = B^{-1}(\bar{p}_t^* - a - A\bar{q}_t)$].

Hence

(20) $$\begin{aligned}
[I + \tfrac{1}{2}(A^{-1}B + D)]\bar{q}_{t+1} &= -A^{-1}Da + [I - \tfrac{1}{2}(A^{-1}B + D)]\bar{q}_t \\
&\quad + A^{-1}(I + \tfrac{1}{2}D)\bar{p}_{t+1}^* - A^{-1}(I - \tfrac{1}{2}D)\bar{p}_t^*
\end{aligned}$$

or (removing the bars and replacing $\bar{p}_t^*$ by $\lambda_t p_t$)

(21) $$q_t = K_0 + K_1 q_{t-1} + K_2 \lambda_t p_t + K_3 \lambda_{t-1} p_{t-1},$$

where

(22) $$K_0 = -[I + \tfrac{1}{2}(A^{-1}B + D)]^{-1}A^{-1}Da$$

(23) $$K_1 = [I + \tfrac{1}{2}(A^{-1}B + D)]^{-1}[I - \tfrac{1}{2}(A^{-1}B + D)]$$

(24) $$K_2 = [I + \tfrac{1}{2}(A^{-1}B + D)]^{-1}A^{-1}(I + \tfrac{1}{2}D)$$

(25) $$K_3 = -[I + \tfrac{1}{2}(A^{-1}B + D)]^{-1}A^{-1}(I - \tfrac{1}{2}D).$$

Since A, B, and D are all diagonal matrices, expression (21) can also be viewed as the equation for the ith good, with $K_0, \ldots, K_3$ (as well as A, B, and D) treated as scalars.

Equation (21) is the discrete analogue to equation (10), and once estimates of $K_0, \ldots, K_3$ are obtained, equations (22)–(25) can be solved for the structural coefficients (ignoring sampling error):

$$(26) \qquad a = \frac{-K_0}{K_2 + K_3}$$

$$(27) \qquad A = \frac{1 + K_1}{K_2 - K_3}$$

$$(28) \qquad B = -4 \frac{K_1 K_2 + K_3}{(K_2 - K_3)^2}$$

$$(29) \qquad D = 2 \frac{K_2 + K_3}{K_2 - K_3}.$$

It will be noted that, in contrast to the nonadditive model, the depreciation rate, D, is just identified.

SHORT-RUN AND LONG-RUN EFFECTS OF INCOME AND PRICE CHANGES

As with the nonadditive model, a key feature of this model is the distinction between short- and long-run effects when income or price changes. We will derive the income effects first. From (4) and (3), we have in the short run $\left(\text{since } \dfrac{\partial s}{\partial x} = 0\right)$:

$$(30) \qquad A \frac{\partial q}{\partial x} = p \frac{\partial \lambda}{\partial x}$$

$$(31) \qquad p' \frac{\partial q}{\partial x} = 1,$$

so that

$$(32) \qquad \frac{\partial q}{\partial x} = A^{-1} p \frac{\partial \lambda}{\partial x}$$

and

$$(33) \qquad p' \frac{\partial q}{\partial x} = (p' A^{-1} p) \frac{\partial \lambda}{\partial x} = 1.$$

Thus

$$(34) \qquad \frac{\partial \lambda}{\partial x} = (p' A^{-1} p)^{-1},$$

so that

$$(35) \qquad \frac{\partial q}{\partial x} = (p' A^{-1} p)^{-1} A^{-1} p.$$

In long-run equilibrium, we have $\dot{s} = 0$, hence differentiating the equilibrium conditions gives

(36)
$$A \frac{\partial \hat{q}}{\partial x} + B \frac{\partial \hat{s}}{\partial x} = p \frac{\partial \hat{\lambda}}{\partial x},$$

(37)
$$p' \frac{\partial \hat{q}}{\partial x} = 1,$$

(38)
$$\frac{\partial \hat{q}}{\partial x} - D \frac{\partial \hat{s}}{\partial x} = 0,$$

where, as before, the "hats" denote long-run equilibrium values. From (36) and (37)

(39)
$$\frac{\partial \hat{q}}{\partial x} = W^{-1} p \frac{\partial \hat{\lambda}}{\partial x},$$

where $W = A + BD^{-1}$.

Then

(40)
$$p' \frac{\partial \hat{q}}{\partial x} = (p' W^{-1} p) \frac{\partial \hat{\lambda}}{\partial x} = 1,$$

so that

(41)
$$\frac{\partial \hat{q}}{\partial x} = (p' W^{-1} p)^{-1},$$

which when substituted in (39) gives

(42)
$$\frac{\partial \hat{q}}{\partial x} = (p' W^{-1} p)^{-1} W^{-1} p.$$

Comparing (35) and (42), we note that the long-run derivative with respect to income differs from the short-run derivative in that $W^{-1} = (A + BD^{-1})^{-1}$ appears in place of A^{-1}. As to the relation between the two derivatives, we now have a choice of saying that a good is subject to habit formation either if the long-run derivative exceeds the short run or if its B_{ii} is positive; the same is true for inventory adjustment. Unlike the nonadditive model the sign of B_{ii} no longer determines whether the short-run or the long-run derivative is greater. We shall see from the empirical results that it makes more sense to look at the derivatives than at B_{ii}, which is nearly always positive.

Turning to the price derivatives, we have in the short run from (4) and (3)

(43)
$$A \frac{\partial q}{\partial p} = p \frac{\partial \lambda}{\partial p} + \lambda I$$

(44)
$$p' \frac{\partial q}{\partial p} = -q'.$$

Therefore

$$(45) \qquad \frac{\partial q}{\partial p} = A^{-1}\left(p\frac{\partial \lambda}{\partial p} + \lambda I\right)$$

and

$$(46) \qquad p'\frac{\partial q}{\partial p} = (p'A^{-1}p)\frac{\partial \lambda}{\partial p} + \lambda p'A^{-1} = -q'.$$

Hence

$$(47) \qquad \frac{\partial \lambda}{\partial p} = -(p'A^{-1}p)^{-1}q' + (p'A^{-1}p)^{-1}\lambda p'A^{-1},$$

so that

$$(48) \qquad \frac{\partial q}{\partial p} = A^{-1}\{-p[(p'A^{-1}p)^{-1}q' + (p'A^{-1}p)^{-1}\lambda p'A^{-1}] + \lambda I\}$$

$$= \lambda A^{-1} - \lambda(p'A^{-1}p)^{-1}pp'A^{-1} - (p'A^{-1}p)^{-1}A^{-1}pq'$$

$$= \lambda A^{-1} - \lambda(p'A^{-1}p)^{-1}A^{-1}pp'A^{-1} - \frac{\partial q}{\partial x}q'$$

[since $(p'A^{-1}p)^{-1}A^{-1}p = \partial q/\partial x$]. If the last term on the right-hand side in (48) is moved over to the left, the result is an equation for the compensated price derivatives

$$(49) \qquad \frac{\partial q}{\partial p} + \frac{\partial q}{\partial x}q' = \lambda A^{-1} - \lambda(p'A^{-1}p)^{-1}A^{-1}pp'A^{-1}.$$

This expression is symmetric, in accordance with the Slutsky equation. It is not hard to show that the diagonal elements are negative, as they should be.

The expression for the vector of long-run price derivatives is similar to (48) except that (as was the case with the income derivatives) $W^{-1} = (A + BD^{-1})^{-1}$ appears in place of A^{-1}, *viz*:

$$(50) \qquad \frac{\partial \hat{q}}{\partial p} = \lambda W^{-1} - \lambda(p'W^{-1}p)^{-1}W^{-1}pp'W^{-1} - \frac{\partial \hat{q}}{\partial x}q';$$

similarly for the compensated derivatives in the long run:

$$(51) \qquad \frac{\partial \hat{q}}{\partial p} + \frac{\partial \hat{q}}{\partial x}q' = \lambda W^{-1} - \lambda(p'W^{-1}p)^{-1}W^{-1}pp'W^{-1}.$$

Like its short-run counterpart, this matrix is symmetric and negative definite.

Although there is not substitution or complementarity in the utility function because A, B, and D are assumed to be diagonal, it follows from these strong independence assumptions that all commodities are substitutes (in the Slutsky sense) in the short run, that is, all compensated short-run cross-price derivatives must be positive. And this is also true in the long run, because of the stability condition (14) which attributes to W the same properties as to A.

In Chapter 7 saving out of disposable income will be viewed as the acquisition of a nondepreciating asset, which leaves consumption to be implicitly determined as a residual. The additive model of this chapter enables this procedure to be tested. Savings can be included as a commodity and the results then compared with the model where savings are excluded. With saving included, the budget constraint involves disposable income rather than total expenditure. The price of savings is taken to be one. In principle, the interest rate should be included in the price, but to do this would involve developing a theory of saving more complex than we care to undertake for the time being.

The treatment of savings as a commodity rather than as a residual has as a consequence that disposable income is used as an explanatory variable not only for savings, but for all other items as well. It is therefore somewhat at variance with the practice elsewhere in this book (except in the equations reported in Chapter 4, section IV). However, our emphasis on PCE as an explanatory variable is not a matter of principle. The dual treatment of savings may in fact be viewed as a further test on the relative merits of these two explanatory variables.

In one respect the treatment of saving in this chapter does not agree with the main implications of Chapter 7, namely that financial assets have a depreciation rate of zero. Unfortunately, however, this is not possible with the present model since D is required to be nonsingular. This means that the savings results in this chapter do not deserve as much weight as those in Chapter 7.

Finally we have to look one difficulty firmly in the face, and pass on, following the proverbial Scottish preacher's example. The theory of the dynamic preference ordering given here is strictly in terms of a single individual, yet we apply it to entire countries. In so doing we ignore the aggregation problem, on which there is a voluminous literature.[6] Rather than add to this inconclusive discussion we simply state as our opinion that of all the errors likely to be made in demand analysis, the aggregation error is one of the least troublesome. As evidence we cite our lack of success in finding significant demographic variables (see the first edition of this book), most of which would capture distributional effects. A formal discussion of aggregation in dynamic models would lead us much too far afield, even if it were likely to be fruitful. We therefore proceed to matters of greater practical importance.

[6] The best work is still Theil (1954). For a more recent summary see Green (1962).

II. Estimation

Equation (21) is the estimating form of the model, and it will be useful to rewrite it here with an error term:

$$(52) \qquad q_t = K_0 + K_0 q_{t-1} + K_2 \lambda_t p_{t-1} + K_3 \lambda_{t-1} p_{t-1} + u_t$$

where the quantities are per capita and the prices are deflated. Since the coefficient matrices are all diagonal, (52) will be interpreted as the equation for the ith commodity. In doing so, however, it should be kept in mind that, although λ varies through time, it is the same for all commodities for any year.

The idea underlying the estimation of the parameters is quite simple: choose a set of λ's such that the estimated values for the individual items of expenditure add up to total expenditure (or income, if saving is treated as a commodity). Once a set of λ's has been chosen, the parameters of (52) can be estimated as the coefficients in the equation

$$(53) \qquad q_t = K_0 + K_1 q_{t-1} + K_2 p_t^* + K_3 p_{t-1}^* + u_t,$$

where $p_t^* = (\lambda p)_t$ and $p_{t-1}^* = (\lambda p)_{t-1}$. Four methods that we have used to estimate the λ's will now be described.

Method I

First, set $\lambda_t = 1$ for all t and estimate equation (53) for each commodity. If the equations were additive, we would have

$$(54) \qquad \sum_{i=1}^{n} \bar{p}_{it} \hat{q}_{it} = \bar{x}_t,$$

where $\bar{p}_{it}$ is the undeflated price of good i in year t, $\hat{q}_{it}$ is the estimated quantity purchased, and $\bar{x}_t$ is income or total expenditure in current dollars (that is, undeflated). But in view of the budget constraint

$$(55) \qquad \sum_i \bar{p}_{it} q_{it} = \sum_i K_{i0} \bar{p}_{it} + \sum_i K_{i1} \bar{p}_{it} q_{i(t-1)} + \lambda_t \sum_i K_{i2} \bar{p}_{it} p_{it}$$
$$+ \lambda_{t-1} \sum_i K_{i3} \bar{p}_{it} p_{i(t-1)},$$

we have

$$(56) \qquad \lambda_t = \frac{\bar{x}_t - \sum_i K_{0i} \bar{p}_{it} - \sum_i K_{i1} \bar{p}_{it} q_{i(t-1)} - \lambda_{t-1} \sum_i K_{i3} \bar{p}_{it} p_{i(t-1)}}{\sum_i K_{i2} \bar{p}_{it} p_{it}}.$$

Therefore an estimate of λ_t can be obtained from

$$(57) \qquad \hat{\lambda}_t = \frac{x_t - \sum_i \hat{K}_{i0} \bar{p}_{it} - \sum_i \hat{K}_{i1} \bar{p}_{it} q_{i(t-1)} - \hat{\lambda}_{t-1} \sum_i \hat{K}_{i3} \bar{p}_{it} p_{i(t-1)}}{\sum_i \hat{K}_{i2} \bar{p}_{it} p_{it}}.$$

The resulting set of λ's are then used to adjust the prices, and the equations are re-estimated using the adjusted prices, and so on. The process continues, iterating on the λ's, until they converge. The initial value λ_0 is always kept at one, so that λ_t $(t = 1, \ldots, T)$ is expressed as a fraction of λ_0.

Although the process does not necessarily converge, our experience has been that it converges after about 20 iterations. In spite of this, the method proved unworkable because the resulting set of λ's was sometimes meaningless. The λ's estimated by this method are very sensitive to the (legitimate) residuals and, indeed, appear to be dominated by them. Since $\hat{\lambda}_t$ in (57) is a function of $\hat{\lambda}_{t-1}$, any errors in $\hat{\lambda}_t$, particularly those early in the period, can accumulate and become magnified through time. Thus a method of estimating the λ's that is less sensitive to the residuals needed to be devised.

Method II

The second method tried is the same as Method I, except that p divided by total expenditure in constant dollars is used in place of p—that is, the estimating equation is

$$(58) \qquad q_t = K_0 + K_1 q_{t-1} + K_2 \lambda_t^* (p/x)_t + K_3 \lambda_{t-1}^* (p/x)_{t-1} + u_t,$$

where the absence of a bar on the x denotes that constant dollars are involved.[7] However, we now have to use a different symbol for λ because the coefficient by which the prices are multiplied is different; in fact, $\lambda_t^* = \lambda_t x_t$.

This method has proved to be much more successful than Method I, for it has always converged, and the resulting set of λ's has nearly always seemed to make sense. But before finally settling on this method, a third method was tried with a view to minimizing the effect of the (legitimate) residuals.

Method III

This method proceeds by estimating equation (52), as with Method I, for each commodity with $\lambda_t = 1$ for all t, and then estimating the λ's as the coefficients in the following regression:

$$(59) \qquad q_{it} - \hat{K}_{i0} - \hat{K}_{i1} q_{i(t-1)} = \lambda_t \hat{K}_{i2} p_{it} + \lambda_{t-1} \hat{K}_{i3} p_{i(t-1)} + w_t$$

$$i = 1, \ldots, n; t = 1, \ldots, T,$$

where K's are estimated in the regression with $\lambda_t = 1$. There are $n \times T$ observations and $T + 1$ independent variables in this regression; the first and last independent variables have n nonzero observations, while the other $T - 1$ independent variables have $2n$ nonzero observations. All other observations are zero. The resulting set of λ's can be used to adjust

---

[7] With p defined as the ratio of $\bar{p}$ to the total PCE deflator, dividing p by x is, of course, equivalent to dividing $\bar{p}$ by $\bar{x}$.

the prices and the process is then iterated in the spirit of the first two methods.

The strength of this method would appear to be that, since the λ's are estimated simultaneously, an error in the estimate of λ for one year does not affect, except possibly in a very general sense, the estimate in any other year. Its theoretical disadvantage is that, unlike in the first two methods, the λ's computed in each iteration do not necessarily give additivity, and this is true, moreover, even if the λ's eventually stabilize. Despite this defect, however, the fact that the λ's are estimated simultaneously should impart some optimal properties to this method and make it a useful check on Method II.

Unfortunately, these expectations were not fulfilled. In an initial trial with only postwar United States data, the λ's appeared to stabilize after about twenty trials and their values seemed reasonable. When the prewar years were added, however, the λ for the last year was negative and there was no apparent tendency to stabilize. Accordingly, this method has been abandoned for the present.

Method IV

The final method involves choosing the λ's so as to minimize the expression:

$$(60) \qquad \Phi(\lambda) = \sum \sum (\bar{p}_{it} q_{it} - \bar{p}_{it} \hat{q}_{it})^2,$$

where

$$(61) \qquad \hat{q}_{it} = \hat{K}_{i0} + \hat{K}_{i1} q_{i(t-1)} + \lambda_t \hat{K}_{i2} p_{it} + \lambda_{t-1} \hat{K}_{i3} p_{i(t-1)}.$$

The "hats" on the K's denote that they are to be taken as given during the minimization. Substituting (61) into (60) and then expanding, we have

$$(62) \quad \Phi(\lambda) = \sum_i \sum_t (\lambda_t^2 \hat{K}_{i2}^2 p_{it}^2 + \lambda_{t-1}^2 \hat{K}_{i3}^2 \bar{p}_{it}^2 p_{i(t-1)}^2 - 2\lambda_t \hat{K}_{i2} \bar{p}_{it}^2 q_{it} p_{it}$$

$$- 2\lambda_{t-1} \hat{K}_{i3} \bar{p}_{it}^2 q_{it} p_{i(t-1)} + 2\lambda_t \hat{K}_{i0} \hat{K}_{i2} \bar{p}_{it}^2 p_{it}$$

$$+ 2\lambda_{t-1} \hat{K}_{i0} \hat{K}_{i3} \bar{p}_{it}^2 p_{i(t-1)} + 2\lambda_t \hat{K}_{i1} \hat{K}_{i2} \bar{p}_{it}^2 p_{it} q_{i(t-1)}$$

$$+ 2\lambda_{t-1} \hat{K}_{i1} \hat{K}_{i3} \bar{p}_{it}^2 p_{i(t-1)} q_{i(t-1)} + 2\lambda_t \lambda_{t-1} \hat{K}_{i2} \hat{K}_{i3} \bar{p}_{it}^2 p_{it} p_{i(t-1)}$$

$$+ \text{terms not involving } \lambda).$$

Differentiating partially with respect to each λ_j ($j = 0, \ldots, T$) and equating the results to zero, we obtain the following system of equations:

$$(63) \quad \lambda_{t-1} \sum_t \hat{K}_{i3}^2 \bar{p}_{it}^2 p_{i(t-1)}^2 - \sum_i \hat{K}_{i3} \bar{p}_{it}^2 q_{it} p_{i(t-1)} + \sum_i \hat{K}_{i0} \hat{K}_{i3} \bar{p}_{it}^2 p_{i(t-1)}$$

$$+ \sum_i \hat{K}_{i1} \hat{K}_{i3} \bar{p}_{it}^2 p_{i(t-1)} q_{i(t-1)} + \lambda_t \sum_i \hat{K}_{i2} \hat{K}_{i3} \bar{p}_{it}^2 p_{it} p_{i(t-1)} = 0$$

$$t = 1, \ldots, T.$$

Altogether, (63) involves $T + 1$ λ's, but only T equations, hence we can set $\lambda_0 = 1$ (as before) and solve for λ_t according to:

$$(64) \quad \lambda_t = [\sum \hat{K}_{i3} \bar{p}_{it}^2 q_{it} p_{i(t-1)} - \sum \hat{K}_{i0} \hat{K}_{i3} \bar{p}_{it}^2 p_{i(t-1)} - \sum \hat{K}_{i1} \hat{K}_{i3} \bar{p}_{it}^2 p_{i(t-1)} q_{i(t-1)}$$
$$- \lambda_{t-1} \sum \hat{K}_{i3}^2 \bar{p}_{it}^2 p_{i(t-1)}^2][\sum \hat{K}_{i2} \hat{K}_{i3} \bar{p}_{it}^2 p_{it} p_{i(t-1)}]^{-1}.$$

From here the procedure is the same as with Methods I and II, the resulting set of λ's being used to adjust the prices and the K's re-estimated. Then a new set of λ's is derived, and so on.

This method does not appear to work either; the quantity $\Phi(\lambda)$ defined in (60) decreases for a number of iterations, but then it stabilizes and finally goes up again. We are therefore left with Method II, which is the only one used for the empirical results in this chapter.[8]

III. Empirical Results I: The United States and Canada

Three sets of equations have been estimated for the United States and two for Canada. We have had to confine the additive model to fewer commodities than the 82 that were analyzed in Chapter 3; having more commodities would not only have made the computations much more difficult, but it would also be contrary to the additivity assumptions made at the beginning of this chapter. These assumptions become more vulnerable as the number of commodities (and hence the possible substitution and complementarity) increases. The model therefore has been applied to eleven categories of expenditure in the United States and to eight in Canada, the categories exhausting total expenditure in each case. The model is first estimated with saving included as a twelfth and ninth commodity, respectively, in which case the budget constraint is disposable income.[9] Then it is estimated without saving, in which case total expenditure is the budget constraint. Finally, for purposes of comparison, the nonadditive model has been applied to the eleven United States categories. These results have already been discussed in Chapter 4, but they are presented again here for ease in comparison.

The periods involved are 1929–1964 for the United States and 1926–1964 for Canada (annual observations for both), with the World War II years excluded (1942–1945 for the United States and 1940–1945 for Canada). The data are in real terms per capita (1958 dollars for the United States and 1949 dollars for Canada), and, as with the nonadditive model, the price is a relative

[8] The model of this chapter would also benefit from the application of Zellner's method for seemingly unrelated equations (see Zellner, 1962); unfortunately this must await another occasion.

[9] Our definition of disposable personal income for the U.S. differs from the Department of Commerce definition in that we exclude personal transfer payments.

price, being the ratio of the implicit deflator for the commodity to the total PCE deflator. Data sources are listed at the end of the book.

Method II has been used in estimating the λ's, that is, the independent variable has been p/x rather than p. Convergence, though always monotonic, has unfortunately also been slow, with more than 40 iterations being required in each application of the model. For the models where saving was not included as a commodity, iterations were continued until the regression-estimated components were within .05 percent of adding up to the given total of income or PCE for each year. When saving is included, however, we set the cutoff point at .10 percent because convergence was even slower and, as will be seen below, the results are inferior to those with saving included.

The pattern that the structural coefficients follow before stabilizing is varied and somewhat surprising. The short-run coefficients and elasticities generally change very little after the first few iterations, but the long-run coefficients are usually very erratic until iteration 30 or so. Actually, even with the cutoff at .05 percent the elasticities are still changing in the third decimal place, and it is apparent that this would continue until the discrepancy is extremely close to zero. But there seemed to be sharply diminishing returns to further iterations, and so they were terminated.

Three-pass least squares was used wherever it appeared likely to improve the final equation, though occasionally the three-pass variable ended up with an insignificant value after the iterative process was completed.

UNITED STATES

1. Additive model: 11 groups (saving excluded)

The results for the additive model applied to the eleven United States categories of expenditure are given in Tables 5.1 and 5.2. Table 5.1 gives the coefficients and their standard errors[10] for the estimating equation, while Table 5.2 presents the structural coefficients, their approximate standard errors, and the income and own-price derivatives and elasticities. Cross-price derivatives and elasticities (both compensated and uncompensated) have also been calculated, but space limitations preclude their inclusion.

For the results to be in keeping with the theory of consumer choice, a_i must be positive and A_{ii} must be negative for all i, and Table 5.2 shows this to be the case. The second part of the stability condition (14) is also satisfied throughout.

With the exception of other durable goods, the pattern of inventory adjustment and habit formation in Table 5.2 is what would be expected, even

[10] Because of the nonlinear element represented by the λ these standard errors should not be taken too literally. They were calculated on the assumption that the estimated λ_t are equal to their true values.

Table 5.1. Coefficients for Estimating Equation* (United States: Eleven Groups, 1929–1941, 1946–1964; 1958 dollars)

Group	K_0	K_1	K_2	K_3	K_4	R^2	S_e	D.W.
Automobile and parts	90.44 (22.76)	.4882 (.1283)	−14.8593 (2.0064)	6.6762 (2.6567)	.3777 (.1995)	.954	8.23	2.03
Furniture and household equipment	94.79 (20.98)	.4501 (.1282)	−7.5941 (.9583)	.9592 (1.6068)	.5165 (.2282)	.991	3.21	1.86
Other durable goods	5.65 (2.80)	.8925 (.0673)	−.9617 (.1881)	.5656 (.2353)	.5944 (.1413)	.994	.97	1.89
Food and beverages	128.91 (30.83)	.8410 (.0498)	−11.3968 (1.9480)	5.5282 (2.4402)		.996	6.37	2.15
Clothing and shoes	72.85 (15.18)	.6046 (.0850)	−5.9409 (1.0458)	2.9644 (1.2949)		.940	3.66	1.72
Gasoline and oil	7.75 (1.37)	.9334 (.0180)	−.7121 (.1304)	.2774 (.1281)		.998	.77	1.75
Other nondurables	24.45 (9.21)	.9113 (.0422)	−3.8759 (.3787)	2.5182 (.4818)	.3161 (.1565)	.999	1.62	1.89
Housing	12.63 (2.59)	.9448 (.0290)	−.7785 (.2687)	−.1354 (.2712)	.4435 (.2336)	.999	1.51	1.94
Household operation	11.98 (2.93)	.9413 (.0235)	−2.5387 (.2330)	1.6644 (.2607)		.997	1.51	1.94
Transportation	15.15 (4.57)	.7934 (.0593)	−1.5364 (.2754)	.6298 (.3814)		.991	1.27	1.77
Other services	24.25 (19.82)	.9587 (.0624)	−7.1814 (1.3531)	4.8364 (1.5749)		.979	5.14	1.63

* $q_t = K_0 + K_1 q_{t-1} + K_2 \lambda_t^* (P/x)_t + K_3 \lambda_{t-1}^* (P/x)_{t-1} + K_4 z_t.$

Table 5.2. Coefficients for Structural Equations (United States: Eleven Groups)

Group	Parameter a	A*	B*	D		Total expenditure Derivative	Total expenditure Elasticity	Price Compensated Derivative	Compensated Elasticity	Uncompensated Derivative	Uncompensated Elasticity
Automobiles and parts	.0420	−.0691	.0050	.7600	SR	.3882	6.34	−1.2118	−1.54	−1.4696	−1.87
	(.0154)	(.0129)	(.0123)	(.2864)	LR	.1109	1.81	−1.6939	−2.19	−1.7675	−2.24
Furniture and household equipment	.1108	−.1695	.1345	1.5514	SR	.1731	2.43	−.5879	−.76	−.7214	−.93
	(.0467)	(.0383)	(.1058)	(.6451)	LR	.0916	1.29	−1.2887	−1.66	−1.3594	−1.75
Other durable goods	.0370	−1.2391	.5020	.5188	SR	.0255	1.24	−.0907	−.47	−.0964	−.49
	(.0232)	(.3084)	(.3790)	(.2877)	LR	.0301	1.46	−.4125	−2.12	−.4192	−2.16
Food and beverages	.0762	−.1088	.0566	.6935	SR	.2561	.71	−.8598	−.21	−1.8679	−.47
	(.0294)	(.0255)	(.0395)	(.3017)	LR	.2659	.73	−3.4216	−.86	−4.4681	−1.12
Clothing and shoes	.0818	−.1802	.0317	.6685	SR	.1600	1.24	−.5609	−.41	−.7840	−.57
	(.0321)	(.0432)	(.0423)	(.2599)	LR	.0561	.44	−.8280	−.60	−.9063	−.66
Gasoline and oil	.0783	−1.9540	1.5822	.8786	SR	.0153	.41	−.0581	−.15	−.0642	−.16
	(.0233)	(.4861)	(.8579)	(.2692)	LR	.0504	1.36	−.7205	−1.83	−.7408	−1.88
Other nondurable goods	.0382	−.2989	.0992	.4247	SR	.0970	.79	−.3561	−.28	−.4847	−.38
	(.0160)	(.0322)	(.0448)	(.1740)	LR	.1147	.94	−1.6051	−1.25	−1.7572	−1.37
Housing	.1964	−3.0242	8.4246	2.8424	SR	.0100	.06	−.0377	−.02	−.0547	−.03
	(.1654)	(2.4507)	(13.8760)	(2.3611)	LR	.1300	.83	−1.7074	−1.08	−1.9276	−1.21
Household operation	.0285	−.4619	.1642	.4160	SR	.0617	.88	−.2372	−.31	−.2842	−.37
	(.0081)	(.0505)	(.0515)	(.1014)	LR	.1097	1.56	−1.5708	−2.03	−1.6543	−2.13
Transportation	.0699	−.8279	.5023	.8371	SR	.0327	.76	−.1355	−.29	−.1508	−.32
	(.0344)	(.2215)	(.4098)	(.4109)	LR	.0307	.71	−.4931	−1.05	−.5075	−1.08
Other services	.0202	−.1630	.0567	.3903	SR	.1610	.78	−.6271	−.26	−.9897	−.41
	(.0180)	(.0366)	(.0365)	(.2126)	LR	.3855	1.86	−4.8064	−1.97	−5.6744	−2.33

* A and B have been multiplied by 100.

though all the B_{ii} are positive. Judged by the short-run and long-run derivatives with respect to total PCE, automobiles and parts, furniture and household equipment, and clothing and shoes are characterized by rather marked inventory adjustment, while gasoline and oil, housing, household operation, and other services are subject to strong habit formation. Food, other nondurables, and transportation, on the other hand, hardly show any dynamic behavior at all. This pattern is the same as is obtained with the nonadditive model (see Table 4.11 above), and it is also broadly consistent, after making allowance for the much higher level of aggregation here, with the results of Chapter 3.

Other than the depreciation rate, the structural coefficients are generally several times their approximate standard errors; D is less significant, but is still usually at least twice its approximate standard error. The greatest uncertainty attaches to the depreciation rate for housing, where the implausibly large D also has a large approximate standard error. The estimating equations are also of a generally satisfactory quality. The coefficients are typically several times their standard errors—indeed, for only furniture and household equipment and housing are these coefficients insignificant by conventional standards—eight of the eleven R^2's are above .99, and thanks to the use of 3PLS, autocorrelation is not a problem. Overall, housing, with its implausibly large depreciation rate, appears to be the least satisfactory equation.

Except for the PCE elasticities for automobiles and parts, the elasticities generally seem reasonable. The short-run elasticities for housing may be on the low side, but these are consistent with the very small adjustment coefficients obtained with the flow-adjustment model for the rent categories in Chapter 4. Certainly there is no problem with the long-run elasticities for housing. The long-run PCE elasticity for automobiles and parts is unreasonably large, and although it is generally agreed to be high, the same might also be said of the short-run PCE elasticity.

The own-price elasticities (compensated or not) are all greater in the long run than in the short run, which is in marked contrast to the nonadditive model, where the identifying restriction on δ implied the same relationship between the short-run and long-run price elasticities as between the PCE elasticities. Indeed, our empirical results in general show that the price elasticity is greater in the long run for all commodities except those that are inferior in the long run or subject to very strong inventory adjustment. It will also be noted in Table 5.2 that the long-run PCE and price elasticities for each commodity are nearly equal except for sign. This phenomenon also occurs in the results for Sweden and is very puzzling.

In addition to the implausibly large depreciation rate for housing, a value of .76 is also obviously too high for automobiles and parts. This value sharply disagrees with that estimated with the nonadditive model (see Table 4.11) and is clearly a major defect in the results.

2. *Additive model: 12 groups (saving included)*

The results for the eleven United States expenditure groups plus saving as a twelfth commodity are tabulated in Tables 5.3 and 5.4.

It is evident from Table 5.4 that the results for the United States are considerably worsened with saving as a commodity in the model. Other durable goods and housing are now major problems, other durables being characterized as an inferior good in the long run, while housing is paraded as inferior in the short run. Neither of these results, needless to say, makes sense. The trouble with other durables is that K_1 is greater than one in the estimating equation, and the problem with housing is that K_3 is greater than K_2, which makes nonsense of the structural coefficients.

Although the short-run income elasticity is now more plausible,[11] the long-run elasticity for automobiles and parts and the depreciation rate are even higher than where saving was excluded from the analysis. Indeed, other than the two categories noted above, automobiles and parts is the category most affected by the addition of saving. This is not surprising, of course, for saving and auto expenditures are undoubtedly substitutes, but the long-run elasticity for autos is too large and is therefore disturbing. The saving equation gives quite plausible short-run and long-run MPS, but the depreciation rate is much too high. It would have been better if K_3 had been made equal to zero for this equation.

The R^2's of the estimating equations are generally little changed with saving in the model, most changes being in the third decimal place. Automobiles and parts and clothing and shoes are exceptions, however, the R^2 for autos dropping about two points and increasing about four points for clothing and shoes.

Perhaps an even more serious defect in the results is not apparent in Tables 5.3 and 5.4. This is that the estimated marginal utility of income is negative for the war years and 1964. Its being negative for the war years is not so serious, since those years do not enter into the calculations of any of the parameters (except λ for 1946); but becoming negative in 1964 is another matter. We will have more to say about this in section V.

[11] Note that we must now deal with income rather than PCE elasticities. Often it is taken as a matter of course that PCE elasticities will be larger than the income elasticity, but whether or not this is true depends on the income elasticity of saving, and it will also differ between the long run and the short run.

Table 5.3. Coefficients for Estimating Equation* (United States: Twelve Groups, 1929–1941, 1946–1964; 1958 dollars)

Group	K_0	K_1	K_2	K_3	K_4	R^2	S_e	D.W.
Automobiles and parts	80.06 (15.82)	.3971 (.1250)	−8.0453 (1.3809)	.9124 (1.3713)		.937	9.62	1.94
Furniture and household equipment	61.29 (12.23)	.5529 (.0988)	−3.6202 (.5808)	−.5118 (.6414)	.3903 (.2077)	.986	3.99	1.70
Other durable goods	3.29 (1.65)	.9832 (.0482)	−.5260 (.0932)	.2682 (.1086)	.5146 (.1909)	.995	.91	1.80
Food and beverages	142.51 (25.41)	.7515 (.0497)	−6.1106 (.8281)	.2064 (1.1337)	.5545 (.1551)	.997	5.94	2.59
Clothing and shoes	66.22 (20.06)	.5831 (.1327)	−2.7347 (.4609)	.5017 (.7518)	.3299 (.2615)	.987	3.72	1.73
Gasoline and oil	7.02 (1.05)	.9281 (.0165)	−.4664 (.0746)	.0703 (.0696)		.999	.72	2.15
Other nondurable goods	17.42 (5.58)	.8902 (.0339)	−1.9046 (.2201)	.9768 (.2385)	.5105 (.1522)	.999	1.69	2.15
Housing	8.00 (2.39)	.8988 (.0370)	−.2838 (.1795)	−.4064 (.1694)	.6737 (.2331)	.999	1.62	2.10
Household operation	13.02 (2.94)	.9115 (.0284)	−1.3401 (.1758)	.4557 (.1768)		.995	1.49	1.49
Transportation	11.49 (2.88)	.8153 (.0444)	−.7121 (.1493)	.0768 (.1954)	.0228 (.1896)	.994	1.26	2.14
Other services	25.90 (15.03)	.9303 (.0557)	−3.9480 (.6424)	1.8845 (.7212)		.982	4.76	1.65
Saving	131.19 (25.76)	−.0518 (.2013)	−4.6845 (.8885)	−.3533 (1.5938)		.916	13.53	1.51

* $q_t = K_0 + K_1 q_{t-1} + K_2 \lambda_t^* (P/x)_t + K_3 \lambda_{t-1}^* (P/x)_{t-1} + K_4 z_t$.

Price

Group	Parameter a	A*	B*	D		Total expenditure Derivative	Elasticity	Price Compensated Derivative	Elasticity	Uncompensated Derivative	Elasticity
Automobiles and parts	.0894 (.0290)	−.1560 (.0430)	.1138 (.0970)	1.5926 (.5267)	SR / LR	.2925 / .1099	5.18 / 1.95	−.3701 / −.7920	−.47 / −1.01	−.5643 / −.8650	−.72 / −1.10
Furniture and household equipment	.1972 (.0745)	−.4996 (.1494)	1.0406 (.7292)	2.6587 (.9879)	SR / LR	.0999 / .0939	1.52 / 1.43	−.1341 / −.6221	−.17 / −.80	−.2111 / −.6946	−.27 / −.90
Other durable goods	.0415 (.0244)	−2.4974 (.5502)	1.5791 (.9252)	.6492 (.3071)	SR / LR	.0215 / .1682	1.13 / 8.85	−.0285 / −.9598	−.15 / −4.94	−.0333 / −.9974	−.17 / −5.14
Food and beverages	.2256 (.0796)	−.2773 (.0672)	.4396 (.2733)	1.8693 (.6898)	SR / LR	.1708 / .2293	.51 / .69	−.2292 / −1.4369	−.06 / −.36	−.9015 / −2.3393	−.23 / −.58
Clothing and shoes	.2046 (.1171)	−.4892 (.1452)	.4173 (.3932)	1.3799 (.7345)	SR / LR	.1002 / .0535	.84 / .45	−.1371 / −.3728	−.10 / −.27	−.2769 / −.4473	−.20 / −.33
Gasoline and oil	.1307 (.0357)	−3.5924 (.8748)	5.0337 (2.5511)	1.4758 (.4086)	SR / LR	.0141 / .0570	.41 / 1.66	−.0200 / −.3818	−.05 / −.97	−.0257 / −.4048	−.07 / −1.03
Other nondurable goods	.0605 (.0215)	−.6560 (.0814)	.3462 (.1441)	.6440 (.2181)	SR / LR	.0751 / .0848	.67 / .75	−.1043 / −.5734	−.08 / −.45	−.2039 / −.6859	−.16 / −.54
Housing	−.6526 (1.7997)	15.4870 (41.9215)	176.0346 (949.7427)	−11.2600 (30.6046)	SR / LR	−.0033 / .0716	−.02 / .50	.0047 / −.4665	−.003 / −.29	.0103 / −.5879	−.006 / −.37
Household operation	.0725 (.0207)	−1.0644 (.1876)	.9498 (.3827)	.9849 (.2479)	SR / LR	.0455 / .0986	.70 / 1.52	−.0658 / −.6719	−.08 / −.87	−.1005 / −.7470	−.13 / −.96
Transportation	.1456 (.0779)	−2.3012 (.8827)	3.2382 (3.0343)	1.6107 (.8524)	SR / LR	.0200 / .0323	.50 / .81	−.0311 / −.2437	−.06 / −.52	−.0404 / −.2599	−.09 / −.55
Other services	.0444 (.0287)	−.3309 (.0683)	.2103 (.1111)	.7076 (.2761)	SR / LR	.1349 / .2690	.70 / 1.40	−.1989 / −1.7518	−.08 / −.72	−.5026 / −2.3575	−.21 / −.97
Saving	.3029 (.2149)	−.2189 (.0900)	.0236 (.2266)	2.3263 (1.6469)	SR / LR	.2989 / .0639	2.92 / .62	−.2322 / −.3251	−.36 / −.51	−.5914 / −.4018	−.92 / −.63

* A and B have been multiplied by 100.

211

Table 5.5. Coefficients for Estimating Equations* (Canada: Eight Groups, 1926–1939, 1946–1964; 1949 dollars)

Group	K_0	K_1	K_2	K_3	K_4	R^2	S_e	D.W.
Food	133.71 (30.69)	.6692 (.0873)	−5.0844 (.6803)	.9068 (1.0261)	.4825 (.1530)	.995	4.05	2.25
Tobacco and alcoholic beverages	4.87 (11.81)	.6296 (.1091)	−1.9979 (.3256)	.3357 (.5459)	.2105 (.2338)	.994	2.07	1.78
Clothing and personal furnishings	36.03 (12.30)	.8068 (.0811)	−3.2862 (.4803)	2.3188 (.6962)	.4508 (.1677)	.993	2.62	1.79
Shelter	4.26 (2.49)	.9954 (.0239)	−.6246 (.1273)	.4076 (.1243)	−.1771 (.1784)	.999	1.15	1.96
Household operation	37.87 (8.21)	.8496 (.0519)	−3.4683 (.2955)	2.3812 (.3554)	.4729 (.1513)	.997	2.06	2.28
Transportation	30.78 (7.44)	.8408 (.0490)	−3.5285 (.4332)	2.3961 (.4405)		.991	3.73	1.74
Personal and medical care and death expenses	3.96 (2.67)	.9896 (.0325)	−1.0042 (.1279)	.8266 (.1314)		.996	1.05	1.72
Miscellaneous	56.83 (23.00)	.5404 (.1910)	−1.7463 (.6429)	.2515 (.8060)	.4707 (.3119)	.968	4.95	1.79

* $q_t = K_0 + K_1 q_{t-1} + K_2 \lambda_t^* (P/x)_t + K_3 \lambda_{t-1}^* (P/x)_{t-1} + K_4 z_t.$

Table 5.6. Coefficients for Structural Equations (Canada: Eight Groups)

Group		Parameter					Total expenditure		Price Compensated		Price Uncompensated	
		a	A^*	B^*	D		Derivative	Elasticity	Derivative	Elasticity	Derivative	Elasticity
Food	SR	.2232 (.0888)	−.2786 (.0622)	.2781 (.1819)	1.3946 (.5562)		.2115	.75	−.5247	−.21	−.9804	−.39
	LR						.0978	.35	−2.0692	−.83	−2.2800	−.92
Tobacco and alcoholic products	SR	.1751 (.0936)	−.6983 (.2067)	.6773 (.6237)	1.4246 (.7665)		.0860	1.19	−.2369	−.38	−.2845	−.45
	LR						.0354	.49	−.7782	−1.24	−.7978	−1.27
Clothing and personal furnishings	SR	.0643 (.0322)	−.3224 (.0572)	.0424 (.0371)	.3452 (.1769)		.8490	1.41	−.4653	−.41	−.6512	−.57
	LR						.0392	.30	−.8657	−.76	−.9052	−.79
Shelter	SR	.0413 (.0254)	−1.9331 (.4624)	.8041 (.4260)	.4206 (.1490)		.0398	.34	−.0884	−.11	−.1238	−.16
	LR						.4803	4.14	−3.8780	−4.94	−4.3046	−5.49
Household operation	SR	.0647 (.0171)	−.3162 (.3132)	.0661 (.0224)	.3717 (.0960)		.1965	1.43	−.4644	−.40	−.6713	−.58
	LR						.0590	.43	−1.2243	−1.06	−1.2864	−1.12
Transportation	SR	.0520 (.0146)	−.3107 (.0445)	.0650 (.0297)	.3823 (.1066)		.2075	2.05	−.4627	−.57	−.6234	−.76
	LR						.0603	.60	−1.2005	−1.47	−1.2472	−1.53
Personal and medical care and death expenses	SR	.0216 (.0150)	−1.0868 (.1469)	.1995 (.0840)	.1940 (.0923)		.0651	1.03	−.1536	−.33	−.1850	−.40
	LR						.1584	2.51	−2.5465	−5.49	−2.6230	−5.66
Miscellaneous	SR	.2845 (.2467)	−.7711 (.4912)	.6937 (1.2771)	1.4965 (1.3101)		.0885	.78	−.2115	−.25	−.2883	−.33
	LR						.0292	.26	−.5651	−.65	−.5904	−.68

* A and B have been multiplied by 100.

CANADA

1. Additive model: 8 groups (saving not included)

The results for the eight Canadian expenditure groups are given in Tables 5.5 and 5.6. For the most part, these results parallel those for the eleven United States groups. Seven of the eight estimating equations have R^2's above .99, most coefficients are several times their standard error, auto-correlation is not a problem, the structural coefficients all have the right sign, and most of them are also several times their approximate standard error.

Despite these favorable features, however, several anomalies are evident in the results. Perhaps the most serious is that tobacco and alcoholic beverages turn up with rather marked inventory adjustment instead of the habit formation that we would normally expect. Unfortunately, no explanation for this is apparent. Another defect is that the long-run elasticities for shelter seem implausibly large, as does also the long-run price elasticity for personal and medical care and death expenses. The long-run PCE elasticity for food, on the other hand, seems a bit low.

Apart from tobacco and alcoholic beverages, the pattern of inventory adjustment and habit formation appears reasonable, although the strength of inventory adjustment for clothing and personal furnishings, household operation, and the miscellaneous category is more than would be expected. Strong habit formation for housing is consistent with the United States results, as is also the habit formation in personal and medical care. In contrast to the United States, automobiles and parts are combined with transportation in the Canadian PCE accounts, hence the more modest Canadian short-run PCE elasticity is appropriate. The long-run elasticity, however, may be too low.

2. Additive model: 9 groups (saving included)

Unlike for the United States, the inclusion of saving in the model leads to improved results for Canada. The results are tabulated in Tables 5.7 and 5.8. The major improvement is in the long-run elasticities, in particular the income elasticity for food and the own-price elasticities for shelter and personal and medical care. Moreover, the depreciation rate for transportation is now more reasonable, and, while still subject to some inventory adjustment, tobacco and alcoholic beverages have come to act less like a durable good, and the same is also true for the miscellaneous services. Food and clothing and personal furnishings are seen to have acquired moderate habit formation. For food this is plausible and in keeping with the results for the United States (although the short-run income elasticity may be a bit low), but it is at odds with clothing in the United States. The Canadian savings equation is quite satisfactory; interestingly enough it is the only item for the United States and Canada with a negative B_{ii}.

Table 5.7. Coefficients for Estimating Equation* (Canada: Nine Groups, 1926–1939, 1946–1964; 1949 dollars)

Group	K_0	K_1	K_2	K_3	K_4	R^2	S_e	D.W.
Food	86.76	.7767	−4.1439	2.3132	.4009	.992	5.38	2.08
	(26.59)	(.0860)	(.8540)	(.7358)	(.1682)			
Tobacco and alcoholic	27.39	.6958	−1.8349	.9668		.993	1.94	1.76
beverages	(4.85)	(.0566)	(.2596)	(.2392)				
Clothing and personal	95.49	.3242	−1.8468	−.1032	.4868	.990	2.99	1.78
furnishings	(25.35)	(.1859)	(.5011)	(.9077)	(.1974)			
Shelter	5.51	.9902	−.5410	.3650		.998	1.12	2.37
	(2.09)	(.0178)	(.1073)	(.0966)				
Household operation	35.66	.8332	−2.8167	2.0825	.3350	.993	2.98	2.10
	(7.64)	(.0559)	(.3783)	(.3446)	(.1563)			
Transportation	29.52	.8126	−2.8223	1.9710		.989	4.24	2.11
	(5.64)	(.0455)	(.4462)	(.4038)				
Personal and medical care	6.76	.9345	−.9212	.7356		.997	.97	1.81
and death expenses	(2.02)	(.0295)	(.1053)	(.0943)				
Miscellaneous	34.06	.6625	−1.5504	.9259	.4612	.967	5.03	1.81
	(14.25)	(.1435)	(.5418)	(.5142)	(.2823)			
Saving	68.46	.1032	−5.8812	3.8264		.938	10.43	1.77
	(11.39)	(.1384)	(.8566)	(.7616)				

* $q_t = K_0 + K_1 q_{t-1} + K_2 \lambda_t^* (P/x)_t + K_3 \lambda_{t-1}^* (P/x)_{t-1} + K_4 z_t.$

215

Table 5.8. Coefficients for Structural Equations (Canada: Nine Groups)

Group	Parameters					Total expenditure		Price			
								Compensated		Uncompensated	
	a	A*	B*	D		Derivative	Elasticity	Derivative	Elasticity	Derivative	Elasticity
Food	.1344	−.2751	.0868	.5670	SR	.1475	.56	−.5263	−.21	−.8357	−.34
	(.0455)	(.0662)	(.0550)	(.1998)	LR	.1495	.57	−1.1847	−.48	−1.4983	−.60
Tobacco and alcoholic beverages	.0978	−.6053	.1580	.6197	SR	.0683	1.01	−.2572	−.41	−.2940	−.47
	(.0219)	(.1073)	(.0926)	(.1446)	LR	.0531	.79	−.4505	−.72	−.4791	−.77
Clothing and personal furnishings	.5477	−.7594	.9235	2.2369	SR	.0541	.44	−.2077	−.18	−.2607	−.23
	(.5501)	(.5123)	(2.0554)	(2.2648)	LR	.0532	.43	−.4556	−.40	−.5077	−.44
Shelter	.0608	−2.1969	.8319	.3885	SR	.0241	.22	−.0733	−.09	−.0941	−.12
	(.0222)	(.4942)	(.3647)	(.1005)	LR	.4289	3.96	−1.5705	−2.00	−1.9414	−2.48
Household operation	.0728	−.3742	.0441	.2997	SR	.1143	.89	−.3970	−.34	−.5143	−.45
	(.0163)	(.0565)	(.0260)	(.0685)	LR	.0846	.66	−.6731	−.58	−.7599	−.66
Transportation	.0616	−.3782	.0561	.3552	SR	.1174	1.24	−.3899	−.48	−.4785	−.59
	(.0131)	(.0697)	(.0362)	(.0784)	LR	.0907	.96	−.6885	−.84	−.7569	−.93
Personal and medical care and death expenses	.0408	−1.1677	.1825	.2241	SR	.0417	.71	−.1357	−.29	−.1553	−.33
	(.0118)	(.1432)	(.0574)	(.0556)	LR	.0620	1.05	−.4390	−.95	−.4682	−1.01
Miscellaneous	.1375	−.6713	.0660	.5044	SR	.0700	.66	−.2295	−.27	−.2886	−.33
	(.0752)	(.2903)	(.1814)	(.2892)	LR	.0391	.37	−.2944	−.34	−.3273	−.38
Saving	.0705	−.1136	−.1367	.4233	SR	.4228	6.51	−.8401	−1.62	−1.0594	−2.04
	(.0138)	(.0266)	(.0262)	(.0859)	LR	.0495	.76	−.3602	−.69	−.3859	−.74

* A and B have been multiplied by 100.

IV. Empirical Results II: The Netherlands and Sweden

THE NETHERLANDS

Two levels of commodity detail have been analyzed for the Netherlands. The first involves sixteen categories of expenditure, while the second is a grouping of the sixteen categories into four broad aggregates. The results are presented in Tables 5.9–5.12. The data are those used by Barten in his extensive analyses of Dutch consumption over the period 1920–1962 (1964, 1968) and are in constant (1938) guilders. Except in computing the λ's, 1940–1948 have been excluded from the analyses.[12]

1. 16 groups

The Dutch results are considerably more mixed than those of either the United States or Canada. A look first at the estimating equations (Table 5.9) will show that, although the fits are generally pretty good, the typical R^2 is not as high as it was with United States or Canadian data. Indeed, for two categories, potatoes, vegetables, and fruit, and especially fish and preserved fish, the R^2's are low as time-series data go.[13] The equations for two other categories, tobacco products and rent, suffer from the defect that A_1 is greater than one. On the positive side, the great majority of coefficients are at least twice their standard error, and autocorrelated residuals, apart possibly from clothing and other textiles, is not a problem.

A number of anomalies are apparent in the structural coefficients and elasticities (Table 5.10). The signs of a and A are reversed for fish, rent has increasing short-run marginal utility, and the depreciation rates are negative for fish, bread, tobacco, and rent. And as if rent did not have enough problems, both PCE elasticities are negative and both own-price elasticities are positive. Rent is an interesting example of an equation with the highest R^2 being the least satisfactory otherwise. It may be noted that Holland has had a severe housing shortage and strict rent control ever since the war, so that it might have been better to omit this item altogether.

The pattern of inventory adjustment and habit formation also presents some problems. Other than meat and meat products, which we would expect to be subject to moderate habit formation instead of strong inventory adjustment, the food items fare quite well. That bread is an inferior good in the long run is in keeping with its long-term downward trend, and little can be said about fish in light of the poor fit of its estimating equation. The Dutch consumption of potatoes, fruits, and vegetables may well be characterized by

---

[12] Barten did not compile data for 1940–1947, and we have had to interpolate those years for computational purposes.

[13] We note that these are the only data in this book for different varieties of foodstuffs.

Table 5.9. Coefficients for Estimating Equation* (The Netherlands: Sixteen Groups, 1920–1939, 1949–1962; 1938 guilders)

Group	K_0	K_1	K_2	K_3	K_4	R^2	S_e	D.W.
Groceries	26.52 (5.55)	.4703 (.1113)	−.9538 (.1639)	.4601 (.1914)		.939	1.29	2.25
Dairy products	4.11 (4.90)	.9218 (.0731)	−.6278 (.1412)	.5789 (.1702)		.969	1.26	2.33
Potatoes, vegetables, and fruits	2.79 (3.09)	.9240 (.0942)	−.3574 (.0915)	.2959 (.1182)		.874	1.11	2.17
Meat and meat products	11.90 (2.59)	.6957 (.0488)	−.6152 (.1236)	.5904 (.1372)		.916	1.38	1.82
Fish and preserved fish	1.37 (.59)	.6992 (.1293)	.0161 (.0296)	−.0377 (.0304)		.571	.36	1.90
Bread	4.15 (2.33)	.6782 (.1483)	.0066 (.0759)	.1500 (.0981)		.908	.62	1.97
Pastry, chocolate, and ice cream	2.16 (1.65)	.9276 (.0614)	−.3125 (.0716)	.2696 (.0786)		.960	.63	1.81
Tobacco products	−2.59 (1.96)	1.1167 (.0699)	−.1657 (.0833)	.2440 (.0912)	−.4061 (.2265)	.989	.62	1.96

Beverages	3.42	.9411	−.4552	.3083		.970	.69	1.75
	(1.09)	(.0372)	(.0779)	(.0944)				
Clothing and other textiles	25.60	.7258	−2.6914	2.3148	.1788	.978	2.49	1.42
	(12.43)	(.1171)	(.2890)	(.3298)	(.2266)			
Footwear	1.32	.9132	−.1587	.1245		.969	.31	1.99
	(.60)	(.0569)	(.0271)	(.0283)				
Household durable goods	33.70	.5528	−1.2717	.4683		.970	1.52	1.83
	(10.05)	(.1471)	(.1484)	(.2756)				
Other durables	3.68	.9622	−.5443	.4027		.973	.94	2.09
	(3.29)	(.1234)	(.1433)	(.1293)				
Rent	−.10	1.0145	.0765	−.0880		.999	.29	1.93
	(.83)	(.0118)	(.0570)	(.0541)				
Fuel, electricity, gas, and water	10.71	.8334	−.6518	.3821	.2048	.992	.81	1.95
	(2.54)	(.0483)	(.1082)	(.1200)	(.2277)			
Other commodities and services	72.69	.6158	−2.7821	1.3141	.3163	.991	3.02	1.99
	(23.62)	(.1338)	(.4858)	(.6504)	(.2586)			

$$* \; q_t = K_0 + K_1 q_{t-1} + K_2 \lambda_t^*(P/x)_t + K_3 \lambda_{t-1}^*(P/x)_{t-1} + K_4 \dot{z}_t.$$

Table 5.10. Coefficients for Structural Equations (The Netherlands: Sixteen Groups)

Group		Parameter				Total expenditure		Price			
								Compensated		Uncompensated	
	a	A*	B*	D		Deriva-tive	Elas-ticity	Deriva-tive	Elas-ticity	Deriva-tive	Elas-ticity
Groceries	.1876	−1.0399	−.0230	−.6984	SR	.0326	1.08	−.1189	−.65	−.1296	−.71
	(.0635)	(.2558)	(.2213)	(.2620)	LR	.0199	.66	−.1181	−.65	−.1246	−.68
Dairy products	.0341	−1.5926	−.0006	.0811	SR	.0240	.65	−.0785	−.39	−.0882	−.44
	(.0436)	(.3795)	(.1928)	(.1855)	LR	.0150	.40	−.0796	−.40	−.0857	−.43
Potatoes, vegetables, and fruit	.0428	−2.9451	.3217	.1882	SR	.0176	.95	−.0425	−.58	−.0460	−.63
	(.0550)	(.8541)	(.5700)	(.2288)	LR	.0264	1.43	−.0986	−1.34	−.1039	−1.42
Meat and meat products	.0987	−1.4065	−.4470	.0411	SR	.0294	.91	−.0874	−.54	−.0978	−.61
	(.0309)	(.3026)	(.1390)	(.1074)	LR	.0021	.07	−.0106	−.07	−.0114	−.07
Fish and preserved fish	−.2550	31.5831	36.4445	−.7999	SR	−.0014	−.46	.0042	.30	.0042	.30
	(.2677)	(34.1850)	(67.4849)	(1.0681)	LR	.0019	.66	−.0094	−.67	−.0094	−.67
Bread	.2890	−11.7012	−30.0340	−2.1832	SR	.0025	.13	−.0112	−.08	−.0117	−.08
	(.3302)	(13.9825)	(61.4027)	(2.3203)	LR	−.0091	−.45	.0648	.46	.0668	.48

Commodity		A	B								
Pastry, chocolate, and ice cream	SR	.0370	−3.3114	.2399	.0127	.85	−.0386	−.52	−.0406	−.55
	LR	(.0305)	(.8408)	(.4172)	.0157	1.04	−.0752	−1.02	−.0778	−1.06
Tobacco products	SR	−.0631	−5.1665	−1.4054	.0085	.54	−.0249	−.34	−.0264	−.36
	LR	(.0526)	(2.1543)	(1.4906)	.0186	1.17	−.0843	−1.13	−.0876	−1.18
Beverages	SR	.0448	−2.5422	.8237	.0137	.96	−.0504	−.60	−.0525	−.62
	LR	(.0208)	(.5487)	(.5198)	.0546	3.82	−.2946	−3.49	−.3031	−3.59
Clothing and other textiles	SR	.0511	−.3447	−.0577	.1289	2.16	−.2659	−.96	−.3495	−1.26
	LR	(.0265)	(.0436)	(.0256)	.0384	.64	−.1642	−.59	−.1891	−.68
Footwear	SR	.0468	−6.7546	1.0194	.0074	1.39	−.0191	−.87	−.0195	−.89
	LR	(.0237)	(1.3081)	(.7107)	.0124	2.33	−.0501	−2.28	−.0508	−2.32
Household durable goods	SR	.1937	−.8924	.3100	.0546	1.82	−.1266	−1.00	−.1443	−1.14
	LR	(.0905)	(.1605)	(.2554)	.0550	1.84	−.2026	−1.60	−.2205	−1.74
Other durables	SR	.0388	−2.0721	.5400	.0203	2.25	−.0606	−1.37	−.0625	−1.42
	LR	(.0347)	(.6008)	(.3696)	.0989	10.99	−.3843	−8.70	−.3939	−8.92
Rent	SR	.0058	12.2487	−.1404	−.0019	−.03	.0108	.02	.0119	.02
	LR	(.0487)	(8.1900)	(.1929)	−.0118	−.21	.1061	.22	.1133	.23
Fuel, electricity, gas, and water	SR	.1036	−1.7734	.5217	.0188	.66	−.0716	−.40	−.0775	−.44
	LR	(.0351)	(.3762)	(.1821)	.0340	1.18	−.1999	−1.13	−.2105	−1.19
Other commodities and services	SR	.1775	−.3945	.0952	.0902	.71	−.2767	−.38	−.4012	−.55
	LR	(.0829)	(.0969)	(.1128)	.0855	.67	−.4214	−.57	−.5395	−.73

* A and B have been multiplied by 100.

Table 5.11. Coefficients for Estimating Equation* (The Netherlands: Four Groups, 1920–1939, 1949–1962; 1938 guilders)

Group	K_0	K_1	K_2	K_3	K_4	R^2	S_e	D.W.
Food	74.08 (14.37)	.5887 (.0748)	−1.8356 (.2184)	1.3400 (.2890)		.966	2.27	2.08
Pleasure goods	2.66 (4.63)	.9729 (.0678)	−.6845 (.1175)	.6353 (.1200)		.984	1.07	1.85
Durables	33.23 (13.40)	.8142 (.0733)	−3.7041 (.2956)	3.2007 (.2788)	.2292 (.2288)	.994	2.77	1.74
Other expenditure	38.93 (15.17)	.8747 (.0499)	3.0851 (.4693)	2.5594 (.5118)	.0302 (.2007)	.996	3.48	1.69

* $q_t = K_0 + K_1 q_{t-1} + K_2 \lambda_t^*(P/x)_t + K_3 \lambda_{t-1}^*(P/x)_{t-1} + K_4 z_t.$

Table 5.12. Coefficients for Structural Equations (The Netherlands: Four Groups)

Group	Parameter					Total expenditure		Price			
	a	A*	B*	D		Deriva-tive	Elas-ticity	Compensated		Uncompensated	
								Deriva-tive	Elas-ticity	Deriva-tive	Elas-ticity
Food	.2333	−.5003	−.1029	.3121	SR	.0962	.68	−.2260	−.29	−.3759	−.49
	(.0661)	(.0747)	(.0309)	(.1275)	LR	.0595	.42	−.1488	−.19	−.2415	−.31
Pleasure goods	.0202	−1.4949	.0704	.7463	SR	.0340	.76	−.0871	−.38	−.1038	−.45
	(.0348)	(.2738)	(.1017)	(.1096)	LR	.0945	2.11	−.2035	−.88	−.2498	−1.08
Durables	.0481	−.2627	−.0155	.1458	SR	.2190	2.10	−.2517	−.53	−.5015	−1.06
	(.0192)	(.0247)	(.0103)	(.0602)	LR	.1599	1.54	−.2334	−.49	−.4158	−.88
Other expenditure	.0690	−.3321	.0175	.1863	SR	.1212	.57	−.3361	−.25	−.6160	−.45
	(.0289)	(.0579)	(.0255)	(.0975)	LR	.1732	.82	−.4165	−.30	−.8165	−.60

* A and B have been multiplied by 100.

habit formation, as the equation suggests. Tobacco, as we anticipate, is subject to strong habit formation, but in view of A_1 being greater than one and the negative depreciation rate, this result has a rather dubious basis.

Apart from rent, which needs no further comment, the results for the rest of the commodities appear to be reasonable. It may seem incongruous for other durables to be subject to habit formation, but included in this category are goods such as sports equipment, toys, and leather goods, whose consumption in the United States we have found to be habit forming. Similarly, habit formation in beverages and footwear is also in agreement with United States results. The lack of a dynamic income effect for household durable goods is puzzling; however, this could conceivably reflect a supply constraint at some time or another during the period.

Despite the rationalizations of the preceding paragraph, it is clear that the dynamic effects for several commodities are too large. This is clearly the case for beverages and other durable goods, where habit formation is unreasonably strong, and for meat, where, as we have already noted, inventory adjustment is implausible to begin with. Part of the problem with the long-run coefficients can be traced to the equations for fish and rent. The implausible structural coefficients for these items are fed into price and income derivatives of the other categories through $p'W^{-1}p$. (The short-run coefficients are also affected, though to a lesser extent, through $p'A^{-1}p$.) This is, unfortunately, a defect of joint estimation.

Another factor contributing to the mixed results here could be that the strong independence assumption underlying the model is not justified. Sixteen commodities may be too many, particularly given the extent to which food is disaggregated. Some evidence to this effect is given by Barten (1964).

2. 4 groups

When the sixteen groups are combined into four, nearly all the anomalies vanish. (See Tables 5.11 and 5.12.) Durables show inventory adjustment, as does (less plausibly) food, but the elasticities are all quite reasonable and the fits are good. This provides support for the remark just made concerning interdependence.

SWEDEN

The Swedish data used are those employed by Bentzel and his associates (1957, 1960) in their exercise to project personal consumption expenditures in Sweden in 1965. Covering the period 1931–1958, the data refer to eight categories of expenditure (the definitions agree fairly closely with the eight groups of Canada) and are in constant (1955) kronor.[14] Method II has been

Table 5.13. Coefficients for Estimating Equation* (Sweden: Eight Groups, 1931–1958; 1955 kronor)

Group	K_0	K_1	K_2	K_3	K_4	R^2	S_e	D.W.
Food and beverages	592.80 (246.69)	.6951 (.1285)	−155.3899 (14.4928)	91.9160 (29.7810)		.978	24.15	1.79
Housing, fuel, and light	−6.40 (33.21)	1.0189 (.0654)	−16.6252 (5.3423)	14.0951 (5.8628)	−.2137 (.1878)	.987	10.91	2.01
Clothing	254.15 (129.29)	.6604 (.1940)	−63.4242 (8.1407)	28.6509 (18.4437)	.3094 (.2895)	.977	19.78	1.85
Household goods	184.09 (56.71)	.5181 (.1513)	−34.6103 (5.0573)	9.3059 (9.2465)	.3967 (.2166)	.973	9.64	2.11
Miscellaneous services	23.62 (10.38)	.7157 (.1138)	−.0240 (1.7190)	2.0327 (1.8938)		.842	2.37	2.19
Travel	30.55 (31.21)	.9568 (.0969)	−40.7464 (11.0073)	34.0941 (11.3190)	.1659 (.2849)	.981	14.96	1.94
Recreation	44.23 (20.23)	.8645 (.0702)	−14.6784 (2.9670)	8.0729 (3.6340)		.990	4.92	1.69
Medical and personal care	21.68 (15.27)	.9423 (.0639)	−12.1167 (2.0358)	9.0776 (2.5820)		.991	3.88	1.82

* $q_t = K_0 + K_1 q_{t-1} + K_2 \lambda_t^*(P/x)_t + K_3 \lambda_{t-1}^*(P/x)_{t-1} + K_4 z_t$.

Table 5.14. Coefficients for Structural Equations (Sweden: Eight Groups)

Group	Parameter					Total expenditure		Price			
								Compensated		Uncompensated	
	a	A^*	B^*	D		Derivative	Elasticity	Derivative	Elasticity	Derivative	Elasticity
Food and beverages	.0240 (.0128)	−.0069 (.0008)	.0011 (.0009)	.5133 (.2732)	SR	.6255	1.00	−4.3847	−.20	−13.3110	−.59
					LR	.6048	.97	−6.3940	−.29	−15.0240	−.67
Housing, fuel, and light	−.0021 (.0106)	−.0657 (.0227)	.0121 (.0126)	.1647 (.2002)	SR	.0805	.45	−.7125	.14	−1.0449	−.20
					LR	−.4786	2.65	9.1873	1.75	11.1630	2.13
Clothing	.0276 (.0197)	−.0180 (.0034)	.0062 (.0056)	.7553 (.5109)	SR	.2879	1.59	−2.1558	−.40	−3.3461	−.63
					LR	.3603	1.99	−3.6951	−.69	−5.1847	−.97
Household goods	.0419 (.0224)	−.0346 (.0083)	.0179 (.0178)	1.1524 (.6212)	SR	.1382	1.56	−1.3042	−.46	−1.5851	−.55
					LR	.1700	1.91	−2.3083	−.81	−2.6538	−.93
Miscellaneous services	.1148 (.1892)	−.8342 (1.4477)	−1.9059 (5.9501)	−1.9533 (3.2653)	SR	.0051	.11	−.0597	−.04	−.0649	−.04
					LR	−.0204	−.46	.3578	.22	.3786	.24
Travel	.0041 (.0045)	−.0261 (.0075)	.0035 (.0031)	.1778 (.1546)	SR	.1872	1.83	−1.6515	−.51	−2.0900	−.65
					LR	.5112	4.99	−4.8390	−1.50	−6.0365	−1.88
Recreation	.0194 (.0112)	−.0820 (.0204)	.0357 (.0292)	.5807 (.3488)	SR	.0563	.78	−.5865	−.24	−.6793	−.28
					LR	.1524	2.11	−2.1821	−.91	−2.4335	−1.01
Medical and personal care	.0102 (.0081)	−.0916 (.0175)	.0208 (.0160)	.2868 (.2085)	SR	.0536	.82	−.5241	−.26	−.6047	−.29
					LR	.1753	2.67	−2.2943	−1.12	−2.5577	−1.24

* A and B have been multiplied by 100.

used in estimating the λ's, and, as before, about 40 iterations were required. The results are tabulated in Tables 5.13 and 5.14.

The results here are generally more plausible than for the Netherlands, but they are not as striking as for the United States and Canada. The poorest equation is quite clearly the one for housing, fuel, and light, where a has the wrong sign, as do also the long-run elasticities. These defects can be traced to A_1 being greater than one in the estimating equation. The only other wrong sign is on the depreciation rate for miscellaneous services, a category which had a downward trend over the entire period and which is therefore quite appropriately indicated to be an inferior good in the long run. The only other commodity that we have found to be an inferior good in the long run is bread in Holland, and D is negative there also. Hence, the negative depreciation rate in these cases may be a defect of the model.

The pattern of dynamic effects is not quite what we would expect to find, but part of the problem may be due to the negative depreciation rate for miscellaneous services and the poor equation for housing, fuel, and light. Food and beverages, recreation, and medical and personal care are each subject to habit formation, which is reasonable enough, but we would ordinarily expect household goods and travel, since this category includes automobiles, to be governed by inventory adjustment. And since clothing behaves like a durable good in the United States, Canada, and the Netherlands we might anticipate the same to hold in Sweden. The PCE elasticities for food and beverages are higher than usually found, but this may be owing to the inclusion of alcoholic beverages.

Except for housing, whose defects have already been discussed, and miscellaneous services, which has a low R^2, the estimating equations are of good quality. The R^2's are at least .97, most coefficients are several times their standard error, and there is no apparent autocorrelation in the residuals.

V. Estimates of the Marginal Utility of Total Expenditure

It was noted in the derivation of the model of this chapter that income does not appear directly as an argument, but indirectly through λ, the marginal utility of income. Thus it is of interest to analyze the marginal utilities that are implicit in the results presented above. These marginal utilities together with the corresponding levels of total expenditure (measured in constant prices) are given in Table 5.15. Only the models with total expenditure are considered here, hence the marginal utilities refer to total expenditure rather

---

[14] The Bentzel data are also available on a 64-commodity breakdown. The results from applying the nonadditive model to these data are reported in Taylor (1968).

Table 5.15. Marginal Utility of Total Expenditure

United States (11 Groups)

Year	x	λ	Year	x	λ
1930	1059.50	1.000	1948	1431.31	.683
1931	1017.41	1.063	1949	1445.58	.650
1932	920.38	1.238	1950	1513.75	.531
1933	900.63	1.178	1951	1503.76	.579
1934	933.74	1.075	1952	1519.49	.596
1935	985.46	1.016	1953	1564.45	.563
1936	1081.58	.872	1954	1568.46	.592
1937	1110.81	.898	1955	1653.10	.461
1938	1079.92	1.004	1956	1666.05	.476
1939	1132.33	.908	1957	1674.57	.513
1940	1174.72	.855	1958	1659.40	.572
1941	1236.64	.757	1959	1728.05	.471
1942	1199.70	.874	1960	1750.57	.477
1943	1227.92	.839	1961	1755.59	.505
1944	1279.92	.763	1962	1813.50	.436
1945	1370.72	.662	1963	1865.20	.380
1946	1434.45	.630	1964	1945.66	.278
1947	1426.42	.692			

Canada (8 Groups)

Year	x	λ	Year	x	λ
1927	556.64	1.000	1946	820.71	.475
1928	601.31	.926	1947	826.89	.528
1929	625.83	.909	1948	793.73	.656
1930	588.52	1.058	1949	812.30	.605
1931	550.38	1.137	1950	849.04	.524
1932	501.85	1.207	1951	843.53	.587
1933	484.84	1.186	1952	873.71	.537
1934	500.59	1.105	1953	898.48	.510
1935	515.76	1.062	1954	892.92	.565
1936	534.34	1.028	1955	934.00	.472
1937	562.92	.981	1956	970.28	.410
1938	549.18	1.044	1957	967.25	.475
1939	559.36	1.010	1958	969.67	.490
1940	600.67	.910	1959	990.10	.441
1941	633.70	.863	1960	1001.40	.441
1942	647.38	.866	1961	1010.97	.443
1943	657.17	.847	1962	1038.50	.390
1944	694.83	.751	1963	1064.67	.347
1945	754.32	.611	1964	1109.80	.249

The Netherlands

Year	x	λ 16 groups	λ 4 groups
1921	477.87	1.000	1.000
1922	469.78	1.065	1.104
1923	465.97	1.086	1.147
1924	462.61	1.118	1.205
1925	476.35	1.091	1.180
1926	486.28	1.055	1.146
1927	499.95	1.011	1.099
1928	506.64	.993	1.073
1929	527.04	.935	.998
1930	527.73	.945	.998
1931	521.88	.982	1.029
1932	516.71	1.005	1.057
1933	500.90	1.073	1.142
1934	495.43	1.089	1.172
1935	510.07	1.045	1.114
1936	504.20	1.064	1.147
1937	499.77	1.080	1.168
1938	526.56	.962	1.021
1939	521.89	.955	1.021
1940	517.33	.956	1.029
1941	512.88	.960	1.044

Year	x	λ 16 groups	λ 4 groups
1942	508.54	.967	1.064
1943	504.31	.975	1.088
1944	500.18	.984	1.115
1945	496.14	.993	1.145
1946	492.20	1.003	1.176
1947	488.35	1.012	1.209
1948	506.68	.962	1.152
1949	509.90	.946	1.134
1950	500.43	.985	1.175
1951	496.85	1.046	1.250
1952	517.72	.978	1.151
1953	543.57	.903	1.026
1954	571.96	.815	.884
1955	610.89	.691	.704
1956	603.44	.727	.715
1957	599.67	.752	.733
1958	616.92	.695	.639
1959	648.87	.585	.463
1960	675.41	.498	.320
1961	707.27	.391	.145
1962	741.90	.278	-.053

Sweden (8 groups)

Year	x	λ
1932	2341.76	1.000
1933	2333.12	1.004
1934	2419.64	.934
1935	2542.51	.891
1936	2654.99	.824
1937	2740.17	.779
1938	2804.42	.764
1939	2940.01	.711
1940	2656.47	.935
1941	2523.79	.993
1942	2464.62	1.000
1943	2527.76	.950
1944	2712.71	.815
1945	2866.41	.712

Year	x	λ
1946	3236.31	.474
1947	3355.51	.452
1948	3402.08	.463
1949	3389.15	.519
1950	3591.43	.398
1951	3492.19	.512
1952	3536.54	.503
1953	3594.71	.491
1954	3721.16	.432
1955	3832.82	.390
1956	4007.27	.322
1957	4058.18	.347
1958	4161.60	.330

Note: All x quantities are in real terms, namely: U.S., 1958 dollars; Canada, 1955 dollars; Netherlands, 1938 guilders; Sweden, 1955 kronor.

than income. Since Method II has been used in estimation, the λ's presented in Table 5.15 have been obtained by dividing λ_t^* of equation (58) by x_t and then renormalized on λ_1 in order to convert λ^* to λ. Marginal utility is thus expressed in terms of the marginal utility of the first year of observation.

To begin the discussion, it will be useful to ask what the λ's should be expected to show. A major premise of the classical theory of consumer's choice is declining marginal utility of income, and since our dynamic model in its limiting long-run form is consistent with classical theory, we should expect λ to decline as total expenditure increases. But this need hold only over long periods of time. In the short run, the state variables can upset this inverse relationship, so that, depending upon the rate of change of income in the recent past, λ and total expenditure may occasionally move in the same direction. Apart from this, perhaps the only other thing to be said *a priori* about the λ's is that they should be positive.[15]

Turning to the empirical results, the first thing to notice is that the inverse relationship between λ and x postulated above (though there are occasional short-term aberrations) is confirmed in each case. Positivity of the λ's fares almost as well, for all are positive except for the final year (1962) for the four Dutch groups. Despite this broad general agreement with expectations, however, an anomaly is apparent in that the λ's, except for Sweden, decline very rapidly in the last two or three years. This is manifested most strongly in the four Dutch groups where λ falls precipitously in the last three years, terminating in the negative value noted above for 1962. At present, we have no explanation for this final drop-off. It is quite at variance with the behavior of the λ's in the other years, and most likely reflects a defect in the estimation procedure.

Looking next at the short-term movements in λ, we see that with few exceptions the inverse relationship between λ and x is maintained year-to-year as well as over the long period. λ is seen to be very sensitive to sharp changes in total expenditure, especially when these follow a period of relatively small changes. When PCE increases after a period of stability, λ decreases sharply, while the reverse is true when PCE decreases after a period of stability. This suggests that the marginal utility curves for goods subject to habit formation are steeper than those subject to stock adjustment.

Since both commodity groups for the Netherlands exhaust total expenditure, we would expect the two sets of λ's to be in close agreement, but this is not the case. The λ's for the four groups show a much wider range of variation, although almost without exception the year-to-year changes all have the

---

[15] This should be true even though the quadratic utility function implies that saturation is eventually reached. Although clearly a defect of this particular function, saturation should hardly be a problem empirically.

same sign. The divergence between the two sets is most marked in the final four years where, as noted above, the λ for the four groups becomes negative. The reason for this divergence is not apparent, though one possible factor is that sixteen categories are too many for the strong independence assumptions underlying the model.

VI. Forecasts for 1965 for the United States and Canada

As a test of the additive model, forecasts for 1965 for the United States and Canada have been prepared and are tabulated in Table 5.16. (Recall that the periods of fit for both countries stop at 1964.) For purposes of comparison, forecasts for 1965 from the nonadditive model are also presented in this table. The nonadditive model forecasts include not only those from the equations for the 11 groups (that is, the equations in Tables 4.10 and 4.12) but also forecasts aggregated from the equations of Chapter 3 for the 82 expenditure categories.[16] It will be easiest to discuss the results in point form.

1. In general, the pattern of over- and under-forecasts with the additive model for the United States is the same as with the nonadditive model.

2. For the United States, the inclusion of saving as a twelfth commodity leads to markedly inferior forecasts, and this also appears to be true, though less decisively, for Canada. Saving is substantially overestimated for the United States and underestimated for Canada. The overestimate for the United States is offset almost exactly by an underestimate of expenditures for automobiles and parts, reflecting once more the interdependence of these two items of "expenditure."

3. The forecasts from the 11-group additive model are clearly superior to those from the nonadditive model. This indicates that simultaneous estimation of demand functions definitely has merit.

4. On balance it appears that the forecasts aggregated from the equations for the 82 expenditure categories are better than the forecasts from the nonadditive aggregate equations (though not better than those from the additive 11-group equations).

VII. Evaluation

The model of this chapter has been designed to integrate our basic dynamic approach of earlier chapters into an additive system of demand functions resting on an underlying utility function. To implement the model empirically

[16] The forecasts in Table 5.16 were made in the early summer of 1967 and are based on data (for the U.S.) from the July, 1966 issue of the *Survey of Current Business*. The nonadditive model forecasts presented in Table 4.14 are based on data from the July, 1968 issue of the *Survey* and therefore differ somewhat from those here.

Table 5.16. Forecasts for 1965 for United States and Canada (per capita, 1958 dollars for U.S., 1949 dollars for Canada)

United States

Group	Actual change	11 groups	12 groups	Nonadditive model PCE	Nonadditive model Disposable income	Nonadditive model Aggregated*
Automobiles and parts	$20.94	$16.05	$10.36	$8.19	$12.32	$10.58
Furniture and household equipment	9.65	9.68	7.53	8.28	4.25	8.33
Other durable goods	3.06	1.19	3.07	3.25	3.75	3.57
Food and beverages	10.64	17.02	17.09	19.66	18.50	20.75
Clothing and shoes	7.69	5.76	5.03	6.42	9.10	6.67
Gasoline and oil	2.19	2.54	2.53	3.50	3.59	3.00
Other nondurable goods	8.38	6.31	5.52	8.84	7.95	7.46
Housing	11.83	11.83	11.47	11.80	11.04	8.36
Housing operation	3.69	5.36	4.66	7.79	7.03	6.54
Transportation	1.88	2.85	2.42	3.83	3.28	2.81
Other services	11.18	12.58	11.24	9.57	10.31	12.38
Personal saving	2.42		12.75			

Canada

Group	Actual change	8 groups	9 groups
Food	$3.04	$10.80	$12.35
Tobacco and alcoholic beverages	4.24	4.85	6.44
Clothing and personal furnishings	2.86	3.76	9.13
Shelter	5.68	5.62	5.90
Household operation	7.03	4.95	6.80
Transportation	12.36	5.56	7.13
Personal and medical care and death expenses	2.62	3.60	4.53
Miscellaneous	8.29	6.99	9.46
Personal saving	22.99		7.17

* Aggregated from the forecasts of the 82 PCE items given in Table 4.6.

232

it has been necessary to make specific assumptions about the form of the utility function, so that the results must be evaluated in light of the quadratic function with independent marginal utilities that we have used.

All considered, the results appear to us to be very good for the United States, of lesser quality but still good for Canada, and mixed for the Netherlands and Sweden. In general, the results for the United States confirm those with the nonadditive model in showing substantial dynamic elements in consumer behavior. With exception of the residual durable goods category, the pattern of stock adjustment and habit formation conform to *a priori* expectations, and magnitudes of elasticities are generally plausible. Moreover, the structural coefficients all have the correct sign and are usually several times their approximate standard errors.

The results for Canada, though they contain more anomalies, in general conform to those of the United States. Substantial dynamic elements also characterize consumer behavior in Canada, and all structural parameters have the correct sign. The results for the Netherlands and Sweden are much less favorable. Dynamic effects are indicated to be present in both of these countries, but numerous anomalies are also apparent, including several structural parameters with wrong signs. The particularly poor results for the 16-commodity breakdown for the Netherlands (as compared with the results for the 4-commodity breakdown) may, as suggested earlier, reflect substitutabilities and complementarities that are at variance with the independence assumptions of the model.

The results obtained from the model of this chapter also shed light on the question of whether total expenditure or disposable income should be used for the budget constraint. The Canadian results slightly favor disposable income, but the United States results quite strongly point to total expenditure, which supports our use of total expenditure in the nonadditive model. As a theory of saving, treating saving as a commodity does not appear to have much to recommend it, though the results for both the United States and Canada indicate a rather marked interdependence between saving and expenditures for autos. Confirmation of this interdependence is provided by the forecasts for 1965 for the United States and Canada. (Speaking of these forecasts, those for the eleven-group equations for the United States, since they are superior to the forecasts from the nonadditive model, provide particularly strong support to the joint estimation of demand functions.)

Finally, the estimates of the marginal utility of total expenditure presented in Table 5.16 provide indirect evidence that the dynamic model of this chapter is an effective vehicle for bringing the theory of consumer behavior to bear on the real world. Classical theory tells us that there should be declining marginal utility of income, and it is reassuring that this is the case with the data of the four countries studied. There is an evident problem in the sharp decline in the λ's at the close of the period of observation, but since this is common to three of the four countries, the fault probably lies with the method of estimation. Indeed, this problem together with the slow convergence of Method II suggests that other methods of estimating the λ's should be explored in future applications of the model.

Appendix to Chapter 5

The Stability Condition for the Additive Dynamic Model

As indicated in the text, it is convenient to derive the convergence condition from a differential equation in s rather than in q. To do so, consider first (5) and (13) in the text, which lead to

$$\text{(A.1)} \qquad\qquad q = h + Hs,$$

where

$$\text{(A.2)} \qquad\qquad h = \frac{x + p'A^{-1}a}{p'A^{-1}p} A^{-1}p - A^{-1}a$$

and

$$\text{(A.3)} \qquad H = (p'A^{-1}p)^{-1}\{A^{-1}pp'A^{-1} - (p'A^{-1}p)A^{-1}\}B.$$

Using (2) we can rewrite (A.1) as

$$\text{(A.4)} \qquad\qquad \dot{s} = h + (H - D)s.$$

If x and p are constant h and H are independent of time, as is D, so (A.4) is the required differential equation in s in which λ does not appear. Since s is a vector, it is of course a system of first-order linear differential equations. Moreover the matrix $H - D$ of this system is symmetric, as can be seen from (A.3). In that case the well-known condition for the stability of the system (A.4) is that $H - D$ is negative definite. This condition is both necessary and sufficient.

Although in principle this settles the matter, a condition involving the negative definiteness of a nondiagonal matrix is difficult to verify in practice. Moreover $H - D$ depends on p, further restricting the usefulness of the condition. We must therefore look for a condition involving only A, B, and D. For this purpose we first observe that if $H - D$ is negative definite, the quadratic form $z'(H - D)z$ must be negative for any z. Now

$$\text{(A.5)} \quad z'(H - D)z = (p'A^{-1}p)^{-1}z'A^{-1}pp'A^{-1}z - z'(A^{-1}B + D)z$$

where the first term has the same sign as $p'A^{-1}p$, since its other factors constitute a square and are therefore positive. Consequently $z'(H - D)z$ will certainly be negative if

$$\text{(A.6)} \qquad\qquad p'A^{-1}p < 0$$

and

$$\text{(A.7)} \qquad\qquad z'(A^{-1}B + D)z > 0.$$

The first of these inequalities requires A to be negative definite, and the second $(A^{-1}B + D)$ to be positive definite, hence $(AD + B)$ to be negative definite. Since A and $(AD + B)$ are both diagonal, this leads immediately to the condition (14) in the text.[1]

It is of some interest to relate the sufficient condition to the estimating equation (21). From (27) we see that (dropping subscripts) $A < 0$ implies that either

$$(A.8) \qquad HK_1 < 0 \quad \text{and} \quad K_2 - K_3 < 0$$

or

$$(A.9) \qquad HK_1 > 0 \quad \text{and} \quad K_2 - K_3 > 0.$$

In our extensive experience with the estimation of equations of the type (21) in demand analysis it has never happened that $HK_1 < 0$, so (A.8) can be ruled out. We have occasionally found $K_1 > 1$, but this has invariably created difficulties with the signs of the short-run and long-run derivatives. Consequently (A.9) can be regarded as an implication of the sufficient condition for stability. By using (28) and (29) it is easy to show that (A.9) also implies (A.7).

---

[1] The above argument only gives us a sufficient condition; we have not succeeded in deriving a necessary condition that is independent of p.

6

Evidence from the 1960–1961 Household Survey

Most of the analysis in this book is based on time series of aggregate consumption. Even though some use was made of household budget data in the early stages of the work (especially in an unsuccessful search for important demographic variables), the principal equations and projections are all derived from time-series analysis. The reasons for this emphasis have already been discussed in Chapter 2; the most important of these is the possibility of applying a dynamic model of demand. Although such a model could be even more effectively applied to so-called panel data,[1] the fact is that the panel data available for the United States cover only a few items of expenditure. It was therefore inevitable that time series should be our main source of data.

Nevertheless, household survey data constitute a valuable body of information on consumers' expenditures, and they should be used at least for purposes of comparison and verification. As we shall see, this is not an easy matter, for there are many differences between the time series produced by the U.S. Department of Commerce and the household surveys undertaken by the U.S. Department of Labor. They are intended to describe the same phenomenon, namely the consumption expenditures of the American people,[2] but they differ not only in methods (which is what makes them useful for comparison) but also in concepts. There appears to be little coordination between the two agencies responsible for consumption data, and as far as one can tell the time series do not incorporate any information from the surveys, except possibly for an occasional benchmark. Any comparison between them is therefore a complicated and not very conclusive enterprise. It is our hope that the comparison attempted here will stimulate more effective coordination at the official level, which should lead to greater accuracy in both types of data and incidentally facilitate the work of future researchers.

---

[1] Also called reinterview data; these are repeated observations on the same households or firms. They were used in Houthakker and Haldi (1960), where a forerunner of our dynamic model was first investigated.

[2] There is a minor difference in coverage in that the time series cover also the military and institutional population and the private nonprofit institutions, whereas the surveys cover only households (including single consumers).

I. The 1960–1961 Survey of Consumer Expenditures (SCE)

In the United States, household surveys are normally undertaken every 10 years by the Bureau of Labor Statistics, with the cooperation of the U.S. Department of Agriculture for the farm population. The most recent survey was made in 1960–1961, and the full tabulations of the results became available in 1966.[3] Although these tabulations are quite detailed, it is even more useful that BLS provides copies of a tape containing details of income and expenditure for each of the 13,748 households in the sample. The use of this tape gives the researcher great freedom in designing his own analyses; most of the tables in this chapter are derived directly from the tape.

The 1960–1961 survey, like its predecessors, is a carefully designed probability sample. Each sample household is assumed to represent a stated number of households in the underlying population, so that it is simple to "blow up" the sample in order to get estimates for the whole population.[4] This is all to the good, but the BLS surveys cannot be rated so highly on the reliability of the figures supplied by the sample households. Most of these are obtained from interview-questions such as "How much did you spend on soap last year?" A skilled interviewer can probably obtain meaningful answers to such questions, but it must be understood that the strain on the respondent's memory is often excessive, so that the answers are no more than guesses.

In some countries this problem is to a large extent met by the use of account books, in which households write down their expenditures as they are made, but in the United States this device has traditionally been frowned upon. It is feared that the use of account books would reduce the response rate to a point where the sample can no longer be considered representative. This fear is not without justification; there is evidently a trade-off between representativeness and reliability, and opinions can differ as to the optimal mixture of the two. The choice is also influenced by the cost of fieldwork, which is higher in the United States than elsewhere. Nevertheless it is permissible to wonder whether the BLS should not give somewhat more weight to reliability than appears to be the case.

---

[3] For a full description see *Bureau of Labor Statistics Report No. 238-13*. We have worked only with the entire sample (urban and rural combined).

[4] If there is anything to criticize in the sampling scheme it is the inadequate representation of high-income households. Optimal estimation of aggregate expenditures requires that every dollar spent have an equal chance of being in the sample, which means, roughly speaking, that a household spending $15,000 a year should have a probability of inclusion five times greater than a household spending $3,000 a year—in fact, even more than five times, because high-income households probably have greater variation in their expenditure patterns and because the response rate may be lower for such households. Admittedly the estimation of aggregate expenditures is only one of the purposes for which surveys are used.

II. *Comparison of Aggregate Consumption Patterns from Time-Series and Survey Data in 1960–1961*

As has been mentioned, there are many conceptual differences between the time series used elsewhere in this book and the household survey data. In particular the classification of expenditures, which concerns us most, is rather different. Some time-series items, in fact, do not appear in the survey at all; apart from fictitious time-series items such as "services rendered without payment by financial intermediaries," which few people will miss, there are of course no survey data on food and clothing for the military, nor for expenditures by foreign visitors to the United States. The treatment of owner-occupied housing is quite different: the time series give an imputed space rental value, the survey gives the actual expenditures by homeowners. Under "religious and welfare expenditures" the time series give the net expenditures of eleemosynary groups; the closest equivalent in the survey are the donations given by households to such bodies. Not infrequently expenditure categories from the time series cannot be identified separately in the survey at all, although in general the survey data are more detailed.

Since our main interest is in the time series, we have attempted to regroup the survey categories to the time-series classification used elsewhere in this book. In several cases this was possible only by combining time-series categories, namely when there was not enough detail in the survey. As will be seen from Tables 6.1 and 6.1a, however, the time-series breakdown has been preserved fairly well. There are undoubtedly several instances where time-series and cross-section items with identical or similar descriptions do not have exactly the same composition, but the available definitions do not make this clear.[5] Sometimes time-series categories which presumably are also covered in the survey could not be located; an example is item 9.7 (flowers, seeds, and potted plants). For these items the cross-section part of Tables 6.1 and 6.1a has been left blank.

Tables 6.1 and 6.1a give the average of the 1960 and 1961 time-series aggregates in current dollars and the "blown up" aggregates of the survey.[6] It also gives these totals as percentages of two concepts which have been labeled PCE_1 and PCE_2; these are, respectively, modifications of the time-series and cross-section totals for personal consumption designed to be as

---

[5] For the survey we have used mostly *Bureau of Labor Statistics Bulletin 237-93* and for the time series the footnotes to Table 2.5 of *The National Income and Product Accounts of the United States 1929–65* (U.S. Dept. of Commerce, 1966).

[6] These totals were derived by multiplying the average expenditure of all households (given in *BLS Bulletin 237-93, supp. 3, part A*) by the estimated number of households in the population, as stated there. This source was used in preference to the data tape because it gives a more detailed breakdown. Wherever possible the survey totals thus derived have been checked against a blowup based on individual household data from the tape, and the agreement was always close.

Table 6.1. Reconciliation of 1960–1961 BLS Survey of Consumer Expenditures and OBE Time-Series Data

Time series			Cross section			
Item	Millions (av. 1960–1961)	% total PCE₁*	Millions	% total PCE₂†	% CS/TS	Item
Food total (minus alcohol)	71,093	25.23	68,274			Food total
			844			Value received without expense
			2,455			Value of home-produced food (urban and rural)
			71,573	27.35	100.7	Total
1.0 Alcoholic beverages	10,618	3.77	4,306			Alcoholic beverages
			144			Value received without expense
			4,450	1.70	41.9	Total
1.1 (minus alcohol)	56,470	20.04	54,693	20.90	96.9	Food prepared at home
1.2 (minus alcohol)	12,217		13,581			Food away from home
1.3 (minus alcohol)	1,268		589			$\frac{1}{3}$ all-expense tours (allocated in thirds to food, transportation, and lodging out of home city)
1.2 + 1.3	13,485	4.79	14,170	5.42	105.1	Total
1.4	1,140	.40	1,530	.58	134.2	Value of home-produced food (rural)
1.5	7,108	2.52	5,032			Tobacco
			53			Value received without expense
			5,085	1.94	71.5	Total

Code	Amount	Percent	Item	Amount	Percent	Index
Clothing (minus 2.4)	33,383	11.85	Clothing, clothing materials, and services	28,673		
2.1	4,513		Value received without expense	2,809		
2.3	23,044		Laundry and cleaning sent out	1,932		
2.7	2,125		Total	33,414	12.77	100.1
2.1 + 2.3 + 2.7	29,682	10.53	Clothing total minus clothing upkeep	25,851	9.88	87.1
2.2	239		Clothing upkeep	2,809		
2.5 + 2.6	3,016		Laundry and cleaning sent out	1,932		
2.8	447		Total	4,741	1.82	128.4
2.2 + 2.5 + 2.6 + 2.8	3,702	1.31		§		
2.4	52	‡				
Personal care (total)	5,558	1.97	Personal care (total)	8,034		
			Value received without expense	238		
			Total	8,272	3.16	148.8
3.1	3,085	1.09	Personal care supplies (total)	4,426	1.69	143.5
3.2	2,474	.88	Personal care services (total)	3,608	1.38	145.8
Housing (total)	47,511	‡	Shelter (total)	36,399		
			Other real estate	388		
			Total	36,787	‡	77.3
4.1	31,589	‡	Owned dwelling, total (actual cost, not space rental value) nonfarm	18,708		
			Owned vacation home	268		
			Total	18,976	‡	60.1

241

(continued)

Table 6.1 (*continued*)

	Time series			Cross section		
Item	Millions (av. 1960–1961)	% total PCE₁*	% $\frac{CS}{TS}$	% total PCE₂†	Millions	Item
4.2	12,461	4.42	116.5	5.55	14,515	Rental dwelling (nonfarm)
					615	Farm dwellings (actual cost, not space rental value of owner occupied)
					353	Farm dwellings, rental
4.3	1,990	‡	48.6	‡	968	Total
					1,940	Lodging out of home city
					589	⅓ all-expense tours
4.4	1,471	.52	171.9	.97	2,529	Total
					13,787	Fuel, light, refrigeration, and water (total)
					15,954	Household operations (total)
					14,695	House furnishings and equipment (total)
Household operation (total)	47,582	16.88	93.4	16.98	44,436	Total
5.1	4,580	1.63	92.0	1.61	4,214	Furniture (total)
					3,791	Major appliances (total)
					409	Small appliances
5.2	4,834	1.72	86.9	1.61	4,200	Total

	Item					
5.3	Housewares (total minus cleaning and laundry equipment)	1,849	.67	596	.23	32.2
	Floor coverings (total)			1,424		
	Other under miscellaneous items (lamps, clocks, pictures, etc.)			1,889		
	Household textiles (pillows, blankets, curtains, draperies)			878		
5.4	Total	4,302	1.53	4,191	1.60	97.4
5.5	Household textiles (sheets, pillowcases, tablecloths, slipcovers, towels, other readymade items, materials, and services)			918		
	Housewares (cleaning and laundry equipment)			154		
5.5	Total	2,869	1.02	1,072	.41	37.4
	Laundry supplies			1,744		
	Cleaning supplies			868		
	Household paper supplies			1,070		
5.6	Total	3,449	1.22	3,682	1.41	106.8
5.7	Insurance on furnishings, equipment, and apparel	1,092		237		
5.11	Other household expenses, total (repairs of furniture, moving, freight, express, storage, postage, writing materials, other expenses)	2,100		3,054		
5.7 + 5.11	Total	3,192	1.13	3,291	1.26	103.1

243

(continued)

Table 6.1 (*continued*)

Time series			Cross section			
Item	Millions (av. 1960–1961)	% total PCE$_1$*	% $\frac{CS}{TS}$	% total PCE$_2$†	Millions	Item
5.8	14,075	4.99	98.0	5.26	13,787	Fuel, light, refrigerator, and water (total minus expenses covered by rent or taxes of owner-occupied housing)
5.8a	5,206				3,290	Gas
5.8b	3,313				4,450	Electricity
					1,050	Gas and electricity (combined bills)
5.8a + 5.8b	8,519	3.02	103.2	3.36	8,790	Total
					1,003	Water
					154	Sewage
					207	Garbage and trash collection
					164	Water, sewage, garbage (combined bills)
					51	Water softening service
5.8c	1,329	.47	118.8	.60	1,579	Total
					3,248	Fuel
					32	Ice
					35	Food freezer rentals
5.8d	4,227	1.50	78.4	1.27	3,315	Total

Code	Item					
5.9	Telephone and telegraph (total)	93.0	1.66	4,342	1.66	4,669
5.10	Domestic service and day nursery care (total)	76.6	1.10	2,884	1.34	3,766
Medical care expenses (total)	Medical care (total)	105.1	7.92	18,802	7.00	19,719
	Value received without expense			1,931		
	Total			20,733		
6.1	Drugs and medicines	102.5	1.44	3,775	1.31	3,683
	Medical appliances and supplies			233		
	Eye care and glasses			875		
6.2	Total	141.9	.42	1,108	.28	781
6.3	Physician's services outside hospital	56.6	1.17	3,059	1.92	5,402
6.4	Dental services	124.2	.98	2,556	.73	2,058
	Other practitioners			146		
	Other medical care			482		
6.5	Total	63.4	.24	628	.35	990
6.6	Direct expenses for hospitalized illness	48.1	.98	2,569	1.89	5,339
6.7	Prepaid care (does not include em-ployer's contribution)	539.0	1.88	4,916	‡	1,468
6.7a					.32	912
6.7b					‡	556
6.3	Physician's services outside hospital			3,059		5,402
6.6	For hospitalized illness			2,569		5,339
6.7a	Prepaid care (does not include em-ployer's contributions)			4,916		912
6.3 + 6.6 + 6.7a	Total	90.5	4.03	10,544	4.13	11,653

(continued)

Table 6.1 (*continued*)

	Time series			Cross section			
Item	Millions (av. 1960–1961)	% total PCE₁*	Millions	% total PCE₂†	% CS/TS	Item
6 (without 6.4 and 6.5)	16,672	5.92	16,100	6.89	108.2	Medical care (total minus dental services and other practitioners)
			1.931			Value received without expense
			$\overline{18,031}$			Total
					108.2	Total
Personal business						
7.1	1,238	‡				
7.2	1,003					
7.5	1,876					
7.6	$\overline{1,490}$					
7.2 + 7.5 + 7.6	4,369	1.55	4,366	1.67	99.9	Miscellaneous, other (interest on loans, other than mortgages and business, bank service charges, legal expenses, fines, marriage, etc., fees, funeral expenses, expenses for raising food for family use, money lost or stolen, money allowances to children, plus other expenses not allocated elsewhere)
7.3	5,228	‡				
7.4	3,594	‡				
7.7	1,075	.38	2,398	.92	223.1	Occupational expenses (union dues, etc., dues to business and professional associations, licenses, tools, etc., not reimbursed by employer)

Item						Description
Transportation (total)	42,295	15.01	41,364			Transportation (total minus other transportation, which becomes 9.4)
			680			Value received without expense
			589			⅓ all-expense tours
			42,633	16.29	100.8	Total
8.1 (total)	38,980	13.83	16,552			Automobile purchase
			21,761			Automobile operation (total)
			275			Car pool
			38,588	14.75	99.0	Total
8.1a	16,870	5.99	16,552	6.33	98.1	Automobile purchase
8.1b	2,392	.85	1,484			Tires and tubes
			556			Batteries and other equipment
			2,040	.78	85.3	Total
8.1c	5,086		789			Lubrication, washing, etc.
			2,360			Repairs and parts
8.1e	312		557			Operating expenses not allocated
			1,738			Registration and other expenses
8.1c + 8.1e	5,398	1.92	5,444	2.08	100.9	Total
8.1d	12,319	4.37	9,499			Gasoline
			680			Motor oil
			10,179	3.89	82.6	Total
8.1f	2,003	.71	4,030	1.54	201.2	Insurance

247

(*continued*)

Table 6.1 (*continued*)

	Time series			Cross section			
Item	Millions (av. 1960–1961)	% total PCE$_1$*		% $\frac{\text{CS}}{\text{TS}}$	% total PCE$_2$†	Millions	Item
8.2 (total)	1,977	.70		79.4	.60	1,570	Public transportation in home city
						1,205	Public transportation out of home city
						589	⅓ all-expense tours
8.3 (total)	1,338	.47		134.1	.69	1,794	Total
8.3	1,338						
12.1	2,318						
8.3 + 12.1	3,646	1.29		49.2	.69	1,794	Same as entry immediately above
						11,068	Recreation (total)
						2,467	Reading (total)
						553	Books, supplies (under education)
						1,217	Other transportation (bicycles, motorcycles, scooters, boats, airplanes)
						777	Value received without expense
Recreation (total)	18,901	6.71		85.1	6.15	16,082	Total
						494	Books, not technical
						267	Books, school (⅓ of books, supplies, and equipment under education)
						54	Other reading
9.1	1,350	.48		60.4	.31	815	Total

248

Code	Item					
	Newspapers			1,423		
	Magazines			493		
9.2	Total	2,271	.81	1,916	.73	84.4
9.3	Toys and play equipment	2,560		944		
9.4	Participant sports	2,118		1,624		
9.9	Other transportation	748		1,217		
9.10	Club dues and memberships	1,230		587		
9.3 + 9.4 + 9.9 + 9.10	Total	6,656	2.36	4,372	1.67	65.7
9.5	Television	3,540		2,102		
	Radio			445		
9.6	Phonograph, etc.	820		875		
	Musical instruments			512		
9.5 + 9.6	Total	4,360	1.55	3,934	1.50	90.2
9.7	Spectator admissions	672	.24	1,333		
	Recreation out of home city			281		
9.8 (total)	Total	1,616	.57	1,614	.62	99.9
9.11	Other recreation	527	.19	202		
	Hobbies			1,060		
	Pets (purchase and care)			1,083		
9.12	Total	1,452	.52	2,345	.90	161.5

Phonograph, etc. and Musical instruments: includes maintenance

249

(continued)

Table 6.1 (*continued*)

	Time series			Cross section		
Item	Millions (av. 1960–1961)	% total PCE₁*	Millions	% total PCE₂†	% $\frac{\text{CS}}{\text{TS}}$	Item
Private education (total)	3,873	1.37	2,355	.90	60.8	Education (total minus books, supplies, equipment)
Religious and welfare activities	4,837	‡	7,650	2.16	158.2	Gifts and contributions to organizations (total)
12.1	2,318	.82				
12.2	1,081	‡	§			
12.3 and 12.4	−1,226	§				

* Total PCE adjusted to eliminate items not found in cross-section data.
† Total PCE minus owned dwellings (actual cost is used in cross-section as opposed to space rental value in time series).
‡ Not included in adjusted total expenditures—no comparable cross-section or time series.
§ Expenditures of military personnel not in cross section.

250

Table 6.1a. Reconciliation of 1960–1961 BLS Survey of Consumer Expenditures and OBE Time-Series Data

	Time series		Cross section		
Item	Millions (av. 1960–1961)	% $\frac{CS}{TS}$	Millions		Item
Total personal consumption	330,197		279,496		Expenditures for current consumption
			2,455		Value of items received without expense
				281,951	Total
minus 2.4	52				
4.1	31,589				
4.3	1,990				
6.7b	556				
7.1	1,238				
7.3	5,228		19,929		Minus owned dwellings total, owned vacation home, and other real estate
7.4	3,594				
11.0	4,837		353		Minus farm dwellings (rented)
12.0	2,173		−20,282		
	278,940		261,669		
	2,318				
add 12.1					
	281,258	93.0	261,669		

251

comparable as possible. From the last line it will be seen that the cross-section total is only 93 percent of the comparable time-series total. This is a large discrepancy, considering that all the known conceptual differences have been removed and that definitional variations in the expenditure categories should cancel out. In money terms the discrepancy is $20 billion.

Over $6 billion of this difference can be attributed to alcohol. That the cross-section figure for alcohol is below the time-series figure is to be expected, but for it to be so far below is really surprising. Although we have generally refrained from taking sides as to which are the better data, it is clear in this case that, backwoods stills aside, the time-series data on alcohol should be very accurate. Some alcoholic beverage expenditures are included in food purchased outside of the home, but even a generous reallocation would stop short of $6 billion. The huge discrepancy therefore points to a substantial "Puritan" element in the household data. The same phenomenon is probably reflected, though to a lesser extent, in the expenditures for tobacco, where the cross-section figure is only 71.5 percent that of the time series.

Other large discrepancies (either as percentages or absolutes) occur in food produced and consumed on the farm (1.4); most of the items in Group II (clothing, accessories, and jewelry), although for clothing as a group the agreement is excellent; both items of personal care (Group III); space rental value of tenant-occupied housing (4.2); lodging away from home (4.4); several items in household operation (Group V); most of the items in medical care (Group VI); tires and tubes (8.1b); gasoline and oil (8.1d); nearly all of recreation (Group IX); private education (Group X); and religious and welfare expenditures (Group XI). For several of these disagreements, there are obvious partial explanations. The cross-section figure for food produced for home consumption includes tomatoes grown in urban backyards, so should be higher than the time-series figure which includes only rural areas. Overlapping categories are a problem in Groups II, V, VI, and IX, and may be instrumental in Group VIII. For Groups X and XI, it may be that some private education expenditures are included in religious and welfare. Group VII, personal business expenses, as already noted, has little representation in the household data.

In contrast to the above categories, the agreement is excellent for food and tobacco (less alcoholic beverages) taken together and for clothing as a group, and pretty good for the household utilities (5.8), automobiles (8.1a), user-operated transportation as a group (8.1), and spectator entertainment (9.8). Despite these close agreements, however, the general pattern in Table 6.1, it will have to be agreed, is one of discrepancy.

To give an overall impression we have tabulated all the comparable categories in Table 6.1 according to the cross-section/time-series ratio, omitting summary items (such as "total food") in order to avoid double counting (see Table 6.2). For the sake of brevity Table 6.2 gives only the lowest numbered item in a consolidated expenditure category (thus the combination of 2.1, 2.3, and 2.7 is listed as 2.1).

Of the 42 items listed in Table 6.2 there are only 14 where the cross-section and time-series totals are within 10 percent of each other. Fortunately these include some of the larger items, such as 1.1 (food consumed at home) and 8.1a (automobiles), though there are a few other large items, in particular 4.2 (rent) and 8.1d (gasoline and oil), where the agreement is far from close. The discrepancy on rent is especially disturbing because this is an item which respondents cannot have much difficulty in recalling accurately or, alternatively, where the Commerce Department should not be far from the truth, especially in a census year such as 1960.

Table 6.2. Expenditure Items According to Cross-Section/Time-Series Ratio

Ratio (in %)	Items	Number
Less than 60	1.0, 5.3, 5.5, 6.3	4
60–79.9	1.5, 5.8d, 5.10, 6.5, 8.2, 9.1, 9.10, 10	8
80–89.9	2.1, 5.2, 8.1b, 8.1d, 9.2	5
90–99.9	1.1, 5.1, 5.4, 5.9, 7.1, 8.1a, 9.6, 9.8	8
100–109.9	1.2, 5.6, 5.7, 5.8a, 6.1, 8.1c	6
110–124.9	4.2, 5.8c, 6.4	3
125–164.9	2.2, 3.1, 3.2, 6.2, 9.12	5
165 and over	4.4, 7.7, 8.1f	3
Total		42

The figures given in this section do not permit us to determine which of the two sources of data is the more accurate; for that we would need a third source, which does not exist.[7] Nevertheless it should be pointed out that on

[7] One important clue is obtained by blowing up some nonexpenditure items. Thus we find that "money income before taxes" according to the survey was $345.4 billion. This figure is conceptually very similar to "personal income" estimated by the Office of Business Economics at $408.9 billion (again taking the mean of 1960 and 1961). The survey figure was therefore only 84.5 percent of the time-series figure. Furthermore, the discrepancy is greater for nonwage than for wage income; for wages the survey gives $258.4 billion, which is 90.1 percent of the corresponding time-series figure of $286.8 billion. For nonwage income the survey figure of $87.0 billion is only 71.3 percent of the time-series figure of $122.1 billion. Similarly, the cross-section/time-series ratio is only 77.9 percent for personal taxes (excluding "personal nontaxes," the treatment of which in the survey is not clear). The "net change in assets and liabilities" in the survey of $11.0 billion compare with a personal savings figure of $19.1 billion estimated by the Office of Business Economics and with $17.6 billion estimated by the Securities and Exchange Commission, giving ratios of 57.6 percent and 62.5 percent, respectively. Since

methodological grounds the time-series data usually inspire more confidence. They are in general based on reports from producers and other sellers, and consequently are of a more objective nature. While such data raise plenty of problems too (for instance in the allocation of sales between households and other customers), they are probably more accurate than the recollections of respondents in a survey. A specific reason for this belief is that industrial data are ultimately derived from accounting records, while the BLS survey relies largely on the participating households' memories.

However this may be, it is clear that the discrepancies demonstrated here cannot be viewed with complacency. Some of them may be attributable to undetected conceptual differences, but this can hardly be the whole story. We hope that our analysis, provisional though it is, will contribute to a reconsideration of the procedures used by both the Office of Business Economics and the Bureau of Labor Statistics, and especially to closer coordination between them. The resulting improvement in the data should be of great benefit to the study of consumer demand.

III. *Variables Used in the Cross-Section Analysis*

By their nature cross-section data are suitable mostly for the study of income effects. Among the households participating in a survey there is not enough price variation to permit the analysis of price effects, particularly since much of the apparent price variation may be attributed to quality differences (see Prais and Houthakker, 1955, chapter viii). The cross-sectional variation in income, on the other hand, is usually very wide; the 1960–1961 sample in particular covers almost the entire range from stark poverty to moderate affluence and is deficient only in really wealthy households. Nevertheless the measurement of income effects poses serious problems which will be discussed in the next section.

It will also be shown there that income, or some proxy for it, is in fact the most powerful variable explaining consumer expenditures in a cross section. Even so it cannot account for more than a modest fraction of the observed variation among households. Several other factors are known to affect consumption patterns. Family composition is so important that no cross-

nonwage income, personal taxes, and saving all tend to be proportionately higher for households with large incomes, this suggests strongly that there are not enough high-income households in the survey, and that the "expansion factors" given by BLS do not make sufficient allowance for this. Unfortunately official data on the distribution of households by income size, by which this explanation could be verified directly, are no longer published. Internal calculations by BLS, made in response to an earlier version of this section, confirm that reweighting the cross-section data by a more realistic income distribution leads to better agreement between the two sets of aggregates.

section analysis can ignore it. The analysis of its effects can be pushed to great lengths, but in the present study this was neither necessary (since the focus is on income effects) nor possible (because of data gaps); only the number of persons has been taken into account. The significance of location and occupation (or more generally social class) is usually somewhat less obvious, and in the present study no attempt has been made to allow for these factors. All the calculations reported here refer to the entire sample, including both urban and rural households.

Another variable to which attention has been given in recent years is income change as contrasted with income level. Our basic dynamic model in the form used for estimation (1.58) also involves income change. While the underlying argument in Chapter 1 was phrased in terms of time series it is clear that this aspect carries over to cross-section data. Fortunately the 1960–1961 survey contains some information on income change; although the dollar amount is not available, households can be divided into five classes according to the size of the year-to-year change. In fact this classification can be made not only for the change from year $t - 1$ to year t (the survey year), but also from $t - 2$ to $t - 1$. Since, as we shall see in section VI below, the results with the more recent income change were discouraging, the earlier income change has not been used in the analysis.

IV. *Income Versus Total Expenditure*

The choice of an appropriate income concept is no less difficult in cross-section analysis than in time-series analysis (Chapter 3, section II; Chapter 5, section III). It cannot be settled by economic theory alone,[8] but must depend at least as much on statistical considerations. The permanent income hypothesis (Friedman, 1957) has been instrumental in clarifying the problem, though it has by no means solved it. According to Friedman, income and consumption can each be divided into a permanent and a transitory component; permanent income determines permanent consumption, and the transitory components are independent of the permanent components and of each other. It follows from this analysis that the income concept should come as close as possible to permanent income, which is itself unobservable. Thus, according to this line of reasoning, an average of measured income over a period of years would usually be a more appropriate concept than the income observed for a single year. Unfortunately, such attempts to reconstruct permanent income rom observations tend to be rather arbitrary.

---

[8] As Hicks (1946, p. 171) has put it.

The dynamic model of consumption on which most of this book is based has much in common with the permanent income hypothesis. Both recognize that the response of consumption to changes in income is spread out over time,[9] but our model is more specific on the time-shape of the response. Our use of PCE instead of income in the time-series analyses is also in line with the spirit, though perhaps not the letter, of the permanent income hypothesis: when habit formation predominates, total expenditure is probably a better indicator of permanent income than is current income. But there is no guarantee that the same holds for cross-section data. As it happens, the matter can be subjected to a quantitative test, and the test gives an unambiguous answer.

For this purpose we took 36 distinct items of expenditure[10] and analyzed the joint variation of their logarithms into principal components.[11] The observations consisted of all the four-person households in the sample. There are of course as many components as there are variables, but the most powerful one accounts by itself for nearly 27 percent of the total variance, and the next four for another 18 percent. Strictly speaking, these components are merely mathematical artifacts, but with luck one is sometimes able to identify those that contribute most to the total variance.

Table 6.3 shows the "factor loadings" of the 36 variables with respect to the first five components. The factor loadings are familiar to economists as the first-order correlation coefficients between each variable and each of the five principal components (since the components are uncorrelated with each other, the factor loadings may also be interpreted as partial correlation coefficients). The "communality" is the sum of squares of the factor loadings and therefore the same as a multiple determination coefficient. The latent

---

[9] Actually Friedman does not include the purchase of durables in consumption, so that his theory applies only to what we call habit-forming commodities.

[10] Not all items appearing in Tables 6.1 and 6.2 could be used because the data tape containing expenditures for individual households is less complete than the printed tabulation underlying the tables. In several cases it was necessary to supplement the data on the tape in order to get items comparable to the OBE classification. This was done by assuming that each household spent as much on an item as the average household in its income group (available from the printed tabulation). Most of the expenditure items for which this procedure had to be followed were small components of a larger item whose more important components *were* reported on the tape. Items that were entirely derived by this method have been ignored in the analyses that follow.

[11] The standard work on principal components analysis is Harman (1960); for a pioneering application to economic time series see Stone (1947). In essence, this technique amounts to finding a linear transformation of a set of variables (here the logarithms of the expenditures) such that the transformed variables are uncorrelated with each other. The variables can be either in terms of deviations from means or in standard measure. Both yield principal components that are uncorrelated, though the transformations are not identical. We have standardized the variables, and logarithms were taken before standardization because double-logarithmic Engel curves usually fit better than linear ones; zero expenditures were put equal to $1.

roots are also sums of squares of the factor loadings in each column; they measure the contribution of each component to the total variance (which is identically equal to the number of variables).

Table 6.3. Correlations of 36 Expenditure Categories With Their First Five Principal Components

	Item	Principal component 1	2	3	4	5	Commu- nality
1	1.0	.496	.186	−.317	−.156	.252	.468
2	1.1	.626	.001	−.312	−.170	−.087	.526
3	1.2, 1.3	.579	.183	.160	−.067	.064	.403
4	1.4	−.356	−.052	.603	.297	.172	.611
5	1.5	.104	.300	−.356	.062	.493	.474
6	2.1, 2.3, 2.7	.750	.189	.130	−.006	.006	.615
7	2.2, 2.56, 2.8	.811	.178	−.046	−.021	−.027	.692
8	3.1	.546	.171	−.109	.168	.043	.369
9	3.2	.645	.136	−.011	−.103	−.073	.451
10	Owned dwellings	.568	−.648	−.060	−.124	.186	.795
11	Rented dwellings	−.240	.765	−.179	.048	−.243	.736
12	4.4	.597	.068	.349	−.184	−.077	.522
13	5.1	.250	.081	.008	.024	.050	.072
14	5.2	.153	.015	.040	.179	.205	.100
15	5.4	.693	.097	.038	−.021	.092	.500
16	5.6	.616	.005	−.190	.143	.095	.446
17	5.8a, 5.8b	.494	−.349	−.112	.035	.066	.384
18	5.8c	.551	−.430	−.326	−.197	.039	.635
19	5.8d	.037	−.176	.169	−.042	.368	.198
20	5.9	.640	−.134	−.191	−.035	−.031	.467
21	6.1	.411	−.111	−.210	.598	−.244	.643
22	6.2	.464	−.030	.195	.092	−.159	.288
23	6.3	.337	−.163	−.192	.569	−.265	.571
24	6.4	.510	−.043	.155	.006	−.239	.343
25	6.5	.716	.090	.005	.050	−.010	.523
26	6.6	−.021	.012	−.109	.403	−.129	.192
27	6.7a	.388	−.139	.046	.160	−.067	.202
28	8.1a	.207	.135	.223	.036	.131	.129
29	8.1b	.143	.061	.289	.381	.393	.408
30	8.1c, 8.1e	.539	.060	.198	.231	.245	.446
31	9.1	.737	.126	.190	−.128	−.086	.619
32	9.3, 9.4, 9.9, 9.10	.751	.100	.018	.017	.113	.588
33	9.5, 9.6	.347	.176	.086	−.056	.041	.164
34	9.8	.687	.258	.032	−.044	.001	.541
35	Private education	.435	.000	.352	−.231	−.316	.467
36	Relief and welfare	.512	−.282	.274	−.019	−.168	.445
	Latent roots	9.611	1.954	1.699	1.493	1.274	

Inspection of the factor loadings reveals that the first component has a fairly high correlation[12] with most of the expenditure items. It is clearly some measure of general purchasing power, but whether it is income, total expenditure, or some other indicator cannot be said without further analysis, which will follow in a moment. The second component shows two strikingly high loadings: a negative one with expenditure on owned dwellings and a positive one with rent. It presumably reflects the tenure status of the household. Other factor loadings disclose that homeowners spend more on utilities and on charity but less on tobacco and on amusements. Two further components can be tentatively identified. The third is highly correlated with food consumed on farms and somewhat less so with farm home expenditures; it is no doubt related to farm residence. The interested reader may like to see for himself how farm residence affects other expenditures. The fourth component is strongly correlated with expenditures on drugs and physicians and more weakly with hospital fees; evidently it represents illness. The fifth component has considerable positive correlation with expenditures on tobacco, on other fuel (mostly heating oil), and on tires, accessories, and other automobile parts; it is negatively correlated with all the health items and with private education. Nevertheless, it would be going too far to link this component with a mysterious population group of robust smokers who send their children (if any) to public schools, heat their homes with oil, and are forever buying things for their cars. The truth of the matter is that we have been lucky to find an interpretation for four components and that the fifth surpasses our comprehension.

Returning now to the first component we shall try to determine its nature by correlating it, and the other four components, with income and total expenditure (see Table 6.4). The first component turns out to be much more closely correlated with total expenditure than with income. In fact, the former correlation is so high (considering that it is based on individual households) that the first component may be described as a close relative of total expenditure.

Moreover, income can be seen to have little or no independent influence and to affect expenditure items only to the extent that it is a proxy for total expenditure. This follows from the fact that the correlation between income and the first component is approximately equal to the correlation between income and total expenditure multiplied by the correlation between total expenditure and the first component.

The unequivocal conclusion is that total expenditure rather than income should be used as an explanatory variable, just as was done in the time-series

---

[12] In evaluating these coefficients, it has to be borne in mind that the observations are of individual households, so that a close fit can hardly be expected.

Table 6.4. Correlation Coefficients Between Selected Variables and the First Five Principal Components (All Variables in Logarithms)

	Variable									
Variable	1	2	3	4	5	6	7	8	9	10
1. Total expenditure	1.000	.672	.034	.644	.546	.932	.132	.006	.007	.034
2. Income		1.000	—	—	—	.660	.013	.014	.032	.014
3. Family size			1.000	.035	.046	.074	.027	.037	.064	.002
4. Foor purchased for off-premise consumption				1.000	.256	.626	.001	.312	.170	.087
5. Purchased meals and food furnished government					1.000	.579	.183	.160	.067	.064
6. First principal component						1.000	0	0	0	0
7. Second principal component							1.000	0	0	0
8. Third principal component								1.000	0	0
9. Fourth principal component									1.000	0
10. Fifth principal component										1.000

analysis. Of course, this conclusion is limited to the particular body of data from which it was derived; it does not necessarily imply that total expenditure is always a better variable than income. The superiority of total expenditure for the survey under consideration may reflect nothing more than the notorious unreliability of respondents' reports on their incomes; total expenditure is not directly reported by households but obtained by adding up individual expenditure, so that it benefits from the canceling of errors. All the same, the common practice, also followed by BLS, of tabulating survey results primarily by income needs reconsideration.[13]

V. Engel Curves

After the choice of the explanatory variables is made, the only major problem that remains is the form of the equations. This is one of the principal issues in cross-section analysis, but for the present purpose it did not seem necessary to pursue it. We have simply used double-logarithmic Engel curves

[13] We have tabulated many items from the data tape by total expenditure, family size, and income change class. These tabulations are available for reproduction upon request.

Table 6.5. Cross-Section Elasticities with Respect to Total PCE and Family Size

Item	PCE elasticity for family size						Elasticities for all family sizes combined		
	1	2	3	4	5	6	PCE	Fam. size	F-Ratio
Total food	.592 (.019)	.529 (.014)	.516 (.024)	.512 (.017)	.503 (.029)	.488 (.019)	.513 (.008)	.332 (.011)	.49
Alcohol (1.0)	2.048 (.018)	1.619 (.079)	1.546 (.069)	1.528 (.060)	1.469 (.111)	1.499 (.093)	1.541 (.037)	−.429 (.048)	1.86
Food purchased* (1.1)	.334 (.025)	.510 (.025)	.593 (.025)	.609 (.029)	.648 (.032)	.702 (.030)	.578 (.014)	.293 (.019)	3.33
Purchased meals (1.2, 1.3)	1.196 (.054)	1.674 (.048)	1.267 (.057)	1.230 (.047)	1.108 (.082)	1.111 (.052)	1.400 (.036)	.005 (.047)	8.42
Farm food (1.4)		−1.408 (.140)	−1.786 (.160)	−1.839 (.232)	−1.726 (.179)	−1.150 (.167)	−1.566 (.077)	1.457 (.101)	1.14
Tobacco (1.5)	.938 (.091)	.749 (.047)	.614 (.047)	.525 (.050)	.521 (.052)	.490 (.039)	.635 (.023)	.047 (.031)	2.71
Clothing	1.214 (.049)	1.115 (.028)	.990 (.026)	.974 (.024)	.930 (.042)	.826 (.027)	1.021 (.017)	.338 (.022)	6.05
Shoes* (2.1, 2.3, 2.7)	1.389 (.060)	1.195 (.027)	1.053 (.029)	1.039 (.024)	1.023 (.037)	.906 (.023)	1.098 (.017)	.403 (.022)	5.69
Shoe repair (2.2, 2.56, 2.8)	1.167 (.047)	1.281 (.044)	1.122 (.022)	1.218 (.068)	1.065 (.060)	1.088 (.067)	1.194 (.024)	−.251 (.031)	2.15
Personal care	.965 (.052)	.897 (.025)	.788 (.026)	.790 (.020)	.749 (.020)	.771 (.021)	.832 (.012)	.079 (.016)	3.62
Toilet articles* (3.1)	.872 (.054)	.767 (.033)	.661 (.034)	.594 (.026)	.628 (.038)	.678 (.022)	.704 (.017)	.280 (.022)	3.37

Barber shops* (3.2)	1.146 (.067)	1.088 (.039)	.977 (.031)	1.067 (.033)	.962 (.047)	.955 (.039)	1.032 (.017)	−.164 (.023)	2.14
Housing*	.851 (.027)	.994 (.023)	1.044 (.040)	1.033 (.033)	1.031 (.052)	1.179 (.035)	1.041 (.016)	−.244 (.021)	1.46
Owned dwelling	.884 (.072)	1.134 (.025)	1.547 (.065)	1.685 (.117)	1.718 (.115)	2.103 (.130)	1.486 (.051)	−.377 (.066)	7.57
Rented dwelling*	.790 (.041)	.752 (.050)	.353 (.117)	.125 (.068)	−.037 (.130)	.259 (.128)	.433 (.051)	−.293 (.067)	4.88
Other housing (4.4)	1.590 (.154)	1.966 (.091)	1.893 (.109)	2.274 (.197)	2.456 (.506)	2.351 (.207)	2.113 (.091)	−.537 (.120)	.67
Household op.*	.795 (.027)	.872 (.019)	.941 (.014)	.951 (.026)	.953 (.030)	.979 (.017)	.918 (.010)	−.086 (.013)	1.79
Furniture* (5.1)	1.550 (.087)	1.603 (.077)	1.661 (.078)	1.295 (.080)	1.393 (.213)	1.123 (.094)	1.482 (.048)	−.179 (.063)	1.53
Kitchen* (5.2)	.986 (.135)	.919 (.071)	.927 (.060)	.824 (.129)	.876 (.147)	.839 (.084)	.889 (.040)	.068 (.052)	.63
China (5.3)	1.767 (.194)	1.572 (.106)	1.340 (.112)	1.279 (.192)	1.246 (.138)	1.153 (.118)	1.411 (.058)	−.081 (.077)	1.52
Other furns. (5.4)	.881 (.064)	1.086 (.056)	1.127 (.058)	1.035 (.063)	.972 (.107)	.992 (.072)	1.065 (.029)	−.086 (.038)	.41
Cleaning prep.* (5.6)	.725 (.019)	.781 (.010)	.751 (.029)	.713 (.034)	.747 (.040)	.770 (.031)	.763 (.011)	.103 (.015)	.79
Household utilities (5.8)	.218 (.040)	.387 (.031)	.539 (.027)	.571 (.051)	.619 (.042)	.752 (.042)	.515 (.021)	.048 (.028)	5.21
Electricity, gas* (5.8a, 5.8b)	.237 (.041)	.382 (.031)	.505 (.028)	.574 (.528)	.587 (.056)	.725 (.043)	.501 (.021)	.056 (.028)	4.50
Water (5.8c)	1.87 (.060)	.736 (.043)	1.081 (.067)	1.129 (.134)	1.102 (.100)	1.654 (.122)	1.022 (.050)	−.191 (.065)	6.22

(continued)

261

Table 6.5 (continued)

Item	PCE elasticity for family size						Elasticities for all family sizes combined		
	1	2	3	4	5	6	PCE	Fam. size	F-Ratio
Fuel (5.8d)	.035 (.097)	.262 (.053)	.438 (.069)	.385 (.085)	.507 (.080)	.621 (.076)	.384 (.032)	.083 (.042)	1.59
Telephone* (5.9)	.873 (.036)	.918 (.033)	1.171 (.083)	1.248 (.095)	1.251 (.137)	1.592 (.097)	1.134 (.041)	−.530 (.054)	3.39
Medical	.660 (.052)	.603 (.028)	.724 (.029)	.805 (.046)	.830 (.048)	.797 (.038)	.697 (.019)	−.187 (.024)	3.90
Drug* (6.1)	.325 (.082)	.371 (.039)	.658 (.050)	.774 (.064)	.852 (.078)	.961 (.054)	.610 (.033)	−.307 (.043)	7.44
Ophthalmic (6.2)	.395 (.073)	.493 (.033)	.826 (.049)	1.159 (.112)	1.177 (.115)	1.259 (.093)	.818 (.046)	−.309 (.061)	11.22
Physicians* (6.3)		.577 (.049)	.794 (.045)	.907 (.087)	.841 (.086)	.940 (.064)	.746 (.031)	−.151 (.041)	3.15
Dentists* (6.4)	1.510 (.137)	1.241 (.049)	1.482 (.096)	1.477 (.092)	1.499 (.061)	1.712 (.123)	1.418 (.040)	−.053 (.053)	2.79
Other prof. services (6.5)	.486 (.134)	.893 (.093)	.952 (.148)	.851 (.135)	.928 (.228)	.956 (.139)	.888 (.060)	−.615 (.078)	1.21
Priv. hosp.* (6.6)		.895 (.134)	.487 (.114)	.449 (.185)	1.027 (.171)	.553 (.143)	.693 (.068)	−.317 (.089)	†
Med. ins.* (6.7a)	.809 (.108)	.834 (.091)	.895 (.092)	.940 (.148)	1.037 (.156)	1.129 (.134)	.918 (.049)	−.309 (.065)	.72
Priv. hosp. (6.3, 6.6, 6.7a)	.792 (.083)	.776 (.064)	.735 (.046)	.771 (.069)	.894 (.088)	.861 (.054)	.784 (.028)	−.243 (.036)	.82
Health related expenditures	.596 (.054)	.545 (.032)	.647 (.034)	.721 (.049)	.735 (.053)	.701 (.038)	.622 (.019)	−.205 (.025)	2.64

262

Item									F
Trans. exp.	1.742 (.058)	1.577 (.040)	1.398 (.034)	1.331 (.059)	1.386 (.049)	1.399 (.038)	1.470 (.023)	−.190 (.030)	4.49
User op. trans.	2.146 (.059)	1.650 (.061)	1.434 (.042)	1.355 (.072)	1.460 (.070)	1.407 (.042)	1.523 (.030)	−.151 (.039)	4.20
New cars* (8.1a)		2.813 (.139)	2.249 (.088)	2.421 (.179)	2.088 (.170)	1.870 (.141)	2.456 (.073)	−.099 (.096)	†
Acc. and parts* (8.1b)	1.601 (.062)	.942 (.083)	.655 (.080)	.532 (.113)	.785 (.092)	.913 (.059)	.815 (.041)	.107 (.054)	2.78
Auto repair (8.1c, 8.1e)	1.874 (.072)	1.350 (.061)	1.183 (.073)	1.027 (.063)	1.184 (.064)	1.265 (.080)	1.247 (.032)	−.204 (.041)	2.55
Auto ins. premiums* (8.1f)	1.666 (.065)	1.383 (.109)	1.314 (.074)	1.233 (.081)	1.467 (.134)	1.579 (.089)	1.395 (.044)	−.394 (.058)	1.42
Recreation	1.048 (.052)	1.141 (.038)	1.104 (.047)	1.011 (.048)	1.112 (.052)	1.106 (.031)	1.120 (.022)	.092 (.029)	3.24
Books (9.1)	1.976 (.167)	1.693 (.151)	1.296 (.078)	1.245 (.108)	1.066 (.133)	1.141 (.068)	1.444 (.064)	.755 (.084)	3.37
Nondurable toys (9.3, 9.4, 9.9, 9.10)	1.924 (.141)	1.648 (.069)	1.298 (.065)	1.065 (.066)	1.224 (.079)	1.212 (.053)	1.427 (.044)	.563 (.057)	8.50
Radio and TV* (9.5, 9.6)	1.212 (.124)	1.236 (.074)	1.234 (.050)	1.092 (.057)	1.283 (.177)	1.199 (.080)	1.224 (.037)	.011 (.049)	.68
Admissions to amusements (9.8)	1.961 (.096)	1.798 (.063)	1.311 (.057)	1.376 (.049)	1.383 (.077)	1.472 (.079)	1.574 (.039)	.163 (.051)	7.20
Private educ. expenses		2.539 (.300)	2.223 (.176)	2.265 (.180)	2.321 (.243)	2.263 (.155)	2.458 (.118)	.769 (.155)	2.42
Religious and welfare	.912 (.068)	.969 (.062)	1.214 (.067)	1.155 (.090)	1.339 (.122)	1.451 (.112)	1.142 (.041)	−.352 (.054)	2.49

Note: Items with an asterisk were entirely derived from the data tape and therefore do not reflect the procedure described in footnote 10, Chapter 6.

† F-ratios for private hospitals (6.6) and new cars (8.1a) were not computed; it is evident from the small standard errors that they would be very large.

263

throughout, relying on their well-established usefulness despite equally well-known limitations.[14] Although linear functions would have been more in keeping with the time-series model, they had to be rejected for the cross-section analysis; the range of variation of total expenditure is much greater in cross sections than in time series, and nonlinearity can therefore not be as easily ignored.

The regressions in this section and the next are calculated from grouped data in order to save computer time. For this purpose the data from the data tape were cross tabulated into seventeen total-expenditure classes and six family-size classes grouped according to the number of persons. For the most part, however, the family-size class consisting of one-person households was left out of the following analysis because of some unusual characteristics; some one-person households, for instance, report very small or even zero expenditures on food and/or housing, which suggests that they were not really separate households at all. Households with six or more persons were treated as one class.

Table 6.5 gives the elasticities with respect to total expenditure for fifty items of consumption (including some groups of items) for each of the six household-size classes, and for the top five household-size classes combined. In the latter case the logarithm of household size has itself been used as a variable. Correlation coefficients are not given because in grouped regressions they do not mean much, but from the standard errors it can be seen that the fit is generally very good.

The table also gives an F-ratio which refers to an analysis of covariance comparing the separate equations for the top five household-size classes with the pooled regression. Each of the separate equations is based on 17-group means and has two parameters, hence fifteen degrees of freedom. The pooled regression is based on 85-group means and has three parameters, so that there are 82 degrees of freedom. For $F_{(15,82)}$ the 5-percent point is at 2.15 and the one-percent point at 3.00. Consequently most of the F-ratios are significant, though in most cases the fit of the pooled regression is not much worse than the combined fits of the separate regressions.

Perhaps the most intriguing feature of Table 6.5 is that for the large majority of items the elasticities for different family-size classes vary monotonically with family size: they either increase or decrease regularly from left to right. This usually remains true even if one-person households are considered along with the other five classes. Thus for item 1.1 (food purchased for off-

---

[14] Further exploration of the problem of functional form is envisaged, however. The modified double-log functions discussed in Houthakker (1960) should provide somewhat better fits, and they also satisfy theoretical requirements, but they do not appear to lend themselves to dynamic generalizations.

premise consumption) the elasticity is nearly twice as large for households of six persons and over as it is for one-person households; almost the exact opposite is found in item 9.1 (books and maps). It is not clear what determines whether the elasticities for an item increase or decrease with family size; this does not appear to be related to either the total-expenditure elasticity or the family-size elasticity (as they appear in the pooled regression). Further study of this problem might be rewarding.[15]

Apart from this question, which is relevant primarily to cross-section analysis, the main interest of Table 6.5 is as a check on the time-series elasticities. This comparison will be undertaken in section VII of this chapter.

VI. *Dynamic Engel Curves*

According to the state-adjustment model in its estimating form (1.58), current purchases of an item are a function of current and past income (or total expenditure) and of past purchases. This model cannot be entirely applied to cross-section data because past purchases are not known. Past income is also unknown, but income change is available in the form of a distribution into five classes ("much higher," "higher," "same," "lower," and "much lower," where "much higher" and "much lower" refer to changes of more than 25 percent, "same" to changes of less than five percent, and the two remaining classes to changes of intermediate magnitude). Despite the absence of past purchases it is of interest to apply this model in truncated form, as follows:

$$(1) \qquad \log q_i = \alpha_i + \beta_i \log x + \sum_j \gamma_{ij} d_j + e_i$$

where q_i is expenditure on the i-th item, x is money income after taxes, and d_j is a dummy variable which assumes the value 1 for the j-th income change class ($j = 1$ for "much higher," $j = 2$ for "higher," $j = 3$ for "lower," and $j = 4$ for "much lower"). Three things should be noted:

a. Income is used as the chief explanatory variable. From the principal component analysis of section IV above we know already that income change is not likely to be a useful variable in conjunction with total expenditure, for if so it should have appeared as a principal component (presumably as one with positive weights for durables and negative weights for habit-forming

---

[15] For an earlier analysis of the influence of family size on Engel curves see Stuvel and James (1950).

Table 6.6. Cross-Section Equations with Income Change

Expenditure item	Intercept	Money income after taxes	Family size	Income-change dummies				R^2	F
				1	2	3	4		
Total food expenditure	3.379 (.087)	.395 (.009)	.385 (.014)					.9361	
	3.337 (.087)	.400 (.009)	.385 (.014)	-.0081 (.0261)	-.011 (.014)	.019 (.018)	.060 (.024)	.9387	2.42
Alcoholic beverages (1.0)	-5.292 (.373)	1.155 (.040)	-.333 (.060)					.7836	
	-5.405 (.378)	1.167 (.041)	-.334 (.060)	-.159 (.114)	-.0083 (.0592)	.098 (.080)	.140 (.103)	.7893	1.54
Food purchased for off-premise consumption (1.1)	2.962 (.092)	.413 (.010)	.375 (.015)					.9312	
	2.899 (.091)	.421 (.010)	.377 (.014)	-.054 (.027)	-.033 (.014)	.0013 (.019)	.064 (.025)	.9364	4.66
Purchased meals food furnished gov. and commercial employees (1.2, 1.3)	-3.897 (2.80)	1.058 (.030)	.129 (.045)					.8574	
	-3.941 (.278)	1.056 (.030)	.200 (.074)	.151 (.084)	.084 (.044)	.088 (.058)	.259 (.076)	.8658	3.57
Farm-produced food (1.4)	9.547 (.530)	-.849 (.057)	1.151 (.085)					.5857	
	9.807 (.516)	-.879 (.056)	1.152 (.082)	-.229 (.157)	.084 (.082)	.092 (.108)	-.549 (.141)	.6234	5.71
Tobacco products (1.5)	.679 (.189)	.435 (.020)	.129 (.030)					.7079	
	.582 (.183)	.442 (.020)	.123 (.029)	.033 (.055)	.038 (.029)	.124 (.038)	.234 (.050)	.7398	6.99
Clothing expenditure	-.569 (.159)	.746 (.017)	.448 (.025)					.9236	
	-.592 (.160)	.746 (.017)	.444 (.025)	.084 (.049)	.033 (.025)	.059 (.034)	.107 (.044)	.9266	2.33

Variable	(1)	(2)	(3)	(4)	(5)	(6)	(7)	R^2	
Shoes, clothing, jewelry (2.1, 2.3, 2.7)	−1.398 (.176)	.801 (.019)	.525 (.028)					.9217	
	−1.413 (.177)	.799 (.019)	.520 (.028)	.100 (.054)	.043 (.028)	.067 (.037)	.108 (.049)	.9247	2.27
Shoe cleaning, other clothing and accessories (2.2, 2.56, 2.8)	−2.842 (.171)	.853 (.018)	.112 (.027)					.9064	
	−2.897 (.170)	.857 (.018)	−.115 (.027)	.055 (.052)	.016 (.027)	.047 (.036)	.146 (.047)	.9107	2.74
Total personal care	−.301 (.126)	.596 (.130)	.181 (.020)					.9115	
	−.358 (.124)	.600 (.013)	.179 (.020)	.038 (.038)	.013 (.020)	.047 (.026)	.136 (.034)	.9180	4.52
Toilet articles and preparations	−.149 (.134)	.480 (.014)	.373 (.022)					.8871	
	−.181 (.132)	.481 (.014)	.369 (.021)	.091 (.040)	.037 (.021)	.065 (.028)	.134 (.036)	.8957	4.70
Barbershops, beauty shops (3.2)	−2.424 (.180)	.773 (.019)	−.053 (.029)					.8803	
	−2.51 (.179)	.783 (.019)	−.053 (.028)	−.050 (.054)	−.022 (.029)	.026 (.038)	.130 (.049)	.8857	2.69
Total housing exp.	.477 (.166)	.711 (.1018)	−.105 (.026)					.8796	
	.443 (.163)	.711 (.018)	−.111 (.026)	.069 (.049)	.055 (.026)	.058 (.035)	.175 (.045)	.8858	3.09
Owned dwellings	−3.262 (4.13)	1.082 (.044)	−.203 (.065)					.7246	
	−3.424 (.414)	1.102 (.045)	−.207 (.065)	−.295 (.125)	−.045 (.064)	.089 (.086)	.146 (.113)	.7365	2.57
Rented dwellings	4.462 (.504)	.145 (.054)	−.243 (.081)					.0535	
	4.629 (.506)	.120 (.055)	−.253 (.080)	.339 (.153)	.134 (.080)	−.049 (.107)	.011 (.138)	.0856	2.00

(continued)

Table 6.6 (*continued*)

Expenditure item	Intercept	Money income after taxes	Family size	Income-change dummies				R^2	F
				1	2	3	4		
Other housing (4.4)	−8.693 (.561)	1.454 (.060)	−.327 (.091)					.7192	
	−8.943 (.566)	1.487 (.061)	−.321 (.089)	−.250 (.171)	−.130 (.089)	−.012 (.120)	.253 (.154)	.7288	2.02
Household operation	1.123 (.124)	.645 (.013)	.038 (.020)					.9181	
	1.1063 (.125)	.645 (.013)	.035 (.020)	.036 (.038)	.022 (.020)	.043 (.026)	.065 (.034)	.9200	1.35
Furniture (5.1)	−4.611 (.352)	1.035 (.038)	−.033 (.056)					.7758	
	−4.476 (.355)	1.014 (.038)	−.042 (.057)	.059 (.107)	.132 (.056)	.056 (.075)	−.060 (.097)	.7826	1.78
Kitchen and other household appliances (5.2)	−.930 (.336)	.588 (.036)	.210 (.054)					.5940	
	−.762 (.331)	.565 (.036)	.206 (.052)	.191 (.101)	.086 (.052)	.101 (.069)	−.223 (.091)	.6204	3.96
China and glassware (5.3)	−5.756 (.423)	.927 (.045)	.067 (.068)					.6640	
	−5.620 (.429)	.904 (.046)	.056 (.067)	.101 (.129)	.162 (.068)	.129 (.090)	−.038 (.119)	.6744	1.82
Other durable household furnishings (5.4)	−2.068 (.201)	.735 (.021)	.037 (.032)					.8465	
	−2.06 (.204)	.731 (.022)	.033 (.032)	.045 (.062)	.043 (.033)	.047 (.042)	.041 (.056)	.8482	.64
Cleaning and polishing preparations (5.6)	−.275 (.127)	.550 (.014)	.199 (.020)					.8998	
	−.304 (.125)	.550 (.013)	.195 (.020)	.016 (.038)	.044 (.020)	.064 (.026)	.123 (.034)	.9068	4.28

Category								R^2	
Total utilities	2.107 (.126)	.390 (.013)	.109 (.020)					.8137	
	2.037 (.124)	.401 (.013)	.113 (.020)	−.133 (.037)	−.050 (.019)	−.011 (.025)	.030 (.034)	.8281	4.77
Electricity, gas (5.8a, 5.8b)	1.714 (.126)	.384 (.013)	.113 (.020)					.8097	
	1.626 (.123)	.396 (.013)	.117 (.020)	−.117 (.037)	−.054 (.019)	.020 (.026)	.049 (.034)	.8274	5.85
Water (5.8c)	−3.58 (.303)	.804 (.033)	−.047 (.049)					.7343	
	−3.733 (.299)	.826 (.032)	−.042 (.048)	−.336 (.091)	−.080 (.047)	−.0021 (.070)	.101 (.082)	.7543	4.64
Other fuel and ice (5.8d)	1.565 (.276)	.286 (.029)	.124 (.044)					.3480	
	1.573 (.273)	.291 (.029)	.129 (.043)	−.280 (.083)	−.043 (.043)	−.144 (.058)	−.091 (.075)	.3903	3.95
Telephone, telegraph (5.9)	−2.010 (.258)	.784 (.028)	−.352 (.041)					.7782	
	−2.133 (.257)	.798 (.028)	−.352 (.040)	−.125 (.078)	−.022 (.040)	.048 (.054)	.176 (.070)	.7889	2.89
Total medical care expense	2.196 (.166)	.452 (.018)	−.086 (.027)					.7402	
	2.104 (.166)	.464 (.018)	−.084 (.026)	−.043 (.050)	−.041 (.026)	−.029 (.035)	.099 (.045)	.7526	2.86
Drug preparations (6.1)	1.064 (.233)	.401 (.025)	−.207 (.038)					.5290	
	.970 (.235)	.414 (.025)	−.202 (.037)	−.128 (.071)	−.072 (.037)	.017 (.050)	.024 (.063)	.5445	1.94
Ophthalmic products (6.2)	−1.944 (.292)	.605 (.031)	−.205 (.047)					.6183	
	−1.971 (.297)	.610 (.032)	−.202 (.047)	−.123 (.088)	−.035 (.047)	−.0065 (.065)	−.036 (.082)	.6219	.54

(continued)

269

Table 6.6 (*continued*)

Expenditure item	Intercept	Money income after taxes	Family size	Income-change dummies				R^2	F
				1	2	3	4		
Physicians (6.3)	−.102 (.283)	.488 (.030)	−.041 (.045)					.5462	
	−.191 (.281)	.499 (.030)	−.043 (.045)	−.084 (.085)	−.0058 (.045)	−.0051 (.057)	.174 (.077)	.5596	1.73
Dentists (6.4)	−5.502 (.396)	1.058 (.042)	.097 (.063)					.7492	
	−5.527 (.396)	1.056 (.043)	.089 (.063)	−.057 (.121)	.086 (.063)	.108 (.084)	.148 (.110)	.7540	1.11
Other professional services (6.5)	−2.723 (.248)	.659 (.026)	−.524 (.040)					.7429	
	−2.764 (.251)	.663 (.027)	−.524 (.040)	−.070 (.076)	−.0017 (.043)	.065 (.053)	.032 (.070)	.7463	.76
Private hospitals and sanitariums (6.6)	3.010 (.530)	.114 (.056)	−.173 (.085)					.0276	
	2.735 (.527)	.155 (.057)	−.156 (.082)	−.200 (.160)	−.257 (.083)	.073 (.111)	.010 (.143)	.0833	3.46
Medical care and hospitalization insurance (6.7a)	−1.080 (.293)	.681 (.031)	−.215 (.047)					.6703	
	−1.074 (.298)	.681 (.032)	−.215 (.048)	−.140 (.093)	.011 (.046)	.0092 (.061)	−.033 (.080)	.6746	.75
Physicians, private hospitals, sanitariums, medical care, hospitalization (6.5, 6.6, 6.7)	1.525 (.200)	.457 (.021)	−.123 (.032)					.6642	
	1.418 (.201)	.470 (.022)	−.121 (.032)	−.048 (.061)	−.053 (.032)	.038 (.043)	.103 (.055)	.6789	2.61
Drug preparations (6.1)	2.647 (.162)	.387 (.017)	−.108 (.026)					.6845	
	2.547 (.161)	.400 (.017)	−.105 (.026)	−.049 (.049)	−.054 (.026)	.025 (.033)	.091 (.044)	.7027	3.49

	const							R^2	F
Total transportation expenditure	−1.187 (.241)	.910 (.026)	−.0014 (.035)					.8517	3.04
	−1.200 (2.40)	.096 (.026)	−.0096 (.038)	.129 (.073)	.085 (.038)	.081 (.050)	.187 (.066)	.8592	
Automobiles and accessories (8.1)	−1.328 (.270)	.910 (.029)	.041 (.044)					.8231	2.77
	−1.320 (.270)	.902 (.029)	.031 (.043)	.140 (.081)	.106 (.042)	.086 (.057)	.182 (.073)	.8313	
New cars and net purchases of old cars (8.1a)	−4.463 (.561)	1.167 (.060)	.017 (.094)					.6371	1.45
	−4.24 (.566)	1.137 (.061)	.0092 (.092)	.206 (.172)	.129 (.089)	−.031 (.119)	−.169 (.154)	.6461	
Tires, tubes, accessories, and parts (8.1b)	−1.560 (.302)	.577 (.032)	.215 (.048)					.6357	1.86
	−1.559 (.304)	.571 (.033)	.206 (.048)	.040 (.093)	.104 (.048)	.108 (.064)	.155 (.084)	.6472	
Automobile maintenance and tolls	−2.925 (.218)	.883 (.023)	−.076 (.035)					.8657	4.19
	−3.00 (.216)	.887 (.023)	.082 (.034)	.050 (.065)	.047 (.034)	.093 (.044)	.228 (.058)	.8749	
Auto insurance premiums, less claims paid (8.1f)	−4.088 (.307)	1.00 (.033)	−.250 (.049)					.8018	3.19
	−4.195 (.306)	1.01 (.033)	2.56	−.077 (.093)	.047 (.048)	.088 (.064)	.268 (.084)	.8123	
Total recreation expenditure	−2.710 (.205)	.933 (.022)	.244 (.033)					.9027	6.17
	−2.727 (.201)	.928 (.022)	.235 (.032)	.168 (.060)	.093 (.032)	.076 (.042)	.227 (.055)	.9122	
Books and maps (9.1)	−6.508 (.284)	.930 (.030)	.848 (.045)					.8794	2.57
	−6.564 (.284)	.931 (.031)	.841 (.045)	.106 (.086)	.063 (.045)	.119 (.060)	.214 (.078)	.8846	

(continued)

Table 6.6 (continued)

Expenditure item	Intercept	Money income after taxes	Family size	Income-change dummies				R^2	F
				1	2	3	4		
Durable–nondurable toys, clubs, and commercial amusements (9.3, 9.4, 9.9, 9.10)	−5.542 (.276)	1.034 (.029)	.689 (.044)					.8900	3.29
	−5.581 (.274)	1.032 (.030)	.681 (.043)	.149 (.083)	.081 (.043)	.118 (.057)	.224 (.075)	.8960	
Radio and television receivers and repair (9.5, 9.6)	−2.716 (.295)	.791 (.032)	.137 (.047)					.7567	1.99
	−2.652 (.297)	.780 (.032)	.130 (.047)	.186 (.090)	.078 (.047)	−.034 (.062)	.082 (.081)	.7649	
Movies, theater, spectator sports (9.8)	−6.841 (.305)	1.123 (.033)	.328 (.049)					.8616	4.82
	−6.917 (.299)	1.124 (.032)	.318 (.047)	.153 (.091)	.094 (.047)	.127 (.063)	.332 (.082)	.8724	
Total private education expenditure	−12.49 (.833)	1.697 (.089)	.926 (.133)					.6891	1.76
	−12.61 (.835)	1.704 (.090)	.912 (.132)	−.325 (.250)	.148 (.132)	.108 (.174)	.428 (.229)	.6984	
Religious and welfare	−3.872 (.307)	1.052 (.033)	−.305 (.049)					.8152	1.52
	−3.83 (.311)	1.046 (.034)	−.307 (.050)	−.153 (.094)	.042 (.049)	.046 (.065)	−.086 (.085)	.8200	
Total expenditure	2.553 (.124)	.678 (.013)	.131 (.020)					.9288	5.15
	2.504 (.122)	.681 (.013)	.128 (.019)	.054 (.037)	.024 (.020)	.056 (.025)	.140 (.033)	.9347	

commodities). It is also somewhat illogical to use total expenditure and income change together; however, we have done so as a check, and the results generally agree with the expectation just stated. Finally the use of income in (1) yields as a by-product a set of regressions without income change which can be compared with the total expenditure regressions of section V.

b. Since there is no dummy variable for the households who reported the same income as in the preceding year, this group is used as the base from which to measure the effects of income change.

c. The regressions were again run on grouped data, but the grouping was not the same as in section V. This time all households were divided into ten income groups (the same as used by BLS in its published tabulations): five family-size groups (2, 3, 4, 5, and 6 and over) and five income-change groups. This would have provided 250 cells, but in some of them there were no households or income was negative, so they had to be left out; 235 cells remained. As before, the cell means were weighted by the number of households in the cells.

Table 6.6 gives for each item a regression involving only income and family size (comparable to the pooled regressions in Table 6.5) and another regression also including a dummy variable for each of the four income-change groups (excluding "no change"). It also gives an F-ratio indicating the significance of the four dummy variables taken together; thus a low value of F implies that the regression with dummy variables does not fit significantly better than the one without them. For 228 and 232 degrees of freedom the 5-percent point of F is 1.26 and the one-percent point is 1.39.

Since it is these F-ratios which come closest to permitting a cross-section test of our dynamic model of consumption we shall discuss them first. It is evidently encouraging that most of the F-ratios are quite high; in fact only 6 out of 51 are not significant at the one-percent level. In conjunction with income and family size, there is an undeniable effect of income change.

Closer examination, however, reveals a disturbing peculiarity. Disregarding past purchases, our model suggests that households whose income has increased will spend relatively less on habit-forming items and relatively more on durables. This is indeed confirmed in such important instances of habit formation as food purchased for home consumption (item 1.1), owned dwellings (roughly corresponding to item 4.1), and gas and electricity (items 5.8a and 5.8b combined), also in a few durable items such as household appliances (item 5.1) and automobiles (item 8.1a). In these and some other items the coefficients of the dummy variables either increase or decrease from left to right, with the positive income-change groups having a sign opposite to that of the negative income-change groups. But a different pattern appears in many other items, namely that the four coefficients are all positive (or, more rarely, all negative). If they are all positive this means that households with unchanged income spend less than households whose income has changed *irrespective of the sign of the income change*. This pattern appears, for instance, in the final item, total expenditure, which according to the results of Chapter 7 should show habit formation. It may be, of course, that this anomaly would disappear if past expenditure were introduced as a variable, but we have no way of verifying this.

Consequently it cannot be claimed that the cross-section test gives much support to the state-adjustment model of consumption. In fact, despite the significant F-ratios it does not even appear that income change contributes a great deal to the cross-sectional explanation of expenditures. This is evident not only from the small increases in R^2 as we pass from the first to the second equation, but also from the virtual equality of the coefficients of income, and of family size, in the two equations. Because of the omission of past expenditures, however, the cross-section results do not contradict the state-adjustment model either.

Finally, a comparison of the elasticities in Table 6.6 with those in Table 6.5 is of some interest. We note first that all the elasticities with respect to income (taken from the first equation for each item in Table 6.6) are smaller in absolute value than the corresponding elasticities with respect to PCE (taken from the pooled regressions in Table 6.5). This is as it should be since the estimated elasticity of PCE with respect to income is .678, and the ratio of the income elasticities to the PCE elasticities is indeed close to two-thirds in most cases. The only important exception is automobiles (item 8.1a) where the PCE elasticity is more than twice as high as the income elasticity; in this case the PCE elasticity was implausibly high.[16]

With one negligible exception all the family-size elasticities in Table 6.6 are algebraically larger than their counterparts in Table 6.5. The reason may be that total expenditure, which we already know to explain more than income, has a positive partial correlation with family size (after income is taken into account). The difference between corresponding family-size elasticities in the two tables is generally between .10 and .15 while the elasticity of total expenditure with respect to family size (after allowance for income) is .131. It appears, therefore, that in Table 6.6 family size picks up some of the effect attributed to total expenditure in Table 6.5.

---

[16] This, incidentally, casts doubt on the objections sometimes voiced against the use of PCE as an explanatory variable on the grounds that it is the sum of the dependent variables and therefore subject to bias (see Summers, 1959, and Liviatan, 1961). According to this line of reasoning the PCE elasticities should be biased toward unity, especially in the case of a large item such as automobile purchases. Actually it is not clear that income is any better from this point of view, since by definition it is equal to the sum of expenditures and savings.

VII. A Check on the Time-Series Results

As has been mentioned, the primary purpose of analyzing the 1960–1961 survey data was to provide a check on the time-series results. A comparison of the total expenditure elasticities obtained from the two sources of information is undertaken in this section, though for reasons already noted it is not possible to make this comparison for all of the time-series categories.[17] The elasticities are given in Table 6.7. The cross-section elasticities are from the pooled regressions for all family sizes (column 8 of Table 6.5); the time-series elasticities (both short-run and long-run) are taken from Table 4.2. Before commencing discussion of the actual numbers, however, several remarks regarding the general nature of income (or PCE) elasticities obtained from the two sources of information are in order.

For PCE elasticities based on cross-section data to be consistent with those obtained from time-series data, the variation implicit in the two sources of information must be homogeneous, but this generally is not the case. Time-series variation is dominated by dynamic, intertemporal factors that are usually absent from cross-section data. As a result, time-series PCE elasticities will largely reflect short-run adjustment to changes in total expenditure, while cross-section elasticities will tend to reflect long-run adjustment.[18] Of course it is possible that not all households will be affected equally by cyclical and other time-varying factors, in which case cross-section elasticities will also reflect some short-run phenomena. The available empirical evidence, however, indicates that the impact of time-varying factors on cross-section variation is small relative to the impact of factors peculiar to individual households. Factors such as family size, age of head of household, race, education of head of household, and so on all vary from household to household, but very little from year to year. Consequently, they are reflected only to a small extent in time-series variation.

These considerations go a long way toward explaining why cross-section elasticities are usually higher than their time-series counterparts, since in terms of flows elasticities are always at least as large in the long run as in the short run. Moreover, unless the household-varying effects, especially family size and age of head, are taken into account, the cross-section elasticity will

---

[17] For those cases where several time-series categories have been combined in order to achieve consistency with a cross-section category, the time-series elasticities are obtained as weighted averages of the elasticities of the constituent items, with the weights being expenditures (current dollar) in 1964. Since the elasticity for an aggregate is not necessarily equal to a weighted average of its components, it would, of course, be better to estimate new equations for the combined items. For present purposes, however, this seems an unnecessary refinement.

[18] See in particular Kuh (1963, chap. vi) and Kuh and Meyer (1957). Moreover, since we are dealing with PCE elasticities, this conclusion is not in conflict with the permanent income hypothesis.

Table 6.7. Comparison of SCE and Time-Series Elasticities

		Elasticities		
			Time series	
SCE code	OBE code	Cross section	SR	LR
3	1.0	1.54	.29	.62
4	1.1	.58	.50	.71
5	1.2 1.3	1.40	1.53	
6	1.4	−1.57	−.61	
7	1.5	.64	.21	.86
9	2.1 2.3 2.7	1.10	1.15	
10	2.2 2.5 2.6 2.8	1.19	.68	
12	3.1	.70	.25	3.74
13	3.2	1.03	.87	1.36
17	4.4	2.11	1.27	
19	5.1	1.48	2.60	.53
20	5.2	.89	1.18	
21	5.3	1.41	.47	.77
22	5.4	1.06	2.09	1.18
23	5.6	.76	.99	1.62
25	5.8a 5.8b	.50	1.29	
26	5.8c	1.02	.87	.59
27	5.8d	.38	.75	
28	5.9	1.13	.32	
30	6.1	.61	.62	3.04
31	6.2	.82	1.29	1.39
32	6.3	.75	.28	1.15
33	6.4	1.42	.38	1.00
34	6.5	.89	1.33	
35	6.6	.69	.37	3.71
36	6.7	.92	.69	2.02
37	6.3 6.6 6.7	.78	.36	2.44
38	6.1 6.2 6.3 6.6 6.7	.62	.46	2.51
41	8.1a	2.46	5.46	1.07
42	8.1b	.82	1.40	1.93
43	8.1c 8.1e	1.25	.90	1.11

Table 6.7 (*continued*)

		Elasticities		
			Time series	
		Cross		
SCE code	OBE code	section	SR	LR
44	8.1f	1.40	.37	1.26
46	9.1	1.44	1.67	1.42
47	9.3 9.4 9.9 9.10	1.43	1.03	2.92
48	9.5 9.6	1.22	3.66	3.33
49	9.8	1.57	.87	2.98
50	10.0	2.46	.27	5.72

overstate the long-run elasticity on the average, since these effects are usually positively correlated with total expenditure.

When we consider dynamic factors other than intertemporal, however, the preceding argument needs to be modified. Even if all households are affected equally by intertemporal phenomena, dynamic adjustment arising from the presence of state variables will still be reflected in survey data. Only in the extremely unlikely event that all households had identical state variables would this not be the case. As has already been noted, however, application of the state-adjustment model of this book to survey data requires observations in two consecutive periods, and since these are not available, use of a conventional static model (as we have done) will lead to a bias in the estimate of the (short-run) PCE elasticity. Except for inferior goods, the state variable is positively correlated with the level of income, hence the bias will be positive for goods characterized by habit formation, and negative for goods subject to inventory adjustment.[19]

A second factor that can contribute to a bias in the cross-section PCE elasticity is the omission of prices. Prices are assumed to be the same for all households in a budget survey, but there are several commodities for which this is not true. Prices may vary among regions or because of discriminatory pricing or quality differences, and if not taken into account, these phenomena are likely to be reflected in the PCE elasticity. With regard to regional differences, it is well known that the price of housing varies from city to city and between urban and rural areas. Regional price differences are also apt

---

[19] This conclusion follows from the theorem on the impact of omitted variables.

to be problems with autos, gasoline, water, and perhaps furniture and household durables. Grouping households by region would, of course, be one way of correcting for these differences, but a better procedure would be to have a direct estimate of the price differentials involved.

Discriminatory pricing is especially likely to be encountered with electricity, gas, and water, where quantity discounts are common.[20] The same phenomenon is present in time-series data, but there the use of a marginal price can effectively overcome the problem. This will not be true with budget data, however, unless a marginal price for each household were available. Since quantity purchased of these items and total expenditure are positively correlated, the effect of quantity discounts will be to bias upward the cross-section PCE elasticity. With regional price differentials, on the other hand, it is impossible to say *a priori* which direction the bias will be.

Still a third reason why cross-section PCE elasticities are likely to be spuriously high is that budget data refer to outlays and do not take quality differences into account. Better quality will be reflected in outlay, but not in quantity (as usually defined), which means that since income and quality are positively related the PCE elasticity will include a price effect. Strictly speaking, therefore, PCE elasticities from budget data should be referred to as outlay elasticities. Time-series data, in contrast, can usually be expressed in real terms, hence the PCE elasticity will more closely approximate a quantity elasticity.[21]

If quantities, as well as outlays, are given in the budget data, it is possible to compute "quality" elasticities by regressing average purchase price per unit on average total expenditure per capita. The quality elasticity can then be defined as the percentage increase in average purchase price divided by the percentage increase in PCE per capita. PCE per capita is used instead of PCE per household since Prais and Houthakker (1955) have found that average purchase price is positively correlated with family income, but is negatively correlated with family size for given income. The difference between the outlay and quality elasticities can then be taken for the quantity elasticity.[22] Unfortunately, however, this procedure cannot be used with the 1960–1961 SCE since quantities were not collected.

---

[20] For a discussion of this phenomenon in the demand for electricity, see Houthakker (1951).

[21] Nevertheless, in most cases the time-series elasticity will still fall short of being a true quantity elasticity because the deflation procedure will not completely remove the quality effect. For example, it will not be removed at all if current outlays are deflated by an average value index; on the other hand, if the price index is of the Lespheres or Paasche type, some, perhaps most, of the quality effects will be removed so long as every quality is included in the index. For further details, the interested reader is referred to Kuh and Meyer (1957).

[22] For the details, see Houthakker and Prais (1955).

Finally, there is the "new goods" effect. It is often argued that consumers tire of a product over time, and in the absence of anything to keep up their interest, expenditures for the product will eventually level off. The appearance of new goods, though, will offset this tendency, and for this reason the time-series PCE elasticity will tend to be high relative to the cross-section elasticity. For this argument to be valid, however, it is necessary that the new goods either be in the same product class or be complementary to the old goods, for if they are competitive, the time-series elasticity will be biased downward rather than upward. It is clear, therefore, that the direction of bias in the time-series PCE elasticity from the "new goods" effect depends on the circumstances.

Also, in interpreting budget data elasticities, it is usually assumed that the same goods are available to all households, but for many goods this is not true. The services of a Mercedes-Benz, for example, are generally not available to a poor household because of an insufficiently developed rental market. Such differential availability of goods will lead to upward biases that may even be greater than the new goods effect with time-series data.

In short, differential availability of goods is likely to be present in some form in both time-series and cross-section data. The direction of bias in the time-series PCE elasticity will depend on whether the new goods are competitive with the old goods. The bias in the cross-section elasticity, on the other hand, will most likely be upward.

It is evident from these paragraphs that reconciling time-series and cross-section PCE elasticities is not an easy undertaking. Because of the unimportance of intertemporal variation in the survey data, the survey PCE elasticities should lie closer to the long-run time-series elasticities than to those calculated for the short run, though inconsistent definitions and omitted variables modify this conclusion somewhat. The major problem with omitted variables is the impossibility of taking the state variables into account with the survey data, and the effect of this, taken in isolation, will be an upward bias in the PCE elasticity for habit-forming goods and a downward bias for goods subject to inventory adjustment. Given the wide range of variation in PCE in the survey data, however, and the fact that the observations are group means, these biases in general might be expected to be small. Biases in the cross-section PCE elasticities can also be anticipated from nonconstancy of prices across households, the fact that the data refer to outlays rather than quantities, and the differential availability of goods. On balance, the net bias from these factors is most likely upward.

With regard to the actual numbers in Table 6.7, however, a rather mixed picture is presented. Although the cross-section elasticity is close to the long-run time-series elasticity for only a few cases, its direction from the short-run time-series elasticity, generally speaking, conforms to expectations—that is, the cross-section elasticity is larger than the short-run time-series elasticity for habit-forming goods and smaller for goods subject to inventory adjustment. This is the strongest statement about the overall compatibility of the results that can be made. As far as individual categories are concerned, the agreement is quite good for the food items (1.1, 1.2, 1.3), clothing and shoes (2.1, 2.3), automobiles (8.1a), and for most of the recreation items in Group IX. On the other hand, the agreement is poor for gas and electricity (5.8a and 5.8b), drug preparations and sundries (6.1), ophthalmic products and orthopedic appliances (6.2), other professional services (6.5), tires, tubes, accessories, and parts (8.1b), and television and television repair (9.5 and 9.6). In each case the cross-section elasticity is perverse in relation to the short-run time-series elasticity. We leave it to the reader to draw his own conclusions as to reasons. The agreement is also very poor for alcoholic beverages (1.0), but this undoubtedly reflects underreporting of expenditures by low-income families in the survey data. All in all, however, the survey data appear to confirm the time-series results for the largest items of expenditure, so that despite the anomalies apparent in the table, there is reason for reassurance.

7

The Dynamics of Total Consumption and Saving

In this chapter we apply dynamic models of demand to total consumption and its complement, savings. To do so we merely have to interpret x_t, as (measured) income and q_t as total consumption, and omit the price terms. (Price changes are reintroduced later on, however.) Various modifications of this simple approach will also be considered. The empirical results obtained in this chapter refer not only to annual observations for the United States, as in previous chapters, but also to quarterly figures that are available only for the postwar period. In addition to the data of the Department of Commerce, the personal savings data from the flow of funds (published by the Board of Governors of the Federal Reserve System) and those published by the Securities and Exchange Commission are also analyzed.[1] Use of these last two sources of data enables a number of definitions of saving to be investigated.

We shall first discuss the basic model (section I), which turns out to do well at first sight but has some unsatisfactory features on closer examination. We then specialize the model by requiring the depreciation rate on consumers' financial assets to be zero (section II), which provides a very simple savings function with reasonable empirical properties, though there is also evidence of a change in the function during the postwar period. The model is next extended to include price changes and the rate of interest (section III), and as final variations, the model is applied to gross saving and gross investment (sections IV and V). The last section is devoted to the projection of saving in 1970 and 1975.

I. The Basic Dynamic Model Applied to Total Consumption

The model described in section II of Chapter 1, which underlies most of the results in this book, can be applied immediately to total consumer

---

[1] For a discussion of the differences, conceptual and otherwise, among the OBE, SEC, and flow-of-funds data on saving, see Taubman (1968).

expenditure, provided we interpret x_t as disposable income and not as PCE, which now becomes q_t. It is then compatible with much contemporary thinking on the consumption function. In particular, linearity with respect to income has been found a good approximation by most students of the subject, but perhaps more important, the basic model gives prominence to habit formation, which has often been stressed in this context, for instance by Duesenberry (1947) and Modigliani (1947), Brown (1952), and Duesenberry, Eckstein, and Fromm (1960). As we shall see in section II below, the model also has a bearing on the effect of asset holdings on saving, which has been stressed by Tobin (1951), Zellner (1957), and others; in fact it will there be shown that habit formation in consumption and asset effects on saving are really two sides of the same coin. Finally, as noted in Chapter 6, section IV, the inertial characteristics of habit formation are in keeping with the spirit of the permanent income hypothesis.

Concerning habit formation, we need only recall the usual argument. When income rises, consumers will not immediately attain the higher level of consumption made possible; when income falls, they will wish to maintain the previously reached consumption level as much as possible. The result is inertia or sluggishness in the adjustment of consumption to income, and this is precisely what our basic model is designed to represent.

While there is nothing new in this emphasis on dynamic adjustment, our model has an advantage over earlier formulations because it is derived from an underlying theory expressed in continuous time. It thereby avoids the arbitrariness common to models initially expressed as difference equations. The length of the period of observation (usually a quarter or a year) does not have any particular significance for the dynamic adjustment process, and should therefore not be used in the theoretical specification of the process. From this point of view, the use of "previous peak income" in the Duesenberry–Modigliani theory of the consumption function is also a crude approximation at best.

The derivation from a continuous-time theory is especially useful when both quarterly and annual data are available. It has often been observed that the marginal propensity to consume (MPC) is lower when estimated from quarterly data than when estimated from annual data. Explanations for this discrepancy vary,[2] though they usually run in terms of a permanent-income theory. But without appealing to the latter theory, our basic model can also shed light on this difficulty. The apparent MPC appears in our estimating equation (39) of Chapter 1 as the coefficient A_2 of Δx_t, and we shall see that A_2 is indeed greater in annual than in quarterly equations. However, what matters from the present point of view is not A_2 but γ, the short-run MPC,

_____

[2] See, for instance, Ackley (1961, chap. ix), Griliches et al. (1962), and Suits (1963).

or γ', its long-run counterpart, and these should be independent of the period of observation. This independence therefore constitutes an important test of the underlying dynamic theory.

While on this subject, it is also interesting to consider the other structural parameters in their relation to the period of observation. To do so we have to go back to equation (37) of Chapter 1; rewritten in the same form as (39) it becomes

$$
(1) \quad q_t = \frac{\alpha \delta \tau^2}{1 - \frac{\tau}{2}(\beta - \delta)} + \frac{1 + \frac{\tau}{2}(\beta - \delta)}{1 - \frac{\tau}{2}(\beta - \delta)} q_{t-\tau} + \frac{\gamma\left(1 + \frac{\tau\delta}{2}\right)}{1 - \frac{\tau}{2}(\beta - \delta)} \Delta x_t
$$

$$
+ \frac{\gamma\delta\tau}{1 - \frac{\tau}{2}(\beta - \delta)} x_{t-\tau},
$$

where Δx_t now stands for $x_t - x_{t-\tau}$. We see then that the parameters α, β, and δ always appear in the combination $\alpha\tau$, $\beta\tau$, and $\delta\tau$, so that γ is the only one that is not multiplied by τ, the period of observation. Hence if we put $\tau = 1/4$, which amounts to using quarterly data if $\tau = 1$ corresponds to a year, then we obtain $\alpha/4$, $\beta/4$, γ, and $\delta/4$. The α, β, and δ estimated from quarterly data therefore must be one-fourth of the α, β, and δ estimated from annual data; this is a further test on the basic model.[3]

Empirical results for the U.S. (data in 1958 dollars per capita) are:

U.S. annual (1929–1941, 1947–1964)

$$
(2) \quad q_t = 9.871 + .695 q_{t-1} + .607 \Delta x_t + .287 x_{t-1}
$$
$$
(21.385) \quad (.177) \qquad (.057) \qquad (.157)
$$

$$
\hat{\alpha} = 18.81 \qquad \hat{\beta} = .26 \qquad \hat{\gamma} = .55 \qquad \hat{\gamma}' = .94 \qquad \hat{\delta} = .62
$$
$$
R^2 = .997 \qquad S_e = 18.10 \qquad D.W. = 2.39
$$

U.S. annual (1947–1964)

$$
(3) \quad q_t = -57.656 + .124 q_{t-1} + .795 \Delta x_t + .857 x_{t-1}
$$
$$
(5.123) \quad (.277) \qquad (.119) \qquad (.268)
$$

$$
\hat{\alpha} = -39.08 \qquad \hat{\beta} = 1.33 \qquad \hat{\gamma} = .58 \qquad \hat{\gamma}' = .98 \qquad \hat{\delta} = 2.89
$$
$$
R^2 = .997 \qquad S_e = 17.08 \qquad D.W. = 1.55
$$

U.S. quarterly (1947–1964, seasonally adjusted annual rates)

$$
(4) \quad q_t = 31.367 + .644 q_{t-1} + .443 \Delta x_t + .354 x_{t-1}
$$
$$
(21.764) \quad (.095) \qquad (.102) \qquad (.091)
$$

$$
\hat{\alpha} = -28.72 \qquad \hat{\beta} = .90 \qquad \hat{\gamma} = .32 \qquad \hat{\gamma}' = .99 \qquad \hat{\delta} = 1.33
$$
$$
R^2 = .990 \qquad S_e = 15.81 \qquad D.W. = 2.09
$$

[3] The matter is slightly complicated by the fact that quarterly national accounts data are customarily expressed as annual rates. This does not change what has just been said about β and δ, but it implies that the quarterly and annual α's should be the same.

Of these three equations, (2) and (4) are the most important; the annual post-war equation is given only because it covers the same period as the quarterly equation. The two principal equations are both quite satisfactory when taken by themselves: except for the intercepts, the estimated coefficients are all significant, and the derived structural parameters all have the expected sign; moreover, the fit is good in both cases, and there is no *prima facie* evidence of serial correlation. Equation (3), based on only eighteen observations, is rather less satisfactory. The coefficient of q_{t-1} is not significant, and the coefficients of Δx_t and x_{t-1} are very close to each other, which suggests that a purely static consumption function would have done just as well.

When we consider (2) and (4) more closely, however, our initial satisfaction has to give way to considerable doubt. In the first place, they are by no means consistent with each other in view of the preceding discussion of the effect of different periods of observations. Even substituting (3) for (2) does not help much in this respect. The calculated values of β and δ, which in theory should be a fourth in (4) of what they are in (2) or (3), are actually much larger. The calculated values of α and γ, which should be the same, are obviously different, even though we cannot calculate the significance of the difference. The only encouraging result of the comparison is that γ', the long-run MPC, is quite similar in (2) and (4), and in fact virtually identical in (3) and (4). Even here it may be objected that a long-run MPC of about .99 in equations (3) and (4) is rather high.

Further doubts, especially about the quarterly equation, arise from inspection of Figures 7.1 and 7.2, showing actual and computed values of per capita consumption. The fit of the annual equation (2) in the postwar period clearly leaves much to be desired, though it does well in the prewar period. More serious, however, are the defects of the quarterly equation. During the years 1950 and 1951 predicted consumption appears to lag one quarter behind actual consumption. Of course we can hardly expect our equation to predict the two buying waves resulting from the Korean War (one in the third quarter of 1950 and the other in the first quarter of 1951), but it is a little disturbing that it is also unable to handle the aftermath of these buying waves. The reason is presumably that the equation treats consumption as habit forming, whereas the hoarding that then took place had just the opposite effect on subsequent consumption.

Even if this defect is charitably overlooked, another and more fundamental inadequacy is revealed by Figure 7.2, particularly in the years after the Korean War. There is a distinct tendency for predicted consumption to be lower than actual consumption in the upswing of the various business cycles, and to exceed it in the downswings. This is especially clear in 1953–1955, in

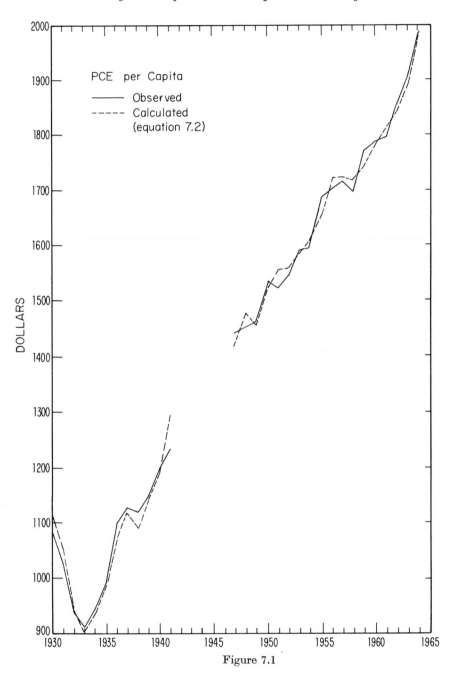

PCE per Capita
——— Observed
- - - - Calculated
(equation 7.2)

Figure 7.1

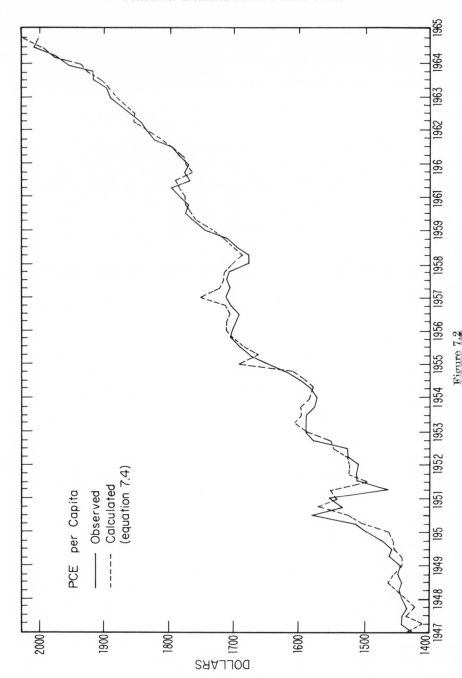

Figure 7.2

the winter of 1957–1958, and in 1961–1962. Here again predicted consumption appears to be one quarter behind actual consumption.

It is instructive to consider the effect of these two inadequacies on the Durbin–Watson coefficient, which in the case of equation (4) failed to reveal anything peculiar in the residuals. The Korean War problem, as is clear from Figure 7.2, leads to sharp swings in the residuals from negative to positive, hence to strong negative serial correlation. The cyclical problem, on the other hand, manifests itself in long strings of residuals of like sign, corresponding to positive serial correlation. As it happens, these two forms of serial correlation virtually cancel each other over the period as a whole, so that the *D.W.* coefficient cannot give a warning.

II. *Saving as the Acquisition of Nondepreciating Assets*

In this section we shall see what a simplified version of the dynamic model can do. The simplification is based on a peculiarity of savings as an object of choice, namely, that the assets acquired through saving are durable and in fact may be assumed to have a depreciation rate of zero. Under the national accounting definition observed in our basic data, saving is essentially the net accumulation of *financial* assets and liabilities, such as money, bonds, shares, equities in unincorporated business,[4] and various forms of nonbusiness debt. Financial assets frequently earn interest or dividends so that it might seem that they have a negative depreciation rate, but this is not the case. Current revenues from investments are included in income and are not counted as an addition to capital, and interest on consumer debt is regarded as an item of expenditure.[5] Capital gains and losses do not appear in the national accounts at all; in principle they may influence consumption and savings, but in practice their influence is hard to detect, and we shall leave them out of the present analysis.[6] The crucial assumption of this section (and of the next) is that, for savings, $\delta = 0$.

The basic model then becomes

$$(5) \qquad\qquad y(t) = \alpha + \beta s(t) + \gamma x(t),$$

$$(6) \qquad\qquad \dot{s}(t) = y(t),$$

where $y(t)$ is savings and $s(t)$ the stock of financial assets. Eliminating $s(t)$ by differentiation we get

$$(7) \qquad\qquad \dot{y}(t) = \beta y(t) + \gamma \dot{x}(t),$$

[4] In the national accounts, all real estate, including owner-occupied dwellings, is assumed to be owned by the business sector. Increases in the stock of durable consumer goods are not included in saving.

[5] There is perhaps an inconsistency here, since such interest might more logically be treated as a deduction from income. The point at issue is not affected by this.

[6] However, see Arena (1965).

and in terms of discrete time periods, with the usual approximation,

$$(8) \qquad y_t = \frac{1 + \frac{1}{2}\beta}{1 - \frac{1}{2}\beta} y_{t-1} + \frac{\gamma}{1 - \frac{1}{2}\beta} \Delta x_t,$$

or more simply

$$(9) \qquad y_t = B_1 y_{t-1} + B_2 \Delta x_t.$$

The result of assuming $\delta = 0$ is therefore to lose two parameters in the estimating equation. It is to be noted, however, that we have not assumed $\alpha = 0$; but α cannot be determined from the estimating equation (9).

The assumption $\delta = 0$ leads to an apparent difficulty with the long-run concepts. In Chapter 1 we defined the static long run by the condition $\dot{s} = 0$, and we see then from (6) that $\hat{y} = 0$. This is as it should be, for in static long-run equilibrium there would be no point in continuing to accumulate a nondepreciating asset. But what about the case of steady long-run growth? We saw in section II of Chapter 1 that the long-run MPC is the same for long-run equilibrium as for steady (linear) growth in income. In the present instance the long-run marginal propensity to save (MPS) is evidently zero in the static case, in accordance with (1.12), and (1.17) implies that the growth rate of savings is also zero. It then follows from (1.18) and (6) that

$$(10) \qquad g_s = \hat{y} = -\frac{\gamma}{\beta} g_x.$$

Hence, in *steady linear growth savings are proportional to the (absolute) growth in income.*[7] If, in accordance with most of the literature, we put the matter in terms of the savings rate and the (relative) growth rate, we find that

$$(11) \qquad \frac{\hat{y}}{x} = -\frac{\gamma}{\beta} \frac{g_x}{x},$$

so that in steady linear growth the savings ratio is proportional to the growth rate. Since $\gamma > 0$ and $\beta < 0$ (financial assets being durable), the constant of proportionality is positive. In view of (1.18) it may be interpreted as a long-run marginal wealth-income ratio.

Similar results can be derived for the case of exponential growth in per

---

[7] The theory of savings developed in this section is therefore closely related to that of Modigliani and Brumberg (developed in 1953), at least in its long-run aspects. Its relation to the work of Friedman (1957), which emphasizes errors in the measurement of income, is rather more remote (see also Chapter 6). Later in this section we shall bring our theory even closer to the Modigliani–Brumberg view by expressing it in aggregate rather than in per capita terms. For an application of the model to international data, see Swamy (1968). It should be noted that so far in this chapter, as everywhere in this book, consumption and income are expressed per capita.

capita income, provided the structural equation (5) is made homogeneous by putting $\alpha = 0$. If we assume

$$(12) \qquad \dot{x}(t) = \rho x(t),$$

where ρ is the growth rate of per capita income, then it is easy to show that y and s will ultimately grow at the same rate ρ. It also follows that

$$(13) \qquad \hat{y}(t) = \frac{\gamma \rho x(t)}{\rho - \beta} = \frac{\gamma \dot{x}(t)}{\rho - \beta},$$

where $\hat{y}(t)$ represents savings in "equilibrium growth," also known as the "golden age." The stock of assets, $s(t)$, does not play any independent part in determining $\hat{y}(t)$, but follows a similarly defined growth path $\hat{s}(t)$.

Translating (13) into a savings ratio we find

$$(14) \qquad \frac{\hat{y}(t)}{x(t)} = \frac{\gamma \rho}{\rho - \beta},$$

which may be compared to (11) by putting $g_x = \rho x$. Although the steady-growth savings ratio is proportional to the growth rate of income in both cases, the proportionality factor is not the same. In (11) this factor is independent of the growth rate, but in (14) it is not. For the growth rates typical in the United States, the difference between (11) and (14) is not negligible; in order to facilitate this comparison, we shall give for each empirical equation not only $-(\gamma/\beta)$ as required by (11) but also $\gamma \rho^* / (\rho^* - \beta)$ according to (14), where ρ^* has been put at .06 for the annual equations and at .015 for the quarterly equations to reflect a typical growth rate of per capita disposable personal income in current prices.[8] As was pointed out earlier, exponential growth is in general more plausible than linear growth, but linear growth between 1961 and 1970 was one of the assumptions of our original projection exercise.

There is more to be said about the theoretical aspects of the present model, but we must leave this to another occasion and confine ourselves to a few brief remarks here. The consumption equation corresponding to (9) can be obtained from the identity $x_t \equiv q_t + y_t$, where q stands for consumption as before, *viz*:

$$(15) \qquad q_t = B_1 q_{t-1} + (1 - B_2)\Delta x_t + (1 - B_1)x_{t-1}.$$

Except for not having an intercept, this equation has the same form as the regular consumption function (equation 1.39), though of course the structural coefficients for the two models have different interpretations and, unlike

---

[8] This incidentally brings out a defect in using undeflated data, for the steady state saving ratios depend directly on the rate of inflation.

equation (1.39), (15) has an identifying constraint corresponding to the restriction on δ. Solving for β_q and β_y, where the subscripts refer to consumption and saving, respectively, we have from equation (1.42)

$$(16) \qquad \beta_q = \frac{2(B_1 - 1)}{B_1 + 1} + \delta_q$$

and

$$(17) \qquad \beta_y = \frac{2(B_1 - 1)}{B_1 + 1}.$$

Hence we have

$$(18) \qquad \beta_q = \beta_y + \delta_q.$$

The stability condition for long-run equilibrium (that is, $\delta_q > \beta_q$) then implies that

$$(19) \qquad \beta_q < 0.$$

This is the basis for the earlier statement that habit formation in consumption and asset effects on saving are really two sides of the same coin.[9]

Focusing on saving rather than consumption brings with it a problem of deflation, however. With the consumption function, a natural deflator is available for both consumption and disposable income, namely, the implicit deflator for total PCE, but this is not the case with the saving function. Indeed, it is not even evident that deflation is warranted in the first place. For these reasons the saving model has been estimated with data in current prices. Another aspect in which the equations with the model of this section differ from those previously reported is that the data are aggregate rather than per capita. Analysis of the population effect (see section VI of Chapter 1) showed this to be unimportant, so that it makes little difference whether per capita or aggregate data are used.

We now come to the empirical results obtained with the model of this section. Those based on Department of Commerce (OBE) data are reported first.[10]

[9] Note that while $\beta_q > 0$ implies $\beta_y < 0$ (assuming the stability condition holds), the converse is not true, that is, $\beta_y < 0$ does not imply $\beta_q > 0$. Thus, it is possible, though highly unlikely, for both β_q and β_y to be negative. It should also be noted that if (15) is estimated without imposing the identifying restriction then (18) may not hold exactly.

[10] The equations reported in the remainder of this chapter were estimated without the benefit of a computer program for 3PLS or one that calculated approximate standard errors of the structural coefficients. Fortunately, however, except for a few cases with *D.W.* coefficients above 2.4, autocorrelation does not appear to be a problem.

U.S. annual (1930–1941, 1947–1966)   OBE data

(20)
$$y_t = .767y_{t-1} + .274\Delta x_t + .853d_t$$
$$\quad\;\;(.054)\qquad\;(.048)\qquad\;\;(.674)$$

$$\bar{R}^2 = .936 \qquad S_e = 2.32 \qquad D.W. = 2.51$$

$$\hat{\beta} = \frac{2(B_1 - 1)}{B_1 + 1} = -.264 \qquad \hat{\gamma} = \frac{2B_2}{B_1 + 1} = .310 \qquad -\frac{\hat{\gamma}}{\hat{\beta}} = 1.17$$

$$-\frac{\hat{\gamma}}{\hat{\beta}}\rho^* = .070 \qquad \frac{\hat{\gamma}\rho^*}{\rho^* - \hat{\beta}} = .057$$

The estimates of B_1 and B_2 are both highly significant, and the stock coefficient is negative, as expected. The estimating equation fits the data fairly well, though the rather high $D.W.$ suggests that some negative auto-correlation in the error term may be present. The linear growth coefficient of (1.17) would imply a saving ratio of 7.0 percent for $\rho^* = .06$; for exponential growth, the saving ratio would be 5.7 percent. The latter in particular is in line with recent experience.

U.S. quarterly (1947–1966, seasonally adjusted annual rates)   OBE data

(21)
$$y_t = .867y_{t-1} + .588\Delta x_t$$
$$\quad\;(.025)\qquad\;(.084)$$

$$\bar{R}^2 = .813 \qquad S_e = 2.51 \qquad D.W. = 2.54$$

$$\hat{\beta} = -.143 \qquad \hat{\gamma} = .650 \qquad -\frac{\hat{\gamma}}{\hat{\beta}} = 4.41 \qquad -\frac{\hat{\gamma}}{\hat{\beta}}\rho^* = .066 \qquad \frac{\hat{\gamma}\rho^*}{\rho^* - \hat{\beta}} = .061$$

The quarterly equation retains many of the features of the annual equation. The steady state saving ratios agree very well with those derived from (20); we recall that $\rho^* = .06$ for the annual equations and $\rho^* = .015$ for the quarterly equations. This is an important point in favor of the structural model. On the other hand, the β's and γ's for (20) and (21) are again not in the expected pattern mentioned at the outset, though the discrepancies are not as striking as they were in section I. This may result in part from the different periods covered by the annual and quarterly equations; postwar annual equations have not been computed for this section.

Equation (21), like its counterpart in the preceding section, appears to be much affected by the violent fluctuations associated with the Korean War. We therefore present a quarterly equation covering only the post-Korean period:

U.S. quarterly (1953–1966, seasonally adjusted annual rates)   OBE data

$$(22) \qquad y_t = .892 y_{t-1} + .497 \Delta x_t$$
$$\qquad\qquad (.026) \qquad (.095)$$
$$\bar{R}^2 = .799 \qquad S_e = 1.98 \qquad D.W. = 2.29$$

$$\hat{\beta} = -.115 \qquad \hat{\gamma} = .526 \qquad -\frac{\hat{\gamma}}{\hat{\beta}} = 4.59 \qquad -\frac{\hat{\gamma}}{\hat{\beta}} \rho^* = .069 \qquad \frac{\hat{\gamma}\rho^*}{\rho^* - \hat{\beta}} = .061$$

This equation differs little from (21). The steady state saving ratios agree well with those derived from the annual equation (they are virtually identical for linear growth). Equation (22) has no apparent autocorrelation in the error term, so that in view of this we should perhaps prefer (22) to (21).

The goodness of fit of the equations of this section cannot be directly compared with those of section I, at least not by means of R^2, since the dependent variables are different. However the "standard error of estimate" (S_e), which is the estimated standard deviation of the dependent variable when the explanatory variables are held constant, is conceptually comparable between the consumption and saving equations, for when income x_t is held constant the standard deviation of q_t is the same as that of $x_t - q_t$. This is complicated somewhat when the consumption equations are in constant prices and the savings equations in current prices, as in the present case, but it is fairly easy to show that, everything else being constant, unremoved price changes common to both the dependent and independent variables will lead to a lower S_e in the saving equations. Empirically, the S_e's, where those of equations (2)–(4) have been multiplied by the mean population for the periods involved in order to convert them to aggregate terms, are somewhat smaller for the saving equations.

We now turn to equations estimated from Securities and Exchange Commission (SEC) and flow-of-funds (FOF) data on saving. (Since these agencies do not prepare estimates of disposable income, we must continue to use OBE disposable income.) The SEC data are not seasonally adjusted, so that three seasonal dummy variables (plus a constant) are included in equation (23).[11]

U.S. quarterly (1953–1966, seasonally unadjusted annual rates)   SEC data

$$(23) \quad y_t = 7.280 + .358 y_{t-1} + 1.408 \Delta x_t - 11.764 D_2 + 3.536 D_3 - 3.284 D_4$$
$$\qquad (2.692) \ (.119) \qquad (.476) \qquad (2.756) \qquad (2.968) \qquad (2.772)$$
$$\qquad\qquad \bar{R}^2 = .565 \qquad S_e = 1.78 \qquad D.W. = 2.41$$

$$\hat{\beta} = -.946 \qquad \hat{\gamma} = 2.07 \qquad -\frac{\hat{\gamma}}{\hat{\beta}} = 2.19 \qquad -\frac{\hat{\gamma}}{\hat{\beta}} \rho^* = .033 \qquad \frac{\hat{\gamma}\rho^*}{\rho^* - \hat{\beta}} = .032$$

[11] The inclusion of seasonal dummies creates a minor problem in that it is no longer possible to restrict B_0 to be zero unless the equation is estimated under the explicit constraint that the sum of the coefficients of the dummy variables is zero. In the usual case where there is a constant term, this restriction is imposed implicitly in unscrambling the seasonal coefficients and the true constant from the estimated coefficients. We have ignored this complication.

U.S. quarterly (1953–1966, seasonally adjusted annual rates)   FOF data

$$(24) \qquad y_t = .892y_{t-1} + .769\Delta x_t$$
$$\qquad\qquad (.014) \qquad (.075)$$

$$\bar{R}^2 = .972 \qquad S_e = 1.43 \qquad D.W. = 2.29$$

$$\hat{\beta} = -.114 \qquad \hat{\gamma} = .813 \qquad -\frac{\hat{\gamma}}{\hat{\beta}} = 7.11 \qquad -\frac{\hat{\gamma}}{\hat{\beta}}\rho^* = .107 \qquad \frac{\hat{\gamma}\rho^*}{\rho^* - \hat{\beta}} = .095$$

Equation (23) with SEC data is clearly the least satisfactory of those presented thus far in this section. The $\bar{R}^2$ is low, and the structural coefficients, with the extremely strong stock adjustment and equally strong short-run marginal propensity to save, make little sense. Moreover, the steady state saving ratios derived from the equation are implausibly low. The equation with FOF data, in contrast, is much more satisfactory. The $\bar{R}^2$ is the highest so far encountered in this section, and the residuals are free of autocorrelation. Even more important, the steady state saving ratios are in line with the recent experience of this definition of saving.[12]

To conclude this section, it seems fair to say that the interpretation of saving as the acquisition of nondepreciating assets is a useful step forward. Problems remain, however, and the model in its present form is incomplete in that changes in the general price level and the rate of interest are not taken into account. These two factors are considered next.

III. Extension of the Zero-Depreciation Model to Include Price Changes and the Rate of Interest

Included among the assets held by savers will be assets (cash and demand deposits, for example) whose values are fixed in dollars. Since the real value of these assets will be affected by general price movements, this implies that unless there are offsetting capital gains or losses among other assets whose values can fluctuate, the real value of the total stock of assets will vary inversely with changes in the general price level. If we assume that the wealth-income relationship that individuals wish to maintain is in real terms, it then follows that the rate of saving will be positively related to the rate of change of prices. A general price increase, for example, will reduce the real value of existing assets, and saving will therefore increase in order to recoup the loss. Thus it is clear that some provision for price changes definitely belongs in the model.

This is easily done by simply including the rate of inflation as a separate explanatory variable. We also take this opportunity to take another factor

[12] The saving figures used in equation (24) are *net* saving of households in the flow-of-funds accounts. This differs from the OBE definition primarily in that the FOF data include net purchases of durable goods (purchases minus capital consun.ption).

into account that has been ignored, namely, the rate of interest. Equation (5) thus becomes

(25) $$y(t) = \alpha + \beta s(t) + \gamma x(t) + \lambda \dot{p}(t) + \xi r(t),$$

where $\dot{p}(t)$ and $r(t)$ are the rate of change of prices and the interest rate, respectively, both measured at time t. Equation (6) remains as it stands. From the discussion of the preceding paragraph, it is evident that we should expect λ to be negative.

A priori assessment of the sign of ξ, on the other hand, is more difficult. In general this sign will depend on the relative strengths of the income and substitution effects arising from a change in r. Ordinarily, the latter is thought to outweigh the former, so that ξ on this reasoning would be expected to be positive. The present approach, however, though it is not inconsistent with the traditional Fisherian theory which gives rise to this result, suggests that ξ ought to be negative. This can be seen most easily in the expression for the long-run equilibrium stock of assets, which is obtained by setting y and $\dot{p}$ in (25) equal to zero and solving for $\hat{s}$:

(26) $$\hat{s} = -\frac{\gamma}{\beta}\hat{x} - \frac{\xi}{\beta}\hat{r}.$$

The coefficient $-\gamma/\beta$, which (as we already know) is the (long-run) equilibrium wealth-to-income ratio, will reflect the opposing forces of the motives to save and time preference, and will be larger the stronger the former are relative to the latter. Since one of the motives for saving is the income earned on assets, it seems reasonable to suppose that for a given income, the desired stock of assets will be smaller the higher the rate of interest is, and conversely. Hence since β is negative, we should expect ξ to be negative also.

The finite approximation of (25) involves nothing new, so that we can proceed directly to the estimating equation:

(27) $$y_t = B_1 y_{t-1} + B_2 \Delta x_t + B_3 \Delta p_t^* + B_4 \Delta r_t,$$

where

(28) $$B_3 = \frac{\lambda}{1 - \frac{1}{2}\beta}$$

(29) $$B_4 = \frac{\xi}{1 - \frac{1}{2}\beta}.$$

Also,

(30) $$p_t^* = \int_t^{t+1} \dot{p}(\tau) \, d\tau,$$

so that Δp_t^* is the first difference of the *within* period changes in prices. With annual data, for example, Δp_t^* could be calculated as the first difference of December-to-December price changes.[13]

---

[13] Since the equations are estimated with undeflated data, we have used Δp_t in place of Δp_t^* in the empirical results that follow.

The empirical results for the extended model of this section follow. The equations estimated from OBE data are given first.[14]

U.S. annual (1929–1941, 1946–1966)   OBE data

$$(31) \qquad y_t = .766 y_{t-1} + .326 \Delta x_t - .324 \Delta p_t - 2.093 \Delta r_t$$
$$\qquad\qquad (.054) \qquad (.058) \qquad (.206) \qquad (1.813)$$
$$\qquad\qquad \bar{R}^2 = .938 \qquad S_e = 2.28 \qquad D.W. = 2.35$$

$$\hat{\beta} = -.265 \qquad \hat{\gamma} = .369 \qquad -\frac{\hat{\gamma}}{\hat{\beta}} = 1.39 \qquad -\frac{\hat{\gamma}}{\hat{\beta}} \rho^* = .083 \qquad \frac{\hat{\gamma}\rho^*}{\rho^* - \hat{\beta}} = .068$$

U.S. quarterly (1953–1966, seasonally adjusted annual rates)   OBE data

$$(32) \qquad y_t = .830 y_{t-1} + .621 \Delta x_t + 2.160 \Delta p_t - 4.797 \Delta r_t$$
$$\qquad\qquad (.033) \qquad (.096) \qquad (.906) \qquad (2.024)$$
$$\qquad\qquad \bar{R}^2 = .828 \qquad S_e = 1.83 \qquad D.W. = 2.12$$

$$\hat{\beta} = -.186 \qquad \hat{\gamma} = .679 \qquad -\frac{\hat{\gamma}}{\hat{\beta}} = 3.65 \qquad -\frac{\hat{\gamma}}{\hat{\beta}} \rho^* = .055 \qquad \frac{\gamma\rho^*}{\rho^* - \hat{\beta}} = .051$$

In terms of the hypotheses stated at the beginning of this section, the quarterly equation is clearly to be preferred, for the coefficients of the two new variables have the correct signs and are both more than twice their standard errors. The sign of the price term in the annual equation is counter to expectations, and the coefficient of Δr_t, though negative, is just barely greater than its standard error. Also, the steady state saving ratios derived from the quarterly equation are more in line with recent experience than those from the annual equation. Autocorrelated residuals are not a problem with either equation.

We next look at the equations estimated with SEC and FOF saving data. As in the preceding section, only quarterly models have been estimated.[15]

U.S. quarterly (1953–1966, seasonally unadjusted annual rates)   SEC data

$$(33) \qquad y_t = 6.592 + .343 y_{t-1} + 1.512 \Delta x_t + 1.164 \Delta p_t - 4.892 \Delta r_t$$
$$\qquad\quad (3.080) \quad (.124) \qquad (.416) \qquad (3.416) \qquad (8.204)$$
$$\qquad\qquad - 10.640 D_2 + 3.764 D_3 - 3.128 D_4$$
$$\qquad\qquad (2.816) \qquad (3.040) \qquad (2.844)$$
$$\qquad\qquad \bar{R}^2 = .551 \qquad S_e = 1.81 \qquad D.W. = 2.43$$

$$\hat{\beta} = -.978 \qquad \hat{\gamma} = 2.252 \qquad -\frac{\hat{\gamma}}{\hat{\beta}} = 2.30 \qquad -\frac{\hat{\gamma}}{\hat{\beta}} \rho^* = .035 \qquad \frac{\hat{\gamma}\rho^*}{\rho^* - \hat{\beta}} = .034$$

---

[14] Δp_t is the first difference in the total PCE deflator. The interest rate used is the yield on long-term government bonds.

[15] The FOF data again refer to net investment of households, i.e., personal saving plus net investment in durable goods.

U.S. quarterly (1953–1966, seasonally adjusted annual rates)   FOF data

$$(34) \qquad y_t = .878 y_{t-1} + .820 \Delta x_t + .569 \Delta p_t - 1.558 \Delta r_t$$

$$\qquad\qquad (.020) \qquad (.087) \qquad (.750) \qquad (1.624)$$

$$\bar{R}^2 = .972 \qquad S_e = 1.44 \qquad D.W. = 2.36$$

$$\hat{\beta} = -.130 \qquad \hat{\gamma} = .921 \qquad -\frac{\hat{\gamma}}{\hat{\beta}} = 6.72 \qquad -\frac{\hat{\gamma}}{\hat{\beta}} \rho^* = .101 \qquad \frac{\hat{\gamma}\rho^*}{\rho^* - \hat{\beta}} = .095$$

The addition of the two new variables does not lead to any improvement in the equation with SEC data [cf. equations (33) and (23)]. Stock adjustment is still extremely strong, and the steady state saving ratios derived from (33) remain implausibly low. Moreover, the coefficients of Δp_t and Δr_t, though both conform to expectations regarding sign, are both smaller than their standard errors. Neither do the new variables add any new explanatory power to the equation estimated from flow-of-funds data, an equation which already is very good [cf. equations (34) and (24)]. The coefficients have hypothesized signs, but once again they are only fractions of their standard errors. It should be noted, however, that the FOF equation involves a concept of saving different from that used in the OBE and SEC equations, in that net purchases of durable goods are included as saving. Since the durable good component of the FOF "saving" figure is substantial (about 50 percent), this is also the case for the stocks of assets implicit in the equation. We should thus hardly expect the durable good component of these stocks to give rise to real balance effect when prices rise. On the contrary, since much of the time the prices of durable goods move with the general price level, we should expect the durable good portion of the FOF saving figure to be negatively related to the change in prices. Thus ξ in equation (35) will reflect opposing forces, a positive one arising from a real balance effect on the financial component of S and a negative one arising from the durable good component of y. Hence the unimportance of Δp_t in (34) is not surprising.

Something else that ought to be mentioned, if only in passing, is that the instantaneous adjustment to inflation postulated in equation (25) may be too simple. An adjustment occurring over a period of time is probably a more appropriate assumption. Such a mechanism could be incorporated into the model by including past price changes in the estimating equation, a procedure which would be especially relevant with quarterly data. Another assumption implicit in equation (25) is a zero elasticity of price expectations with respect to current price changes, and this too is probably an exaggeration. Specifying the formation of price expectations, however, is a tricky task, and lack of time has precluded any exploration of this as well as of a more realistic inflation adjustment mechanism. These qualifications should therefore be kept in mind in interpreting the results of this section.

IV. Gross Saving of Households

In this section, we extend the model to an even broader concept of saving than that used in equations (24) and (34), namely, gross savings of households. The latter is defined in the flow-of-funds accounts as the sum of personal saving, expenditures for durable goods, and depreciation on residences. Gross saving thus differs from net saving in that depreciation is excluded from the latter. However, this means that the zero-depreciation model is no longer appropriate, and the general model with $\delta \neq 0$ must be used instead. The data are quarterly and the period of observation is 1953–1966.

U.S. quarterly (1953–1966, seasonally adjusted annual rates)   FOF data

$$(35) \qquad y_t = 1.363 + .768 y_{t-1} + .782 \Delta x_t + .038 x_{t-1}$$
$$\qquad\qquad (.946) \quad (.061) \qquad (.077) \qquad (.014)$$

$$\bar{R}^2 = .995 \qquad S_e = 1.32 \qquad D.W. = 2.42$$

$$\hat{\alpha} = 26.91 \qquad \hat{\beta} = -.205 \qquad \hat{\gamma} = .863 \qquad \hat{\delta} = .057 \qquad \frac{\hat{\gamma}\hat{\delta}}{\hat{\delta} - \hat{\beta}} = .245$$

The fit of this equation is very good, and with exception of the intercept the coefficients are multiples of their standard errors. In view of the fact that S includes nondepreciating financial assets as well as durable goods, a low value for δ is warranted, and the long-run marginal propensity to "save," though high, is not implausibly so. There is some suggestion of negative autocorrelation in the error term, but not enough to detract from the general high quality of the equation.

In addition to analyzing gross saving as an aggregate, we have also estimated a model with separate equations for personal saving and expenditures for durables in which it is assumed that personal saving is influenced by both the stock of financial assets and the stock of durable goods, and similarly for expenditures for durable goods. Recall that one of the findings with the additive model in Chapter 5 was an interaction between saving and automobile expenditures. The structural equations for saving and durables expenditures considered simultaneously therefore become

$$(36) \qquad \begin{aligned} y_1(t) &= \alpha_1 + \beta_{11} s_1(t) + \beta_{12} s_2(t) + \gamma_1 x(t) \\ y_2(t) &= \alpha_2 + \beta_{21} s_1(t) + \beta_{22} s_2(t) + \gamma_2 x(t), \end{aligned}$$

where y_1 and y_2 denote saving and durables expenditures, respectively, and similarly for s_1 and s_2. The stock-flow relationships remain as before:

$$(37) \qquad \begin{aligned} \dot{s}_1(t) &= y_1(t) \\ \dot{s}_2(t) &= y_2(t) - \delta s_2(t). \end{aligned}$$

The usual finite approximation and elimination of s_1 and s_2 yields estimating equations of the form:

(38)
$$y_{1t} = K_0 + K_1 y_{1(t-1)} + K_2 y_{2(t-1)} + K_3 \Delta x_t + K_4 x_{t-1}$$
$$y_{2t} = L_0 + L_1 y_{1(t-1)} + L_2 y_{2(t-1)} + L_3 \Delta x_t + L_4 x_{t-1},$$

where $K_0, \ldots, K_4, L_0, \ldots, L_4$ are functions of the structural parameters in (36) and (37). Unfortunately, the functions are very complicated and cannot readily be solved for the structural parameters. Because of this, discussion of the empirical results must be confined to the estimating equations. Quarterly OBE data for the period 1953–1966 have been used to estimate the equations that follow:

U.S. quarterly (1953–1966, seasonally adjusted annual rates)   FOF data

(39) $y_{1t} = 3.346 + .671 y_{1(t-1)} + .057 y_{2(t-1)} + .495 \Delta x_t - .003 x_{t-1}$
              (1.510) (.103)   (.113)   (.112)   (.018)

$$\bar{R}^2 = .813 \qquad S_e = 1.91 \qquad D.W. = 1.98$$

(40) $y_{2t} = -1.268 + .169 y_{1(t-1)} + .744 y_{2(t-1)} + .315 \Delta x_t + .025 x_t$
              (1.140) (.078)   (.085)   (.085)   (.013)

$$\bar{R}^2 = .984 \qquad S_e = 1.44 \qquad D.W. = 2.03$$

Empirical interest in these two equations lies in the coefficients for $y_{1(t-1)}$ and $y_{2(t-1)}$. *A priori*, we should expect $y_{1(t-1)}$ to be fairly important in explaining y_2, but for y_1 to be relatively independent of $y_{2(t-1)}$. This follows from the lumpy nature of most durable goods which necessitates some saving prior to purchase. There is of course a great deal of purchase on credit, which puts the expenditure prior to saving, but the former almost certainly predominates in United States consumer spending. The empirical results are consistent with this reasoning, for the coefficient of $y_{2(t-1)}$ is less than its standard error in (39), while the coefficient of $y_{1(t-1)}$ is about twice its standard error in (40).

V. Gross Investment of Households

We now leave household saving for a moment to consider an equation for gross investment of households which is defined in the flow-of-funds accounts as the sum of residential construction, expenditures for durable goods, and expenditures of nonprofit organizations for plant and equipment. If gross saving and gross investment were both known accurately they would be identical, but in fact there is a considerable statistical discrepancy. As with gross saving in the preceding section, it is again necessary to use the general model with $\delta \neq 0$.

U.S. quarterly (1964–1966, seasonally adjusted annual rates)   FOF data

(41)
$$y_t = 4.513 + .239y_{t-1} + .880x_t + .145x_{t-1}$$
$$(3.270) \quad (.123) \qquad (.269) \qquad (.029)$$
$$\bar{R}^2 = .932 \qquad S_e = 4.60 \qquad D.W. = 2.26$$

$$\hat{\alpha} = 1.311 \qquad \hat{\beta} = -1.048 \qquad \hat{\gamma} = 1.303 \qquad \hat{\delta} = .180 \qquad \frac{\hat{\gamma}\hat{\delta}}{\hat{\delta} - \hat{\beta}} = .191$$

The only anomaly apparent in this equation is in the short-run marginal propensity to invest, which at first sight seems implausibly high. However, strong stock adjustment, which is to be expected, and a depreciation rate, which also does not seem out of line, yield a long-run marginal propensity to invest that agrees well with historical experience.

VI. Forecasting Performance of the Saving Equations

The criteria by which the underlying models have been judged so far are plausibility of the estimated parameters, consistency between annual and quarterly equations, and goodness of fit. The application of these criteria has led to encouraging results, particularly for the (personal) saving equation where $\delta = 0$. Nevertheless, it is useful to test these equations more searchingly by looking at their forecasting performance after the period of observation. Since the saving equations use data through 1966, there is sufficient new evidence at the time of writing to make such a test worthwhile.[16]

With dynamic equations containing lagged values of the dependent variable, there are two ways of making conditional forecasts. For instance, if data through period t have been used in estimating the equation, and we require a forecast for period $t + 2$, we can use either (using the zero-depreciation model for illustration)

(42)
$$\hat{y}_{t+2} = B_1 y_{t+1} + B_2 \Delta x_{t+2}$$

or

(43)
$$\hat{y}_{t+2} = B_1 \hat{y}_{t+1} + B_2 \Delta x_{t+2}$$

where

(44)
$$\hat{y}_{t+1} = B_1 y_t + B_2 \Delta x_{t+1}.$$

In (42) the actual value of y_{t+1} is used, while in (45) the value of y_{t-1} used is itself a forecast. This distinction is of considerable importance in evaluating

[16] The following calculations are all based on the figures appearing in the July, 1968 and January, 1969 issues of *The Survey of Current Business*, the 1967 and 1968 *Economic Report of the President*, and the *Flow of Funds*, 3rd quarter, 1968. These figures will no doubt be revised in subsequent issues.

an equation, especially when it is to be used for long-term projection. Projections based on (42) are to some extent self-correcting, because they use intervening information, whereas (43) is in the nature of a straightforward extrapolation. The latter test is therefore more stringent and also more relevant. We can rely on (42) only if we are primarily interested in short-term projection; in fact, for $t + 1$, (42) coincides with (43).

In order to facilitate comparison between the different equations, the forecasts and actual values are shown in terms of the saving ratio in the accompanying tables. Except for Table 7.3, the forecasts are based on (43).

It is seen from Table 7.1 that the annual equations underestimate saving in 1967 and 1968, though the estimates for 1968, especially from equation (20), are very close to the actual figure. [Recall that equation (31) differs from (20) in that it includes the first differences in the PCE deflator and the yield on long-term government bonds; both refer to personal saving.] Given the fact that the saving rate in 1967 reflected a sharp jump over 1966 to a post-Korean high, a rather large underestimate is hardly surprising.

Table 7.1. U.S. Annual Saving Equations: Actual and Projected Values of the Saving Ratio * (in percent)

Equation	1967	1968
Actual	7.4	6.9
(20) 1929–1966	6.5	6.8
(31) 1929–1966	6.5	6.6

* Data for 1968 are preliminary.

This same tendency is also apparent in the quarterly forecasts for 1967 (Table 7.2), though in contrast to the annual forecasts, the quarterly estimates tend to be too high in 1968. The biggest discrepancy is for the fourth quarter of 1967 when the saving rate reached 7.8 percent, and except for the third quarter the forecasts for 1968 from equations (21) and (22) are very good. The inclusions of changes in the PCE deflator and of the yield on long-term government bonds definitely leads to inferior forecasts, as was not the case with the annual model. On the other hand, since they give virtually identical forecasts, there is little to choose between the post-Korean equation [equation (22)] and the equation estimated from data covering the entire postwar period. It is interesting to note that the quarterly equations forecast the annual saving ratio in 1967 better than the annual equation: the projected figures from the 1953–1966 equation, obtained by adding up the quarterly projections, are 7.0 percent compared with 6.5 percent from (20).

Table 7.2. U.S. Quarterly Saving Equations: Actual and Projected Values of the
Saving Ratio* (in percent)

Equation	1967				1968			
	I	II	III	IV	I	II	III	IV
Personal saving								
Actual	7.4	6.8	7.4	7.8	7.1	7.5	6.3	6.9
(21) 1947–1966	7.1	6.9	6.8	6.8	7.3	7.4	6.9	6.9
(22) 1953–1966	7.1	7.0	6.9	6.9	7.3	7.4	7.1	7.0
(32) 1953–1966	7.8	7.3	6.9	6.7	7.5	7.7	7.5	7.5
Net saving								
Actual	10.8	10.4	10.7	11.7	11.2	11.9	10.6	
(24) 1953–1966	11.1	9.9	10.0	10.6	10.7	10.3	10.3	
Gross saving								
Actual	23.5	23.2	21.9	24.5	24.0	24.7	23.5	
(35) 1953–1966	23.3	22.7	22.4	22.2	22.6	22.5	21.9	
Gross investment								
Actual	21.9	22.2	22.9	24.0	21.8	24.2	23.2	
(41) 1953–1966	21.7	21.4	21.5	21.6	22.2	22.0	21.2	

* Data for 1968-IV are preliminary.

Turning now to the two flow-of-funds definitions of saving, we see that
there is a tendency to underpredict not only in 1967 but in 1968 as well. With
net saving, however, it is encouraging that the most accurate estimates are at
the ends of the period of forecast. The projections of gross investment of
households also tend to be underestimates, and exhibit about the same error
as the projections of gross saving.

To illustrate the difference between the forecasting equations (42) and (43),
Table 7.3 shows the quarterly projections from (22), which appears to be our
best savings equation, using either the fourth quarter from 1966 or the
quarter preceding the projection as the base. The second line is identical with
the corresponding one in Table 7.2. It is clear that (42), which uses more
information, does not project as well as (43).[17] The reason presumably is that
this information, though relevant conceptually, is too much affected by error.
The saving ratios computed from quarterly National Accounts data are rather
erratic, and the minor fluctuations in the "actual" figures may be merely
errors of measurement. Consequently a forecast based on (43) which pays no
attention to these minor fluctuations is more reliable than one that does.

[17] Equation (35) in Table 7.2 is the only equation for which this is not true.

Table 7.3. U.S. Quarterly Equation (22): Projected Saving Ratios, Using (42) and (43)* (in percent)

Base of projection	1967				1968			
	I	II	III	IV	I	II	III	IV
Actual	7.4	6.8	7.4	7.8	7.1	7.5	6.3	6.9
Saving in 1966-IV	7.1	7.0	6.9	6.9	7.3	7.4	7.1	7.0
Actual saving in preceding quarter	7.1	7.2	6.8	7.3	8.0	7.2	7.2	6.3

* Data for 1968-IV are preliminary.

This also suggests that in the presence of errors of measurement we should not rely too much on the comparison of actual and calculated values of the observations in judging a regression equation containing a lagged dependent variable. In such a comparison it is natural to use (42), that is, to use actual values for the lagged dependent variable. Perhaps it would be more illuminating to use the equivalent of (43). But then the problem would arise of what value of the dependent variable should be used as a point of departure. This question needs further study.

VII. Conclusions and Projections for 1975

The application of the dynamic model to total consumption or saving appears to be a definite advance. If the dynamic model is specialized by putting the depreciation rate of net financial assets equal to zero, very satisfactory saving equations result. The best equations obtained are satisfactory in at least five aspects.

1. The structural parameters derived from them are in accordance with expectations.

2. The equations fit well during the period of observation.

3. They provide fairly reliable projections after the period of observation.

4. They fit in with the best previous work on saving, especially with the work of Modigliani and his associates.

5. They do not depend upon the particular definition of saving employed.

Even so, a number of problems remain, which have been noted as they became apparent in the preceding sections. In particular, it is disturbing that the agreement between the quarterly and annual parameters is not better. On the other hand, the results suggest several directions to extend the model.

One such direction, suggested by the results of section IV, would be to disaggregate gross saving to specific durable goods and to broad categories of financial assets and then to estimate the demands for these simultaneously. The additive model of Chapter 5 would provide a natural vehicle for doing this.

Finally, we give some projections of the personal saving rate for 1975 in line with the original purpose of this book. We shall use equation (22) to make the projections, since it appears to be the best of our saving equations. In the absence of a more specific assumption, we have taken the growth rate of aggregate disposable personal income to be the same as the growth rate of aggregate GNP. It will be recalled that a growth rate of 4.3 percent per year in real GNP underlies the projections of Chapter 4. Since equation (22) is based on current dollar data, it is necessary to include an inflation factor, and we shall take this to be 3.0 percent per year for the period as a whole, allowing for the more rapid inflation that has already taken place in the initial years. We therefore take the (annual) ρ to be .073. Moreover, it is sufficiently accurate to assume that by 1975 the quarterly equation will have reached the equilibrium corresponding to steady state growth. We then find that $\rho = .018$, with linear growth, leads to a 1975 saving ratio of 8.3 percent. With exponential growth, the 1975 saving ratio would be 7.1 percent.

8

Evaluation

At this point we shall draw together what we consider the major results and conclusions of our investigation. Though we have never lost sight of the fact that the original objective was to provide several sets of projections of personal consumption expenditures in 1970, much of our research energy, and especially so in this edition, has fallen into two other clearly defined areas. These are the derivation and empirical estimation of the dynamic model of consumer behavior and the treatment of several formal econometric problems encountered in estimating the equations and making the projections. Hence the investigation as a whole can be described as a thorough-going study in econometrics.

I. Empirical Results

We feel that the empirical results have justified our initial enthusiasm for the dynamic model, if only because in many instances the long-run elasticities differ markedly from the short-run elasticities. Of the 81 regression equations estimated in Chapter 3, 79 are dynamic, and in most cases the stock coefficient, depreciation rate, total PCE, and price elasticities are plausible. The results of Chapters 5 and 7 show the dynamic model to even better advantage. In addition, use of the dynamic model has largely sidestepped the problems with autocorrelation of the error term, though the Monte Carlo experiments of Chapter 2 suggest that autocorrelation in a projection context may not be as serious a problem as many (including ourselves) had previously believed.

Moreover, use of the dynamic model has enabled us to obtain the highly interesting finding that consumption in the United States is characterized more by habit formation than by inventory adjustment. This conclusion is based on the fact that, of the 65 categories with stock coefficients, 46 of the coefficients are positive. These 46 categories account for 61 percent of total expenditure in 1964. In addition, the positive stock coefficients for the aggregate consumption functions estimated in Chapter 7 corroborate the predominance of habit formation.

A second major empirical finding is that prices (relative to income) play a fairly modest role in explaining United States consumption. Prices appear in only 44 of the 81 equations, while total expenditure appears in 79. Both this result and the predominance of habit formation may reflect the relatively high level of income in the United States. If income is high enough, it is possible for nearly all commodities to become subject to habit formation. And as income grows, prices cease being a factor in the consumption of many commodities. Additional empirical support for this contention is offered by the Swedish consumption study of Taylor (1968).[1] There it was found that, at income levels roughly half those in the United States for essentially the same period of time (1931–1958), inventory adjustment is more widespread than habit formation, while prices play a more important role. Still other evidence, though of a mixed nature, is provided by the recent application of the dynamic model to 37 categories of Canadian consumption by Schweitzer (1967). If the hypothesis has any substance, we should expect the strength of habit formation in Canada, where the per capita income is between that of Sweden and of the United States, to be stronger than in Sweden but weaker than in the United States, and the reverse for the relative importance of prices. Schweitzer's results conform to the expectation with respect to prices, but not with respect to the strength of habit formation. Habit formation appears to be even more widespread in Canada than in the United States. Thus, the relationship between the pervasiveness of habit formation and the level of per capita income must be left an open question for the present.

Turning now to the cross-section results, the poor reconciliation of the cross-section data for 1960 and 1961 from the Survey of Consumer Expenditures with the OBE time-series data stands out, and makes use of the survey data to check the time series results a problematic undertaking. Moreover, even if consistency were not a problem, the extensive dynamism in United States consumption behavior strongly argues against the use of equations estimated from survey data in time-series contexts until such time as panel (or reinterview) data become available. Besides the poor reconciliation of the OBE and SCE data, the other important empirical finding of Chapter 6 is the importance of total expenditure rather than income as the budget constraint (with cross-section data) that was revealed by the principal component analysis of 36 items of expenditure.

Chapter 5 shows that state adjustment can be successfully incorporated into a system of demand equations that is obtained by utility maximization. The results with the additive model agree very well with those obtained with the nonadditive model, and provide evidence that total expenditure (vis-à-vis

---

[1] This study uses the same data as were used with the additive model in Chapter 5; 64 commodity categories are analyzed in all.

income) is also the more appropriate budget constraint with time-series data. Finally, the application of the additive model to consumption in Canada, the Netherlands, and Sweden shows that substantial state adjustment also exists in these countries.

II. The Projections for 1970 and 1975

Beyond the fact that, with few exceptions, they are insensitive to the relative prices, there is little that is objective to be said about the projections for 1970 and 1975. For the most part we believe them to be plausible, and we have noted where this is not the case. The accuracy of the predictions for 1965 from the 82-group equations and for 1965, 1966, and 1967 from the 11-group equations serves to increase the confidence that we can place in the projections, but it is an inescapable fact that time remains the ultimate judge.

III. Formal Econometric Results

Perhaps the most interesting formal econometric results are those obtained in the Monte Carlo experiments of Chapter 2. Though much still remains to be done on both formal and empirical levels, these experiments provide several interesting insights into the sample estimating and projecting properties of dynamic equations. In particular, it was interesting to find that projecting from the structural equation is inefficient and results in considerable bias. It was also interesting to find that the projections from the 3PLS equations are unbiased, though they are less efficient than the biased OLS projections.

The Monte Carlo results also bring home the fact that choosing the projecting equation cannot be done in a vacuum. Clearly, there is a difference between a structural equation and a good projecting equation. In order to assess properly a projecting equation, we need to know how and in what context a projection is to be used. In particular, we need to know the utility function (or at least the cost function) of the policy-maker using the projections, for with this knowledge we could weight such "costs" as bias and variance in choosing the projecting equation.

In estimating the basic dynamic model, we were led to develop a simple quadratic programming procedure for taking into account an overidentifying restriction on the depreciation rate. Though the procedure itself is short of novel, it does offer some insights into the multicollinearity of the predictors. The results here are certainly suggestive for future research.

Equally suggestive for future research are the results of section VI of Chapter 7 which show that predictions made over several quarters or years that do not use intervening information on the lagged dependent variable are generally more accurate than those that do. Indeed, the whole question of finding criteria for judging the quality of an equation with a lagged dependent variable in the presence of errors of measurement needs investigation.

Our study has also served as an empirical testing ground for the three-pass least-squares method for estimating models with the lagged dependent variable as a predictor. In general, we must conclude that the technique has proven successful in that we were able to estimate many equations in the face of substantial autocorrelation in the OLS residuals.

If we confess to some satisfaction with the results of this econometric investigation, this may be merely because experience has taught us not to expect too much. It is not often that a relatively untried theoretical approach (such as our dynamic model) survives an extensive confrontation with a broad range of stubborn facts (such as the detailed personal-consumption-expenditure data for the United States). On the whole it survived better than we had dared to hope. In view of somewhat similar results achieved by Stone and his associates, we may conclude that *an explicitly dynamic formulation should now become part and parcel of demand analysis*. Although improvements can and should be made both in the dynamic theory and in its application, the days of the traditional, essentially static, approach would seem to be numbered.

DATA SOURCES

REFERENCES

INDEX

Data Sources

I. Annual United States Data

(1) Personal consumption expenditure (in 1958 dollars). Sources: 84-commodity breakdown, Bureau of Labor Statistics worksheets; 11-commodity breakdown, *The National Income and Product Accounts of the United States 1929–1965* and subsequent July issues of the *Survey of Current Business* (both are publications of the Office of Business Economics, U.S. Department of Commerce). Data in current dollars are from the same sources. The regressions of Chapters 3 and 5 incorporate revisions made through August, 1966: the aggregate consumption equations of Chapter 7 incorporate revisions through July, 1965.

(2) Personal saving (in both current and 1958 dollars). Sources: OBE data, *National Income and Product, 1929–1965* and July issues of the *Survey of Current Business*. The regressions of Chapter 6 incorporate revisions through July, 1967.

(3) Personal disposable income (in both current and 1958 dollars). Sources: same as for (1).

(4) Population of the United States in thousands (including armed forces overseas). Source: *Statistical Abstract of the United States, 1965*.

(5) Yield on 3–5-year U.S. government bonds. Source: *Federal Reserve Bulletin*, various issues.

(6) Percentage of the population older than 18 years. Sources: For 1930, 1940, and 1950, figures were taken from the *Census of the Population*. The in-between years were obtained by interpolation by the formula $x_{10} = x_0(1 + r)^{10}$ where x_{10} represents the census year 10 years ahead of x_0. For 1951–1964 the figures were taken from various issues of the *Statistical Abstract of the United States* and *Current Population Estimates, Series P-25* (published by the Bureau of the Census, U.S. Department of Commerce).

(7) Percentage of the population living on farms. Source: *Economic Report of the President*, 1966.

(8) Number of shares sold on the New York Stock Exchange. Sources: *Historical Statistics of the United States from Colonial Times to 1957*, Series X-373 (p. 659).

(9) Disposable farm income (in 1958 dollars). Sources: *Farm Income Situation*, *1965* (published by the U.S. Department of Agriculture). The total PCE deflator was used to deflate the current dollar series.

II. Quarterly United States Data

(10) Total personal consumption expenditure (in both current and 1958 dollars). Sources: same as for (1). The quarterly aggregate consumption equations of Chapter 7 incorporate data revisions through July, 1965. Quarterly population figures were obtained by linear interpolation between successive annual figures.

(11) Personal saving. Sources: OBE data, same as for (2); SEC data, Securities and Exchange Commission, *Statistical Bulletin*, various issues; flow-of-funds data, Board of Governors, Federal Reserve System (data used were those on tape storage at the FRS computation center in Washington). The quarterly personal saving equations incorporate data revisions through mid-year 1967.

(12) Disposable personal income. Sources: same as for (1).

(13) Yield on 3–5-year U.S. government securities. Source: same as (5).

III. Canada

(14) Personal consumption expenditure (in 1949 dollars). Sources: *National Accounts, Income and Expenditure, 1926–1956* and various issues of Canadian *National Accounts*. (These are published by the Dominion Bureau of Statistics.)

(15) Disposable personal income (in 1949 dollars). Sources: same as (14).

(16) Population of Canada. Sources: *Canada Yearbook*, various volumes.

IV. The Netherlands

(17) The Dutch consumption data are taken from A. P. Barten, "Het verbruik door gezinshuishoudingen in Nederland 1921–1939 en 1948–1962," Report 6604 of the Econometric Institute of the Netherlands School of Economics. Population figures are taken from various volumes of the *Demographic Yearbook* of the United Nations.

V. Sweden

(18) The Swedish consumption data are taken from R. Bentzel *et al.* (1957), *Den privata konsumtionen i Sverige 1931–1965* (Stockholm: Almqvist and Wiksells) and R. Bentzel *et al.* (1960), *IUI's Konsumtionprognos for ar 1965* (Stockholm: Almqvist and Wiksells). Population figures are taken from various volumes of the *Demographic Yearbook* of the United Nations.

References

Ackley, G. N. (1961), *Macroeconomic Theory*, Macmillan and Company.

Allen, R. G. D., and Bowley, A. L. (1935), *Family Expenditure*, London, Staples.

Almon, C. (1966), *The American Economy to 1975*, Harper and Row.

Arena, J. J. (1965), "Postwar Stock Market Changes and Consumer Spending," *Review of Economics and Statistics*, vol. 47, no. 4.

Barten, A. P. (1964), "Consumer Demand Functions under Conditions of Almost Additive Preferences," *Econometrica*, vol. 32, no. 1–2.

Barten, A. P. (1968), "Estimating Demand Equations," *Econometrica*, vol. 36, no. 2.

Bentzel, R. et al. (1957), *Den privata konsumtionen i Sverige 1931–65*, Stockholm, Almqvist and Wiksells.

Bentzel, R. et al. (1960), *IUI's Konsumtionsprognos for ar 1965*, Stockholm, Almqvist and Wiksells.

Brown, T. M. (1952), "Habit Persistence and Lags in Consumer Behavior," *Econometrica*, vol. 20, no. 1.

Christ, C. F. (1956), "Aggregate Econometric Models," *American Economic Review*, vol. 46, no. 3.

Christ, C. F. (1967), "Econometrics in Economics: Some Achievements and Challenges," *Australian Economic Papers*, vol. 6, no. 9.

Crockett, J. (1960), "Demand Relationships for Food," in *Consumption and Savings*, Friend and Jones, ed., University of Pennsylvania.

Duesenberry, J. S. (1947), "Some New Income-Consumption Relationships and Their Implications" (abstract), *Econometrica*, vol. 15, no. 2.

Duesenberry, J. S. (1949), *Income, Saving, and the Theory of Consumer Behavior*, Harvard University Press.

Duesenberry, J. S., Eckstein, O., and Fromm, G. (1960), "A Simulation of the United States Economy in Recession," *Econometrica*, vol. 28, no. 4.

Durbin, J. R., and Watson, G. S. (1951), "Testing for Serial Correlation in Least Squares Regression, II," *Biometrica*, vol. 38.

Farrell, M. J. (1952), "Irreversible Demand Functions," *Econometrica*, vol. 20, no. 2.

Farrell, M. J. (1959), "The New Theories of the Consumption Function," *Economic Journal*, vol. 69.

Ferber, R., and Verdoorn, P. J. (1962), *Research Methods in Economics and Business*, Macmillan and Company.

Friedman, M. (1957), *A Theory of the Consumption Function*, Princeton University Press.

Gollnick, H. (1968), review of first edition of *Consumer Demand in the United States* by H. S. Houthakker and L. D. Taylor, *Econometrica*, vol. 36, no. 1.

Gossen, H. H. (1854), *Entwicklung der Gesetze des menschlichen Verkehrs, und der daraus fliessenden Regeln für menschliches Handeln*, Berlin, Prager.

Green, H. A. J. (1962), *Aggregation In Economic Analysis*, Princeton University Press.

Griliches, Z. (1961), "A Note on Serial Correlation Bias in Estimates of Distributed Lags," *Econometrica*, vol. 29, no. 1.

Griliches, Z. (1967), "Distributed Lags: A Survey," *Econometrica*, vol. 35, no. 1.

Griliches, Z., Maddala, G. S., Lucas, R., and Wallace, N. (1962), "Notes on Estimated Aggregate Quarterly Consumption Functions," *Econometrica*, vol. 30, no. 3.

Harman, H. H. (1960), *Modern Factor Analysis*, The University of Chicago Press.

Hicks, J. R. (1946), *Value and Capital*, 2nd ed., Oxford, The Clarendon Press.

Houthakker, H. S. (1951), "Some Calculations on Electricity Consumption in Great Britain," *Journal of the Royal Statistical Society*, vol. 114, part III.

Houthakker, H. S. (1960), "Additive Preferences," *Econometrica*, vol. 28, no. 2.

Houthakker, H. S. (1961), "An International Comparison of Personal Savings," *Bulletin de l'Institut International de Statistique*, vol. 38, no. 2.

Houthakker, H. S. (1962), "On a Class of Dynamic Demand Functions" (abstract), *Econometrica*, vol. 30, no. 3.

Houthakker, H. S. (1963), "Some Problems in the International Comparison of Consumption Patterns," in *Le Rôle et l'évaluation des besoins de bien de consommation*, ed. R. Mossé, CNRS, Paris.

Houthakker, H. S. (1965), "New Evidence on Demand Elasticities," *Econometrica*, vol. 33, no. 2.

Houthakker, H. S., and Haldi, J. (1960), "Household Investment in Automobiles," in *Consumption and Savings*, Friend and Jones, ed., University of Pennsylvania.

Houthakker, H. S., and Tobin, J. (1952), "Estimates of the Free Demand for Rationed Foodstuffs," *Economic Journal*, vol. 62, no. 245.

Klein, L. R. (1958), "The Estimation of Distributed Lags," *Econometrica*, vol. 26, no. 4.

Klein, L. R., and Goldberger, A. S. (1955), *An Econometric Model of the United States, 1929–1952*, North-Holland Publishing Company.

Koyck, L. M. (1954), *Distributed Lags and Investment Analysis*, North-Holland Publishing Company.

Kuh, E. (1963), *Capital Stock Growth: A Microeconometric Approach*, Amsterdam, North Holland.

Kuh, E., and Meyer, J. R. (1957), "How Extraneous Are Extraneous Estimates?" *Review of Economics and Statistics*, vol. 39, no. 4.

Leser, C. E. V. (1963), "Forms of Engel Functions," *Econometrica*, vol. 31, no. 4.

Liviatan, N. (1961), "Errors in Variables and Engel Curve Analysis," *Econometrica*, vol. 29, no. 3.

Malinvaud, E. (1966), *Statistical Methods of Econometrics*, Chicago, Rand McNally.

Malinvaud, E. (1961), "Estimation et prévision dans les modèles autorégressifs," *Revue de L'Institut International de Statistique*, vol. 29, no. 2.

Meyer, J. R., and Glauber, R. R. (1964), *Investment Decisions, Economic Forecasting, and Public Policy*, Harvard Business School.

Meyer, J. R., and Kuh, E. (1957), *The Investment Decision*, Harvard University Press.

Modigliani, F. (1947), "Fluctuations in the Savings Ratio: A Problem in Economic Forecasting" (abstract), *Econometrica*, vol. 15, no. 2.

Modigliani, F., and Brumberg, R. (1953), "Utility Analysis and Aggregate Consumption Functions: An Attempt at Integration," unpublished.

Modigliani, F., and Brumberg, R. (1954), "Utility Analysis and the Consumption Function: An Interpretation of Cross Section Data," in *Post-Keynesian Economics*, ed. K. K. Kurihara, Rutgers University Press.

Nerlove, M. (1958), *Distributed Lags and Demand Analysis*, Agricultural Handbook Number 141, United States Department of Agriculture.

Nerlove, M. (1960), "The Market Demand for Durable Goods: A Comment," *Econometrica*, vol. 28, no. 1.

Nicholson, J. L. (1949), "Variations in Working Class Family Expenditure," *Journal of the Royal Statistical Society*, vol. 112.

Orcutt, G. H., and Winokur, H. S. (1969), "First Order Autoregression: Inference, Estimation and Prediction," *Econometrica*, vol. 37, no. 1.

Perry, G. L. (1967), "Consumer Demand in the United States: A Review Article," *American Economic Review*, vol. 57, no. 4.

Prais, S. J. (1952), "Non-Linear Estimates of the Engel Curve," *Review of Economic Studies*, vol. 20.

Prais, S. J., and Houthakker, H. S. (1955), *The Analysis of Family Budgets*, Cambridge University Press.

Prest, A. R. (1948), "National Income of the United Kingdom," *Economic Journal*, vol. 58, no. 229.

Schultz, H. (1938), *The Theory and Measurement of Demand*, University of Chicago Press.

Schweitzer, T. T. (1967), "Elasticities of Canadian Consumer Items," Economic Council of Canada.

Stone, J. R. N. (1947), "On the Interdependence of Blocks of Transactions," Supplement to the *Journal of the Royal Statistical Society*, vol. 9, nos. 1–2.

Stone, J. R. N. (1954), "Linear Expenditure Systems and Demand Analysis: An Application to the Pattern of British Demand," *Economic Journal*, vol. 64.

Stone, J. R. N., and Prais, S. J. (1953), "Forecasting from Econometric Models: A Further Note on Derationing," *Economic Journal*, vol. 63.

Stone, J. R. N. et al. (1954), *The Measurement of Consumers' Expenditure and Behaviour in the United Kingdom, 1920–1938*, vol. 1, Cambridge University Press.

Stone, J. R. N., and Croft-Murray, G. (1959), *Social Accounting and Economic Models*, Bowes and Bowes.

Stone, J. R. N., and Rowe, D. A. (1960), " The Durability of Consumers' Durable Goods," *Econometrica*, vol. 28, no. 2.

Stone, J. R. N., and Rowe, D. A. (1966), *The Measurement of Consumers' Expenditure and Behaviour in the United Kingdom, 1920–1938*, vol. II, Cambridge University Press.

Stuvel, G., and James, S. F. (1950), "Household Expenditure on Food in Holland," *Journal of the Royal Statistical Society*, Series A, vol. 113.

Suits, D. B. (1958), "The Demand for New Automobiles in the United States, 1929–1956," *Review of Economics and Statistics*, vol. 40.

Suits, D. B. (1963), "The Determinants of Consumer Expenditure: A Review of Present Knowledge," in *Impacts of Monetary Policy*, one of the research studies prepared for the Commission on Money and Credit, Prentice-Hall, Inc.

Summers, R. (1959), "A Note on Least Squares Bias in Household Expenditure Analysis," *Econometrica*, vol. 27, no. 1.

Swamy, S. (1968), "A Dynamic Personal Savings Function and its Long-Run Implications," *Review of Economics and Statistics*, vol. 50, no. 1.

Taubman, P. (1968), "Personal Saving: A Time Series Analysis of Three Measures of the Same Conceptual Series," *Review of Economics and Statistics*, vol. 50, no. 1.

Taylor, L. D. (1968), "Personal Consumption Expenditure in Sweden, 1931–1958," *Review of the International Statistical Institute*, vol. 36, no. 1.

Taylor, L. D., and Wilson, T. A. (1964), "Three-Pass Least Squares: A Method for Estimating Models with a Lagged Dependent Variable," *Review of Economics and Statistics*, vol. 46.

Theil, H. (1954), *Linear Aggregation of Economic Relations*, Amsterdam, North Holland.

Theil, H. (1961), *Economic Forecasts and Policy*, North-Holland Publishing Company.

Tobin, J. (1951), "Relative Income, Absolute Income and Savings," in *Money, Trade, and Economic Growth, Essays in Honor of John Henry Williams*, Macmillan and Company.

Tsujimura, K., and Sato, T. (1964), "Irreversibility of Consumer Behavior in Terms of Numerical Preference Fields," *Review of Economics and Statistics*, vol. 46.

Wold, H., and Jureen, L. (1953), *Demand Analysis, A Study in Econometrics*, John Wiley and Sons.

Yule, G. U. (1926), "Why Do We Sometimes Get Nonsense Correlation Between Time Series?" *Journal of the Royal Statistical Society*, vol. 89, no. 1.

Zellner, A. (1957), "The Short-Run Consumption Function," *Econometrica*, vol. 25, no. 4.

Zellner, A. (1962), "An Efficient Method of Estimating Seemingly Unrelated Regression Equations and Tests for Aggregation Bias," *Journal of the American Statistical Association*, vol. 57, June 1962.

Index